Instructor's Manual to Accompany
Papalia/Olds

HUMAN
DEVELOPMENT

Sixth Edition

Thomas L. Crandell
Corinne H. Crandell
Broome Community College

McGRAW-HILL, INC.
New York   St. Louis   San Francisco   Auckland   Bogotá
Caracas   Lisbon   London   Madrid   Mexico City   Milan   Montreal
New Delhi   San Juan   Singapore   Sydney   Tokyo   Toronto

This book is printed on recycled, acid-free paper containing a minimum of 50% recycled de-inked fiber.

Instructor's Manual to Accompany Papalia/Olds
HUMAN DEVELOPMENT
Sixth Edition

Copyright © 1995 by McGraw-Hill, Inc. All rights reserved.
Printed in the United States of America. The contents or
parts thereof may be reproduced for use with
HUMAN DEVELOPMENT
Sixth Edition
by Diane E. Papalia and Sally Wendkos Olds
provided such reproductions bear copyright notice, but may not
be reproduced in any form for any other purpose without
permission of the publisher.

ISBN 0-07-048762-6

3 4 5 6 7 8 9 0 BKM BKM 9 0 9 8 7 6

CONTENTS

PREFACE

TO THE INSTRUCTOR

This *Instructor's Manual* is designed to provide assistance in planning an introductory course in human life-span development with the sixth edition of *Human Development*, by Diane E. Papalia and Sally Wendkos Olds, as the primary text.

In any course, there are at least three critical elements: the instructor, the students, and the instructional medium--usually the textbook.

• The instructor's interest in and enthusiasm for the material are usually apparent to students; the instructor's professional knowledge enriches class sessions; and there is certainly no substitute for the instructor's careful planning before class sessions.

• Another vital element is, of course, the students. Typically, students enroll in a course in life-span development for a variety of reasons: at some institutions, the course is required for general education or for a program such as teaching or nursing, but many students elect the course because of personal interests. Students may also vary tremendously in their preparation for college work and in their academic progress; for the instructor, awareness of students' motivations and skills is indispensable.

• The textbook is also an essential component of the course. The text covers far more material than even the best-prepared instructor can hope to convey, and it is often the student's most enduring, if not most intensive, exposure to the field. Most instructors find that a well-planned and well-written textbook can bridge any gaps between their own interests and background in human development and the motivations and preparation of their students.

We are sure you will find that Papalia and Olds's *Human Development* helps you make the most of the course for yourself and your students. It is exceptionally well written; our own students invariably say they enjoy reading it. Also, it has been carefully planned to provide balanced coverage. The authors have taken pains to note racial and cultural variations in development, and they give substantial attention to all phases of the life span. Perhaps most important, there is an admirable blend of up-to-date empirical work with objective and critical evaluations and discussions of practical implications. In making *Human Development* your primary text, you have already taken an important step toward success in teaching the course.

USING THE INSTRUCTOR'S MANUAL

Just as the text was written for many kinds of students, this manual has been written for many kinds of instructors. Some of you are new to college teaching, some are new to teaching the life-span development course, and some are "veterans" in both respects. Whatever your background and experience, this manual is designed to help you optimize your use of *Human Development* and its supplements.

For the novice, the manual can be an indispensable tool for planning lectures, discussions, and classroom activities, and for evaluating students and the course itself. More experienced instructors will probably prefer to use the manual as a resource for new ideas, to be combined with teaching approaches that they have already used successfully.

The *Instructor's Manual* has eighteen chapters, corresponding to the eighteen chapters of *Human Development*, and a resource appendix. Each chapter of the manual has the following sections: Introduction, Chapter Outline, Key Terms, Learning Objectives, Chapter Summary and Teaching Recommendations, an updated list of Audiovisual Materials, Lecture Outlines (including current reference citations), Topic for Debate, Topics for Discussion, Projects and Class Exercises, and Essay Questions.

The first four sections--Introduction, Chapter Outline, Key Terms, and Learning Objectives--are based closely on the textbook and also correspond to sections of the *Study Guide*. They all provide a quick overview of the chapter and, in addition, will highlight chapter topics with which you may be unfamiliar.

Introduction

The introduction (which appears on the opening page of each chapter of the manual) is a brief preview of the textbook chapter, noting the main topics that the chapter considers.

Chapter Outline

The chapter outline is a list, in outline format (I, A, 1, a, etc.) of all the headings and subheadings in the text chapter. Since the heading system in the text chapters is both detailed and logical, the outline gives a very

clear picture of the organization, or framework, of the text material and of how topics and subtopics are related.

Key Terms

The list of key terms reproduces all the important vocabulary highlighted in the textbook and defined in its glossary. The terms are listed alphabetically in the *Study Guide* and *Instructor's Manual* but by order of appearance at the end of each chapter in the text. Each key term has a page reference indicating where it is discussed in *Human Development*.

Learning Objectives

Each learning objective corresponds to a major principle or concept discussed in the main text. The learning objectives let the students know in advance what the important learning outcomes are for each chapter. Key terms are in *italics* where they may appear in a learning objective.

Chapter Summary and Teaching Recommendations

You might think of the chapter summaries as a guided tour through the textbook. Each summary provides a detailed description of the text chapter, along with suggestions for elaborating on selected points in the text material. (We often identify topics that have prompted questions from our students. You may want to comment on these topics in class.)

Audiovisual Materials

The lists of audiovisual materials include many recent films and videos. General comments on audiovisual materials, a list of distributors, and further information about speakers are given in the appendix.

Our listing of audiovisual materials is far from exhaustive. In compiling the lists, we have tried to emphasize materials that are reasonably recent and available or materials that may be dated but are considered to be classics in the field of human development. Most of the materials are 30 to 60 minutes in length.

Distributor and date (when known) are indicated for each film or video with the exception of the videos selected from a media publication entitled "Films for the Humanities and Sciences" (coded FFHS). These videos are dated according to the publication date of the brochure, which is 1994.

As we note in the appendix, we encourage you to preview materials before using them in class. Nearly every "veteran" instructor has had the embarrassing experience of relying on a brief summary of a film or video (from an instructor's manual or a distributor's catalog), only to find that the content, the length, or both, have only the vaguest resemblance to the description. Most instructors also find previewing indispensable as a way of identifying points they will want to highlight for students' attention.

There is a small collection of video laser discs and computer software related to the field of psychology that may be used to supplement the text. Most emphasize the biological aspects of psychology (such as how neurons function, how the body reacts to stress, explanations of DNA, delivery and birth of a baby, etc.). So, if you wish to start using this instructional medium, contact your McGraw-Hill representative.

Guest Speakers

Suggestions for guest speakers and ideas about where and how to find guest speakers are provided after the Audiovisual section.

Lecture Outlines

Several lecture outlines--which include references for background reading--are provided in each chapter of the manual. They deal with topics of contemporary importance that are likely to arouse students' interest and concern. Each of them takes up material discussed in the text or a closely related issue.

Most instructors will probably want to use these outlines as a framework or starting point for their own lectures. The outline provides an organizational framework, but some supplement (reflecting the instructor's professional or personal background and interests and background readings) will almost certainly be necessary.

Topic for Debate

The topics for debate by students are related to topics in the text that are likely to arouse the greatest interest and emotions. Each debate topic begins with some background material and also includes one or more references to give the students further information. Suggestions for working with the debate format are given in the appendix.

Note that many of the topics for debate could also be effectively addressed through a class discussion (see below).

Topics for Discussion

Each chapter of the manual has several sets of questions developed for guiding class discussions. Like the topics for debate, these are based on material in the text that is most likely to be interesting and provocative.

Again, you will find general ideas and recommendations for discussions in the appendix. Note also that many of these questions could be adapted--or used as is--for essay examinations.

Projects and Class Exercises

The projects and exercises are special assignments to be done by individual students or groups of students. Many involve research in the form of reading, interviews, or both-- followed by a paper or a report to the class as a whole--and thus can give students some idea of scholarship and fieldwork.

The suggested projects and exercises deal with issues raised in the text or closely related issues. Their purpose is to prompt students to consider the implications or practical applications of course material.

Many of the projects are intended as individual assignments; depending on the size of your class, and on your teaching load, you may prefer to use them as an option for extra credit rather than a course requirement.

The group exercises are intended for groups of 3 to 5 students to complete during a class session. The guidelines for implementing the debates and discussions may be helpful in deciding how to incorporate these exercises into your course. Depending on the size of your class, you can either assign students to groups (this is recommended for small classes) or allow students to form their own groups (this is recommended for larger classes). (A sample group project assignment sheet that we use is in the Appendix of this *Instructor's Manual*.)

We have found from student feedback that this is probably one of the most realistic, meaningful assignments students have had during their college experience.

With regard to grading, one option is to have each group turn in a single set of answers for the exercise and award the same grade to all group members. Another option is to use a weighted formula which results in each student's receiving two scores: one for his or her individual effort and the second for the group's combined effort. The two scores, weighted as you see fit and then added together, yield the student's grade for the exercise.

Essay Questions

Several essay questions are provided for each chapter, and each is followed by an "answer guideline" which will give instructors (and assistants who may be grading tests) criteria for evaluating students' responses.

Although these essay questions are intended primarily for examinations, they could--with some modification or elaboration--serve as a basis for planning additional class discussions or special projects.

Most instructors will probably want to use these chapter-by-chapter resources in somewhat modified form, in accordance with their own interests and teaching styles. Our main objective in developing them has been to prompt creative thought about the course, classroom activities, and evaluation methods.

Appendix:
General Resources

In the appendix, you will find a selected bibliography of handbooks and readers, information about distributors of audiovisual materials and guest speakers, suggestions for implementing and evaluating the debates and class discussions, and suggestions for evaluating your course.

This appendix is likely to be most useful before the semester begins, particularly for instructors who are new to college teaching or to teaching the human development course. It offers references for background reading and possibilities to consider in designing the course. Equally important, some of the resources described in this section--most notably, audiovisual materials and guest speakers--must be scheduled well in advance. We therefore suggest that you examine the appendix before preparing your course syllabus.

USING THE SUPPLEMENTS

The usefulness of *Human Development* is enhanced by the supplemental materials that accompany it.

Study Guide

The *Study Guide* with readings (prepared by Thomas Crandell and George Bieger) gives students general information on study techniques, individual differences in learning, and taking tests. Specific learning objectives and many self-test items (both of a factual and conceptual nature) are provided for each chapter. It also includes chapter previews, outlines, and lists of key terms. In addition, each chapter of the *Study Guide* has a reading selection from a professional journal or a popular source--related to topics in the textbook.

Many first-year college students (and even more advanced students) have fairly weak study skills and need assistance in structuring their study time and focusing their study efforts. The *Study Guide* has been developed to optimize their learning for comprehension and retention.

Test Bank

The *Test Bank*, prepared by Dr. Thomas Moye, includes approximately 2,000 multiple-choice items.

The questions in the *Test Bank* are presented chapter by chapter and have been developed to reflect the learning objectives in the *Study Guide* and the *Instructor's Manual*.

The multiple-choice questions for each chapter are of two kinds: those dealing essentially with informational or factual material, and those dealing essentially with concepts or applications or analysis of factual material.

A key is given for each item, indicating the answer and the page or pages in the textbook where the answer can be found. For multiple-choice questions, the key also indicates whether the item is factual (F) or conceptual (C).

The *Test Bank* can be used with test-generating systems available for both Apple and IBM PC microcomputers.

Note that essay questions with answer guidelines for each chapter in the text are provided in this *Instructor's Manual* (rather than in the *Test Bank*).

Overhead Transparencies

The set of overhead transparencies includes 50 color transparencies of illustrations. You will undoubtedly find that many of them provide very effective supplements for your lectures.

ACKNOWLEDGMENTS

The authors sincerely thank Dr. T. Ellen Hill and Colleen Crandell for their contributions to this *Instructor's Manual*. Their assistance added greatly to the quality and completeness of the final manuscript.

We also thank Beth Kaufman, our editor at McGraw-Hill, for her encouragement and critical observations regarding the content of this manual. Especially, we thank Jane Vaicunas for her continued support of our work.

Corinne Crandell

Thomas Crandell

CHAPTER 1
ABOUT HUMAN DEVELOPMENT

INTRODUCTION

Chapter 1 provides an overview of the field of human development from both theoretical and research perspectives. Several important issues are discussed, including:

- A historical presentation of the study of human development leading to the current life-span view.

- The influences on human development, ranging from those which are purely individual to those common to specific (cross-cultural) groups.

- Correlation, nonexperimental methods, experimental methods, and data-collection techniques used to discover more about human nature, as well as the framework of ethical considerations for conducting research on human subjects.

- The four dominant theories of development: psychoanalytic, learning, cognitive, and humanistic, and the role they play in helping to explain, interpret, and predict and modify human behavior and guide future research.

    The authors' intent in this textbook is to provide the reader with practical information based on research with human subjects, as much as is currently available--and to portray people as unique individuals with the capacity to change and to influence their own development.

CHAPTER OUTLINE

I. HUMAN DEVELOPMENT: THE SUBJECT AND THE TEXT

  A. WHAT IS HUMAN DEVELOPMENT?
  B. HOW THIS BOOK APPROACHES HUMAN DEVELOPMENT
    1. We Celebrate the Human Being
    2. We Respect All Periods of the Life Span
    3. We Believe in Human Resilience
    4. We Recognize that People Help Shape Their Own Development
    5. We Believe That Knowledge Is Useful

II. HUMAN DEVELOPMENT: THE STUDY AND ITS HISTORY

  A. ASPECTS OF DEVELOPMENT
    1. Physical Development
    2. Intellectual (Cognitive) Development
    3. Personality and Social Development
  B. PERIODS OF THE LIFE SPAN
  C. INDIVIDUAL DIFFERENCES IN DEVELOPMENT
  D. INFLUENCES ON DEVELOPMENT
    1. Types of Influences: Sources and Effects
      a. Internal and external influences
      b. Normative and nonnormative influences
    2. Contexts of Influences: An Ecological Approach
    3. Timing of Influences: Critical Periods
  E. HOW THE STUDY OF HUMAN DEVELOPMENT HAS EVOLVED
    1. Studies of Childhood
    2. Studies of Adolescence, Adulthood, and Aging
    3. Life-Span Studies

III. HUMAN DEVELOPMENT: RESEARCH METHODS

  A. CORRELATION

  B. NONEXPERIMENTAL METHODS
    1. Case Studies
    2. Observation
      a. Naturalistic observation
      b. Laboratory observation
      c. Evaluation of observational studies
    3. Interviews
  C. EXPERIMENTAL METHODS
    1. Variables and Groups
    2. Sampling and Assignment
    3. Types of Experiments
      a. Laboratory experiments
      b. Field experiments
      c. Natural experiments
    4. Comparing Experimentation with Other Methods
  D. DATA COLLECTION DESIGNS FOR STUDYING DEVELOPMENT
    1. Cross-Sectional and Longitudinal Studies
    2. Sequential Studies
  E. ETHICS OF RESEARCH
    1. Ethical Issues
      a. Informed consent
      b. Deception
      c. Self-esteem
      d. Privacy
    2. Ethical Standards

IV. HUMAN DEVELOPMENT: THEORETICAL PERSPECTIVES

  A. THEORIES AND HYPOTHESES
  B. PSYCHOANALYTIC PERSPECTIVE
    1. Sigmund Freud: Psychosexual Theory
      a. Id, ego, and superego
      b. Defense mechanisms
      c. Stages of psychosexual development
    2. Erik Erikson: Psychosocial Theory
      a. Erikson's approach
      b. Erikson's eight crises
    3. Jean Baker Miller: Relational Theory
    4. Psychoanalytic Perspective
  C. LEARNING PERSPECTIVE: BEHAVIORISM AND SOCIAL-LEARNING THEORY
    1. Behaviorism
      a. Classical conditioning
      b. Operant conditioning
    2. Social-Learning Theory
    3. Evaluation of Learning Perspective

D. COGNITIVE PERSPECTIVE
    1. The Cognitive-Stage Theory of Jean Piaget
        a. Cognitive structures
        b. Principles of cognitive development
    2. Evaluation of Piaget's Theory
    3. Information-Processing Approach
E. HUMANISTIC PERSPECTIVE
    1. Abraham Maslow: Self-Actualization and the Hierarchy of Needs
    2. Evaluation of Humanistic Theory

V. A WORD TO STUDENTS

organization (36)
psychoanalytic perspective (24)
psychosexual development (25)
psychosocial development (29)
punishment (32)
qualitative change (3)
quantitative change (3)
random sample (19)
reinforcement (32)
relational theory (29)
sample (19)
scheme (35)
scientific method (14)
shaping (33)
social-learning theory (33)
superego (25)
theory (23)

KEY TERMS

accommodation (page 36)
adaptation (36)
assimilation (36)
behaviorism (30)
case studies (14)
classical conditioning (31)
cognitive development (34)
cognitive perspective (34)
cohort (9)
control group (19)
correlation (14)
critical period (10)
cross-sectional study (21)
cross-sequential study (22)
data (23)
defense mechanisms (25)
dependent variable (19)
ecological approach (9)
ego (25)
environmental influences (8)
equilibration (36)
experiment (17)
experimental group (19)
extinction (33)
heredity (8)
human development (3)
humanistic perspective (37)
hypothesis (23)
id (25)
independent variable (19)
interview (17)
laboratory observation (16)
learning perspective (30)
longitudinal study (21)
naturalistic observation (16)
operant conditioning (32)

LEARNING OBJECTIVES

After finishing Chapter 1, students should be able to:

1. Explain what is meant by the study of *human development*. (p. 3)

2. Differentiate between *quantitative* and *qualitative* changes in development. (p. 3)

3. List four major steps applied in the study of *human development* and give an illustration of each. (p. 5)

4. Recall the four major aspects of the self in which growth and change occur and describe an example of each. (p. 6)

5. Name and briefly describe eight periods of development within the life span. (pp. 7-8)

6. Distinguish between internal and external influences on development and cite an example of each. (p. 8)

7. Differentiate between normative and nonnormative influences on development. (pp. 8-9)

8. On the basis of the *ecological approach* to development, briefly describe the four different levels of *environmental influence*. (p. 9)

9. State how cross-cultural research is applied in the study of human development. (p. 10)

10. Define the concept of *critical period* and how this concept relates to human development. (p. 10)

11. Explain how societal and medical progress in the 19th century caused adults to take a new view of childhood. (pp. 11-12)

12. Explain the life-span approach to understanding human development. (p. 12)

13. Define the term *scientific method* and explain its application to psychological research. (p. 14)

14. Describe *correlation*, the research technique that examines the statistical relationship between variables. (p. 14)

15. Name and describe the three categories of nonexperimental methods for collecting data. (pp. 14-17)

16. Define the following terms as they relate to *experimental* research: (pp. 17-19)
    a. *independent variable*
    b. *dependent variable*
    c. *experimental group*
    d. *control group*
    e. *random sample*

17. List the three types of *experiments*, give an example of each, and cite advantages and disadvantages of each. (pp. 19-20)

18. Critique the *experimental* method over the *nonexperimental* methods. (p. 20)

19. Compare and contrast the three methods of *data* collection design. (pp. 21-22)

20. In your own words, summarize each of the following issues as it relates to the ethics of human research: informed consent, deception, self-esteem, privacy, and ethical standards. (pp. 22-23)

21. Define the following research terms: (p. 23)
    a. *theory*
    b. *data*
    c. *hypothesis*

22. Briefly describe the goals of the *psychoanalytic perspective*, and name the physician who is attributed with having originated it. (p. 24)

23. Summarize what Freud meant by each of these terms: (p. 25)
    a. *id*
    b. *ego*
    c. *superego*

24. List and define Freud's five stages of *psychosexual development*. (pp. 25-28)

25. Explain in your own words each of Erik Erikson's eight *psychosocial development* crises of development and indicate at approximately what ages these occur. (pp. 27-30 and Table 1-6)

26. Summarize the *relational theory* and identify its founder. (p. 29)

27. Critique the *psychoanalytic perspective*. (p. 30)

28. Explain the two major theories comprised by the *learning perspective*: (pp. 30-33)
    a. *behaviorism*
    b. *social-learning theory*

29. Briefly describe the *cognitive* perspective of development and name its major proponent. (p. 34)

30. Identify and describe Piaget's four stages of *cognitive development* and indicate at approximately what age each occurs. (p. 34)

31. Critique Piaget's cognitive-stage theory. (p. 36)

32. Define what is meant by the information-processing approach to *cognitive development*. (p. 37)

33. Explain the major beliefs of the *humanistic perspective*, and name the person who is credited with its development. (p. 37)

34. Briefly describe Maslow's hierarchy of needs that motivate human behavior. (p. 38)

35. Critique the *humanistic perspective* to human development. (p. 38)

CHAPTER SUMMARY AND TEACHING RECOMMENDATIONS

The chapter opens by focusing on one aspect in the life of Anna, the adopted daughter of Diane Papalia, one of the authors of the textbook. The story of Anna--her problems with early language development and the eventual correction of those problems-- illustrates how the study of human development can enable us to understand and help children and adults.

The authors follow this example with a definition of human development as the "scientific study of the quantitative and qualitative ways people change over time." Definitions and examples of both quantitative and qualitative change are provided, and the *Study Guide* includes this distinction as one of the learning objectives for the chapter. The chapter continues with a presentation of the authors' perspectives on human development.

In teaching the chapter, you may want to call students' attention to the distinction between quantitative and qualitative change, and point out that the different theoretical perspectives discussed later in the chapter differ in their emphasis on the two types of change. Another point to note about the definition of human development is that both quantitative and qualitative changes are related to time and age factors. These variables, however, are neither causal nor explanatory.

The chapter identifies three developmental processes--physical, intellectual, and personality-social--and eight periods of the human life span (with approximate age ranges for each). Although the authors stress that the three kinds of developmental processes are interrelated and that the age ranges are arbitrary, these points could certainly bear repetition in class. In describing influences on human development, the authors identify internal (or hereditary) and external (or environmental) influences, distinguish between normative and nonnormative influences, and present the concept of critical periods. The authors note that critical periods are more apparent in some developmental processes (e.g., language development) than in others (e.g., social development). Again, this point bears repetition in class, both at this point as well as later in the course, when specific influences of development are identified.

The authors also present the concept of "environmental systems" and describe how developmentalists use this systems approach to study the effects of environment upon human development, especially through cross-cultural research studies. The chapter continues with a brief discussion of how the study of human development from childhood through adulthood has itself evolved.

The chapter then gives an overview of nonexperimental and experimental approaches to studying human development and describes the strengths and weaknesses of each approach. For students who have taken an introductory psychology course, much of this material will be familiar. It is important to call students' attention, nonetheless, to the authors' statement that only the experimental approach can test cause-effect hypotheses. With regard to cross-sectional and longitudinal strategies for data collection, the formidable practical barriers to conducting longitudinal research (particularly in studying adult development) are worth noting. These barriers, you could emphasize, also exist with the sequential strategies. Also, point out that, for ethical reasons, experimentation is often not an option in the study of many important topics in human development.

The chapter concludes with a discussion of developmental theories and hypotheses, outlining four major theoretical perspectives: psychoanalytic, learning, cognitive, and humanistic. As a general introduction to this section, you might point out that this is only one way of classifying perspectives on development and that students may well encounter other classification schemes if they take a more advanced course in child, adolescent, or adult development. In our experience, students often react quite negatively (albeit with considerable curiosity) to the psychoanalytic (particularly the Freudian) and learning perspectives, while reacting much more positively to the cognitive and humanistic perspectives. Whether or not your own students react this way, you may want to use their reactions as a starting point for debate or discussion (in addition to the options for debate and discussion we provide later). At least, you might consider calling students' attention to the contributions (as well as the limitations) of the psychoanalytic and learning approaches, and to the limitations (as well as the strengths) of the humanistic approach.

These points could provide a basis for a student debate or class discussion (see Topic for Debate and Topics for Discussion).

Boxes in Chapter 1 are "The Purpose of Cross-Cultural Research" and "What Longitudinal Studies Can Tell Us."

AUDIOVISUAL MATERIALS

Distributor, date, and running time are given for each film or video. Distributors' addresses are listed in the appendix (General Resources). If a film or video is not in color, there is a notation (BW) to that effect.

Child development. (IM, 1992, video, 30 min.) Presents a historical overview of the contributions of Locke, Rousseau, Freud, Erikson, Bowlby, Watson, Gessell, Piaget, and modern theorists to the field of developmental psychology.

Infancy to adolescence. (IM, 1990, video, 2 volumes, 60 min. each) David Hartman and eminent researchers in psychology, biology, anthropology, and sociology investigate major theories of human development.

Research methods. (IM, 1975, video, 35 min.) This program addresses the impact psychological research can have on the average person. It explains what sound scientific research methods are and what makes these methods so important.

Jean Piaget. (IM, 1969, 2 parts, 40 min. each) This 2-part interview with the developmental psychologist illuminates key concepts of his theory.

Carl Rogers. (IM, 1969, 2 parts, 50 min. each) Dr. Carl Rogers compares the humanistic model of personality with other theories of personality.

B. F. Skinner on behaviorism. (IM, 1977, video, 28 min.) B. F. Skinner discusses behavior modification, behavioral technology, and the uses of positive reinforcement in shaping human behavior.

Freud: The hidden nature of man. (IM, 1970, video, 29 min.) Using dramatized interviews with Sigmund Freud, this video assesses the psychologist's theories of psychoanalysis, the Oedipus complex, the unconscious, and the id, ego, and superego.

What right has a child? (CRM, no date information available, approximately 15 min.) Describes UN Declaration on Children's Rights and children's reaction to it.

Everybody rides the carousel. (YU, 1982, approximately 25 min.). Describes Erikson's theory of life-span personality development.

LECTURE OUTLINES

Lecture 1: What Is Life-Span Developmental Psychology?

I. Definition, foci, and goals

Life-span developmental psychology is the description, explanation, and optimization of changes within the individual from birth to death, and of differences between individuals. This definition indicates two foci, or objects of study, and two goals.

A. Foci.
  1. Changes within the individual--how any one person changes from birth to death. Examples:
     a. Physical changes include changes in health, athletic abilities, endurance, etc.
     b. Intellectual changes include changes in memory, language ability, etc.
     c. Personality changes include changes in values, moral reasoning or behavior, etc.
  2. Differences between individuals-- how different people change in different ways during life. Examples:
     a. Social class differences can be found in patterns and rates of physical growth.
     b. Sex differences can be found in rates and patterns of language development.
     c. Cultural differences can be found in moral development.
B. Goals.
  1. Description--What changes occur within any individual? How do different people change in different and similar ways? The goal here is simply to provide a portrait or profile of changes occurring during life.

2. Explanation--Why do people change as they grow older? The goal here is to account for the changes that occur during life.
3. Optimization--How can human development be optimized? When changes which occur during development and ways in which different people change are described, we can usually identify some patterns that are more desirable than others (e.g., robust health in old age as opposed to chronic illnesses; age-appropriate skills in reading, writing, and mathematics as opposed to learning delays). The goal here is to ensure that as many people as possible experience these more desirable or more adaptive patterns of change.

II. Illustration of the foci and goals

Foci and goals can be illustrated in terms of developmental studies of auditory sensitivity; this illustration summarizes many studies of age differences in hearing done with many populations.

A. Description. Measurements of auditory sensitivity indicate:
 1. Age differences; this suggests individual change within individuals.
 2. Variations in age differences between individuals; differences are greater among urban groups than among rural groups.
B. Explanation. Differences between urban and rural groups suggest at least one possible explanation for change--exposure to noise. Patterns of differences between individuals often suggest explanations, but not always.
C. Optimization. Since it is desirable to maintain good hearing as long as possible, can we use the suggested explanation to prevent hearing loss? Two approaches to optimization:
 1. Alleviative--If change has already occurred, what can be done to minimize its impact?
 2. Preventive--If change has not yet occurred, what can be done to prevent it from occurring?

III. Major assumptions

Life-span developmental psychology makes two major assumptions.

A. Development as a lifelong process. Important changes occur during all periods of life from birth to death. This assumption can be contrasted with an orientation toward biological growth (the idea that development has an end point, that a state of absolute maturity occurs).
B. Pluralistic view of development. The pluralistic view emphasizes that:
 1. Not all important ways in which people change are processes starting at conception and ending at death.
 2. A variety of influences cause developmental change. Three major categories of influences of development:
  a. Normative age-graded influences. These affect most people, and--within a given culture--at about the same age. In any one culture, there will be some normative age-graded events; but many such events will be different from one culture to another.
  b. Normative history-graded influences. These are major historical events or processes so large in scope that they affect the lives of virtually everyone who is living when and where they take place (e.g., depressions and wars). The impact of these events on the individual varies depending on the age at which they are experienced.
  c. Nonnormative life events. These are experiences that most people do not have, but that have profound impact on those who do have them.

References for Lecture 1

Baltes, P. B., Reese, H. W., & Lipsitt, L. P. (1977). *Life-span developmental psychology: Introduction to research methods*. Monterey, CA: Brooks/Cole.
Freiberg, K. L. (1992). *Human development: A life-span approach*. Boston, MA: Jones and Bartlett.
Rice, F. P. (1992). *Human development: A life-span approach*. New York: Macmillan.

Lecture 2: Developmental Research Methods

I. Collecting data: Three basic designs.

Scientists can get information about human development (in order to describe, explain, and optimize) through three basic research designs.

A. Cross-sectional design compares behavior of people of different ages at the same point in time.
   1. There is a problem with the cross-sectional design: Members of different age groups are also members of different cohorts.
   2. Despite this problem, the cross-sectional design is the most widely used of all.
B. Longitudinal design studies the same people for years to see how their behavior changes. This design has several problems:
   1. Age changes may or may not be maturational (they may be affected by time of measurement and by practice).
   2. Such studies give information about only one cohort.
   3. There are practical problems in implementing the longitudinal design:
      a. Considerable time and money are required.
      b. The study may outlive the researcher or researchers.
      c. Subjects may drop out (they may move away, die, or simply choose to end their participation).
      d. Subjects who remain in the study may not be representative.
      e. If the study involves performance, subjects who remain may show practice effects.
      f. Measures used in the study may become outdated.
C. Time-lag design compares members of different generations at same age.
   1. This implies that measurements must be done at different times.
   2. This is the least-used design.

II. Collecting data: Sequential designs

Because none of the three basic designs gives straightforward answers to questions about development, three more complex sequential research designs have been developed.

A. Sequential designs are all ways of combining two of the basic designs to get more complete answers to questions about human development.
B. Sequential designs are seldom used, since the time and money requirements are as problematic as with longitudinal designs.

References for Lecture 2

Baltes, P. B., Reese, H. W., & Lipsitt, L. P. (1977). *Life-span developmental psychology: An introduction to research methods.* Monterey, CA: Brooks/Cole.
Burnand, Gordon. (1993). *Human development: Childhood, adolescence, and personality in terms of a unifying theoretical system.* High Wycombe: Leadership.
Kaplan, Paul S. (1993). *The human odyssey: Life-span development.* Minneapolis/St. Paul: West.

Lecture 3: World Views and Theories

I. Scientific theories

What are scientific theories, and what is their function?

A. Definition: A theory is a description of currently known ideas important in understanding a phenomenon and of relationships among those ideas.
   1. This definition applies to all scientific fields, not just human development.
   2. Since the definition specifies that a theory includes currently known ideas and their interrelationships, a theory must often be revised to account for new data as current knowledge and ideas change.
B. Functions of scientific theories.
   1. Organize existing knowledge based on earlier research.
   2. Identify new topics for continued research. (The new knowledge resulting from further research may lead to revision of the original theory.)

II. Theories of human development

How can theories of human development be classified? The textbook presents many theories of human development. With so many theories, it is useful to identify groups of theories with similar underlying assumptions. Three categories of theories--or models--are generally identified, on the basis of their assumptions about human nature, about the kinds of changes that occur as humans develop, and about the causes of these changes. Every theory of development (not only those described in the text) is consistent with one, and only one, set of assumptions.

A. Learning model: behaviorism.
   1. Assumption about human nature: Humans are basically reactive; i.e., environment affects and determines behavior.
   2. Assumption about changes in behavior: Changes are only quantitative.
   3. Assumptions about causes of changes in behavior: Behavior is caused by two kinds of learning-- classical and operant conditioning.
   4. Learning model: Social-learning theory
      a. Assumption about human nature: Humans are active contributors to learning.
      b. Assumption about changes in behavior: Changes are quantitative and continuous.
      c. Assumption about causes of changes: Behavior is learned by direct observation and imitation of models within a given social context.
B. Cognitive model (Piaget).
   1. Assumption about human nature: Humans are active rather than reactive.
   2. Assumption about changes in behavior: Changes are only qualitative (not quantitative). Stages of development can be identified by such changes.
   3. Assumption about causes of changes: Changes in behavior reflect changes in thinking or ways of processing information.
C. Humanistic model.
   1. Assumption about human nature: Humans are basically good and unique.
   2. Assumption about changes in

behavior: Humanists emphasize the potential for self-development. No insights into the process of development are offered; rather, the emphasis is on becoming a better person.
   3. Assumptions about causes of changes: Changes occur as a result of humans' freedom to choose, to be creative, and to achieve self-realization.

References for Lecture 3

Baltes, P. B., Reese, H. W., & Lipsitt, L. P. (1977). *Life-span developmental psychology: Introduction to research methods.* Monterey, CA: Brooks/Cole.
Flavell, J. (1993). *Cognitive development.* Englewood Cliffs, NJ: Prentice-Hall.
Ford, D. (1992). *Developmental systems theory: An integrative approach.* Newbury Park, CA: Sage.
Nsamenang, A. (1992). *Human development in cultural context: A third world perspective.* Newbury Park, CA: Sage Publications.
Puckett, J. & Reese, H. W. (Eds.) (1993). *Mechanisms of everyday cognition.* Hillsdale, NJ: Erlbaum.
Reese, H. & Overton, W. (1970). *Models of development and theories of development.* In L. R. Goulet & P. B. Baltes (Eds.), *Life-span developmental psychology: Research and theory.* New York: Academic.

TOPIC FOR DEBATE

What Are Appropriate Ethical Guidelines for Research on Human Development

Background

The text outlines ethical issues of concern in any type of research involving human participants; these issues include privacy, self-esteem, freedom from deception, and informed consent. The authors also mention the guidelines of the American Psychological Association for research with human subjects and note that most colleges and universities have established review boards to ensure that research conducted at the institution conforms to relevant ethical standards.

Few would dispute that some set of ethical guidelines is necessary to protect human research subjects. Furthermore, many scientists and practitioners would agree that such guidelines are particularly important in research on human development, since developmental research often involves vulnerable populations (e.g., people who are very young, very old, developmentally disabled, institutionalized, or considered to be "at risk").

However, there is also concern regarding the actual implementation of guidelines and the impact of guidelines on research.

Unquestionably, some research topics cannot, ethically or even legally, be studied in any way that would demonstrate cause-effect relationships (e.g., causes of spontaneous abortion, causes of dementia). But other research involves more subtle issues; and in some cases, implementing ethical guidelines for research procedures may influence the results. For example, if adolescent subjects in a study of the relationship between teaching style and students' achievement are informed of the purpose of the research, that in itself might affect the outcome. Also, people who agree to participate in a particular study after being fully informed of its purposes and procedures may not be representative of the population of interest--e.g., volunteers for a study of the impact of retirement planning on satisfaction with retirement may not be representative of all retirees. In these instances, well-founded ethical concerns may have an unintended impact: they may preclude the gathering of information that has important scientific, practical, or clinical value.

Debate plan

Using this background, and information from additional sources (selected references are provided below), student panels should debate the following positions:

Position A. Current ethical guidelines for research with human participants are too lax and do not adequately protect participants in developmental research.

Position B. Current ethical guidelines for research with human participants are too strict and hamper the conduct of research that might optimize development.

References for the debate

For the most part, students should be responsible for gathering material to support their arguments. The references below are intended as a starting point for student research.

American Psychological Association. (1982). *Ethical principles in the conduct of research with human participants.* Washington, DC: American Psychological Association.
Blanck, P. D., Belleck, A. S. & Rosnow, R. L. (1992, July). Scientific rewards and conflicts of ethical choices in human subjects research. *American psychologist,* 959-965.
Cassel, C. K. (1988). Ethical issues in the conduct of research in long term care. *The gerontologist, 28,* (Suppl.), 90-96.
Fethe, C. (1993, June). Beyond voluntary consent: Hans Jonas on the moral requirements of human experimentation. *Journal of medical ethics,* 99-103.
Moody, H. R. (1988). From informed consent to negotiated consent. *The gerontologist, 28* (Suppl.), 64-70.
Stone, R. (1993, March 26). Eyeing a project's ethics. *Science.* 1820.

TOPICS FOR DISCUSSION

Topic 1: Strengths and Weakness of Various Developmental Research Approaches

1. Begin by asking the students to define the cross-sectional and longitudinal approaches (textbook page 21).

2. With these definitions as a basis, the discussion could include the following questions:
    a. What can be concluded from group differences in a cross-sectional study? What <u>cannot</u> be concluded?
    b. What can be concluded from change over time in a longitudinal study? What <u>cannot</u> be concluded?

3. What problems is a researcher likely to encounter in conducting a longitudinal study of personality development between the ages of 20 and 80?

4. In what kinds of research situations would a cross-sectional study probably be most useful and most feasible?

5. In what kinds of research situations would a longitudinal study probably be most useful and most feasible?

6. Ask the students to define the sequential strategies (page 22). The ensuing

discussion could include the following questions:

a. Developmental scientists often consider sequential strategies more adequate than cross-sectional and longitudinal approaches. Why would this be the case?

b. What practical problems would come up in the implementation of a sequential study?

Topic 2: Developmental Perspectives

1. Ask the students to identify the perspectives discussed in the text and one or more theorists identified with each perspective (pages 24-38).

2. With this basis, the discussion could include the following questions:

a. In which theory is the role of the environment given the greatest stress? Why do the students consider this theory the most "environmental?"

b. In which theory is the individual accorded the greatest role in affecting his or her own development? Why have the students chosen this theory?

c. Which theory would place the greatest responsibility on parents for the way their children develop?

d. Which is the best example of a "life-span" theory?

PROJECTS AND CLASS EXERCISES

Group Exercise: Applying Developmental Perspectives

The following exercise should involve a group of no more than five students; the group should turn in one set of written answers at the end of the class session. During the previous class session, advise students to prepare for the exercise by reviewing the text section on developmental perspectives.

A case study. Deborah Shore, age 45, works for a small corporation in the Research and Development department. When she first became a member of the department 15 years ago, Deborah was an unusually creative and productive researcher; her efforts quickly resulted in raises and promotions within the department and earned her the respect of her

colleagues. Now, Deborah finds herself less interested in doing research; she is no longer making creative contributions to her department, although she is making contributions to its administration. She is still respected by the coworkers who have known her since she joined the firm, but not by her younger coworkers.

Group members should analyze the case study from the psychoanalytic, learning, and humanistic perspectives: how would a theorist from each perspective explain Deborah's development? Which perspective do group members believe provides the most adequate explanation, and why?

Project 1: Researching Institutional Guidelines for Ethical Research

Ask the students to research the procedures followed at your institution for protecting human research subjects. If there is an institutional review board, have the students find out who serves on the board and what backgrounds the board members bring to the review process. If possible, students should interview one or more board members. If there is no review board at your institution, ask the students to develop a hypothetical board, identifying the types of individuals needed on it.

Project 2: Autobiographies

Have the students write autobiographies in which they trace milestones in their own physical, intellectual, and personality-social development. They should also identify the major normative age-graded events, normative history-graded events, and nonnormative events they have experienced and speculate about how each event has affected their development.

ESSAY QUESTIONS

---

1. Define *critical period* and identify an aspect of development in which the concept applies well and one in which it does not apply.

Answer guideline. An acceptable answer will note that a critical period refers to a well-demarcated period of development during which an influence will have maximum impact. Aspects of development for which the concept applies well include prenatal physical

development and language development.
Aspects for which the concept does not apply
well include personality development during
adulthood and learning practical or
occupational skills.

2.   Define normative age-graded event,
      normative history-graded event, and
      nonnormative event. Contrast these three
      types of influence and give examples of
      each.

Answer guideline. An acceptable answer will
note that normative age-graded events are
experienced by most people at similar ages,
that normative history-graded events are
experienced by virtually all who are living
when they occur, and that nonnormative
events are experienced by few but are likely to
have profound effects. The two normative
events differ from nonnormative events in the
numbers of individuals that they are likely to
affect.

3.   Distinguish *qualitative change* and
      quantitative change and give an example
      of each in human development.

Answer guideline. Qualitative change is
change in kind, organization, or basic
structure; examples would include changes in
the nature and organization of cognitive
abilities at different points in development.
Quantitative change is change in the amount of
a quality which itself does not change;
examples include increases in vocabulary,
changes in the frequency of aggressive
behavior, and increases in height or weight.

4.   Define *theory* and *hypothesis* and explain
      the relationship between them.

Answer guideline. A theory is a set of
related statements explaining and interpreting
data (basic information gathered through
research). A hypothesis is a prediction of the
outcome of an experiment. Hypotheses are
based on theories; theories suggest an
explanation for a phenomenon, and a
hypothesis is based on this explanation and
tested through research.

5.   Define *correlational* studies. Describe
      three nonexperimental methods of
      developmental research. What is a
      problem with nonexperimental methods?

Answer guideline. Correlational studies
involve measuring two or more characteristics

in a group of people and measuring the extent
to which these characteristics are associated
with one another. The major problem with
nonexperimental research is that it cannot test
hypotheses regarding cause-and-effect
relationships. Nonexperimental methods
include the following: (1) case studies--
studies of a single individual, (2) naturalistic
observation--observations of people's behavior
in real-life settings, (3) laboratory observa-
tion--observation and recording of peoples'
behavior in a fixed setting, (4) interview
method--asking people to report their attitudes
or opinions or describe their experiences.

6.   Relative to other methods, what are
      advantages and disadvantages of
      experimental research methods?

Answer guideline. In an experiment, the
researcher manipulates an independent variable
and observes the effect upon a dependent
variable. Advantages of an experiment are
that it can test cause-and-effect hypotheses and
that it can more easily be replicated by other
researchers. A disadvantage of experiments is
that they can be designed with such a narrow
focus that they become meaningless or trivial
and that they may lack generalizability.

7.   Give an example of a longitudinal and a
      cross-sectional study of language
      development; what types of conclusions
      would each study permit?

Answer guideline. An example of a
longitudinal study would be observing the
same children from birth to age 5 to see how
their use of language changes over that time.
Such a study would reveal whether changes
occur within individual children but not
whether these changes would be observed in
future cohorts of children. An example of a
cross-sectional study would be observing
children in different age groups (say, ages
6 months, 12 months, 18 months, 24 months,
30 months, 36 months, 42 months, 48 months,
54 months, and 60 months) and comparing
their use of language. This study would
reveal age differences in children's use of
language, but it would not indicate whether
any individual child's use of language changes
with age.

CHAPTER 2
CONCEPTION THROUGH BIRTH

INTRODUCTION

Chapter 1 examined the subject of human development and discussed several research methods and theoretical perspectives that are used in the study of various aspects of human development. **Chapter 2** discusses what the most current research has found about the beginning of human development, the period from conception until birth. Several issues are covered, including:

- Fertilization and the basic genetic principles that describe the mechanisms of heredity.

- One of the most perplexing questions in the study of human development: whether human nature is primarily inherited or learned.

- Stages of prenatal birth, including germinal, embryonic, and fetal.

- Methods of assessing development before birth, such as amniocentesis, chorionic villus sampling, blood sampling, and umbilical cord sampling.

- Various influences in the prenatal environment which can affect the developing fetus.

- The benefits and dangers associated with genetic testing.

- The stages of the birth process and various settings for childbirth available today.

The chapter also discusses the interaction between heredity and environmental influences on the developing organism.

CHAPTER OUTLINE

I. FERTILIZATION

A. HOW DOES FERTILIZATION TAKE PLACE?
B. WHAT CAUSES MULTIPLE BIRTHS?
C. WHAT DETERMINES SEX?

II. HEREDITY AND ENVIRONMENT

A. WHAT IS THE ROLE OF HEREDITY?
1. Mechanisms of Heredity: Genes and Chromosomes
2. Patterns of Genetic Transmission
   a. Mendel's laws
   b. Dominant and recessive inheritance
   c. Sex-linked inheritance and other forms
3. Genetic and Chromosomal Abnormalities
   a. Defects transmitted by dominant inheritance
   b. Defects transmitted by recessive inheritance
   c. Defects transmitted by sex-linked inheritance
   d. Chromosomal abnormalities
4. Genetic Counseling
B. HOW DO HEREDITY AND ENVIRONMENT INTERACT?
1. "Nature versus Nurture": Hereditary and Environmental Factors
   a. Hereditary and environmental influences on traits
   b. Maturation
2. Ways to Study the Relative Effects of Heredity and Environment
3. Some Characteristics Influenced by Heredity and Environment
   a. Intelligence
   b. Personality
4. Some Disorders Influenced by Heredity and Environment
   a. Alcoholism
   b. Schizophrenia
   c. Infantile autism
   d. Depression
5. The Importance of the Environment

III. PRENATAL DEVELOPMENT

A. STAGES OF PRENATAL DEVELOPMENT
1. Germinal Stage (Fertilization to about 2 Weeks)
2. Embryonic Stage (2 to 8-12 Weeks)
3. Fetal Stage (8-12 Weeks to Birth)
B. THE PRENATAL ENVIRONMENT
1. Maternal Factors
2. Prenatal Nourishment
3. Maternal Drug Intake
4. Other Maternal Factors
5. Paternal Factors: Environmental Influences Transmitted by the Father

IV. BIRTH

A. STAGES OF CHILDBIRTH
B. METHODS OF CHILDBIRTH
1. Medicated Delivery
2. Natural and Prepared Childbirth
3. Cesarean Delivery
4. Medical Monitoring
C. SETTINGS FOR CHILDBIRTH

KEY TERMS

alleles (page 51)
amniocentesis (61, Box 2-1)
autosomes (49)
cesarean delivery (83)
chorionic villus sampling (61, Box 2-1)
chromosomes (50)
concordant (65)
depression (69)
dizygotic twins (47)
DNA (deoxyribonucleic acid) (50)
dominant inheritance (50)
Down syndrome (58)
electronic fetal monitoring (84-85)
embryonic stage (70)
fertilization (46)
fetal alcohol syndrome (FAS) (76)
fetal stage (72)
gametes (46)
gene (50)
genetic counseling (59)
genetics (49)
genotype (51)
germinal stage (70)
heredity (49)
heterozygous (51)
homozygous (51)

independent segregation (51)
infantile autism (67)
karyotype (59)
maternal blood test (61, Box 2-1)
maturation (63)
medicated delivery (82)
monozygotic twins (47)
multifactorial inheritance (52)
multiple alleles (52)
natural childbirth (83)
ovulation (46)
personality (66)
phenotype (51)
prepared childbirth (83)
recessive inheritance (51)
schizophrenia (67)
sex chromosomes (49)
sex-linked inheritance (52)
spontaneous abortion (70)
temperament (66)
teratogenic (73)
ultrasound (62, Box 2-1)
zygote (46)

LEARNING OBJECTIVES

After finishing Chapter 2, students should be able to:

1. Describe the processes leading to conception: (p. 46)

2. Identify and explain the two mechanisms which produce multiple births. (pp. 47-48)

3. Name and describe the mechanism that determines a baby's sex. (p. 49)

4. Explain how *heredity* is determined at *fertilization*. (pp. 49-50)

5. Explain briefly how hereditary traits are transmitted--as separate units or as a group. Name the scientist responsible for this finding. (p. 50)

6. Recall the principles that govern the transmission of inherited traits. (pp. 50-52)

7. Differentiate between what is meant by *dominant*, *recessive*, and *sex-linked inheritance*. (pp. 51-52, 57)

8. Distinguish between *phenotype* and *genotype*. (p. 51)

9. List some of the birth defects which are caused by *genetic* and *chromosomal* abnormalities. (p. 52)

10. Explain how hereditary and environmental factors interact to influence human nature. (pp. 52, 56-65)

11. Describe the methods for prenatal diagnosis of birth defects. (pp. 61-62, Box 2-1)

12. Define *maturation* and explain how it can be affected by environmental forces. (p. 63)

13. List some of the benefits and dangers of genetic testing. (p. 64, Box 2-2)

14. Describe the various methods for studying the relative effects of *heredity* and environment. (pp. 65-67)

15. Explain how certain characteristics and disorders are influenced by both *heredity* and environment. (pp. 67-69)

16. List and describe the three stages of prenatal development. (pp. 70-73)

17. Identify and explain some of the maternal factors that influence prenatal development. (pp. 73-80)

18. Describe and explain some of the paternal factors that influence prenatal development. (pp. 80-81)

19. List and describe the three stages of childbirth. (p. 81)

20. Name and explain the various methods of childbirth. (pp. 82-84)

21. List some alternative settings for childbirth. (p. 85)

22. Compare and contrast some of the differences in maternity care in western Europe and the United States. (p. 86, Box 2-5)

CHAPTER SUMMARY AND TEACHING RECOMMENDATIONS

At the opening of the chapter, fertilization is defined, the ovum and sperm are described, and the life span of each gamete is specified. Two causes of multiple births are explored, and the authors distinguish between dizygotic and monozygotic twins. The discussion of conception continues with information on sex determination, X and Y chromosomes, and male vulnerability to disorders throughout the life span.

The section "Heredity and Environment" begins with a description of DNA and the normal human set of 23 pairs of chromosomes. The distinction between mitosis and meiosis is explained before a discussion of the chief patterns of genetic transmission: dominant, recessive, sex-linked, and multifactorial. In our experience, many students (especially those who do not have a strong background in biology or genetics) are confused by this material. We would advise being quite specific about how much detail you expect students to master. And, if you plan to test heavily from this section of the chapter, you would be well advised to spend at least one class session explaining the material. Furthermore, you might call students' attention to the authors' statement that most characteristics are influenced by multifactorial patterns of genetic transmission as well as by environmental influences.

The section "Heredity and Environment" continues with discussions of genetic and chromosomal abnormalities (with special attention to Down syndrome) and genetic counseling. The authors then discuss how physiology, intelligence, personality, and certain disorders can be influenced by the interaction of heredity and environmental factors. This section closes with a discussion of the importance of the environment.

The section "Prenatal Development" opens with a description of each of the three stages of prenatal development: germinal, embryonic, and fetal. Following is a discussion of ways in which prenatal development is affected by environmental factors; you might remind students of the concept of "critical periods" in the context of this section. The section outlines the developmental impact of maternal nutrition, drug intake, illness, blood-type incompatibility, medical x-rays, age, and other environmental hazards, as well as paternal factors.

The section "Birth" opens with an explanation of the three stages of labor and the various methods of childbirth: medicated, natural, prepared, and cesarean. You might identify local organizations and agencies providing "childbirth preparatory education." Electronic fetal monitoring is presented as a means of prenatal assessment. You might wish to note recent criticisms of fetal monitoring raised by feminist scholars of obstetrical procedures in light of calls for minimal intervention in the birth process. The chapter concludes with a discussion of alternative settings for giving birth; with reference to this section, you may wish to comment on the increasing prominence of nurse-midwives.

Boxes in Chapter 2 are "Prenatal Assessment," "Genetic Testing," "Shyness," "Reducing Risks during Pregnancy," and "Maternity Care in Western Europe and the United States."

AUDIOVISUAL MATERIALS

Distributor, date, and running time are given for each film or video. Distributors' addresses are listed in the appendix (General Resources). If a film or video is not in color, there is a notation (BW) to that effect.

Developmental phases before and after birth. (FFHS, 1994, video, 30 min.) This program examines the development of the fetus in utero and the child during the first year.

Psychological development before birth. (FFHS, 1994, video, 30 min.) The development of the individual can be followed in utero.

Abortion clinic. (PBS, 1983, Video, approximately 60 min.) Includes interviews with physicians and counselors at an abortion clinic, and interviews with protestors outside the clinic.

The process of birth. (FFHS, 1994, video, 30 min.) This program shows how different cultures and different individuals within the same culture respond to questions concerning the birth process.

The development of the human brain.
(FFHS, 1994, video, 40 min.) This
program follows the physiological
development of the human brain from
conception through the growth of the
neurological system in utero to the
moment of birth.

Fetal rights. (FFHS, 1994, video, 28 min.)
An examination of the obligations of the
mother to her unborn child and her rights
to privacy and control over her own
body.

Genetics. (FFHS, 1994, video, 30 min.)
The medical advances and the ethical
issues developing from the human
genome project.

Genetic screening. (FFHS, 1994, video,
26 min.) The role of genetic screening in
detecting abnormalities in adult genes,
which in turn can predict whether genes
in a child might be affected.

Guest speakers

Hospitals are one possible source of guest
speakers on topics in this chapter. Check with
local hospitals to see if their maternity
departments offer childbirth education; if so,
they may be able to provide a guest speaker
on birth, prenatal development, or both. If
there is a medium- to large-sized hospital
nearby, you may be able to locate a speaker
on genetic counseling.

LECTURE OUTLINES

Lecture 1: The Nature-Nurture Issue

I. General controversy

Are behavior and development determined by
genetic factors, by environmental factors, or
by both, and--if by both--in what combination?
This has been a major, and long-term,
controversy.

A. Before psychology emerged as a field, the
issue was addressed by philosophers and
theologians.

B. Within the field of psychology, the issue
has been discussed since the earliest
scholarly writings, before the eighteenth
century.

II. Controversy within psychology

Within psychology, the question "nature or
nurture?" has been asked in various ways.

A. The question has been asked about the
development of many characteristics,
including personality, intelligence,
susceptibility to psychiatric conditions
(e.g., schizophrenia and depression),
special skills, and talents.

B. The question has been asked in different
forms at different points in the history of
developmental psychology as a science.

1. "Which one?"
   a. In the first approach to the
      question, philosophers and the
      earliest psychologists asked,
      "Which one?" That is, they
      asked, "Is nature or nurture the
      determining factor?" At this
      point, it was assumed that one
      or the other factor was solely
      responsible for behavior and
      development.
   b. Note that this approach was
      illogical. Proponents of either
      side of the argument could
      never prove their own viewpoint
      or disprove their opponents',
      since one can observe influences
      of heredity only by observing
      an individual in some
      environment, and the individual
      so observed always has genetic
      characteristics. Therefore, one
      cannot separate effects of
      heredity and environment to
      study one or the other as the
      sole determinant.

2. "How much?"
   a. In the second approach (lasting
      until the mid-twentieth century),
      scientists acknowledged that
      nature and nurture are both
      involved in determining
      behavior and development.
      Their efforts were now directed
      at determining the relative
      influence of each factor. The
      question thus became, "How
      much?" (rather than "Which
      one?"). This approach was
      based on the notions that
      heredity and the environment
      were completely independent of
      each other and that their
      separate influences were simply
      added together.
   b. Note that the "How much?"
      approach was not really

different from the earlier "Which one?" approach, since "which one" can be seen as a special case (0 percent and 100 percent) of "how much."

   3.   "How?"
       a.   Currently, most scientists take an interactionist approach. This approach includes two assumptions:
          (1) Both nature and nurture are involved in all behavior and development.
          (2) These two sources of influence are inseparable.
       b.   Thus, the question can now be phrased as, "How do nature and nurture combine or interact to influence behavior and development?"

References for Lecture 1

Bigner, J. (1994). *Individual and family development: A life-span interdisciplinary approach.* Englewood Cliffs, NJ: Prentice-Hall.

Lerner, R. M. (1976). *Concepts and theories of human development.* Reading, MA: Addison-Wesley.

Lecture 2: Genetic Counseling

I. Genetic disorders

Genetically based developmental disorders are of two types: chromosome-related and gene-related.

A.   Chromosome-related problems.
   1.   These occur if there is some abnormality of an entire chromosome or a set of chromosomes.
   2.   Best-known example: Down syndrome, or trisomy 21.

B.   Gene-related disorders.
   1.   Some occur when an individual inherits two recessive genes coding for a disorder; others occur when an individual inherits an abnormal trait carried on a dominant gene.
   2.   Examples: Sickle-cell anemia, cystic fibrosis, Tay-Sachs disease, Rh incompatibility.

II. Genetic counseling

Genetic counseling is a process designed to help a couple determine the probability that they will bear a child with a genetically based developmental disorder. The goal of genetic counseling is to promote an informed decision about reproduction. It is not intended as a process through which a decision is made for a couple.

A.   Genetic counseling as a process of communication. Information is exchanged between counselor and couple. In this process, primarily factual information is exchanged.
   1.   Phase 1: Counselor to client.
       a.   Nature of the disease; its impact on those who have it; its prognosis.
       b.   Alternatives for treatment.
   2.   Phase 2: Client to counselor.
       a.   Personal medical background; results of medical tests. This information allows evaluation of the couple's genetic stock (are the parents carriers of gene-related problems?).
       b.   Family medical history. Does any disease "run in the family"?
   3.   Phase 3: Counselor to client. On the basis of test results and personal and family medical background, <u>What is the probability that the couple will bear an afflicted child?</u> The counselor does not tell the couple what to do on the basis of this information.

B.   Referral for genetic counseling.
   1.   Clients are typically referred by a physician, or they seek counseling on their own initiative.
   2.   Reasons for referral.
       a.   Family history of disease (especially if a couple has previously had a child with a gene-related problem).
       b.   Age of the mother (over 35).
       c.   Age of the father (over 55).

C.   Prenatal diagnosis. This is a part of genetic counseling if a woman is already pregnant when counseling is sought. Counseling should then also provide information about diagnostic techniques: what a given technique can and cannot reveal; what risks are involved. Two techniques are used especially often:
   1.   Amniocentesis.
   2.   Ultrasound.

D.   Problems with genetic counseling.
   1.   Problems with communication.
       a.   One criticism of genetic counseling is its almost

exclusive focus on exchanging factual information; there may be too little attention to emotional issues.

    b.   The factual information that is exchanged is technical and therefore confusing to many clients who have no background in medicine or genetics.

  2.   Often, there is no follow-up.

E. Impact of genetic counseling. There is evidence that knowledge of genetically based disorders is gained through genetic counseling. A brief questionnaire is used in many facilities, and responses typically indicate gains in knowledge.

References for Lecture 2

Allen, W. & Ostrer, H. (1993). Anticipating unfair uses of genetic information. *American journal of human genetics, 53,* 16-21.

Alper, J. & Natowicz, M. (1993). Genetic discrimination and the public entities and public accommodations titles of the Americans with Disabilities Act. *American journal of human genetics, 53,* 26-32.

Bonnicksen, A. (1992). Genetic diagnosis of human embryos. *The Hastings Center report, 22,* S5-S11.

Draper, E. (1992). Genetic secrets: Social issues of medical screening in a genetic age. *The Hastings Center report, 22,* S15-S18.

Faden, R. & Kass, N. (1993). Genetic screening technology: Ethical issues in access to tests by employers and health insurance companies. *The journal of social issues, 49,* 75-88.

Michael, M. & Buckle, S. (1990). Screening for genetic disorders: Therapeutic abortion and IVF. *Journal of medical ethics, 16,* 43-47.

Nolan, K. (1992). First fruits: Genetic screening. *The Hastings Center report, 22,* S2-S4.

(1993). *Prescribing our future: Ethical challenges in genetic counseling.* New York: Aldine de Gruyter.

TOPIC FOR DEBATE

Do Pregnant Women Have a Right to Refuse Medical Treatment Aimed at Safeguarding the Health of the Fetus?

Background

The 1980s witnessed several court cases in which a pregnant woman's right to refuse medical treatment came into conflict with the potential of certain treatment approaches to safeguard the health of the fetus. In most of these cases, physicians had recommended cesarean deliveries but women were unwilling to accept the recommendation. In other instances, physicians had wanted to hospitalize women with certain health problems (e.g., diabetes or abnormal bleeding) but the women were unwilling to comply. In still other instances, physicians recommended an intrauterine transfusion deemed necessary for the fetus's survival, but the women refused. Typically, the courts have given greater weight to concern for the fetus than to the woman's rights.

Perhaps the most celebrated case was that of "Angela C.," a terminally ill pregnant woman whose own death was imminent. Although she was willing to undergo medical treatment which would allow her to survive to the twenty-eighth week of gestation (when the fetus would be viable), she, her family, and her physician had also agreed that her own comfort and care should be the guiding force behind all medical decisions. Hospital attorneys, however, sought and received a court order mandating a cesarean section at the twenty-sixth week of gestation; both Angela and the fetus died shortly after the operation.

Several arguments can be made in defense of such court decisions. Medical advances are constantly increasing the survival rates of infants who are born prematurely; with these advances, the importance of protecting the rights of the fetus also grows. Some people might maintain that, by forgoing an abortion, a pregnant woman has accepted a moral responsibility to protect the welfare of the fetus. And, since states can require vaccination and other health safeguards for children, court-ordered prenatal treatment might be regarded as a logical extension of these requirements.

Equally strong arguments can be made against the courts' position. Medical opinions about the necessity of particular treatments for a fetus's survival (as well as judgments about the probable success of these treatments) are fallible. Furthermore, most of the cases so far have involved minority-group women, non-English-speaking women, poor women, or teaching hospitals--or all of these. Thus, one could maintain that these women are being exploited (as more privileged women would never be), often for purposes of medical education. Some observers have held that these women's right of privacy is violated by such court decisions. Since men and nonpregnant women are normally deemed competent to accept or reject medical advice, pregnant women should be accorded the same privilege.

Debate plan

Using this background, and information from additional sources (one reference appears below), student panels should debate the following positions:

Position A. Society has an obligation to protect the unborn, and courts should therefore compel pregnant women to comply with medical procedures in the best interest of the fetus.

Position B. Pregnant women should be conferred the same rights to make decisions about their bodies as are granted to men and to nonpregnant women.

References for the debate

(1991). The battle between mother and fetus: Fetal protection policies in the context of employment discrimination: International Union, UAW V. Johnson Controls, Inc., 111 S. Ct. 1196. *Hamline law review, 14*, 403-426.
(1992). Fetal rights: Protecting fetal rights may diminish women's rights. *The futurist, 26*, 54-55.
Blank, R. (1992). *Mother and fetus: Changing notions of maternal responsibility.* New York: Greenwood Press.
Goode, S. (1988). A mother's body, a fetus' fate. *Insight*, 54-55.
Hojat, M. (1993). The world declaration of the rights of the child: Anticipated challenges. *Psychological reports, 72*, 1011-1022.

TOPICS FOR DISCUSSION

Topic 1: Environmental Influences on Prenatal Development

1. Ask students to summarize the major events of the three stages of prenatal development (textbook, pages 70-73).

2. Ask students to identify the impact on prenatal development of one or more of the following: maternal nutrition, maternal drug intake, maternal illness, external environmental hazards, and paternal factors (pages 73-81).

3. How does the concept of "critical periods" (see Chapter 1) apply to the issue of environmental influences on prenatal development?

4. What are the difficulties inherent in precisely identifying environmental influences on prenatal development? (page 73)

Topic 2: Methods of Childbirth

1. What are the different types of anesthetics used in medicated deliveries? Explain the arguments of both the supporters and the opponents of medicated delivery. (page 82).

2. What is involved in prepared childbirth? Compare parental responses to natural and prepared birth. (page 83)

3. For what reasons are cesarean deliveries usually performed? What risks are involved in cesarean birth? (pages 83-84)

4. Describe one "alternative setting" for giving birth. What advantages and disadvantages would this setting offer? (pages 85-87)

PROJECTS AND CLASS EXERCISES

Group Exercise: Intervention in Adolescent Pregnancy

Typically, adolescent pregnancies are considered "high-risk" pregnancies. On the basis of the section "Prenatal Environment" in the text (pages 73-81), group members should identify at least two environmental influences of special concern for pregnant teenagers and explain why these factors are important. Next, group members should outline a possible workshop or pamphlet for pregnant teenagers in which the selected environmental influences are explained.

Project 1: Historical Changes in Methods of Childbirth

Ask students to interview their mothers (and grandmothers, if possible), asking about their experiences with childbirth. Students could also compare/contrast their father's (and grandfathers', if possible) experiences with childbirth. Students should write a paper summarizing these childbirth experiences and comparing them with the contemporary experiences described in the text.

Project 2: Genetic Influences on Development

Ask students to research one of the genetic and chromosomal abnormalities described in the text. The resulting paper should include the inheritance pattern for the disorder, the prognosis, and suggestions for optimizing the development of afflicted individuals.

Project 3: Interaction of Genetic and Hereditary Influences on Development

Ask students to select one of the characteristics influenced by heredity and the environment and write a paper summarizing the evidence supporting the impact of both genetic and environmental factors.

ESSAY QUESTIONS

---

1. Describe the process of fertilization, and explain when (in relation to ovulation) fertilization can occur.

Answer guideline. An acceptable answer will note that sperm and ovum fuse to form a new cell, that both sperm and ovum are gametes, and that the resulting new cell is a zygote. Since spermatozoa remain active for 48 hours after copulation and since ova can be fertilized for 24 hours after ovulation, copulation is most likely to result in fertilization 24 hours before and after ovulation.

2. Define the four patterns of genetic transmission discussed in the text.

Answer guideline. Dominant inheritance: Competing alleles are inherited, but only one (the dominant one) is expressed. Recessive inheritance: Two recessive alleles are inherited and only then is the recessive allele expressed. Sex-linked inheritance: Recessive genes carried on the X or Y chromosome are transmitted differently to males and to females. Multifactorial inheritance: Characteristics are affected by many genes, as well as by environmental factors.

3. Identify and describe two means of studying the influences of heredity and the environment.

Answer guideline. Twin studies examine the concordance rates for identical and fraternal twins. Consanguinity studies examine "family resemblances." Adoption studies compare adopted children's resemblances to biological and adoptive parents and siblings. Prenatal studies examine links between pregnancy experiences and birth outcomes. Comparison of actual histories identifies links between reported child rearing and developmental outcomes. Environmental manipulation changes diet, exercise, etc., and compares the effects with those observed in a control group. Selective breeding of animals determines the extent to which selective breeding promotes or inhibits the expression of a trait.

4. Define the various types of genetic and chromosomal abnormalities discussed in the text, and give an example of each.

Answer guideline. Defects transmitted by dominant inheritance: An abnormal trait is carried on a dominant gene; each child has a 50-50 chance of being affected (assuming that only one parent is affected). Examples are achondroplasia and Huntington's disease. Defects transmitted by recessive inheritance: An abnormal trait is carried on a recessive gene; a child must receive the recessive gene from both parents to be affected; the probability of being affected is 1 in 4 for children of two "carrier" parents. An example is Tay-Sachs disease. Defects transmitted by sex-linked inheritance: An abnormal trait is carried on the X chromosome of an unaffected mother; the trait usually shows up only in males. An example is hemophilia. Abnormal chromosomes: An entire set of chromosomes (rather than a single gene or one pair of genes) is abnormal. Examples are Down syndrome, Klinefelter's syndrome, Turner's syndrome, and the XYY and XXX syndromes.

5. Identify the three stages of prenatal development, and specify a major event of each stage.

Answer guideline. Germinal stage (fertilization to 2 weeks): Major events are cell division, increasing complexity of the zygote, and implantation in the wall of the uterus. Embryonic stage (2 to 8-12 weeks): Major events are development of the major organ systems of the body and generally rapid growth and development. Fetal stage (8-12 weeks to birth): Major events are appearance of the first bone cells and growth and refinement of the organ systems established during the embryonic stage.

6. Explain the importance of good nutrition during pregnancy.

Answer guideline. Good nutrition during pregnancy is associated with fewer complications of pregnancy and birth, and with healthier babies. Poor nutrition during pregnancy is associated with development of fewer brain cells during the prenatal period, stillbirth, low birthweight, death in the neonatal period, and health problems in the neonatal period.

7. Describe techniques of prenatal assessment.

Answer guideline. Amniocentesis: A sample of amniotic fluid is drawn from the uterus and analyzed to detect genetic defects; this procedure is performed at the fifteenth to sixteenth week of pregnancy. Chorionic villus sampling (CVS): Tissue is taken from projections of membrane around the embryo and tested for the presence of various conditions; CVS is performed during the first trimester. Maternal blood tests: Blood taken from the mother at the fourteenth to fifteenth week of pregnancy can be tested for alpha fetoprotein (AFP); AFP levels may indicate Down syndrome or defects in the formation of the central nervous system. These tests can also detect sickle-cell disease, Tay-Sachs disease, and thalassemia. Ultrasound: High-frequency sound waves are directed into a woman's uterus, and a sonogram (a picture of the fetus and placenta) is produced; ultrasound can detect multiple pregnancies or anatomical defects in the fetus or uterus and determine whether a fetus has died.

8. Describe the three stages of childbirth.

Answer guideline. In the first stage of childbirth, the cervix dilates; this is the longest stage. In the second stage, the infant moves through the cervix and vaginal canal and emerges from the mother's body. In the third stage, the umbilical cord and placenta are expelled.

9. Describe three types of drugs used in medicated deliveries.

Answer guideline. With general anesthesia, the mother is completely unconscious. Regional anesthesia blocks the nerve pathways carrying pain sensations to the brain. Analgesics relax the mother. All are transmitted to the fetus through the placenta, and all may result in decreased respiration, decreased responsiveness, and decreased alertness.

CHAPTER 3
PHYSICAL DEVELOPMENT IN INFANCY AND TODDLERHOOD

INTRODUCTION

In **Chapter 3** we learn that the first year of life is usually one of rapid physical growth, more so than at any other time in the child's life, with stabilized regulation of all major systems of the body.

- The first four weeks of life are the neonatal period. Physical characteristics, body systems, and brain and reflex behavior of the neonate are thoroughly discussed.

- At birth, immediate medical and behavioral assessment is crucial to predict a baby's health status. The Apgar Scale, various screening tests, and the Brazelton Scale are all used to examine the health of a newborn.

- Low-birthweight babies are at a higher risk of potential complications; several recommendations are made for preventing or overcoming the physiological and psychological problems of these babies. Also examined are the topics of postmaturity, infant mortality, sudden infant death syndrome (SIDS), and immunization.

- A neonate's initial reflex behaviors will disappear during the first year or so, being replaced by deliberate behaviors. More recent research examines the importance of early sensory stimulation for all newborns. Three principles of infant development are explained: head to toe, inner to outer, and simple to complex.

- Infant variations in daily cycles of nourishment, sleep, wakefulness, and activity are thoroughly described.

- Infants are able to make sense of their perceptions, and they can discriminate in the areas of sight, hearing, taste, smell, touch, and pain. Sensory systems of newborns are explained in detail.

- The developmental differences between boys and girls are briefly examined.

- The interaction of heredity and environment as it affects the timing of milestones of motor development is discussed, along with a multicultural view of motor development.

CHAPTER OUTLINE

I. THE NEONATE

A. PHYSICAL CHARACTERISTICS
B. BODY SYSTEMS
1. Circulatory System
2. Respiratory System
3. Gastrointestinal System
4. Temperature Regulation
C. THE BRAIN AND REFLEX BEHAVIOR
1. Growth and Development of the Brain
2. A Newborn's Reflexes
D. THE NEWBORN'S HEALTH
1. Effects of Birth Trauma
2. Medical and Behavioral Screening
   a. Immediate medical assessment: The Apgar Scale
   b. Neonatal screening for medical conditions
   c. Assessing responses: The Brazelton Scale
3. Low Birthweight
   a. Who is likely to have a low-birthweight baby?
   b. Cross-cultural aspects of low birthweight
   c. Consequences of low birthweight
   d. Treatment of low-birthweight babies
4. Postmaturity
5. Infant Mortality
6. Sudden Infant Death Syndrome
E. IMMUNIZATION FOR BETTER HEALTH

II. DEVELOPMENT DURING THE FIRST 3 YEARS OF LIFE

A. PRINCIPLES OF DEVELOPMENT
1. Top-to-Bottom Development
2. Inner-to-Outer Development
3. Simple-to-Complex Development
B. STATES OF AROUSAL: THE BODY'S CYCLES

III. STATES OF AROUSAL: THE BODY'S CYCLES

A. GROWTH AND NOURISHMENT
1. Influences on Growth
2. Breastfeeding
   a. The benefits of breastfeeding
   b. The cultural context of breastfeeding
3. Bottle Feeding
4. Cow's Milk and Solid Foods
B. THE SENSES
1. Sight
   a. Depth perception
   b. Visual preferences
2. Hearing
3. Smell
4. Taste
5. Touch and Pain
C. MOTOR DEVELOPMENT
1. Milestones of Motor Development
   a. Head control
   b. Hand control
   c. Locomotion
2. Environmental Influences on Motor Development
3. Can Motor Development be Speeded Up?
D. HOW DIFFERENT ARE BOYS AND GIRLS?

KEY TERMS

LEARNING OBJECTIVES

After finishing Chapter 3, students should be able to:

1. Describe some common physical characteristics of the *neonate*. (pp. 92-93)

2. Compare the demands on the major body systems before and after birth. (pp. 93-94)

3. Box 3-1 addresses a child's development of motor skills in various cultures. Comment briefly on the findings on this topic. (pp. 99-100)

4. Briefly describe the growth and development of the human brain. (pp. 94-96)

5. Describe the differences between the *Apgar Scale* and the *Brazelton Scale*. (pp. 96, 98-99)

6. The authors have given considerable information about the relationship between low birthweight and health complications. List several factors which can contribute to low birthweight, some of the consequences of low birthweight, and how it is treated. (pp. 100-103)

7. Explain postmaturity and its effect on newborns. (pp. 103)

8. Define *SIDS* and explain some findings about what may cause it. (pp. 104-105)

9. Compare rates of immunization in the U.S. and other countries and account for the discrepancies. (pp. 105-107)

10. Briefly describe the following three principles about babies' growth and development: *top-to-bottom* development, *inner-to-outer* development, *simple-to-complex* development (pp. 107-108)

11. List and briefly explain an infant's *states of arousal*. (pp. 108-110)

12. Discuss how heredity and environment interact in the process of physical growth. (p. 111)

13. Comment on the nourishment of newborns in the following areas: breastfeeding, bottle feeding, cow's milk and solid foods (pp. 111-112)

14. Describe what the normal infant's capacities seem to be in each of the following sensory systems: sight, hearing, smell, taste, touch and pain (pp. 113-117)

CHAPTER SUMMARY AND TEACHING RECOMMENDATIONS

The neonatal period is defined and described, together with a discussion of the neonate's adjustment from intrauterine to extrauterine life. A discussion of central nervous system (CNS) development during the prenatal period and infancy follows; you may wish to call students' attention to the importance of nutrition during the first months of life (discussed later in the chapter) in light of early neurological development. This initial section on the neonate concludes with a description of the newborn's reflexes.

The authors describe methods of neonatal assessment (Apgar, medical screening, and Brazelton Neonatal Behavioral Assessment Scale); they next discuss the effects of birth trauma. The chapter continues with an extensive discussion of low birthweight and how it relates to the infant mortality rate. At this point, a class discussion of social policy and infant mortality could be in order (see Topics for Discussion). This section of the chapter closes with a discussion of sudden infant death syndrome (SIDS).

In the next section--"Development During the First 3 Years of Life"--the authors present three developmental principles and describe infants' states. The chapter continues with a discussion of issues related to infants' growth and nourishment, with emphasis on the advantages of breastfeeding. Although the authors acknowledge that the quality of the developing parent-infant relationship is more important than the feeding method chosen, you may wish to stress the legitimacy of the need, or simply the decision, to bottle-feed.

"Development During the First 3 Years of Life" continues with a description of early sensory and motor capacities, including a brief discussion of the Denver Developmental Screening Test. With regard to the Denver test, you might want to note some of the problems with attempts to assess cognitive functioning early in life. The authors discuss environmental influences on development, and they provide a "Window on the World" box describing cross-cultural differences in the timing of motor development.

Following the discussion of environmental influences, the authors review experimental efforts to accelerate various aspects of motor development. Although the criticisms offered are well taken, you may also want to point out the advantages that sensory stimulation and enrichment (e.g., voices, motion, touch) can offer for the developing bond between parents and infant. The chapter concludes with a brief discussion of gender differences and similarities in infancy.

Boxes in Chapter 3 are "How Universal Is 'Normal' Development?" "When Does Obesity Begin, and What Should Be Done about It?" "Should Baby Boys Be Circumcised?" "Are 'Walkers' Worth the Risk?" and "Putting Research Findings to Work."

AUDIOVISUAL MATERIALS

Distributor, date, and running time are given for each film or video. Distributors' addresses are listed in the appendix (General Resources). If a film or video is not in color, there is a notation (BW) to that effect.

Preemies: The price tag. (AJN, 1983, video, approximately 30 min.) Topics include the varied costs (financial, medical, emotional) of premature birth.
The first 365 days in the life of a child. (FFHS, 1994, video, 13-part series, 28 min. each) This 13-part series shows the normal development of an average healthy child during the first year of its life.
Cross-cultural differences in newborn behavior. (PSU, 1980, approximately 10 min.) Shows neonates from varied racial and ethnic groups (Caucasian, Navajo, Aborigine, African) to illustrate behavioral differences.
Mothers, fathers, and babies. (FFHS, 1994, video, 30 min.) This program observes the role of breastfeeding in different cultures and its effect on the role of the father.
The postpartum blues. (FFHS, 1994, video, 19 min.) Women discuss the physical and

psychological demands on them immediately after childbirth; an obstetrician explains the physical and hormonal changes that take place during pregnancy and childbirth.
The second year in the life of a child. (FFHS, 1994, video, 4-part series, 28 min. each) Following on *The First 375 Days in the Life of a Child*, this segment follows toddlers through the second year. Once again, the developmental patterns are those of the average child. Like all averages, these present general guidelines.

Guest speakers

Local hospitals may again be your most useful resource for possible speakers. The pediatrics department may be able to help you locate a Brazelton examiner or a neonatal intensive care nurse. In addition, you might check to see if your community has a support group for parents of SIDS infants; if so, that group (or a more general support group for bereaved parents) might be able to provide a speaker.

LECTURE OUTLINES

Lecture 1: Neonatal Assessment

I. Neonatal period

A. Definition: The neonatal period is probably most commonly defined as the first 28 days of life.
B. Importance.
  1. In terms of physiology, this is a period of major adjustment. Processes such as eating, elimination, and temperature regulation must adapt to life outside the uterus.
  2. In terms of assessment, this is the first time that behavior is available for extensive observation.

II. Neonatal assessment: definition and goals

Assessment of neonates is defined in a specific way and has certain specific goals.

A. Definition: Neonatal assessment is systematic evaluation of the newborn.
B. Goals: Neonatal assessment has three goals.
  1. To identify abnormalities calling for early intervention.

2. To study individual differences apparent at birth.
3. To study newborns' behavior as an influence on early relationships with caregivers.

III. Types of neonatal assessment

There are three general types of neonatal assessment: screening tests, neurological examinations, and behavioral assessment.

A. Screening tests.
   1. These are relatively quick and simple to administer.
   2. Apgar scale. This is the most widely used; it is routinely done in the delivery room at 1 and 5 minutes after birth. It evaluates five characteristics of the newborn; a low Apgar score signals possible health problems. The Apgar test allows identification of serious problems needing immediate intervention.
   3. Screening tests for medical conditions. These can be administered directly after birth and can often detect such rare conditions as PKU, hypothyroidism, and galactosemia. When detected early, such defects can be correctable.
B. Neurological examinations.
   1. These are more extensive than screening tests and are not routinely used. Most infants don't need them, and they are costly to administer because they demand considerable time and skill.
   2. Their purpose is to evaluate the maturity and functioning of the CNS; they examine reflexes, muscle tone, and physical condition.
C. Behavioral assessments.
   1. These are also more extensive than screening tests and are not routinely used.
   2. Their purposes are to study individual differences among newborns and to study newborns' behavior for implications about relationships with caregivers. Most applications of such tests are in research.
   3. Brazelton Neonatal Behavioral Assessment Scale (BNBAS) is most widely used.
      a. Items on BNBAS include reflexes, reactions to different kinds of stimulation, and spontaneous behaviors.
      b. BNBAS is usually administered by a psychologist, early in the neonatal period (usually during the first 3 days after birth, when the infant is still in the hospital).
      c. Administration procedures are flexible: to elicit an infant's best performance (rather than a typical performance), the order of items may be varied and items may be repeated.

References for Lecture 1

Bayley, N. (1993). *Manual for the Bayley scales of infant development*. New York: Psychological Corporation.
Oliwenstein, L. (1992). Medical research on SIDS. *Discover, 13,* 87.
Osofsky, J. (Ed.) (1987). *Handbook of infant development*. New York: Wiley.

Lecture 2: Principles of Early Physical Development

I. Milestones of motor development

Motor development during the first 2 years of life incorporates several major milestones:

A. 1 month: holding head erect.
B. 8 months: sitting without support.
C. 1 year: standing, walking.
D. 2 years: climbing stairs.

II. Processes in motor development

Achieving these milestones depends on two general processes of development. These processes depend on both maturation and experience.

A. Development of muscle strength, allowing the infant to move muscles steadily against the force of gravity.
B. Establishment of neural control over muscles, leading to more voluntary and less reflexive activity.

III. Sequence of motor development

Motor abilities advance for different muscle groups at different points in development. Three general principles govern the sequence of acquiring motor abilities.

A. Cephalocaudal principle: literally, "head to tail."
   1. Prenatal development of hands and arms

occurs before that of legs and feet.
2. After birth, infants gain voluntary and sophisticated use of arms and hands before legs and feet.
B. Proximodistal principle: literally, "near to far."
1. Prenatally, structures closer to the trunk develop before structures farther out. For example, vital organs develop before limbs, and limbs develop before fingers and toes.
2. With respect to motor development, infants gain voluntary and sophisticated use of structures closer to the trunk before structures farther from the center of the body (e.g., an infant can reach with the arms before using the hands and fingers to grasp and hold).
C. Hierarchical integration: "simple to complex."
1. Infants first master simple motor abilities; these are later combined into more complex abilities (e.g., infants first can reach, then can grasp, then can keep hold of objects); finally, these skills are combined to reach for an object, grab it, and hold on to it while drawing it toward oneself.
2. This principle could also be applied to other developmental processes, such as cognitive development.

Note: Lecture 2 closely follows the material presented in Chapter 3 of the textbook, and therefore no specific references are cited. However, the references on infant development in the appendix to this manual (General Resources) could be used to elaborate on or supplement the lecture.

TOPIC FOR DEBATE

Are Efforts to Accelerate Early Development Ethically Acceptable?

Background

In Chapter 3 of the textbook, the authors describe a variety of efforts to speed up early motor development; in later chapters, they review attempts to accelerate early cognitive and even social and moral development. These efforts have met with mixed success, depending on their nature and focus, and on the criteria used in evaluating success.

Proponents of such efforts raise a number of arguments for their scientific and practical

standpoint. Identification of environmental factors which cause developmental progress-- as well as the identification of developmental processes that seem to be relatively immune to environmental influence--is of enormous value. More practically, this information could suggest means of intervening in cases of developmental delays and of optimizing normal development through environmental enrichment.

Critics of such efforts, on the other hand, raise a number of questions about these supposed benefits. From a scientific standpoint, one might argue that simply because one demonstrates that a particular environmental intervention can accelerate development, one has not proved that this or a similar intervention normally does govern development. If generalizing from an experimental to a normal context is, in that respect, unwarranted, then one must be even more cautious about using experimental results as a basis for intervention in cases of abnormal development. Another concern is that efforts to accelerate development may unnecessarily raise parents' anxieties, their competitiveness, or their need for achievement. In essence, one might argue that there is simply no compelling need to hasten the achievement of developmental milestones that will be attained naturally as a result of maturation.

Debate plan

Using this background, and information from additional sources (selected references appear below), student panels should debate the following positions:

Position A. Research aimed at speeding motor development in infancy is of such potential scientific and practical value that any potential risks are far outweighed.

Position B. The risks of research aimed at accelerating development are not outweighed by its potential value.

References for the debate

Bijou, S. W. & Baer, D. M. (1978). *Behavior analysis of child development.* Englewood Cliffs, NJ: Prentice-Hall.
Bornstein, M. (1992). *Development in infancy: An introduction.* New York: McGraw-Hill.

(1992). *Future directions in infant development research.* New York: Springer-Verlag.

TOPICS FOR DISCUSSION

Topic 1: Early Nutrition

1. Ask students to identify some of the effects of diet on infants' growth and physical development (textbook pages 110-111).

2. Ask students to summarize the advantages (described in the text) of breastfeeding over bottle feeding and to note possible disadvantages of breastfeeding as compared with bottle feeding. Ask students to identify circumstances under which a woman might reasonably choose to bottle-feed (pages 111-113).

3. Ask students to speculate about changes in society, in social policy, or in both that would make it easier for parents to provide optimal nutrition for infants. (Examples: more nutritious commercial baby food, better and more accessible parent education, more extensive income support and nutritional supplement programs, greater flexibility in the workplace for nursing mothers.)

Topic 2: Low Birthweight and Social Policy

1. It is sometimes said that our current rates of low birthweight and infant mortality are indicators of a number of social problems. Why might this statement be made? (pages 100-104)

2. What kinds of social changes could be most effective in reducing the incidence of low birthweight and infant mortality? (pages 101-103, 105-107)

PROJECTS AND CLASS EXERCISES

Group Exercise: Sudden Infant Death Syndrome

Working in groups, students should develop a set of written answers to the following questions:

1. What are the characteristics of SIDS infants?

2. What are the characteristics of parents of SIDS infants?

3. What is the most important service that could be provided to parents of SIDS victims and to other family members? Why do you consider this service so important?

Project 1: Historical Changes in Views of the Neonate

Have students review a child-care manual published within the last 5 years and evaluate the accuracy of its presentation of the newborn's sensory capacities. Then have them compare this contemporary presentation with a child-care manual published before 1960--preferably, before 1940.

Project 2: Portrayals of Early Gender Differences

Have students review portrayals of male and female infants in various popular media, such as television programs, television advertising, and magazines. Students should write a paper evaluating the accuracy of these portrayals in light of the material presented in the text and supplementary materials obtained through library research.

ESSAY QUESTIONS

1. Describe the growth of the brain before and after birth.

Answer guideline. Brain growth is most rapid during the prenatal period and the early years of life. Before birth, most of the cells of the mature brain have already been formed. Shortly after birth, brain cells become more specialized and migrate to the cerebral cortex, or to subcortical layers, and connections between these areas of the brain are formed. Within the first 2 months, this process is more or less completed. Thereafter, the brain continues to grow, reaching 66 percent of its adult weight by the end of the first year and 80 percent of adult weight by the end of the second year. The brain is virtually at adult size by age 12.

2. What is the importance of reflex behaviors in the newborn?

Answer guideline. Students should note that many of the reflexes described in the text have apparent functions for survival (e.g., sucking and rooting), or promote parent-infant bonding (e.g., grasping), or both. Students could also note that the presence or absence of these reflexes can indicate neurological maturity of the neonate.

3. Identify the three approaches to neonatal screening discussed in the text and note the purpose of each.

Answer guideline. The Apgar test is performed routinely at 1 and 5 minutes after birth to identify infants in need of lifesaving treatment. Screening for medical conditions (e.g., PKU) is also performed routinely at birth to detect correctable but potentially serious conditions. The BNBAS is used primarily as a research tool to identify ways in which infants respond to their environment.

4. Describe two types of low-birthweight babies and explain the consequences of low birthweight.

Answer guideline. All low-birthweight babies weigh less than 5 1/2 pounds at birth. There are two types of low-birthweight babies. Preterm babies are born before the thirty-seventh gestational week; small-for-date babies weigh less than 90 percent of all babies born at the same gestational age. These two types are not mutually exclusive. Consequences of low birthweight include difficulty in maintaining normal body temperature; vulnerability to infection; immature reflexes (including reflexes necessary for survival); a higher incidence of hypoglycemia, jaundice, and bleeding in the brain; lungs that are too weak to sustain breathing; and a higher incidence of death in the neonatal period.

5. Identify the three principles of development discussed in the text and give an example of each.

Answer guideline. Cephalocaudal: Development proceeds from the head to the lower parts of the body. Proximodistal: Development proceeds from the center to the outer parts of the body. Simple to complex: In acquiring skills, complex skills build on simple ones.

6. Describe the five states of infants.

Answer guideline. Regular sleep: closed eyes, regular breathing, no movements except for startle responses, no response to mild stimulation. Irregular sleep: closed eyes, irregular breathing, muscle twitches, and smiles or grimaces in response to sound or light. Drowsiness: open or closed eyes, irregular breathing, some activity, and some response (e.g., facial expression, erection) to stimuli. Alert inactivity: open eyes, quiet movement (looking, moving head or limbs). Waking activity and crying: open eyes, much activity; activity may increase in response to stimuli.

7. Identify hereditary and environmental influences on growth.

Answer guideline. Genetics has an important influence on height and weight; gender and racial differences in physical stature are readily apparent. Environmental influences on growth include health, nutrition, living conditions, and medical care.

8. Describe the Denver Developmental Screening Test.

Answer guideline. This test was designed to identify children whose motor development is abnormal; it covers gross motor skills (e.g., rolling over, catching a ball) and fine motor skills (e.g., grasping a rattle, copying a circle) that should occur between 1 month and 6 years of age. The test also covers language development (e.g., vocabulary) and personal and social development (e.g., smiling spontaneously, dressing independently). Norms are provided to indicate the ages at which 25 percent, 50 percent, 75 percent, and 90 percent of children master each skill. A child is considered developmentally delayed if he or she does not master a skill by the time that 90 percent of all children do; a child is thought to need special attention if he or she shows delays in two or more sectors of development.

CHAPTER 4
INTELLECTUAL DEVELOPMENT IN INFANCY AND TODDLERHOOD

INTRODUCTION

Chapter 3 discussed the physical development of the baby from birth through toddlerhood. **Chapter 4** continues the examination of that early stage of life but shifts the focus to intellectual development. Contrary to earlier beliefs, the infant is capable of significant learning and not only responds to the environment but works actively to alter it.

- This chapter explores the intellectual capabilities of the newborn and examines the processes by which the developing infant begins to interact with the environment in order to render it meaningful. Topics which are introduced include maturation, habituation, conditioning, and infant memory.

- Three different approaches to studying intellectual development will be evaluated: the psychometric, Piagetian, and information-processing approaches.

- The major intellectual accomplishment of infancy--the development of language--is outlined and will be examined from the view of learning theory and nativism. Also, a variety of factors influencing language development are discussed.

- The chapter concludes with a discussion of the child's emerging sense of competence and how it is acquired and develops relative to parents' child-rearing styles.

CHAPTER OUTLINE

KEY TERMS

Piagetian approach (135)
prelinguistic speech (146)
psychometric approach (133)
representational ability (138)
schemes (136)
sensorimotor stage (135)
visible imitation (139)
visual-recognition memory (142)

LEARNING OBJECTIVES

After finishing Chapter 4, students should be able to:

1. Distinguish between *learning* and *maturation*. (pp. 128-129)

2. Explain *habituation*. (p. 129)

3. Define and give an example of the following types of conditioning: (pp. 130-131) classical and operant (instrumental) conditioning

4. Describe how *classical conditioning* and *operant conditioning* can combine to produce complex learning. (p. 131)

5. Describe the concept of infant memory. (pp. 131-132)

6. Briefly compare and contrast the three approaches to studying intellectual development: *psychometric approach, Piagetian approach, information-processing approach* (p. 133)

7. Define *intelligent behavior* and explain some problems in trying to measure intelligence in infants and toddlers. (pp. 132-134)

8. Explain the significance of developmental tests. (p. 134)

9. Explain *cognitive development* in Piaget's *sensorimotor stage* and define his terminology: *circular reactions, schemes, object permanence, causality, representational ability* (pp. 135-138)

10. List and briefly describe the 6 substages of Piaget's *sensorimotor stage*. (pp. 135-138)

11. Explain the pros and cons of the *sensorimotor stage* concept, and define the following terms: *invisible imitation, visible imitation, deferred imitation* (pp. 138-142)

12. Explain how information processing in infancy is related to intelligence, and give an example of each of the following: *visual-recognition memory, novelty preference, cross-modal transference* (pp. 142-143)

13. Briefly relate the cultural difference of the Chinese and American approaches to child development that Professor Gardner found in his 1989 study in China. (p. 144)

14. Describe the development of *prelinguistic speech*. (pp. 148-149)

15. Explain the significance of the babbling of hearing-impaired children. (p. 147)

16. Describe the development of *linguistic speech* and explain how vocabulary grows in young children. (pp. 148-149)

17. Explain how children learn to create sentences and list three characteristics of early speech. (pp. 149-150)

18. Compare and contrast *learning theory* and *nativism* as approaches to language acquisition. (pp. 150-151)

19. Define *child-directed speech* ("motherese") and explain its influence on language development. (pp. 151-153)

20. Give three suggestions for talking with babies and toddlers at different stages of language development. (p. 154)

21. Briefly explain the topic of delayed language development. (p. 153)

22. Explain what influences competence, and give a few suggestions for enhancing a child's competence. (pp. 155-156)

23. Describe some findings of studies using the Home Inventory. (pp. 155-157)

CHAPTER SUMMARY AND TEACHING RECOMMENDATIONS

The chapter opens with a definition of learning and distinguishes between learning and maturation. Different types of learning observed in young infants (including habituation, classical conditioning, and operant conditioning) are described. At this point, you might note that all these forms of learning continue to be important throughout the life span and that their importance in this context may have to do with demonstrating the variety of things infants can learn and the various means by which infants can learn. The initial section of the chapter concludes with a brief discussion of infants' memory.

In the next section, "Studying Intellectual Development: Three Approaches," the authors define intelligence; the section continues with a review of the psychometric, Piagetian, and information-processing views of intelligence. In discussing this section of the chapter, you might want to indicate that predicting later IQ on the basis of performance on an assessment made in infancy is rarely necessary (except for research purposes) and in any event is rarely accurate: poor prediction is cited as a general problem of the psychometric approach.

Another important point to call to students' attention is the importance of Piaget's theory as a stimulus for a diverse and vast body of research documenting cognitive competence in infancy; in our experience, students are apt to greet his theory with skepticism when they learn that his timetable of development has not been perfectly confirmed through subsequent research.

The authors present language development as a central part of cognitive development; this point bears special emphasis, together with a more general statement that language development can be seen as a critical intersection of physical, cognitive, and social development. The nativist and learning-theory positions on language development are presented, and the stages of prelinguistic and linguistic speech are reviewed. This section includes a discussion of the importance of caregivers' speech for language development and a description of "motherese."

The chapter closes with an overview of the growth of competence. Competence is defined on the basis of findings from the Harvard Preschool Project, which is described in detail. In discussing this section, you might reiterate the authors' point that infants and children undoubtedly influence parenting styles, just as parenting is a critical influence on children's development.

Boxes in Chapter 4 are "Eastern and Western Learning Styles," "What the Babbling of Hearing-Impaired Babies Tells Us about the Development of Language," "Talking with Babies and Toddlers," and "How Parents Can Help Their Children to Be More Competent."

AUDIOVISUAL MATERIALS

Distributor, date, and running time are given for each film or video. Distributors' addresses are listed in the appendix (General Resources). If a film or video is not in color, there is a notation (BW) to that effect.

Piaget on Piaget. (YU, 1977, approximately 40 min.) Includes descriptions of Piaget's classic studies of infant intelligence.

The developing child: the crucial early years. (FFHS, 1994, video, 26 min.) This program deals with ways in which mental growth can be assisted in infants and young children.

Sex roles: charting the complexity of development. (IM, 1991, video, 60 min.) Beginning with a look at the cultural ramification of sex roles and the myths associated with them, this program examines three theories of socialization: Freudian, social-learning, and cognitive-developmental.

The infant mind. (IM, 1992, video, 30 min.) Jean Piaget's stage theories of object permanence and sensory-motor development are explained and challenged in this new investigation of infant learning.

Baby talk. (IM, 1985, video, 60 min.) Beginning with the radical reappraisal of linguistic development that stemmed from the studies of Noam Chomsky, this video investigates the development of language.

First adaptations. (IM, 1992, video, 30 min.) This program shows how infants' sleeping patterns contribute to mental organization and later to learning abilities and illustrates how the brain develops as the infant attains higher levels of cognitive processing.

Language and thinking. (IM, 1992, video, 30 min.) Examining research on language development, this program investigates the role of the brain in facilitating and processing language during early childhood.

Basic parenting skills. (IM, 1990, video, 60 min.) In an entertaining manner, this program examines the "three R's of parenting"--routine, respect, and resourcefulness. The program also presents strategies for coping with the frustrations of being a new parent.

Guest speakers

Possible sources of guest speakers include local community mental health centers, which may be able to refer you to a professional skilled in making psychometric assessments of very young children. Such a person could probably give much more concrete meaning to the text's discussion of difficulties in applying this approach with infants and toddlers. In addition, CMHCs may help you contact an "infant stimulation" program or a "parent effectiveness training" program; either program may be able to provide a speaker.

LECTURE OUTLINES

Lecture 1: Piaget's Theory

I. What is Piaget's theory?

This is a theory of cognitive development: how thinking, reasoning, etc., change with age and how intelligence changes with age. Cognitive development is represented as a sequence of stages.

A. Intelligence is qualitatively (as opposed to quantitatively) different at different periods of development.
B. Individuals differ in how quickly or slowly they progress through the stages, but the sequence of stages is invariant: various forms of intelligence always appear in the same order.
C. The stages are also functionally invariant: two basic characteristics of intelligence appear in all stages.
  1. Organization: Abilities, concepts,

etc., are used in a coordinated way (not unrelated to each other). Organization is different at different stages, but some form of organization exists at each stage.
  2. Adaptation: Intelligence is always a tool or mechanism for dealing with tasks and demands presented by the environment. Two processes allow adaptation to occur.
    a. Assimilation: New information is taken in and fitted into existing knowledge.
    b. Accommodation: New information is again taken in and fitted into existing knowledge, but previous ideas and concepts must be modified.

II. How did Piaget study cognitive development?

Piaget's methodology was very personal.

A. Piaget observed his own three children. This was especially important to his ideas about infants' intelligence.
  1. He made very careful, detailed observations and records of those observations.
  2. Many of his observations have been confirmed by research with larger, more representative samples of infants.
B. Piaget also administered the Binet test. His interest was in wrong answers and the reasoning behind answers. He questioned children about these answers, using the clinical method. The clinical method is a flexible approach to discovering children's concepts and reasoning, as opposed to the quantitative measures of intelligence used in the psychometric approach.
C. He also undertook later research with children, again using the clinical method but not starting with "wrong" answers on the Binet test. Instead, he presented various types of tasks designed to discover children's reasoning processes and beliefs about the world.

References for Lecture 1

Amann-Gainotti, M. (1992). Contributions to the history of psychology: Jean Piaget, student of Pierre Janet. *Perceptual and motor skills, 74,* 1101-1115.

Beilin, H. (1992). Piaget's enduring contribution to developmental psychology. *Developmental psychology, 28,* 191-204.
Flavell, J. H. (1963). *The developmental psychology of Jean Piaget,* New York: Van Nostrand Reinhold.
Ginsburg, H. P. & Opper, S. (1988). *Piaget's theory of intellectual development* (3rd ed.). Englewood Cliffs, NJ: Prentice-Hall.

Lecture 2: Piaget's Sensorimotor Period

I. The sensorimotor period

This is the first stage of cognitive development, from birth to approximately 2 years. Many of Piaget's ideas about this period were based on his observations of his own children.

II. Stages within the sensorimotor period

The sensorimotor period is divided into six substages. Note that all ages given for these stages are approximate.

A. Stage 1, birth to 1 month. Infant has reflexes and reflexlike abilities--schemes. Schemes are very primitive skills, applied in wide variety of situations. They are important as building blocks for further development and are elaborated and coordinated throughout this period. (Note: The term schema is often used instead of scheme.)
    1. Example of a reflex: sucking.
    2. Examples of reflexlike behavior: grasping, looking.
B. Stage 2, 1 to 4 months.
    1. First sign of accommodation of schemes: Infant performs schemes differently in different situations (e.g., sucking differently on a nipple and on a thumb; grasping a rattle differently from a blanket).
    2. First sign of coordination of schemes: Infant will look at an object and reach for it.
    3. Primary circular reaction: Infant makes a new response that produces some sensation and then repeats the response again and again.
C. Stage 3, 4 to 8 months.
    1. Motor recognition: First sign of ability to represent objects, actions, and experiences mentally. (Infant sees a familiar object and makes a reduced form of the motion usually

made with that object.)
    2. Generalizing assimilation: When infants encounter a new object or situation, they apply an existing scheme to it.
    3. Secondary circular reaction: Infant makes a new response that produces environmental effects and repeats the response so that its effects are repeated.
D. Stage 4, 8 to 12 months. Further coordination of schemes: These are now coordinated in means-end sequences. One scheme is performed in order to be able to perform another.
E. Stage 5, 12 to 18 months. Tertiary circular reactions: Infant performs a new action producing an effect in the environment and then repeats the action with variations.
F. Stage 6, 18 to 24 months. Mental experimentation: A sign of more advanced mental representation. Child now seems to "think through" a sequence of actions before performing them (that is, representing mentally what will be done and what its consequences will be).

III. Major accomplishment of the sensorimotor period: Object permanence

There are several steps in the development of object permanence.

A. Early in the first year: If the infant is playing with a toy which falls out of the crib, he or she doesn't look for it ("out of sight, out of mind"). Infant doesn't distinguish between an object and actions on an object; is not aware that an object continues to exist when not being acted on.
B. Later in the first year: Infant will look for a hidden object if he or she is actually reaching for it when it is hidden.
C. Early in the second year: Infant will now search for a hidden object whether or not he or she is reaching for it when it is hidden.
    1. This shows a stronger grasp of the concept.
    2. The infant now makes the "A not B" error. The object is hidden in one place and the infant finds it there several times; then the object is hidden in a second place while

the infant watches. Infant looks for the object where it was last <u>found</u>, not where it was last <u>hidden</u>.

D.   End of the second year: Infant no longer makes the "A not B" error. Infant will consistently look for an object where it was last hidden, rather than where it was last found and thus has a mature concept of an object.

References for Lecture 2

Amann-Gainotti, M. (1992). Contributions to the history of psychology: Jean Piaget, a student of Pierre Janet. *Perceptual and motor skills, 74,* 1011-1015.
Beilin, H. (1992). Piaget's enduring contribution to developmental psychology. *Developmental psychology, 28,* 191-204.
Ginsburg, H. P. & Opper, S. (1988). *Piaget's theory of intellectual development* (3rd ed.). Englewood Cliffs, NJ: Prentice-Hall.

Lecture 3: On Talking to Children: "Motherese"

I. Characteristics of "motherese"

What kinds of linguistic environments do caregivers provide for children? Studies of mothers' speech to young children, older children, and adults demonstrate the unique characteristics of "motherese."

A.   Philips (1973). Philips studied the speech of white middle-class mothers to their 1-year-old sons and to an adult. Differences in the speech samples included the following:
1.   Speech to sons used shorter sentences and fewer verbs, modifiers, function words, and verb forms.
2.   Vocabulary in speech to sons was less diverse and more concrete.
B.   Snow (1972). Snow compared mothers' speech to their 2-year-old children with their speech to their 10-year-old children. Differences in the speech samples included the following:
1.   Speech to younger children was less complex structurally (as in Philips's study) and more repetitious, and it included fewer pronouns.
2.   These differences were much less pronounced when mothers spoke into a tape recorder (without the child present) and were instructed to

talk as if they were speaking to a child of age 2 or age 10. This suggests that children themselves provide critical cues or feedback governing adults' speech modifications.
C.   Shatz & Gelman (1973). Shatz and Gelman studied linguistic input provided by older children. Their findings included the following:
1.   Older children provide a substantial proportion of younger children's linguistic input.
2.   Four-year-olds modified their speech depending upon the age of the listener, much as adults did.

II. Significance of "motherese"

"Motherese" may facilitate language learning by providing linguistic input at an optimal level of complexity.

A.   Difficult constructions are avoided.
B.   Repetitions (exact and paraphrased) make up a large portion of the input.
C.   Infants and toddlers pay greater attention to taped presentations of "motherese" than to taped speech addressed to an adult.

References for Lecture 3

Bloom, L. (1991). *Language development from two to three.* Cambridge; New York: Cambridge University Press.
Burleson, B., Delia, J., & Applegate, J. (1992). Effects of maternal communication and children's social-cognitive and communication skills on children's acceptance by the peer group. *Family relations, 41,* 264-272.
(1993). *Language and cognition: A developmental perspective.* Norwood, NJ: Ablex.

TOPIC FOR DEBATE

Are Efforts to Instill or Enhance Parenting Skills Warranted?

Background

Several research projects document the potential value of early intervention to optimize infants' intellectual and social development. At the beginning of this century, Skeels and Dye apparently forestalled retardation in orphans' cognitive development through environmental intervention. More recently, some intervention efforts to enhance mothers' parenting skills and self-concepts, in particular, and to improve their children's intellectual and social environments more generally have met with success. These recent programs include the Milwaukee Project, the Parent-Child Development Centers, the Levenstein Toy Demonstration program, and the Auerbach-Badger Mothers' Discussion groups.

Although such intervention programs may be costly, the social costs of the long-term consequences of parenting practices which do not foster children's competence (or which actually lead to "familial retardation") are far higher. Many people would include in such costs the expense of providing remedial education and services for children who have difficulties with school adjustment; also, the social costs of juvenile delinquency and chronic unemployment.

Concerns can certainly be raised regarding these programs, however. Some observers consider the definitions of competence and optimal developmental outcomes--cited as goals of the programs--to be culturally biased, reflecting white middle-class values and overlooking the strengths of nonwhite and nonwestern cultures. Others note that, even on the assumption that these "optimal outcomes" should be fostered, the parenting practices which would lead to them have not yet been clearly delimited. Also, it is likely that many approaches to parenting lead to desirable patterns of development--not only the approaches that have been identified thus far. Furthermore, the child's own contribution to achieving these outcomes may have been underestimated.

Debate plan

Using this background, and information from additional sources (selected references appear below), student panels should debate the following positions:

Position A. Early intellectual development should be optimized through interventions aimed at enhancing parenting skills.

Position B. Current efforts to optimize early intellectual development are overzealous or even misguided.

References for the debate

Bigler, R. & Liben, L. (1992). Cognitive mechanisms in children's gender stereotyping: Theoretical and educational implications of a cognitive-based intervention. *Child development, 63,* 1351-1363.
Hudley, C. & Graham, S. (1993). An attributional intervention to reduce peer-directed aggression among African-American boys. *Child development, 64,* 124-138.
Slaughter, D. T. (1983). Early intervention and its effects on maternal and child development. *Monograph of the society for research in child development*, 48(48), Serial No. 202.
(1993). *Family-centered early intervention with infants and toddlers: Innovative cross-disciplinary approaches.* Baltimore: Brookes.

TOPICS FOR DISCUSSION

Topic 1: Learning and Memory in Infancy

1.   Ask students to identify the types of learning in infancy that are described in Chapter 4 of the text.

2.   Which of these types seem to be most prominent during infancy and toddlerhood? Which seem to be most prominent in the students' own lives as young adults (or older adults)? (Refer to the material on textbook pages 129-132.)

Topic 2: Approaches to Studying Intellectual Development

1.   Ask students to summarize the psychometric view of intelligence and how intelligence is assessed with this approach (pages 133-134).

2.   Ask students to identify problems that one would be likely to encounter in making a psychometric assessment of a toddler. Ask them for suggestions about how the problems could be overcome (pages 133-134).

3.   Ask students to identify the potential values and potential dangers of a psychometric assessment of a toddler's intelligence (pages 133-135).

4. Ask students to note differences between the psychometric and the Piagetian approaches to studying intellectual development (pages 133-142).

5. Ask students to summarize the information-processing approach to how intelligence works and to explain its significance in predicting intelligence (pages 142-143).

Topic 3: Theories of Language Acquisition

1. Ask students to summarize the nativist and the learning-theory approaches to explaining language acquisition (pages 150-151).

2. Ask students to judge--on the basis of the material presented in the text--whether nativism or learning theory currently has greater empirical support. Ask them to describe the type or types of evidence needed to provide definitive support for one theory over the other (pages 150-151).

3. Ask students to identify implications of each theory for parenting.

PROJECTS AND CLASS EXERCISES

Group Exercise: Defining and Assessing Infants' Intelligence

Working in groups, students should develop their own definition of *intelligence* as it would apply to a 2-year-old and develop a means of assessing intelligence as they have defined it.

The group's definition of *intelligence* can be one of those discussed in the text or an original one. Either way, the group should also present a written rationale for the definition.

The assessment procedure that the group develops should have two parts: a general overview of the procedure (e.g., time and materials required, setting for administration, who would administer the procedure, etc.), and two or more sample items.

Project 1: Piagetian Observations

Students should read Piaget's descriptions of his observations of his infants and attempt to replicate them with a sibling, a nephew or niece, or a neighbor of the appropriate age.

The students should then write a paper comparing the results of their observations with those of Piaget and discussing possible reasons for differences.

Note: Sources for Piaget's descriptions include Piaget's chapter in Carmichael's manual of child development, Ginsburg and Opper's book on Piaget, Flavell's books on cognitive development, and studies by Amann-Gainotti and Beilin.)

Project 2: Language Development

Students should collect 5- to 10-minute tape-recorded samples of the speech of a 12-month-old, an 18-month-old, a 24-month-old, a 30-month-old, and a 36-month-old child. Students should write a paper describing as much background information as possible on each child, each child's use of language, and similarities and differences between these speech samples and the text's description of stages of language development.

ESSAY QUESTIONS

1. Distinguish between classical and operant conditioning, and give an example of how each is apparent in infants' behavior.

Answer guideline. In classical conditioning, an association between a "neutral" stimulus and a reflexive response is formed. In operant conditioning, a behavior becomes more frequent or less frequent through association with consequences. An example of classical conditioning is a child blinking at the sight of a camera because of previous experiences with flashbulbs. An example of operant conditioning is an infant learning to suck more on a nipple that activates a tape of his or her mother's voice rather than on a nipple that produces the voice of a strange woman.

2. Discuss infants' memory abilities.

Answer guideline. Evidence for infants' memory abilities includes their ability to learn through both classical and operant conditioning. If infants could not remember, they could neither form associations between unconditioned and conditioned stimuli nor modify their behavior in reaction to its consequences. Furthermore, infants' ability to habituate to a familiar stimulus indicates that they recognize the stimulus. Research has also shown that very young infants can remember actions effective in activating mobiles for as long as 2 months.

3.   Explain the three approaches to studying intelligence outlined in the chapter.

Answer guideline. The psychometric approach attempts to measure intelligence; in this approach, only quantitative changes in intelligence occur as the individual develops. In the Piagetian approach, the organization and functioning of intelligence are studied; this approach is based on the belief that qualitative changes in these aspects of intelligence occur as the individual develops. The information-processing approach involves the study of how individuals process, store, and retrieve information using the abilities defined as intelligence.

4.   Describe problems in the use of intelligence tests in infancy.

Answer guideline. Problems include difficulties in interpreting an infant's behavior (or failure to behave) during a testing session, poor reliability of scores on these tests, and inaccurate predictions of later intelligence based on infants' scores.

5.   Describe the cognitive concepts central to Piaget's sensorimotor stage of intellectual development.

Answer guideline. During the sensorimotor period (birth to approximately 2 years), infants normally acquire the concepts of object permanence (the realization that an object continues to exist even when out of sight) and causality (the recognition that certain events cause certain other events). Acquisition of both concepts proceeds through six substages of the sensorimotor period and requires approximately the first 2 years of life.

6.   What are the strengths and weaknesses of Piaget's theory?

Answer guideline. Strengths: The theory has generated an impressive body of research (much of it confirming Piaget's original observations) and has been the basis for efforts to measure early intellectual development. Weaknesses: The specific timetable of cognitive milestones that Piaget

proposed may need some modification in light of Baillargeon's work on object permanence and Moore and Meltzoff's work on imitation.

7.   Identify forms of prelinguistic speech and explain the importance of these early forms of communication.

Answer guideline. Forms of prelinguistic speech include crying, cooing, babbling, accidental imitation, and deliberate imitation. The importance of prelinguistic speech includes its impact on emotional bonding with the caregiver.

8.   Describe the four stages of language development discussed in the text.

Answer guideline. Stage 1 (prespeech): Infants make a variety of sounds that progress in a fairly set sequence from crying to cooing and babbling, accidental imitation, and then deliberate imitation. Stage 2 (first words): Babies begin linguistic speech, the use of spoken language to convey meaning. Stage 3 (first sentences): Infants initiate the ability to combine two words together to express a single thought. Stage 4 (early syntax): Children's speech becomes longer and more complex; although they omit many parts of speech, they get their meaning across, and they are fluent speakers.

9.   What are the characteristics of "motherese," and what is its importance?

Answer guideline. Characteristics include a high voice pitch, short words, short sentences, slowed speech, greater frequency of questions, and greater frequency of repetitions than are used in speech addressed to adults. "Motherese" seems to be important in its encouragement of vocalization by the infant and in its focus on simple, concrete topics (about which young children may find it easier to talk).

10.   Summarize the differences between the "A" and "C" mothers in the Harvard Preschool Project.

Answer guideline. Compared with the "C" mothers, "A" mothers were better able to design a safe and interesting physical environment for their children, acted more effectively as "consultants" for their children by being available but not hovering, and were better able to exert control as needed (setting reasonable and consistent rules, and using distraction and physical separation rather than punishment).

11. According to the text, what can parents do to enhance children's competence?

Answer guideline. Parents can have the greatest influence on their children's competence between the ages of 6 to 8 months and 2 years. At that time, the quality (rather than the quantity) of contact with parents is critical; parents should be responsive to the child's needs for help. However, parents should not hover over the child, since children need to learn how to gain an adult's attention. Talking to the child is important, as is providing a safe and interesting physical environment; the child should have physical freedom to explore and interesting things to explore.

CHAPTER 5

PERSONALITY AND SOCIAL DEVELOPMENT IN INFANCY AND TODDLERHOOD

INTRODUCTION

Chapter 5 begins with a discussion of early personality development. According to Erik Erikson, infants and toddlers experience the first two crises in a series of eight that influence personality development throughout life. These include *basic trust versus mistrust* and *autonomy versus shame and doubt*. Suggestions on reducing negative behavior and encouraging self-regulation are provided.

- Emotions form a fundamental element of personality. Self-awareness appears to emerge in the following sequence: physical self-regulation, self-description, and emotional response to wrongdoing. The ability of infants to show their emotions through crying, smiling, and laughing is examined, and the mutual-regulation model is presented to explain how emotions are communicated between infant and adult.

- Early differences in emotional response are indicative of future personality development. Some emotional reactions may stem from differences in temperament. Nine fairly stable components of temperament are given, as are a variety of temperamental influences.

- Also examined are personality differences between the sexes, which appear to be mostly socially influenced.

- The topic of socialization--how children learn the behaviors their culture deems appropriate--is looked at closely. Mothers play a central role in their child's development. The mother-infant bond and father-infant bond are critiqued, and research on mother-infant attachment is presented.

- Separation anxiety and stranger anxiety, which appear during the second half of the first year, are discussed. Research on disturbances in family relationships--including institutionalization, hospitalization, and child abuse/neglect are presented.

- Studies about the influence of sibling relationships are presented.

- The impact of early day care is discussed, with suggestions provided on selecting good child care. Research is summarized on how day care affects a child's cognitive, social, and emotional development.

CHAPTER OUTLINE

I. EARLY PERSONALITY DEVELOPMENT

A. TRUST VERSUS MISTRUST
B. AUTONOMY VERSUS SHAME AND DOUBT

II. EMOTIONS: THE FOUNDATION OF PERSONALITY

A. HOW INFANTS' EMOTIONS ARE STUDIED
B. HOW EMOTIONS DEVELOP: THE EMERGING SENSE OF SELF
C. HOW INFANTS SHOW THEIR EMOTIONS
   1. Crying
   2. Smiling
   3. Laughing
D. HOW EMOTIONS ARE COMMUNICATED BETWEEN INFANTS AND ADULTS
   1. Mutual-Regulation Model
      a. "Reading" the emotions of another person
   2. Social Referencing

III. DIFFERENCES IN PERSONALITY DEVELOPMENT

A. TEMPERAMENTAL DIFFERENCES
   1. Components of Temperament
   2. Three Patterns of Temperament
   3. Influences on Temperament
   4. Effects of Temperament on Adjustments: "Goodness of Fit"
B. GENDER DIFFERENCES

IV. THE FAMILY AND PERSONALITY DEVELOPMENT

A. THE MOTHER'S ROLE
   1. The Mother-Infant Bond
      a. Is there a critical period for mother-infant bonding?
      b. What do babies need from their mothers?
   2. Attachment: A Reciprocal Connection
      a. Studying attachments
      b. Patterns of attachment
      c. How attachment is established
         (1) What the mother does
         (2) What the baby does
      d. Changes in attachment
      e. Long-term effects of attachment
      f. Critique of attachment research
B. THE FATHER'S ROLE
   1. Bonds and Attachments between Fathers and Infants
   2. How Do Fathers Act with Their Infants?
   3. What Is the Significance of the Father-Infant Relationship?
C. STRANGER ANXIETY AND SEPARATION ANXIETY
D. DISTURBANCES IN FAMILY RELATIONSHIPS
   1. Institutionalization
   2. Hospitalization
   3. Child Abuse and Neglect
      a. Causes of abuse and neglect
         (1) Abusers and neglecters
         (2) Victims
         (3) Families
         (4) Communities
         (5) Cultures
      b. Effects of abuse and neglect
      c. Combating abuse and neglect
      d. Preventing sexual abuse

V. RELATIONSHIPS WITH OTHER CHILDREN

A. SIBLINGS
   1. How Children React to the Arrival of a New Baby
   2. How Siblings Interact
B. SOCIABILITY

VI. THE IMPACT OF EARLY DAY CARE

A. COGNITIVE DEVELOPMENT
B. SOCIAL DEVELOPMENT
C. EMOTIONAL DEVELOPMENT

KEY TERMS

ambivalent (resistant) attachment (page 177)
attachment (176)
autonomy versus shame and doubt (163)
avoidant attachment (177)
basic trust versus basic mistrust (162)
battered child syndrome (185)
child abuse (185)
depression (170)
disorganized-disoriented
  attachment (177)
emotions (165)
ethological approach (174)
mother-infant bond (175)
mutual regulation model (168)
negativism (164)
neglect (185)
nonorganic failure to thrive (185)
personality (162)
secure attachment (177)
self-awareness (166)
self-regulation (164)
separation anxiety (183)
sexual abuse (185)
social referencing (169)
socialization (174)
strange situation (177)
stranger anxiety (183)
temperament (171)

LEARNING OBJECTIVES

After finishing Chapter 5, students should be able to:

1. Describe the significance of the following developmental stages, according to Erik Erikson: basic trust versus basic mistrust, autonomy versus shame and doubt (pp. 162-164)

2. List and briefly explain the three stages in which self-awareness emerges. (pp. 166-167)

3. List and describe the three ways in which babies are able to show their emotions. (pp. 167-168)

4. Describe the significance of the *mutual-regulation model* and provide an example of what can happen when this model breaks down. (pp. 168-169)

5. Explain how babies "read" the emotions of others and display *social referencing*. (p. 169)

6. Define *temperament* and, in your own words, explain what is meant by each of the following terms pertaining to a baby's *temperament*: easy child, slow-to-warm up child, difficult child, goodness of fit (pp. 171-173)

7. Describe how, in a research study on gender differences, strangers tended to react to a supposedly male baby and a supposedly female baby. (pp. 173-174)

8. Explain what babies need from their mothers by defining these two concepts: *ethological approach* and *mother-infant bond* (pp. 174-175)

9. Define *attachment* and briefly describe the four patterns of attachment observed in the *strange situation*. (pp. 176-177)

10. Compare and contrast the mother's role, as well as the baby's role, in establishing attachment. (pp. 178-179)

11. Describe recent findings about fathers' interactions with young children. (pp. 180-182)

12. Distinguish between *stranger anxiety* and *separation anxiety*. (p. 183)

13. Briefly describe how babies may react to the following changes in their lives: institutionalization and hospitalization (pp. 183-185)

14. List some of the causes of *child abuse* and *neglect*, as well as some of the ways in which they can be prevented. (pp. 185-187)

15. What is the reaction of most children to a new sibling? (pp. 187-188)

16. Describe sociability and its significance in a child's development. (p. 189)

17. Explain how day care may affect the following aspects of a youngster's development: cognitive, social, and emotional (pp. 190-194)

CHAPTER SUMMARY AND TEACHING RECOMMENDATIONS

This chapter opens with a discussion of Erikson's crises of basic trust versus basic mistrust and of autonomy versus shame and doubt. Guidelines are provided for encouraging self-regulation and for reducing negative behaviors. In discussing this material, you might also want to mention Erikson's work on cross-cultural patterns of development and his general concern for the social context of development.

A section called "Emotions: The Foundation of Personality" follows. The authors discuss infants' emotions; how emotions develop; and how infants express emotions through crying, smiling, and laughing. The mutual-regulation model, which suggests that infants play an active part in regulating their emotional states, is presented. This section ends with a discussion of how infants "read" the emotions of others and how they display social referencing after about six months of age.

The next section--"Differences in Personality Development"--explains how temperament is a source of individual differences; it also describes the New York Longitudinal Study. This study identified the three most common patterns of temperament: easy, difficult, and slow-to-warm-up. The authors make the critical point that temperament and--more specifically--the "fit" between an infant's temperament and the parents' expectations and behavior can affect developmental outcomes. You may wish to reiterate this point in class, noting the need for parents to recognize and adapt to their infant's temperament. This section concludes with a brief discussion of gender differences in infancy. The authors note that parents typically behave differently with sons and daughters; you may want to add that infants are exposed to many other potential agents of sex-role socialization (e.g., grandparents, siblings, babysitters, neighbors, and the media).

The chapter includes an extensive section called "The Family and Personality Development." The authors note social trends having an impact on development and ways in which developmental research has begun to examine the impact of these changes

systematically. Bonding is discussed, and the authors point out that there is apparently no "critical period" for bonding (although the first few days of life are undoubtedly important).

The authors present a detailed discussion of mother-infant attachment. Patterns of attachment--secure, avoidant, ambivalent, and disorganized-disoriented--are described; moreover, the long-term consequences of these early patterns of attachment are outlined, along with effects of other caregivers. The authors describe research on the consequences of maternal employment (work for pay) and nonmaternal care; in this section, they point out that personality development may be negatively affected, especially for sons, depending on a number of circumstantial factors. In our experience, students who are also parents greet this section with understandable concern. Thus, it is important to emphasize a number of points in discussing this material. For example, you might note that (1) given high-quality nonmaternal care and "quality time" with the mother, there may be no adverse impact on development, (2) a full-time mother who resents forgoing opportunities for personal growth or career development may have a far more negative impact on her children than a fulfilled "part-time" mother, and (3) research on the impact of maternal employment and nonmaternal care is itself too "young" to identify truly long-term effects (such as outcomes in adulthood).

The section continues with a substantial discussion of the father's role and of stranger and separation anxiety. In discussing this material, you might want to call students' attention to the authors' suggestions for minimizing infants' distress upon separation.

This section concludes with a discussion of disturbances in family relationships, including child institutionalization, hospitalization, child abuse and neglect. The authors summarize the characteristics of abusers, neglecters, and victims; factors believed to contribute to abuse and neglect; and alternative treatments for abusers and neglecters. Students are invariably fascinated by this material and would benefit from addressing the topic in class and perhaps evaluating it in the context of their own experiences.

The chapter continues with "Relationships

with Other Children," a section including a description of how infants develop a sense of "sociability."

The final topic covered in this chapter is the impact of early day care on children's cognitive, social, and emotional development. The quality of day care in the United States is examined, and suggestions are provided for needed improvements.

Boxes in Chapter 5 are "Reducing Negativism and Encouraging Self-Regulation," "How a Mother's Depression Affects Her Baby," "How to Choose a Good Day Care Center," "How Sweden Cares for Parents and Children," and "Putting Research to Work."

AUDIOVISUAL MATERIALS

Distributor, date, and running time are given for each film or video. Distributors' addresses are listed in the appendix (General Resources). If a film or video is not in color, there is a notation (BW) to that effect.

Mother love. (PSU, 1960, BW, approximately 30 min.) Although this film is quite old, it presents Harlow's classic research on the importance of "contact comfort."

First feelings. (IM, 1992, video, 30 min.) This video features interviews with Jerome Kagan, Mary Ainsworth, and Alan Sroufe, who explain their research on infant attachment. The video also considers how children are active participants in their own emotional development.

Toddler. (IM, 1992, video, 30 min.) The fine line between a toddler's need for others and need for autonomy is explored in this program. The video contrasts the development of a securely attached toddler with that of a child whose mother is in prison.

In the land of giants. (IM, 1991, video, 57 min.) Urie Bronfenbrenner characterizes the family as "the most efficient means for making human beings human." This program examines models of behavior and codes of discipline used to mold children to a culturally desirable social image.

No more secrets. (FFHS, 1994, video, 24 min.) The stories of sexually abused children and of adults who were abused as children and how children can be encouraged to share their secret.

Child abuse. (FFHS, 1994, video, 19 min.) A therapist describes the common characteristics of offenders and a clinical social worker discusses the effects of physical and sexual abuse on a child.

Social services and child abuse. (FFHS, 1994, video, 28 min.) This specially adapted Phil Donahue program examines reports of agencies unable or unwilling to prevent vicious and sometimes fatal child abuse.

Having a mentally handicapped baby: a crack in the crystal. (FFHS, 1994, video, 50 min.) The agonies and joys, as well as the endless cycle of questions, that families face when confronted by mental handicap in their child.

Prodigies: Great expectations. (FFHS, 1994, video, 52 min.) The problems and privileges of brilliant children.

Children of Perestroika. (FFHS, 1994, video, 60 min.) This sad and charming documentary featuring children from the Siberian city of Kemerovo shows how perestroika and glasnost have affected the children.

Everybody rides the carousel, Part 1. (PF, 1976, approximately 20 min.) Covers Erikson's stages of trust versus mistrust, autonomy versus shame and doubt, and initiative versus guilt.

Guest speakers

As noted earlier, students are typically quite interested in the topic of child abuse; there are many possible sources of guest speakers on this topic. One approach is to have a police officer from the local youth services division come to your class. Other sources of speakers include a local chapter of Parents Anonymous, a social worker or another mental health professional specializing in child and family services, and a worker or director at a day care center (since day care staffs are typically trained to detect abuse and are legally required to report suspected abuse).

LECTURE OUTLINES

Lecture 1: Parent-Infant Bonding and Attachment

I. Definition

Attachment is defined as a close, reciprocal bond between parent and infant.

II. Perspectives on attachment

There are various perspectives on attachment. Two of them are psychoanalytic theory and Ainsworth's approach.

A. Psychoanalytic theory: A warm, gratifying relationship with the mother is crucial for normal personality development.
B. Ainsworth: Studies of the formation of parent-infant attachment throughout the early years of development.
  1. Methodology. Observation and analysis of the "strange situation" (a sequence of seven timed episodes involving mother, infant, and stranger).
  2. Stages of attachment.
    a. Birth to 3 months: Infant shows interest in people in general through attachment behaviors (e.g., looking, smiling, reaching). There is some preference for the regular caregiver, but it is not consistent.
    b. 3 months to 6-7 months: Infant consistently shows a preference for the regular caregiver by attachment behaviors.
    c. By approximately 12 months: Infant continues to express a preference for and attachment to the regular caregiver by earlier attachment behaviors. In addition, locomotion becomes an attachment behavior. Normally, a securely attached infant uses the regular caregiver as a secure base from which to explore the environment.
    d. Stranger anxiety and separation anxiety: These also occur toward the end of the first year, regardless of the pattern of attachment. They are usually explained in terms of infants' growing cognitive abilities.

III. Attachment and early mother-infant contacts

The importance of very early mother-infant contact for attachment was initially examined by Klaus and Kennell.

A. Methodology. Longitudinal study of two groups of mothers having first babies in a large metropolitan university hospital. Mothers agreeing to participate were randomly assigned to one of two groups:
  1. "Standard contact." This group saw infants at feeding times.
  2. "Extended contact." This group saw infants for one of the first two hours after birth, at feeding times, and during several extra visiting periods per day.
B. Findings. Researchers observed differences between the mother-infant pairs as the infants developed.
  1. At 1 month: "Extended contact" mothers expressed greater concern and attention during their infants' physical exams, soothed their infants more during the exam, fondled their infants more, and had greater eye contact with their infants during feedings.
  2. At 1 year: "Extended contact" mothers continued to be more attentive during their infants' physical exams; those who were working reported missing their infants more than the "standard contact" mothers who were working.
  3. At 2 years: "Extended contact" mothers encouraged their infants to talk more and used more explanations in talking to the infants. "Standard contact" mothers used more commands in talking to their infants and generally talked to their infants less.
C. Implications. This study suggested that contact with the infant immediately after birth has a critical impact; later research suggests that this early contact may be important but is not critical (secure attachment is quite possible without it).

D. Consequences. Klaus and Kennell's study was conducted in the early 1970s, before hospital policies permitted much contact at all between parents and infants. Since its findings were disseminated, hospitals have responded with practices such as rooming in, allowing fathers and other family members into delivery rooms, and flexible visiting policies for maternity wards.

References for Lecture 1

Cox, M., Owen, M. & Henderson, V. (1992). Prediction of infant-father and infant-mother attachment. *Developmental psychology, 28,* 474-483.
Klaus, M. H. & Kennell, J. H. (1982). *Parent-infant bonding.* St. Louis: Mosby.
Mallinckrodt, B. (1992). Childhood emotional bonds with parents, development of adult social competencies, and availability of social support. *Journal of counseling psychology, 39,* 453-461.
Thevenin, T. (1993). *Mothering and fathering: The gender differences in child rearing.* Garden City, NJ: Avery.

Lecture 2: Father-Infant Relationships

I.   Background

The study of father-infant relationships was largely neglected until the early 1970s, for several reasons.

A. Influence of psychoanalytic theory. Psychoanalytic theory stresses the importance of the mother-infant relationship almost exclusively. The father is seen as important primarily as a figure in the Oedipus or Electra complex

B. Cultural views of gender roles. Home and family were seen as women's exclusive province; the workplace was seen as men's province.

C. Fathers were not as available for home-based observational research.

II.   Research findings

Findings from research since the early 1970s on father-infant relationships include the following:

A. Research on fathers' reactions to newborns.

1. Fathers were eager to interact with newborns.
2. Fathers interacted somewhat differently from mothers: they smiled less and talked less to the infant but held and rocked the infant more than mothers did.

B. Observations and reports from mothers and fathers regarding fathers' early involvement in caring for infants.

1. Fathers almost always took less responsibility for routine caregiving (e.g., feeding, bathing, diapering).
2. When involved in routine care, fathers were as capable as mothers (e.g., infants ate as much when fed by the father as they did when fed by the mother).

C. Research on father-infant attachment.

1. Fathers generally spend less time than mothers in interaction with infants (many studies document this). But if their interaction is responsive, infants typically do show attachment to fathers as well as to mothers.

2. Increased father-infant interaction has an effect on attachment. In one study of 20 fathers with 1-year-old sons, according to the fathers' and mothers' reports, the fathers spent relatively little time taking care of their sons and spent less time in general with their sons than the mothers did.

   a. Initial observations of all 20 father-infant pairs measured frequency of attachment behaviors directed toward fathers.

   b. After initial observation, fathers were randomly assigned to one of two groups:

      (1) Experimental group. Fathers were instructed to spend an extra 30 minutes per day for 1 month playing with their sons (in addition to their normal routines).

      (2) Control group. Father were given no instructions to increase their interaction with their sons.

   c. After one month of intervention, father-infant pairs were again observed for frequency of attachment behaviors.

(1) Experimental group. Infants showed increased frequency of attachment behaviors directed toward the father (but no change in frequency of attachment behaviors toward the mother).

(2) Control group. Infants showed no change in frequency of attachment behaviors directed toward either parent.

References for Lecture 2

French, S. (Ed.) (1992). *Fatherhood.* London: Virago.
Hewlett, B. (Ed.) (1992). *Father-child relations: Cultural and biosocial contexts.* Hawthorne, NY: Aldine De Gruyter.
O'Connell, M. (1993). *Where's Papa? A father's role in childcare.* Washington, DC: Population Reference Bureau.

Lecture 3: Child Abuse

I.   Definition

Defining child abuse is difficult because it can take so many forms.

A.   Today, four forms of child abuse are recognized.
  1.   Physical abuse (harmful physical actions against a child; e.g., inflicting head injuries, breaking bones, burning, and poisoning).
  2.   Emotional abuse (imparting lasting psychological trauma).
  3.   Sexual abuse (incest, molestation, and rape).
  4.   Neglect (e.g., inadequate nutrition, medical care, or clothing).
B.   Legal definition of abuse, provided by the Federal Child Abuse Prevention and Treatment Act (PL 93-247), specifies physical or mental injury, sexual abuse, negligent treatment, or maltreatment of a child under age 18 by a person responsible for the child's welfare under circumstances indicating that the child's health or welfare had been harmed or threatened.

II.   Incidence

Unknown. Reported cases increase yearly, but it is difficult to estimate how many unreported cases occur.

III.   Recognition as a social problem

There are indications of early concern over child abuse. Although attention to child abuse as a national social problem is relatively recent, the problem itself is not at all new.

A.   1920s: A pediatrician studying childhood injuries published the suggestion that parents may have caused these injuries in some cases. This suggestion was greeted with widespread skepticism.
B.   1961: Kempe (another pediatrician) described the "battered child syndrome" at a professional meeting of pediatricians. The audience was shocked.

IV.   Misconceptions and facts

There are many misconceptions about child abuse.

A.   One misconception is that it is rare and confined to poor and disadvantaged groups. Fact: Although the actual incidence is unknown, we can safely say that child abuse is not rare and that it occurs at all levels of society.
B.   Another misconception concerns the characteristics of abusive parents; it is incorrectly believed that all abusing parents are psychotic, criminal, or retarded--a view known as the psychiatric model of child abuse. Fact: Actual characteristics of abusing parents include the following:
  1.   Experience of abuse during their own childhood.
  2.   Negative perception of the abused child. The child is seen as disappointing (perhaps because of unrealistic expectations) or unlovable.
  3.   Stress and crisis in their own lives.
  4.   Lack of support network of family and friends.

V.   Intervention

Experts believe that most abusing parents can be helped to stop abusing, permanently. Following are approaches to intervention in cases of child abuse.

A.   Early detection. Early detection is important--even vital--to ensure the child's survival and safety and to prevent the child from growing into an abusive parent.

1. Early detection requires widespread involvement in reporting cases of suspected abuse: this is legally mandated in all states for anyone dealing with children in the course of his or her work.
2. It also requires some protection for people who report abuse. Individuals reporting suspected abuse are now legally protected from liability.
3. It also requires adequate reporting. Reports should be made to a county department of social services or human services, or to an abuse hot line, or to the police.

B. Family counseling.
C. As a last resort, the abused child is removed from the home and placed in a foster home. Parental rights may be terminated.

References for Lecture 3

Corby, B. (1993). *Child abuse: Towards a knowledge base.* Buckingham; Philadelphia: Open University Press.

Fryer, G. (1993). *Child abuse and the social environment.* Boulder, CO: Westview Press.

Green, A. (1993). Child sexual abuse: Immediate and long-term effects and intervention. *Journal of the American academy of child and adolescent psychiatry, 32,* 890-902.

TOPIC FOR DEBATE

What Is the Best Approach for Dealing with Child Abuse?

Background

It is difficult to remain unaware of the deep and widespread social concern expressed over the tragedy of child abuse and neglect. Despite this concern, the frequency of reported incidents of abuse and neglect increases annually. Although few would deny that child abuse and neglect are among our gravest national problems, there is sharp disagreement over what causes the problem and how to eradicate it.

There are several ideas about the source of child abuse. According to the psychiatric model, abuse results from a parent's

abnormality, a parent's history of a pathologically punitive childhood, or both. The sociological model proposes that factors such as social problems (including unemployment, substance abuse, poor housing, and poverty) and cultural attitudes toward violence are the source of the problem. Finally, the social-situational model sees the complex social situation in which abuse occurs (including parents' and children's personal characteristics and parents' attitudes and beliefs) as the root of the problem.

With this diversity of views about the source of child abuse and neglect, it is not surprising that intervention approaches are also varied. There are a variety of psychiatrically based approaches, involving therapy for the abuser, the victim, the entire family, or all of these. In some cases, the focus is on modifying the parent's or the child's behavior, or both. Some observers hold that child abuse and neglect can be eliminated only through massive social change aimed at altering our views of children and of violence, abolishing poverty and unemployment, and providing decent housing and health care for all.

One feature common to most intervention efforts is a concern for both safeguarding the interests of the child and maintaining family unity. Accordingly, abused children are removed from the home only in extreme situations, and abusers are sometimes not prosecuted. An abusing mother or father's parental rights are terminated only as a last resort. Few would criticize concern for the child's welfare as a guiding principle; however, some people question how well the child's interests are served by efforts to maintain the unity of an abusive family.

Debate plan

Using this background, and information from additional sources (selected references appear below), student panels should debate the following positions:

Position A. An abused child's interests are best served by removing the child or the abusing parent from the home and by criminal prosecution of the abusing parent.

Position B. Child abusers are victims, just as their children are; all possible efforts should be made to keep the family together and provide therapy and support.

References for the debate

Benedict, L. & Zautra, A. (1993). Family environmental characteristics as risk factors for childhood sexual abuse. *Journal of clinical child psychology, 22,* 365-74.

Benson, C. (1991). Battered half. *Canadian forum,* 70, 14-16.

Dodge, K. A., et al. (1990). Mechanisms in the psychology of violence. *Science,* 250, 1678-1683.

Jellinek, M. S., et al. (1990). Protecting severely abused and neglected children: An unkept promise. *New England journal of medicine,* 323, 1628-1630.

Mondale, W. (1993). Child abuse: Issues and answers. *Public welfare, 51,* 24.

TOPICS FOR DISCUSSION

Topic 1: Early Personality Development

1. Ask students to summarize the first two of Erikson's critical developmental stages, basic trust versus mistrust and autonomy versus shame and doubt (textbook pages 162-164).

2. Ask students to provide some suggestions for reducing negative behaviors and for encouraging self-regulation in young children (page 165).

Topic 2: Crying as Emotional Expression

1. Ask students to list and describe the various types of cries discussed in the chapter (page 167).

2. Ask students to relate the description of crying in this chapter to the discussion of prelinguistic speech in Chapter 4 (pages 146-148, 167).

Topic 3: Temperament and Parenting

1. Ask students to describe the three patterns of temperament summarized in the chapter (pages 171-172).

2. The chapter discusses influences on temperament; ask students for suggestions about how their early life experiences may have affected their own temperament (pages 172-173).

Topic 4: Parent-Infant Attachment

1. Ask students to explain Ainsworth's three main patterns of attachment in one-year olds (page 177).

2. Ask students how both the mother's and the father's behavior could affect the bond with their child (pages 178-182).

3. Ask students how an infant's temperament could affect the process of attachment to a parent (pages 171-173, 176-180).

Topic 5: Child Abuse

1. Ask students to identify some of the factors cited in the text as possible causes of child abuse; ask them which they believe to be the best explanation (pages 185-186).

2. Ask students what each of the causal factors cited in the text implies about intervention in cases of child abuse. Which of these approaches to intervention seems the most feasible? (pages 185-187)

PROJECTS AND CLASS EXERCISES

Group Exercise: Implications of Temperament for Parenting

Working in groups, students should identify a "type" of parent (e.g., single parent, teenage parent, low-income parent, dual-career couple) that is most likely to be distressed because an infant has a "difficult" temperament. The group should explain why they believe this type of parent would have particular problems with a difficult infant.

Next, the group should write (or outline) an informational brochure for the selected type of parent. The brochure should include an explanation of temperament in general and of the difficult temperament in particular, and give suggestions for parents of difficult infants.

Project 1: Observing Infants and Toddlers

Have students observe infants and toddlers in public places (e.g., shopping malls, parks, religious centers, grocery stores). Depending on the emphasis in your own course, you might ask them to make notes of adults' behavior toward the children, and vice versa; of children's behavior toward other children; of differences between behavior directed at boys and girls, etc. Whatever behavior is selected for observation, ask students to write a paper comparing their own observations with the material presented in the chapter.

Project 2: Depictions of Infants' and Toddlers' Behavior

Have students review the explanations of stranger anxiety, separation anxiety, temperament, and negativism in three or more child-care manuals. Using the text's explanation of these phenomena, students should write a paper critically evaluating the depictions in the manuals.

ESSAY QUESTIONS

---

1.   What is the significance of the infant's cry, and how should parents respond to a crying infant?

Answer guideline. Crying may communicate hunger, anger, pain, frustration, or any combination of these; crying should be regarded as a form of prelinguistic speech. Parents are best advised to respond promptly to an infant's cries; this communicates to infants that their needs will be reliably met.

2.   Discuss the indications of the sense of self in infancy.

Answer guideline. One set of initial signs of the sense of self are the "self-conscious" emotions (e.g., empathy, jealousy, shame, guilt, and pride), which appear by the end of the second year; also by that age, children develop a sense of self-awareness, or knowledge that they are separate from other people and things. Another early sign of the sense of self is self-recognition, the ability to identify oneself in a mirror; this ability usually appears by the age of 18 months.

3.   Describe the three patterns of temperament outlined in the text, and suggest how a parent would help a child with each pattern adjust to a new food.

Answer guideline. Easy: The child is generally contented in mood, has moods of moderate intensity, is regular in biological

functioning, and adapts well to new people, to change, to new situations, and to frustration. This child would need little special effort on the parents' part to adjust to a new food. Difficult: The child has intense and often negative moods, has irregular rhythms of biological functioning, has tantrums in the face of frustration, and is generally suspicious of novelty (new people, new foods, new situations, new routines). Parents would need to be flexible, patient, and firm in helping this child adjust to a new food. Slow to warm up: The child has mildly intense positive and negative moods, has moderately regular patterns of biological functioning, and initially has a negative reaction to novelty but eventually adapts. Parents would also have to be patient and flexible and let this child "set the pace" in adjusting to a new food.

4.   Discuss gender differences during infancy.

Answer guideline. Research has not identified many consistent differences between male and female infants' behavior. However, researchers have found differences in the ways adults behave toward male and female infants. Depending on an infant's supposed sex, adults tend to attribute different meanings to the infant's cries, to offer the infant different toys, and to direct attention to infants with different purposes.

5.   Evaluate the evidence suggesting a "critical period" for the formation of the mother-infant bond.

Answer guideline. Klaus and Kennell proposed that there was a critical period for bonding between mother and infant in the first few hours after birth. Their evidence was a longitudinal study comparing mother-infant pairs who had extensive early contact and mother-infant pairs who had more restricted contact during the first few days after birth. However, later research has failed to replicate the long-term differences that Klaus and Kennell identified.

6.   Define attachment and describe three patterns of attachment.

Answer guideline. Attachment is an active, reciprocal, and affectionate relationship (specifically between a caregiver and an infant). Secure attachment: Caregiver is used as a base for exploration; infants can separate from the caregiver as long as they are readily able to return. Avoidant attachment: Infants show no distress when the caregiver leaves and avoid the caregiver when he or she returns; infants do not reach for the caregiver in times of need, are typically angry, and dislike both being held and being put down. Ambivalent attachment: Infant is anxious before the caregiver's departure and quite distressed when the caregiver does depart; when reunited, the child seeks contact with the caregiver but also resists contact.

7.   What are the consequences of maternal employment for mother-infant attachment?

Answer guideline. The effects vary, depending on many factors, including the mother's satisfaction with her marriage, whether the mother works full time or part time, why the mother is working, the age of the child, the sex of the child, the temperament of the child, and the quality of substitute care the infant receives. The most negative consequences for mother-infant attachment seem to occur for infants who experience unstable or poor-quality care during their first 12 months, and for boys. Infants with a difficult temperament also seem to suffer more from maternal employment than other infants.

8.   Summarize differences and similarities in fathers' and mothers' interaction with infants.

Answer guideline. Similarities: Fathers typically bond with babies soon after birth, are about as responsive to infants as mothers, speak to infants using "motherese," and have physiological reactions to infants' distress that is similar to mothers' reactions. Differences: Fathers typically have a less active role in caretaking and thus are somewhat less responsive than mothers; they play more with infants than mothers do; and they have different "rhythms" of interaction from those of mothers.

9.   Define stranger anxiety and separation anxiety, and discuss factors that influence them.

Answer guideline. Stranger anxiety is fear of an unfamiliar person; separation anxiety is distress at the departure of a familiar caregiver. Both types of anxiety usually appear during the second half of an infant's first year. Both seem to be influenced by

cognitive factors, attachment patterns, and other factors. Cognitive influences on these types of anxiety include the infant's increased memory capacity, which enables the infant to detect unfamiliar individuals and to distinguish between the presence and absence of the familiar caregiver. Attachment is related to these types of anxiety in that securely attached infants tend to experience less separation anxiety; however, securely attached infants who are distressed at separation from the caregiver also tend to express greater stranger anxiety than other infants. Other factors that are related to these types of anxiety are the number of adults with whom an infant has been reared, the infant's temperament, and the situation in which separation or a stranger is encountered.

10.   Identify and describe sources of parental deprivation in infancy and toddlerhood.

Answer guideline. Death and divorce: Toddlers may react to these sources of separation with great distress (whining, crying, clinging, sleep disturbances, bed-wetting), although they do not always understand that death means a permanent separation from the parent. Institutionalization: When institutions fail to provide plenty of interaction with stable caregivers and active meaningful experiences, infants may decline in intellectual functioning, develop major psychological problems, or even die. Hospitalization: As the length of time in a hospital increases, an infant or toddler's intellectual functioning may decline (until the child returns home) unless caregivers provide the child with a great deal of attention; hospitalized infants may also experience three stages of separation anxiety (protest, despair, detachment). Other temporary separations: If the separation continues for longer than 4 consecutive weeks, and the child has been separated from both parents, the child is likely to be disturbed. However, the extent of the child's reaction depends on the reason for the separation; reactions such as antisocial behavior are more likely when the reason for the separation is family discord than when it is a more favorable circumstance (e.g., vacation, illness).

11.   Describe approaches to combating child abuse and neglect.

Answer guideline. Approaches to prevention would include support for parents who feel

overwhelmed by parenting, particularly
parents of children with special needs. In
order to stop abuse and neglect, the child or
parent may have to be removed from the
home, although this should be a last resort.
Treating abusive adults as criminal offenders
may also be effective in combating abuse.
Improved means of detecting abuse and better
procedures for reporting suspected abuse must
also be developed.

CHAPTER 6
PHYSICAL AND INTELLECTUAL DEVELOPMENT IN EARLY CHILDHOOD

INTRODUCTION

The discussion of physical and intellectual development in early childhood in **Chapter 6** begins a pattern that will continue through most of the remainder of the textbook. Each period of development (early childhood, adolescence, etc.) will be discussed in two chapters: the first will deal with physical and intellectual development during that period, and the second, with personality and social development during that period.

- Chapter 6 begins by describing the physical growth and change of children aged 3 to 6 and examines the effect of nutrition on growth and health.

- The early childhood years are basically healthy; yet, some health problems do exist. Various minor and major illnesses as well as common accidental injuries are described, with particular attention given to the topic of children with AIDS. Several factors affecting children's health are discussed.

- Children's sleep patterns and sleep disturbances and how they change during early childhood are discussed, as well as the topic of bed-wetting.

- Large-muscle, small-muscle, and hand-eye coordination are briefly described.

- In the area of intellectual development, Chapter 6 examines how memory, speech, and intelligence develop and function during early childhood. It focuses on Piaget's preoperational stage of cognitive development and modifies his theories with recent research findings.

- Recent research is presented and evaluated on the effects of the quality of day care, preschool, and kindergarten programs.

CHAPTER OUTLINE

PHYSICAL DEVELOPMENT

I. PHYSICAL GROWTH AND CHANGE

    A. HEIGHT, WEIGHT, AND APPEARANCE
    B. STRUCTURAL AND SYSTEMIC CHANGES
    C. NUTRITION

II. HEALTH

    A. HEALTH PROBLEMS IN EARLY CHILDHOOD
       1. Minor Illnesses
       2. Major Illnesses
          a. AIDS in children
       3. Accidental Injuries
    B. INFLUENCES ON HEALTH
       1. Exposure to Illness
       2. Stress
       3. Poverty

III. SLEEP PATTERNS AND PROBLEMS

    A. NORMAL SLEEP PATTERNS
    B. SLEEP DISTURBANCES
    C. BED-WETTING

IV. MOTOR SKILLS

    A. LARGE-MUSCLE COORDINATION
    B. SMALL-MUSCLE AND EYE-HAND COORDINATION

INTELLECTUAL DEVELOPMENT

V. ASPECTS OF INTELLECTUAL DEVELOPMENT

    A. DEVELOPMENT OF MEMORY: INFORMATION PROCESSING
       1. Influences on Children's Memory
          a. General knowledge
          b. "Mastery motivation" and study activities
       2. Unusual Activities and New Experiences
       3. Social Interactions

    B. COGNITIVE DEVELOPMENT: PIAGET'S PREOPERATIONAL STAGE
       1. The Symbolic Function
          a. Indications of the symbolic function
       2. Achievements of Preoperational Thought
          a. Understanding of identities and function
       3. Limitations of Preoperational Thought
          a. Centration
          b. Irreversibility
          c. Focus on states rather than on transformations
          d. Transductive reasoning
          e. Egocentrism
       4. Assessing Piaget's Theory
          a. Do young children understand cause and effect?
          b. How animistic are young children?
          c. How egocentric are young children?
          d. How well can young children classify?
          e. Can cognitive abilities be accelerated?
    C. DEVELOPMENT OF LANGUAGE
       1. Using Words, Sentences, and Grammar
       2. Speaking to Others: Social Speech
       3. Speaking to Oneself: Private Speech
    D. DEVELOPMENT OF INTELLIGENCE
       1. Assessing Intelligence by Traditional, Psychometric Measures
       2. What do Scores on Intelligence Tests Mean?
          a. Stanford-Binet Intelligence Scale
          b. Wechsler Preschool and Primary Scale of Intelligence, Revised (WPPSI-R)
       3. The "Zone of Proximal Development"
       4. Parents' Influence on Children's Intelligence

a.   Providing an environment for learning
b.   "Scaffolding"
c.   The father's role
d.   The mother's role: when mothers are employed

VI.   THE WIDENING ENVIRONMENT

A.   PRESCHOOL AND DAY CARE
    1.   How Good Preschools Foster Development
    2.   Montessori Preschools
    3.   Compensatory Preschool Programs
       a.   Project Head Start
       b.   Long-term benefits of compensatory education
B.   KINDERGARTEN

KEY TERMS

animism (page 218)
centration (215)
conservation (215)
decenter (215)
deferred imitation (214)
egocentrism (217)
enuresis (208)
fine motor skills (209)
gross motor skills (209)
intelligence quotient (IQ) tests (224)
irreversibility (215)
preoperational stage (214)
private speech (223)
Project Head Start (233)
recall (212)
recognition (212)
reliable (224)
scaffolding (214)
social speech (223)
standardized norms (224)
Stanford-Binet Intelligence Scale (225)
symbol (214)
symbolic function (214)
symbolic play (214)
transduction (214)
transitional objects (208)
valid (224)
Wechsler Preschool and Primary Scale of Intelligence (WPPSI-R) (225)
zone of proximal development (ZPD) (225)

LEARNING OBJECTIVES

After finishing Chapter 6, students should be able to:

1.   Describe changes during early childhood in the following areas: height, muscular, weight, structural (pp. 200-201)

2.   Explain the vital role of nutrition on children's health. (p. 201)

3.   List some of the common childhood illnesses, accidental injuries, and other factors that influence health. (pp. 201-204)

4.   Discuss some of the physical and psychological effects of AIDS on children. (p. 202)

5.   How does poverty affect young children, and what recommendations are made to improve the situation for children most at risk? (pp. 204-206)

6.   Describe patterns of sleep and some common sleep disturbances in early childhood. (pp. 207-208)

7.   List some biological and environmental facts about bed-wetting and explain some of the approaches used to deal with this. (pp. 208-209)

8.   Describe eye-hand coordination and some of the characteristic motor skills, both large- and small-muscle, that are present or develop in early childhood. (pp. 209-210)

9.   Explain how memory is developed and operates in early childhood and define the following terms: *recognition, general knowledge, recall, mastery motivation* (pp. 212-213)

10.   Describe children's thinking process during the *preoperational stage* of cognitive development. (p. 214)

11.   Explain the following concepts associated with *preoperative* thinking: *symbol, deferred imitation, symbolic function, symbolic play* (p. 214)

12. Compare and contrast the achievements and limitations of *preoperational* thought and explain the following terms: *centration, animism, irreversibility, egocentrism, transduction* (pp. 215-218)

13. Briefly critique Piaget's theory and comment on the following questions: (pp. 218-221)
    a. How *animistic* are young children?
    b. How *egocentric* are young children?
    c. How well can young children classify?
    d. Can cognitive abilities be accelerated?

14. Describe the development and use of language in early childhood. (pp. 221-222)

15. What are the cognitive benefits a child derives from speaking to others and from speaking to himself or herself? (pp. 223-224)

16. Describe the purpose of measuring young children's intelligence, then name and describe the three major psychometric intelligence inventories mentioned in the text. (pp. 224-225)

17. How do parents influence children's intellectual development? (pp. 225-227)

18. Explain how preschools foster development and describe the views of both Montessori and compensatory preschool programs. (pp. 228-234)

19. What is kindergarten like in American schools today? (pp. 234-235)

CHAPTER SUMMARY AND TEACHING RECOMMENDATIONS

The chapter opens with a description of physical growth and change: the authors discuss the rate of growth, gender differences in physical development, changes in children's bodily structures, and changes in physical systems. You might want to note the importance of hereditary and maturational factors in these growth processes. The authors discuss the importance of nutrition for young children; in this context, you might want to point out parental and social influences on early physical development.

In the section headed "Health," the authors describe minor and major illnesses common in early childhood, as well as childhood accidents. In discussing the section on accidents, you could refer back to the discussion of child abuse and neglect in Chapter 5. This section continues with an overview of the health consequences of such environmental factors as exposure to illnesses, stress, poverty, and homelessness. In this context, you could ask students to consider types of social change needed to improve the health status of all young children (see Topics for Discussion, below).

Normal sleep patterns during the preschool years are described in the following section, as are night terrors, nightmares, sleepwalking, and sleeptalking. In addition, the causes and treatments of bed-wetting (enuresis) are presented.

In "Motor Skills" the authors describe advances in large-muscle coordination, small-muscle coordination, and eye-hand coordination.

The chapter has an extensive section on aspects of intellectual development. Changes in memory--including the superiority of recognition over recall as well as several influences on children's memory--are described. The authors next discuss Piaget's stage of preoperations, noting achievements of this stage (development of the symbolic function, understanding of functions, understanding of identity) and limitations of preoperational thought (centration, irreversibility, focus on states rather than transformations, transductive reasoning, egocentrism, animism). In a critique of the theory, the authors present recent research suggesting that Piaget may have overestimated young children's language capacity and thus underestimated their other cognitive skills. It is important to call this critique to the students' attention, but it is equally important to note the significance of Piaget's description of a unique form of intellectual functioning characteristic of the preschool years.

The section on intellectual development continues with a description of young children's use of language, including a discussion of the characteristics and functions of both social speech and private speech. The section concludes with an overview of psychometric approaches to studying preschoolers' intelligence; the Stanford-Binet and the Wechsler Preschool and Primary Scale of Intelligence, Revised (WPPSI-R) are described, and noncognitive factors influencing performance on intelligence tests are noted. The latter point is particularly important to emphasize in class; you might want to add that any test score is fallible and that if an IQ test score does not seem to reflect an individual's actual abilities, retesting may be in order. You might also point out that test results should always be considered in the context of as much background information about an individual as can be obtained.

The chapter closes with a section called "The Widening Environment," in which various approaches to early childhood education and day care are considered. The authors point out ways in which programs have changed to meet both working parents' needs and children's needs for intellectual and social enrichment. The authors describe various approaches to preschool education (including the Montessori method) and review research documenting the short- and long-term benefits of Project Head Start. The chapter concludes with a description of kindergarten, including the recent change to all-day kindergarten in many communities.

Boxes in Chapter 6 are "Encouraging Healthy Eating Habits," "How Homelessness Affects Children," "Helping Children to Sleep Well," "Theories of Mind," "Should Preschool Be About the Three R's?" and "Preschools in Three Cultures."

AUDIOVISUAL MATERIALS

Distributor, date, and running time are given for each film or video. Distributors' addresses are listed in the appendix (General Resources). If a film or video is not in color, there is a notation (BW) to that effect.

The preschooler's mind. (IM, 1992, video, 30 min.) This program reveals the dramatic changes in cognitive ability that occur during the preschool years. It examines Jean Piaget's theory of development and criticisms of the theory, focusing on cross-cultural

criticisms and the phenomenon of *decalage*.

Cognitive development. (IM, 1990, video, 30 min.) Focusing on the influential theories of Jean Piaget, this program explains the stages of cognitive development through examples of children's cognitive skills at various levels of development.

Nanny care. (FFHS, 1994, video, 26 min.) This program discusses how to find a nanny and keep the cost of finding one within reason; the obligations of parents as employers are also presented.

Day care grows up. (FFHS, 1994, video, 52 min.) New societal attitudes about child care and solutions evolving from those attitudes is presented.

How does the mind grow? (IM, 1991, video, 60 min.) Defining cognition, this video examines the three major schools of thought on cognitive development and two types of theories that have developed from them. It investigates Piaget's theory, showing children at each stage of development. It then explores Case's information-processing approach.

Preschool physical development. (IM, 1994, video, 30 min.) This program examines the child's physical development during the preschool ages of three to six--a period of rapid growth in physical skills.

Preschool mental development. (IM, 1994, video, 30 min.) Focusing on the mental development of children during the preschool years, this lesson reviews the stages of development in the Piagetian model and compares this model with the behavioristic approach to mental development and learning.

Guest speakers

You may want to invite a pediatrician or pediatric nurse to talk to the class about health problems in early childhood, and about preventive health measures parents should take. Another possible source of a speaker on young children's health and nutrition is your city or county department of human services: a program on maternal and child health could be a source of a speaker discussing locally available nutritional-support programs for young children.

LECTURE OUTLINES

Lecture 1: Preoperational Intelligence

I.   The preoperational period

The preoperational period is the second major stage in Piaget's theory. It lasts from about 2 years to about 6 or 7 years of age.

II.   Language development in the preoperational period

The major advance of this period is the development of language--the symbolic function.

A.   Whereas an infant uses action to acquire and express information, a preschooler uses representations to acquire and express information.

B.   Two types of representations are used during preoperations.
1.   Signs (words, numbers) have socially shared meanings.
2.   Symbols ("made-up" words) have idiosyncratic meanings.
3.   Preschoolers may use symbols as if they were signs. (This is one major limitation of preoperations.)

III. Other characteristics of preoperational thought

In general, these other characteristics reflect limitations (relative to later stages) more than advances.

A.   Egocentrism. There are several indications of egocentrism. (But note that recent research reviewed in the text suggests that this limitation may have been overestimated.)
1.   Using symbols as if they were signs.
2.   Not considering a listener's need for information in communication. (Example: a 3-year-old explaining a game or telling a baby-sitter where something is.)
3.   Spatial misconceptions. A child believes that everyone else "sees" things as he or she does.

B.   Lack of conservation. Preoperational children are unable to conserve: they do not understand that fundamental characteristics (e.g., size, weight,

amount) of a substance remain the same despite changes in appearance.   Several limitations of preoperational thought are seen in preschoolers' response to conservation problems:
1.   Centration. The child focuses on only one of several dimensions relevant to a problem or situation.
2.   Static thinking. The child attends only to the initial and end states of a problem--not to the process of transformation.
3.   Irreversible thinking. The child seems unable to imagine a process of transformation being undone.

C.   World view. Another set of limitations on preoperational thought involves concepts and beliefs about the world that seem to make sense to children at this stage of intellectual development
1.   Animism. Children believe that inanimate objects have characteristics of living things (have sensations, eat, sleep, etc.).
2.   Artificialism. This has two aspects.
a.   Children believe that living things are "manufactured" (e.g., one could make a puppy out of mud or stone).
b.   Children believe that all physical phenomena are made by humans for human purposes (e.g., snow exists so that children can build a snowman; sunshine exists so that children can play outside). Note: Egocentrism is also apparent here.
3.   Realism. Children believe that "psychological" entities have properties of physical objects (e.g., size, shape, color, mass). For instance, ideas are indicated by a light bulb over one's head, or by cartoon-like "balloons"; dreams are like movies in the child's room at night and would be visible to anyone else in the room.

References for Lecture 1

Beilin, H. (1992). Piaget's enduring contribution to developmental psychology. Developmental psychology, 28, 191-204.

Flavell, J. H. (1993). *Cognitive development.* (3rd ed.). Englewood Cliffs, NJ: Prentice-Hall.

Ginsburg, H. P. & Opper, S. (1988). *Piaget's theory of intellectual development.* (3rd ed.). Englewood Cliffs, NJ: Prentice-Hall.

(1993). *Language and cognition: A developmental perspective.* Norwood, NJ: Ablex.

Lecture 2: Day Care

I.   The need

There is an increased need for high-quality day care--a need which reflects contemporary increases in women's employment outside the home, dual-career couples, and single-parent families. These are international trends.

II.   Responses in Europe

Scandinavia and eastern Europe have various types of day care (center-based, family-care, subsidies for baby-sitters) sponsored by state and local governments and by employers. In most countries, these provisions are inadequate (relative to parents' needs), but they are significant as examples of governmental and corporate support for working parents and their children.

III. Responses in the United States

Provisions for day care in the United States are far less adequate than those in Europe.

A. Definition. In the United States, day care is defined as custodial care (as opposed to education or enrichment) of preteenage children during parents' working hours.
This definition is somewhat arbitrary.
1. Education or enrichment may be provided at day care centers, but these are not the primary purposes of the facilities.
2. Nursery schools, preschools, and kindergartens may provide supervisory care for children during part of the day, but these are not considered day care facilities unless they offer full-day care specifically adapted to the schedules of working parents.

B. Policy. The United States has at present no national policy on day care.
1. There is no consensus in the federal government (or in most state and local governments) that providing day care is appropriate or important. (This contrasts, of course, with policies on providing public schooling).
2. Possible reasons for the absence of a national day care policy.
a. There is disagreement over the ideal nature of day care or the appropriate form for it to take.
(1) Disagreement over its purposes: custodial care? education? enhancement of health? etc.
(2) Disagreement over its appropriate sponsorship: federal government? state or local governments? corporations?
(3) Disagreement over who should administer day care: early childhood specialists? specialists in educational administration?
b. Documentation of the need for day care has been haphazard. Despite widespread awareness of the increasing number of working parents, there are few systematic studies providing data on a national, regional, or state-by-state basis regarding several points.
(1) How these parents' children are currently being cared for.
(2) How these parents would prefer for their children to be cared for.
(3) How many parents would like to work and could find work but currently do not work because of lack of day care.
c. There are fears regarding the economic consequences of facilitating out-of-home employment by mothers during periods of

unemployment and
recession.

C. Governmental responses: historical
background.
1. World War II: Women were
needed to work in industry, and
thus many local school systems
housed and administered day care
centers. These centers were
disbanded after the war.
2. "War on poverty" (1960s): Day
care was provided by Project
Head Start, although it was
intended as a federally funded
compensatory education program
rather than a day care program.
3. "Patchwork" efforts during the
1970s, 1980s, and early 1990s.
a. There is government
support of preschool
education for handicapped
children (but this fits the
definition of day care used
here only if extended
daytime programming is
provided for the purpose of
assisting working parents).
b. There is a tax credit for
privately purchased day
care.
D. Response by public schools. The
response of public schools to the need
for day care has been slow and
tentative, owing to budgetary limitations
and (until recently) limited space and
staffs, as well as to resistance from
some legislators and taxpayers.
1. Potential importance of public
school involvement in providing
day care: Such care would be
available to virtually all parents;
and it would become one of the
major institutions of socialization.
2. Recent forms of involvement: In
some communities, all-day
kindergarten and extended
daytime and after-school programs
for older children exist.
3. Possible incentive for
involvement: Declining
population of school-age children
has yielded surplus space and
personnel in many communities.
E. Response by industry. There has been
very little corporate response in the
United States. Most existing corporate
centers are in health care settings,
universities, and nonprofit institutions.

References for Lecture 2

Barbee, A. (1993). Political agendas versus
research agendas: The day care dilemma.
*Journal of social behavior and personality,
8*(1), 13-16.

Lamb, M. (Ed.) (1992). *Child care in
context: Cross-cultural perspectives.*
Hillsdale, NJ: Erlbaum.

Mallory, B. & New, R. (1994). *Diversity
and developmentally appropriate practices:
Challenges for early childhood education.*
New York: Teachers College Press.

Rust, F. (1993). *Changing teaching,
changing schools: Bringing early childhood
practice into public education: Case studies
from kindergarten.* New York: Teachers
College Press.

Scarr, S. (1993). Childcare research: Issues,
perspectives, and results. *Annual review of
psychology, 44*, 613-644.

Lecture 3: Communication in Early Childhood

I. **Egocentrism and children's
communication**

Children's egocentrism has important
implications for their communication.

A. Piaget's studies. Piaget discussed
limitations of young children's abilities
to communicate with a listener. He
classified most preoperational children's
speech as egocentric but found that
egocentricity decreased with age.
1. Egocentric speech is not
addressed to a listener and is
carried on with no apparent
concern for signs of understanding on a listener's part. Piaget
identified three categories:
a. Repetition (echolalia):
Repeating words or
syllables for their own sake
(e.g., "She's in her house,
her house, her house").
b. Collective monologue:
Another person is the
stimulant and recipient of
the child's speech, but this
person's response is not
considered as the
"conversation" progresses
(e.g., Adam: "Now we can
play with my puppy."
Joan: "My mom is prettier
than your mom."

Adam: "My puppy can dig holes." Joan: "I'm as pretty as my Mom").

   c. Monologue: Soliloquies produced as though the child were thinking aloud.

2. Egocentric speech is contrasted with sociocentric (social) speech. The latter is framed in order to communicate with a listener and moderated or elaborated on the basis of feedback from the listener.

B. Study by Krauss et al. Egocentric speech can create difficulties in young children's efforts to communicate. This is illustrated in a study by Krauss and others (briefly described in the text).

1. Subjects: 4- and 5-year-old children.

2. Task: Communication about abstract graphic designs.

   a. These designs were reproduced on wooden blocks with a hole in middle that could be stacked on a rod. Speaker and listener had identical sets of blocks.

   b. Listener's blocks were spread on a table in front of him or her. Speaker received blocks (from a dispenser) in a predetermined order. Speaker and listener were separated by a wooden partition and could not see one another or one another's blocks.

3. Object: Speaker was to describe each block as it was received and stacked on the rod; speaker and listener were to create identical stacks of blocks.

4. Results:

   a. Generally, performance was poor (there were almost always some errors) when both speaker and listener were preoperational.

   b. With an adult speaker and a preoperational listener, the child was able to duplicate the speaker's stack (thus, the problem was apparently not in understanding).

   c. When preoperational children served as listeners to their own tape-recorded descriptions of the blocks, there was better duplication of the stacks than when another child attempted to reproduce the stack. (This suggests that the children's speech could be fairly described as idiosyncratic.)

C. Comparative studies. More recent research, described in the text, indicates that children's communication is less egocentric in other tasks.

II. Problems in adult-child communication

There are at least two major sources of problems in communication between adults and children.

A. Children are often confused by adults' use of metaphors.

B. Adults may overestimate children's linguistic abilities. For example, Piaget's overestimation of children's language skills (despite his view that their language is egocentric) led him to underestimate their general cognitive capability. (This is discussed in the text.)

III. Individual variation

There are several sources of individual differences in young children's ability to communicate.

A. Maturation. Effects of maturational level are especially apparent in studies of retarded children.

1. Low correlation between communication ability and age.

2. Higher correlation between communication ability and measures of physical maturation.

B. Practice. Opportunities to practice communicating and reinforcement for communicating are influential.

1. Studies of children in institutions have found that their language ability often lags behind that of home-reared children. Institutionalized children's speech is seldom reinforced, and there is little adult modeling of speech.

2. Language development of twins and triplets is often slower than that of singletons. This may

reflect less parental practice with and reinforcement of each child.

References for Lecture 3

Beilin, H. (1992). Piaget's enduring contribution to developmental psychology. *Developmental psychology, 28,* 191-204.
Flavell, J. (1993). *Cognitive development. (3rd ed.).* Englewood Cliffs, NJ: Prentice-Hall.
Spodek, B. (Ed.) (1993). *Handbook of research on the education of young children.* New York: Macmillan; Toronto: Maxwell MacMillan.

TOPIC FOR DEBATE

Should Parents Teach Children Before the Children are Old Enough to Enter School?

Background

Parents have always wanted the best for their children. Today, with advancing technology, increasing competitive pressures, and the "information explosion," many parents wonder how they can best prepare their children for a fulfilling, successful adult life. Some believe that this preparation is best accomplished by initiating teaching early, so that their children may have an edge on the competition right from the start. Almost any toy store reflects this belief with displays of plastic letters and numbers, toy computers and calculators, and electronic gadgets designed to teach spelling, math, letters, and numbers.

Some experts in early child development urge parents to begin academic instruction well before the child enters school. These experts argue that young children are naturally curious and eager to learn; thus, teaching the child can also be quite rewarding for the parents. Furthermore, they point out that most parents teach infants and preschoolers quite a lot anyway, through toilet training and instruction in dressing and personal grooming, manners, and simple household chores. Extending this teaching process to more "academic" areas is both natural and logical. Finally, these experts claim that children who receive preschool instruction from their parents receive the best "head start" possible and will usually do better than other children in school.

Other child development specialists disagree, however. Although these professionals do not deny young children's curiosity and desire to explore and learn, they argue that parents' efforts to channel or focus this energy too narrowly can be stressful for young children. They also warn that early teaching at home can actually have negative effects on children, including inhibiting their natural initiative and making them too dependent on their parents for direction and esteem. Moreover, they argue, there is no convincing evidence that early teaching at home has any measurable or long-lasting benefits on later performance in school.

Debate plan

Using this background, and information from additional sources (selected references appear below), student panels should debate the following positions:

Position A. Teaching young children before they enter school is one way for parents to give their children a head start on academic success.

Position B. Teaching young children before they enter school imparts no substantial or lasting advantage and may have negative consequences.

References for the debate

Elkind, D. (1986, May). Formal education and early childhood education: An essential difference. *Phi delta kappan.*
Elkind, D. (1986). *The miseducation of children: superkids at risk.* New York: Knopf.
Gibbings, E. (1989). The head start child and the superbaby: Enrichment versus acceleration. *Dissertation abstracts international, 50*(6-B), 2645.
Keister, E. & Keister, S. (1990). Give your child an edge. *Reader's digest, 137,* 103-107.
Vinovskis, M. (1993). Early childhood education: Then and now. *Daedalus, 122,* 151-176.

TOPICS FOR DISCUSSION

Topic 1: Nutrition, Health, and Poverty

1.   Ask students to summarize changes in children's nutritional needs during the preschool years (textbook page 201).

2. Ask students to identify the minor and major illnesses of early childhood discussed in the chapter. Ask them to identify preventive measures that parents can take to minimize the probability of minor and major illnesses (pages 201-203).

3. The text asserts that "poverty is unhealthy." Ask students to explain several ways in which poverty impairs young children's health. Ask them to identify current programs which attempt to minimize the impact of poverty on young children. Ask them to suggest additional types of programs that should be implemented (pages 204-207).

Topic 2: Implications of Children's Memory Capacity for Parenting

1. Ask students to summarize young children's typical performance on recognition tasks and recall tasks (page 212).

2. Ask students to identify factors which might influence young children's recall or recognition (pages 212-213).

3. Ask students to suggest steps parents could take to ensure that preschoolers remember information important for their safety (e.g., address and telephone number, rules about safe play areas inside and outside the home).

Topic 3: Intelligence Testing

1. Ask students to review the basic assumptions of the psychometric approach to studying intelligence (presented earlier in the text). Have them identify the two major intelligence tests used with preschoolers (pages 224-225).

2. Ask students to suggest possible negative and positive effects of intelligence testing in early childhood. Ask them to consider circumstances under which negative and positive effects would be most likely to occur.

Topic 4: Compensatory Preschool Programs

1. Ask students to describe Project Head Start, including the motivation for

establishing the program and some of the features included in it (pages 233-234).

2. Ask students to identify short- and long-term benefits of Project Head Start (pages 233-234).

3. Ask students to speculate about ways in which compensatory preschool programs like Project Head Start could be most effectively expanded.

PROJECTS AND CLASS EXERCISES

Group Exercise: Health Education for Young Children

Working in groups, students should plan an educational unit covering nutrition, health, and safety for use with preschoolers and kindergartners. Their plan should reflect the material in the chapter and should take young children's cognitive and linguistic characteristics into account.

The group's written product should include (1) an outline of the content of the unit; and (2) a description of how the content would be presented, given the intellectual abilities of preschoolers. For example, how long would each lesson be? What kinds of pictures or other audiovisual materials would be used? How would this content be integrated with the children's other activities in preschool or kindergarten?

Project 1: Preoperational Concepts

Have students interview two or more preschoolers. The students should devise their own questions, but these questions should all be aimed at determining the extent to which animism and artificialism characterize the children's thinking.

The students should write a paper in which they thoroughly describe their questions and the children's answers, note differences between the responses of different children, and interpret the children's responses. In particular, students should attempt to explain differences between these children's responses and those of the children that Piaget studied.

Project 2: Young Children's Memory

Have students administer a simple recall and recognition task (like the one described on page 213 of the text) to a young child. After the task, the students should question the child about memory, devising their own questions. The questions should be directed toward determining the child's awareness of demands placed on memory and of his or her own memory skills. For example, the students might ask the child what he or she did to try to remember objects seen; or what kinds of things people can do to be sure of remembering things; or what kinds of things the child finds hardest to remember.

Students should write a paper describing the child's recall and recognition, their interview questions, and the child's responses to the questions.

Project 3: Evaluating Day Care

Students should visit one or more day care centers and evaluate each center using the practices recommended on pages 228-230 as a guideline; they should also request a fee schedule from each center. Then they should write a paper summarizing their evaluation of each center.

Note: Stress that, unless some of the students are really potential clients of the center (or will be during the next few months), they should contact the director beforehand to explain the actual purpose of the visit, obtain permission to visit, and schedule their visit so as to minimize disruption of the center's schedule.

ESSAY QUESTIONS

---

1. What changes in children's appearance occur during the preschool years, and what gender differences are apparent in these changes?

Answer guideline. Children become less chubby and more slender and athletic in appearance. Body proportions change: the trunk becomes relatively larger and the head relatively smaller than before. Generally, boys have more muscle tissue and girls have more fatty tissue; boys tend to be slightly taller and heavier than girls until puberty.

2. What are the major threats to health during early childhood?

Answer guideline. Most major illnesses of early childhood (e.g., measles, rubella,

mumps, whooping cough, diphtheria, polio) are controlled through vaccination, but they can still be a threat if parents or communities do not provide vaccination. Other major illnesses are infrequent in early childhood; these include cancer, heart disease, influenza, and pneumonia. Today, the major health threat in early childhood is accidental injury.

3. How can illness be good for children, according to the text?

Answer guideline. Illness can have physical, cognitive, and emotional benefits for young children's development. Illnesses help children build up their physical immunity and thus are physically beneficial. In addition, illnesses can make children more attentive to sensations and enhance their awareness of the body. By learning to cope with physical discomfort, children may also gain a greater sense of competence. Finally, illness is an experience that can help children empathize with others.

4. How does poverty influence health during early childhood?

Answer guideline. Poverty is the factor most strongly associated with poor health in early childhood. Poor children are usually not well nourished and do not receive proper medical care, and their families tend to live in overcrowded, unsanitary housing. Furthermore, poor parents may be too overwhelmed by the demands of survival to give their children adequate supervision.

5. Describe normal and pathological sleep patterns of early childhood.

Answer guideline. Normal sleep patterns include bedtime rituals, playing quietly in bed (for toddlers), and use of transitional objects (for older children). Pathological sleep patterns include fear of the dark, fear of being left alone, nightmares (frightening dreams remembered after awakening), night terrors (awakening suddenly in a state of panic for unknown reasons), sleepwalking, and sleeptalking.

6. Describe young children's recognition and recall, and identify influences on young children's memory.

Answer guideline. Young children usually do well in recognition tasks, such as identifying previously presented toys from a larger group of toys; even children as young as age 2 usually recognize approximately 80 percent of previously presented objects. Young children's recall (when they must reproduce information) is much poorer; even 4-year-olds rarely recall much more than one-third of the requested information. Young children's memory performance is influenced by such factors as their motivation, their general knowledge, their exposure to novel events, and the amount of socialization they receive during an experience.

7. Describe the achievements and limitations of the preoperational stage of cognitive development.

Answer guideline. One achievement of the preoperational stage is mastery of the symbolic function; children use the symbolic function through language, deferred imitation, and symbolic play. Other achievements of the symbolic function are enhanced understanding of functional relationships (although children do not necessarily understand the specific type of function relating two events) and of identity (understanding that something stays the same despite changes in appearance). Limitations of the preoperational stage are difficulty in distinguishing reality from fantasy, centration in thinking (exclusive and inappropriate focus on one aspect of a situation), irreversibility in thinking (failure to understand that an action can be undone), focus on beginning and ending states rather than on processes of transformation, transductive reasoning (reasoning from particular to particular), and egocentrism.

8. According to the text, in what respects may Piaget have underestimated preoperational children's intellectual capacities?

Answer guideline. Recent research suggests that young children may have a better understanding of cause-effect relationships, less tendency toward animism, less tendency toward egocentrism, and more advanced ability to classify objects than Piaget originally suggested. These discrepancies appear to reflect Piaget's possible overestimation of young children's language capabilities as well as the use in recent research of tasks more familiar and more interesting to children.

9. Describe ways in which parents can enhance young children's intellectual achievement.

Answer guideline. Parents may influence preschool children's performance on intelligence tests by providing an environment for learning. This environment would include intelligent, sensitive, attentive, and accepting parents who use relatively sophisticated language with the child; who encourage the child's independence, creativity, and curiosity; who read to the child; and who teach the child to do things.

10. Describe good day care and its possible benefits.

Answer guideline. Characteristics of good day care include a high adult-to-child ratio; little turnover among the staff; staff members who have training in child development and are sensitive to young children; and staff members who are able to be firm, stimulating, and affectionate with children. Good day care may provide children with physical, cognitive, and social benefits. Children in well-run centers may have more advanced language development and may be more motivated than their peers; and children from disadvantaged families may not show declines in IQ.

11. What are potential benefits of a good preschool program?

Answer guideline. A well-planned and well-implemented preschool program can have a number of benefits for children, particularly for only children and children with only one sibling. A good program provides a child with many new kinds of activities and choices among activities; children's experience with choosing helps them to learn about themselves and experience success in different areas (provided that activities are planned for children's physical and cognitive abilities). Children can also learn interpersonal skills, including how to cooperate and how to deal with anger, conflict, and frustration. More generally, children can learn to enjoy school and feel confident that they can learn and enjoy learning.

CHAPTER 7

PERSONALITY AND SOCIAL DEVELOPMENT IN EARLY CHILDHOOD

INTRODUCTION

Chapter 7 presents several theories about personality development in early childhood to help us understand how young children begin to perceive their place in the world around them. Many factors can influence a child's development in this stage--fears, friends, parenting styles, siblings, etc.

• According to Erikson, the chief developmental crisis of early childhood is the development of a balance between initiative and guilt. The ways in which parents deal with their children strongly influence this stage.

• Several types of theories attempt to explain how young children acquire gender identity: the psychoanalytic approach, the social-learning approach, the cognitive developmental theory, and the gender-schema theory.

• Gender differences, gender roles, and gender stereotyping are discussed in detail from both the biological and environmental perspectives.

• Childhood fears are examined briefly. The development of aggressive (or passive) tendencies is explained along with a section devoted to the detrimental effects of televised violence and a practical section on guiding children in watching television.

• Parents' influence on the development of prosocial (or altruistic) behavior--or the lack of it--is covered in detail, as is the effect of rewards and punishment on children's behavior.

• In addition, parenting styles--authoritarian, permissive, and authoritative--are presented, with some practical suggestions on effective parenting.

• Research on siblings' influence--or the lack of it--is also covered. The discussion includes findings of a study on China's policies toward the one-child family.

• Finally, play is examined as both a social aid and a cognitive activity. Play is influenced by parents, type of day care, and gender.

CHAPTER OUTLINE

I. IMPORTANT PERSONALITY DEVELOPMENTS IN EARLY CHILDHOOD

A. INITIATIVE VERSUS GUILT
B. IDENTIFICATION
C. GENDER IDENTITY
D. PSYCHOANALYTIC THEORY
E. SOCIAL-LEARNING THEORY: OBSERVING AND IMITATING MODELS
   1. How Identification Occurs
   2. Effects of Identification
   3. Evaluating Social-Learning Theory
F. COGNITIVE-DEVELOPMENTAL THEORY: MENTAL PROCESSES
   1. Gender Identity and Gender Constancy
G. GENDER-SCHEMA THEORY: A "COGNITIVE-SOCIAL" APPROACH
   1. Evaluating the Cognitive Theories

II. ASPECTS AND ISSUES OF PERSONALITY DEVELOPMENT

A. GENDER
   1. How Different Are Girls and Boys?
   2. Attitudes Toward Gender Differences
      a. Gender roles and gender typing
      b. Gender stereotypes
      c. Androgyny: A different view of gender
   3. How Do Gender Differences Come About?
      a. Biological influences
      b. Family influences
      c. Media influences
      d. Cultural influences
B. FEARS
   1. What Do Children Fear and Why?
   2. Preventing and Dealing with Fears
C. AGGRESSION
   1. Triggers of Aggression
   2. Reinforcement
   3. Frustration and Imitation
   4. Televised Violence
   5. Reducing Aggression
D. ALTRUISM: PROSOCIAL BEHAVIOR
   1. Origins of Prosocial Behavior
   2. Encouraging Prosocial Behavior: What Parents Do
E. CHILD-REARING PRACTICES
   1. Parents' Use of Reinforcement and Punishment
      a. Reinforcement
      b. Ineffective punishment: "rewarding with punishment"
      c. Effective punishment: When does punishment work?
   2. Parents' Styles and Children's Competence: Baumrind's Research
      a. Three parenting styles
      b. Evaluation of Baumrind's conclusions
   3. Determinants of Child-Rearing Styles
   4. Parents' Love and Maturity
F. RELATING TO OTHER CHILDREN
   1. The Only Child
   2. Brothers and Sisters
   3. First Friends
      a. Behavior patterns and choice of playmates and friends
      b. Family ties and popularity
G. PLAY
   1. The Importance of Play
   2. Perspectives on Play
      a. Social and nonsocial play
      b. Cognitive play
      c. Imaginative play
   3. Influences on Play: Parents, Day Care Centers, and Gender

KEY TERMS

aggressive behavior (page 250)
androgynous (247)
authoritarian parents (257)
authoritative parents (257)
behavior modification (255)
cognitive play (263)
gender (241)
gender constancy
   (gender conservation) (241)
gender differences (246)
gender identity (241)
gender roles (241)

gender schema (241)
gender-schema theory (241)
gender stereotypes (246)
gender-typing (246)
identification (241)
imaginative play (265)
initiative versus guilt (241)
permissive parents (257)
prosocial behavior (254)
sex differences (245)
social play (263)

LEARNING OBJECTIVES

After finishing Chapter 7, students should be able to:

1. Explain Erikson's third psychosocial crisis, *initiative versus guilt*, and its resolution. (pp. 240-241)

2. Define the following terms as they relate to a child's personality development: *identification, gender identity, gender roles* (p. 241)

3. Briefly explain Freud's psychoanalytic theory as it pertains to child development at this age. (p. 242)

4. Describe and evaluate the social-learning theory of personality development. (pp. 242-243)

5. Briefly explain and evaluate Kohlberg's cognitive-developmental theory of *gender differences* and behavior. (pp. 244-245)

6. Describe and evaluate the *gender-schema* theory of gender development. (pp. 244-245)

7. List some *gender differences* and some similarities between boys and girls. (pp. 245-246)

8. Explain some factors that might contribute to *gender stereotyping*. (pp. 246-247)

9. Define *androgyny* as it relates to gender. (p. 247)

10. Explain what research tells us about the following influences on *gender differences*: biological influences, family influences, media influences, cultural influences (pp. 247-249)

11. List some common childhood fears, and explain why young children seem to develop fears. (pp. 249-250)

12. Explain why *aggressive behavior* seems to appear in early childhood. (pp. 250-251)

13. Explain what research tells us about violence on television and the relationship between children's behavior and the programs they watch. (pp. 252-253)

14. List some suggestions for reducing children's violence and aggression. (pp. 253-254)

15. Define altruism (or *prosocial behavior*) and explain some influences that encourage it. (pp. 254-255)

16. Briefly explain the following terms and explain how they influence a child's personality development: *behavior modification*, ineffective punishment, effective punishment (pp. 255-256)

17. Identify the three styles of parenting researched by Baumrind and briefly describe typical behavior patterns of children raised primarily according to each style. (pp. 257-258)

18. Referring to Box 7-2, "Window on the World," describe the findings from the studies of raising only children in China. (p. 260)

19. Explain the research pertaining to relationships between siblings. (pp. 259, 261)

20. List some suggestions for helping children make friends. (pp. 261-263)

21. How does play benefit children at this stage of development, and differentiate between *cognitive play* and *imaginative play*? (pp. 263-266)

22. Compare and contrast how a child's play is influenced by parents, day care centers, and gender. (pp. 266-267)

CHAPTER SUMMARY AND TEACHING RECOMMENDATIONS

The chapter opens with an overview, "Important Personality Developments in Early Childhood." Erikson's third crisis of personality development, initiative versus guilt, is discussed, as are the outcomes of its successful or unsuccessful resolution for young children. How children develop identity, particularly gender identity, is examined in detail; also, several theoretical perspectives addressing identity formation are presented and evaluated. The psychoanalytic theory is discussed, and the Oedipus and Electra complexes and their resolution are described. The next theory reviewed is the social learning theory; you might want to call students' attention to the fact that identification is a central concept both in this theory and in Freudian theory, but the term is used quite differently in the two theories. Kohlberg's cognitive-developmental approach and Bem's "cognitive-social" approach are discussed next; in this context, it is useful to point out that these theories of personality development rely on Piaget's theory of cognitive development.

The next section of the chapter reviews research on several aspects of personality development. Gender similarities and differences, gender roles, and gender-typing are extensively discussed. The authors also review research on young children's gender stereotypes, and they identify biological, familial, and cultural sources of gender differences. The authors include a section on androgyny; you might want to note that raising "androgynous" children is a goal for many contemporary parents, and the literature on early personality development may have an entirely different cast in the next generation, if these parents are successful.

The authors next describe research on a variety of topics having to do with personality, including sources and treatment of common fears of early childhood, influences on childhood aggression including televised violence, and the development of prosocial behavior.

A section on ways in which parenting practices influence young children follows. In this discussion, two points--the greater effectiveness of reinforcement over punishment, and the effectiveness of authoritative parenting--are particularly important; you might want to use them as a basis for a lecture or class discussion (see Lecture Outlines and Topics for Discussion).

The next section focuses on relationships with other children--both siblings and friends. The authors trace age-related changes in sibling relationships, individual differences in young children's friendship patterns, and influences on young children's friendship patterns.

The chapter closes with a discussion of research findings related to various forms of children's play. Also summarized are the main influences on play--parents, day care centers, and gender.

Boxes in Chapter 7 are "Guiding Children's Television Viewing," "A Nation of Only Children," "Helping Young Children to Make Friends," and "Imaginary Playmates."

AUDIOVISUAL MATERIALS

Distributor, date, and running time are given for each film or video. Distributors' addresses are listed in the appendix (General Resources). If a film or video is not in color, there is a notation (BW) to that effect.

The emerging personality. (IM, 1994, video, 30 min.) This program surveys the components of personality and the influences that shape it. Four major theories of personality development are discussed: Sigmund Freud's psychoanalytic model, Erik Erikson's psychosocial model, social-learning model, and Margaret Mahler's separation-individual model.

Preschool social development. (IM, 1992, video, 30 min.) This program examines how children between the ages of three and six develop a sense of self, gaining greater self-control and self-reliance.

In the land of giants. (IM, 1992, video, 57 min.) Urie Bronfenbrenner characterizes the family as "the most efficient means for making human beings human." This program examines models of behavior and codes of discipline used to mold children to a culturally desirable social image.

Adoption and assisted reproduction: A look at the children. (FFHS, 1994, video, 26 min.) New biological options and shifting social mores have redefined traditional concepts about parenting and the average American family. This program looks at some examples and examines the effects of these choices on children.

Play and imagination. (IM, 1992, video, 30 min.) By tracing the developmental course of play and imagination from infancy through adolescence, this program shows how play enhances social-emotional and cognitive skills. Footage of Mexican and American mothers playing with their children illuminates cultural differences in play. The program also considers the roles of toys and television in shaping imagination.

Sex roles: Charting the complexity of development. (IM, 1991, video, 60 min.) Beginning with a look at the cultural ramification of sex roles and the myths associated with them, this program examines three theories of socialization: Freudian, social-learning, and cognitive-developmental. It analyzes how each theory views the nature-versus-nurture controversy. It explores the impact of sex-role stereotypes on the developing child.

Culture and education of young children. (IM, 1985, video, 16 min.) This discussion with Carol Phillips focuses on how programs for young children can be designed to show respect for cultural diversity, thereby enhancing the richness of a child's education.

Guest speakers

A preschool teacher, a kindergarten teacher, a director of a day care center, or an administrator in early childhood education would be an excellent choice for a guest speaker. Such a professional could address many of the chapter topics--particularly aggression, prosocial behavior, play, fearfulness, and friendship--on the basis of extensive experience with young children. You might also contact your local community mental health center for the names of child psychologists or family therapists in your area; these professionals could speak about childhood fears, abnormal levels of aggression in young children, sibling conflict, or parenting problems and their effects on young children.

LECTURE OUTLINES

Lecture 1: Two Theories of Sex-Role Development

I.   **Cognitive-developmental theory**

Cognitive-developmental theory was outlined by L. Kohlberg.

A.   Social development in general and sex-role development in particular reflect children's intellectual development as described by Piaget.

B.   Sex-role development takes place in two stages: gender identity and gender constancy.

1.   Gender identity: 2-3 years.
a.   Children can identify their own gender and other people's gender.
b.   But this identification is made on the basis of superficial physical clues (e.g., hairstyle, clothing).
c.   Children believe that gender can change if these superficial physical characteristics are changed.

2.   Gender constancy: 5-6 years.
a.   Children now understand that gender is a permanent personal characteristic which does not change with changes in appearance or interests.
b.   Several related changes occur at this time.
(1) Gender is used as a basis for classifying behavior, objects, and interests.
(2) Children imitate behaviors considered appropriate for their own gender because of a desire to master these behaviors--not because of rewards or punishments.
(3) Persons, things, and behaviors associated with a child's own gender are more highly valued than those associated with the other gender; but this reference is less consistent for girls than for boys. There are at

least three possible reasons for this difference.
  (a) It may reflect an early awareness of status differences within the culture.
  (b) It may reflect value judgments based on perceptual cues and a preference for things that are larger, stronger, etc.
  (c) It may reflect the fact that girls generally enjoy greater tolerance from others for "cross-sex" behavior.

C. Cognitive-developmental theory is closely tied to Piaget's ideas about development. Children are viewed as active participants in the process of sex-role development: the environment provides information, but the child actively shapes that information into cognitive structures.

II. Social-learning theory

Social-learning theory is used to explain many aspects of development, including acquisition of sex roles.

A. This theory stresses the importance of reinforcement for children's gender-appropriate behavior and of punishment for--or extinction of--gender-inappropriate behavior
  1. Parents are held to treat boys and girls differently and to have different expectations for them; the text reviews research indicating that these differences are present from birth.
  2. However, note also that some studies contradict the notion that parents' treatment of boys and girls is markedly different.
B. Social-learning theory also stresses the importance of generalization. The consequences of one gender-appropriate or gender-inappropriate behavior are applied to similar behaviors and situations.
C. Finally, social-learning theory emphasizes the importance of observation and imitation.
  1. Children note physical similarities between themselves and older

children or adults of their own gender.
  2. Children imitate behavior of others of their own gender; such imitation is particularly likely in two circumstances:
    a. When the model is admired or loved.
    b. When the model is perceived as powerful or important.
  3. Thus, parents and other significant adults are potential models.

References for Lecture 1

Bigler, R. & Liben, L. (1992). Cognitive mechanisms in children's gender stereotyping: Theoretical and educational implications of a cognitive-based intervention. *Child development, 63*, 1351-1363.
Fagot, B. (1993). Gender-role development in young children: From discrimination to labeling. *Developmental review, 13*(2), 205-224.
Kohlberg, L. (1966). A cognitive developmental analysis of children's sex-role concepts and attitudes. In E. E. Maccoby (Ed.), *The development of sex differences*. Stanford, CA: Stanford University Press.
Signorella, M. (1993). Developmental differences in children's gender schemata about others: A meta-analytic review. *Developmental review, 13*(2), 147-183.

Lecture 2: Children and Television

I.   Concerns

Concerns have been raised about children and television, and particularly about programming directed at children.

A. Many people hold that there is not enough programming to serve children's educational and informational needs.
B. Also, children who watch adult-oriented programming may be adversely affected by its content (e.g., criminality and violence).
C. There is also concern about television advertising directed toward children.
  1. Children lack the cognitive sophistication needed to evaluate advertisers' claims.
  2. Children may be unable to distinguish between programs and commercials, unless broadcasters make this distinction explicit.

II. Research

Much research on the impact of television on children was done in the 1960s and 1970s. Several major topics were studied.

A. Children's social learning from television, including their learning of gender, racial, and occupational stereotypes.
B. Potential educational uses of television.
C. Children's strategies for understanding television plots and stories, and for understanding television advertising.
D. Effects of televised violence on children's aggressive behavior. This has been the most extensively researched topic. The major investigator was Bandura of Stanford University.
   1. Studies of effectiveness of filmed versus live models of aggression in inducing aggression in children found that filmed models were more effective.
   2. Other investigators found that cartoon and fantasy models of aggression were as effective as "real-life" models in inducing aggression in children.
   3. On the basis of a review of this research and related material, the Presidential Commission on the Causes and Prevention of Violence concluded (1969) that children do learn aggressive behavior from films and television.

III. Intervention

The report of the Presidential Commission motivated efforts to regulate children's television programming.

A. Nongovernmental efforts
   1. Action for Children's Television (ACT).
     a. Goal: to increase the viewing options available to children.
     b. Proposals, early 1970s (these have not been implemented, but they are important as an initiative for improving programming):
       (1) Require stations to provide a minimum number of hours per week of daily programming for children (ACT wanted 14 hours per week).
       (2) Eliminate all commercial sponsorship from children's television.
   2. FCC: Children's Television Report and Policy Statement (1974). This was the FCC's response to ACT's proposals.
     a. Broadcasters were directed to provide programming specifically designed for children's needs.
     b. With regard to advertising, "host selling" (use of program characters to promote products) should be discontinued; also, program content and commercials should be clearly distinguished.
B. Governmental efforts
   1. Reagan administration's "marketplace approach"
     a. Use of FCC guidelines for all programming (including children's programming)
     b. Reliance on marketplace competition, rather than regulations, to ensure adequate audience service. (The assumption here is that audiences will support only programming that meets their needs.)
     c. Rationale: With respect to children's programming, it was noted that video programming was increasingly available through alternative means (e.g., PBS, cable stations, VCRs) and was no longer solely the responsibility of commercial networks.
   2. Children's Television Education Act, proposed in 1985. This was a landmark legislative proposal.
     a. It would establish a minimum of 7 hours per week for children's educational programming.
     b. It would require the FCC to conduct inquiries into the implications of programs created to promote toys or other children's products.

References for Lecture 2

Barry, D. (1993). Screen violence and America's children. *Spectrum, 66*, 37-42.
Berry, G. & Asamen, J. (Eds.) (1993).

Children and television: Images in a changing sociocultural world. Newbury Park, CA: Sage.

Gortmaker, S. L., et al. (1990, Winter). The importance of television viewing on mental aptitudes and achievement: A longitudinal study. *Public opinion quarterly, 54,* 594-604.

Hayes, D. & Casey, D. (1992). Young children and television: The retention of emotional reactions. *Child development, 63,* 1423-1436.

Holden, C. (1992). Does TV stunt neural development? *Science, 258,* 738.

Kunkel, D. L. & Watkins, B. A. (1985). *Children and television.* Washington Report of the SRCD, I (4).

Lecture 3: Punishment

I.   Research approaches

It is difficult to do research on the effectiveness of punishment in controlling young children's behavior; there are obvious ethical constraints. However, three general approaches are used.

A.   There are some studies of punishment in controlling animals' behavior.

B.   There are retrospective studies involving parents' reports of their child-rearing practices.

C.   There are also some laboratory studies. Many of these involve manipulating various aspects of punishment to determine its effect in constraining children from playing with attractive but forbidden toys when the children are later observed covertly.

II.   Effectiveness of punishment

Laboratory studies have yielded findings about factors influencing the effectiveness of punishment.

A.   Timing: Early punishment is more effective than later punishment.
   1.   Most effective timing: Verbal punishment delivered as a child initiates a forbidden act (e.g., as the child reaches for a forbidden toy during a punishment-learning session).
   2.   But timing interacts with other factors that can influence the effectiveness of punishment.

B.   Intensity: More intense punishment is more effective than less intense punishment.
   1.   In lab studies with children, intensity of punishment was varied; this involved increasing or decreasing the volume of an aversive tone delivered as children touched a forbidden toy.
   2.   With high-intensity punishment, timing usually had less effect than it did with low-intensity punishment. But there were exceptions to this-- situations that may induce anxiety levels incompatible with learning. There are at least two explanations.
      a.   Distinction between "good" and "bad" behavior is subtle relative to children's cognitive complexity.
      b.   The child may be uncertain as to what response would avoid the punishment.

C.   Relationship between agent and recipient of punishment: Punishment is more effective when delivered by a person with whom the child has a warm, affectionate relationship than when delivered by a cold, impersonal agent. Such punishment may take two forms.
   1.   Presentation of aversive consequence (verbal or physical rebuke).
   2.   Withholding of positive consequence (agent's affection).

D.   Reasoning: Punishment combined with reasoning is more effective than either punishment delivered alone or reasoning delivered alone. Reasoning also interacts with other factors.
   1.   With reasoning, late-delivered punishment is as effective as early-delivered punishment. (Thus, if punishment must "wait until your father gets home," be sure that the father explains the reason for the punishment.)
   2.   With reasoning, low-intensity punishment is as effective as high-intensity punishment.
   3.   With reasoning, punishment delivered by an impersonal agent is as effective as punishment delivered by affectionate agent.
   4.   Reasoning (and periodic reminders of reasons) may substantially prolong the effectiveness of punishment.

E.   Consistency: Inconsistent punishment is worse than no efforts at all to control child's behavior.

III. Negative effects

Punishment can have some undesirable consequences.

A.   When used to control aggression, punishment may actually provide a child with a model of aggressive behavior.
B.   Punishment can impair the relationship between agent and child.
    1.   The child may be motivated to avoid the agent, if this is possible.
    2.   Or--if avoiding the agent is not possible--the child may become passive or withdraw emotionally from the relationship.

IV. An alternative to punishment

Reinforcement of incompatible responses is an alternative to punishment.

References for Lecture 3

Newell, P. (1989). *Children are people too: The case against physical punishment.* London: Bedford Square Press.
Rich, J. (1993). Discipline and moral development. *High school journal, 76*(2), 139-144.
Whitmore, E. (1993). The association between punitive childhood experiences and hyperactivity. *Child abuse and neglect, 17*(3), 357-366.

TOPIC FOR DEBATE

Should Parents Foster Traditional Gender Roles or Androgyny in Children?

Background

There are several reasons for arguing that distinct male and female roles are an inevitable and desirable facet of society. Biologically based physical sex differences are, of course, an undeniable fact of life. Some sociobiologists assert that these differences are only the most observable innate differences between the sexes, and that there are genetic bases for gender differences in behavior, personality, and abilities.

Some psychologists have also argued that gender differences in behavior are both unavoidable and desirable. Several developmental theories--including psychoanalytic theory, cognitive-developmental theory, and cognitive-social theory--hold that the emergence of gender differences in behavior is inextricably linked with normal processes of personality and intellectual development. In other contexts, some psychologists have proposed the existence of a "parental imperative" whereby both men and women fulfill distinct roles and express distinct sets of personal characteristics in order to provide complementary resources for their children. From a sociological and historical viewpoint, one might argue that maintaining traditional male and female roles is necessary for cultural continuity.

Nonetheless, there are also strong arguments in favor of abandoning traditional gender roles and evolving more androgynous roles for men and women. Many psychologists disagree with the notion that gender differences are linked with other processes of normal development; they argue that most gender differences in behavior are learned--and that these differences are not particularly adaptive. Furthermore, many feminists and sociologists note that views of "innate" or "natural" gender differences have been used as a rationale for discrimination against women and men, particularly in the workplace.

Androgyny has been proposed as an aspect of personality that may be more adaptive, for both women and men, than distinct gender differences in personality and behavior. An androgynous person is one who cannot be readily classified as "masculine" or "feminine" across all situations. Rather, such a person possesses characteristics traditionally ascribed to both sexes and is able to draw on all these characteristics as a situation demands. A society in which most members were androgynous rather than masculine or feminine would be quite different from our contemporary society, but it might function at least as well.

Debate plan

Using this background, and information from additional sources (selected references appear below), student panels should debate the following positions:

Position A.   Parents should be encouraged to instill traditional masculinity in their sons and traditional femininity in their daughters.

Position B.   Parents should be encouraged to raise androgynous sons and daughters.

References for the debate

Bem, S. L. (1974). The meaning of psychological androgyny. *Journal of consulting and clinical psychology, 42,* 155-162.

Boldizar, J. (1991). Assessing sex typing and androgyny in children: The children's sex role inventory. *Developmental psychology, 27,* 505-515.

Lombardo, J. & Kemper, T. (1992). Sex role and parental behaviors. *Journal of genetic psychology, 153,* 103-113.

Robinson, J. (1993). Emotional communication in mother-toddler relationships: Evidence for early gender differentiation. *Merrill-Palmer quarterly, 39*(4), 496-517.

Sandberg, D., Meyer-Bahlburg, H., & Yager, T. (1993). Feminine gender role behavior and academic achievement: Their relation in a community sample of middle childhood boys. *Sex roles, 29,* 125-140.

TOPICS FOR DISCUSSION

Topic 1: Theoretical Perspectives on Gender Differentiation

1. Ask students to summarize the psychoanalytic, social-learning, cognitive-developmental, and gender-schema perspectives on the development of masculinity and femininity (pages 242-245).

2. Ask students to identify one or more implications for parenting of each viewpoint.

3. Ask students which perspective places the most emphasis on environmental influences on gender differentiation.

4. Ask students which explanation for the emergence of masculinity and femininity they find most acceptable, and why.

Topic 2: Gender and Personality Development

1. Ask students to summarize how recent studies on gender have dispelled many of the traditionally held behavioral and psychological differences between boys and girls (page 246).

2. Ask students to explain the main sources of gender differences and to defend their choice of the factor they believe is most responsible for imparting gender-biased attitudes in children today (pages 247-249).

Topic 3: Parenting Styles

1. Ask students to summarize the text's descriptions of authoritarian, permissive, and authoritative parents (pages 257-258).

2. The text portrays authoritative parents as most effective in rearing competent preschoolers. Remind the students of the differences in infants' temperament described earlier in the text. Ask them to consider the potential effectiveness of the permissive and authoritarian styles of parenting for children fitting each temperamental category.

Topic 4: The Importance of Play

1. Ask students to list and briefly describe the various types of play defined in the chapter (pages 263-266).

2. Ask students to describe how play can contribute to children's physical, intellectual, emotional, and social development (pages 263-266).

3. Ask students to specify what types of play they would most encourage in their own children, and why. Ask them to specify what (if any) types of play they would discourage in their own children, and why.

PROJECTS AND CLASS EXERCISES

Group Exercise: Helping Children Form Friendships

Students working in groups should use the box on page 263 of the text ("Helping Young Children to Make Friends") as a basis for this exercise. The group should select two of the suggestions included in the box and describe at least three specific, concrete things they would do to implement each suggestion they choose. Ask the group members to plan their implementation in a specific context: they should assume the role of a preschool teacher who has just had a new child join the class;

they are to suppose that the child's family has just moved from out of town and that the child does not know any children in the school or neighborhood.

Project 1: Gender and Personality

Have students watch some children's television programs and advertising, examine some children's toys and their packaging, read some children's books, and listen to some children's recordings, looking for evidence of sex-role socialization. Students should write a paper comparing these contemporary influences with those they remember from their own childhood and discussing the implications of the differences and similarities they find.

Project 2: Children's Gender Stereotypes

Students should interview a preschool boy and a preschool girl to determine the children's beliefs about differences between boys and girls. Interview topics should include what differences the children believe exist and why the children think these differences exist. Students should write a paper describing the interviews and interpreting them in the context of the psychoanalytic, social-learning, cognitive-developmental, or gender-schema approaches to early personality development.

Project 3: Children's Television

Students should watch several children's television programs. On the basis of their observations, they should write a paper analyzing the aspects of these programs that could encourage aggressive and prosocial behavior in young children.

Project 4: Rewards and Punishment

Students should write a paper in which they recall how their own parents used rewards and punishment to shape their behavior. Students who have young brothers and sisters could supplement their recollections with observations of their parents' present approach to child rearing. Students should also explain how (and why) they would use rewards and punishments differently from their parents.

ESSAY QUESTIONS

1.   Distinguish the concept of *identification* in psychoanalytic theory and in

social-learning theory.

Answer guideline. In psychoanalytic theory, identification is a process through which children see themselves as similar to the same-sex parent; through identification, children relieve the anxiety aroused by the Oedipus or Electra complex. In social-learning theory, identification is the result of observing and imitating a model; through identification, children come to believe that they have the same desirable characteristics as the model.

2.   Describe the cognitive-developmental and gender-schema theories of the development of gender.

Answer guideline. According to cognitive-developmental theory, children classify themselves as male or female and then organize their behavior around that classification. Children first acquire gender identity (awareness that they are male or female) and only later acquire gender conservation (knowledge that they will always be male or female). According to gender-schema theory, children organize information around the concept of gender because of their awareness of gender-based definitions of people throughout society. Once children have acquired the gender schemas of their society, they construct a self-concept that is consistent with their gender schema.

3.   Describe gender differences in personality that are apparent among preschoolers.

Answer guideline. There are few personality differences related to gender in the preschool years. The clearest differences are that boys tend to be more aggressive than girls and that girls tend to be more empathetic than boys.

4.   Describe the major sources of gender differences outlined in the chapter.

Answer guideline. Biological influences include hormonal balance and differences in brain functioning. Cultural influences include social roles deemed appropriate for men and women, and parents' differential treatment of sons and daughters. Media influences include how many male and female characters are seen on television and in what kinds of roles. Family influences include the encouragement of gender-typed activities by parents, the different ways parents relate to boys and girls, and the rise in one-parent families.

5.   Why is play described as the "work of the young"?

Answer guideline. Children grow in many ways through play. Play can benefit physical development through exercise; it can enhance cognitive development through observation of functional relationships and through sensory stimulation; finally, it can benefit emotional and social development through fantasy, role-playing, and interaction with other children.

6.   Describe the forms of social play and nonsocial play outlined in the text.

Answer guideline. Unoccupied behavior: The child watches anything of momentary interest, plays with his or her own body, or simply moves around. Onlooker behavior: The child watches other children playing; he or she may talk to the other children or ask questions but does not enter into play activities.
Solitary independent play: The child plays alone with toys not being used by other children in the vicinity and is not attentive to what other children are doing.
Parallel play: The child plays independently, but play activity brings the child into the vicinity of other children; the child may play with toys like those being used by other children, but his or her use of the toys is not affected by the other children's uses.
Associative play: The child plays with other children, their conversation concerns the content of their play, and toys are shared; but there is no organization of the children's activity toward a goal or product.
Cooperative (or organized, or supplementary) play: The child plays in a group organized around attempting to achieve a purpose (make a product, dramatize a situation, play a formal game, etc.); one or two children direct the activity of the group, and the efforts of one child are supplemented by the actions of others in order to reach the goal.

7.   In what ways can childhood fears be effectively treated?

Answer guideline. Parents should react to children's fears with acceptance, reassurance, and encouragement to express fears openly. However, parents should not allow children to avoid feared objects, people, or situations; this would deprive the child of opportunities to learn that the fear is unfounded (if that is the case). If a child's fear impedes his or her activities, more extensive treatment (e.g., systematic desensitization) could be appropriate.

8.   What factors appear to trigger aggression in children?

Answer guideline. Reinforcement may be a trigger, if a child succeeds in achieving a goal through aggression. Frustration has been identified as a trigger for aggression in some laboratory studies. And modeling--of other children's aggression, a punitive adult, or a live or cartoon character observed on television--seems to be a powerful influence on aggression.

9.   What can parents do to help their children develop altruism?

Answer guideline. Parents can encourage prosocial behavior and altruism in their children by modeling these behaviors; by encouraging the children to be empathic and to consider others' reactions; by holding high (but clear, consistent, and reasonable) standards for their children's behavior; and by directing their children toward media that promote prosocial behavior and altruism.

10.   Describe the three styles of parenting outlined in the chapter.

Answer guideline. Authoritarian parents value control and obedience, hold children to a uniform standard of conduct, and punish transgressions severely. They are detached, less warm than other parents, discontented, withdrawn, and distrustful.

Permissive parents value self-expression and self-regulation, make few demands on children, set few rules but explain reasons for any rules that are set, rarely punish, and are relatively warm.

Authoritative parents value individuality and social values; control children's behavior through reasoning rather than punishment or withdrawal of affection; respect children's interests, opinions, and personalities; and are loving, consistent, firm, and encouraging. These parents tend to produce the most self-reliant, self-controlled, assertive, and content children.

CHAPTER 8

PHYSICAL AND INTELLECTUAL DEVELOPMENT IN MIDDLE CHILDHOOD

INTRODUCTION

In Chapters 6 and 7, the development of children through kindergarten was discussed. Now, in **Chapter 8**, the discussion is shifted to the child of elementary school age. Whereas Chapter 6 focused on the physical and intellectual development of the preschooler, **Chapter 8** examines the physical and intellectual development of the 6- to 12-year-old.

- Elementary school years are marked by further growth, strength, and agility and the mastery of skills that first appeared or were just learned during early childhood.

- Health, fitness, and safety represent important aspects of a child's development. Such topics as vision, dental health, general fitness, and childhood accidents are covered.

- Studies conducted several decades ago suggest that boys excel in motor skills, but more recent research indicates that boys and girls have similar motor abilities.

- Probably the most significant aspect of development at this age is the fact that children spend a large proportion of their time in school. Intellectual development takes place in the context of formal schooling, entry into which coincides with significant changes in the way children think and organize knowledge. Piaget's stage of concrete operations is discussed in detail .

- Moreover, in middle childhood, moral and ethical thinking begins to develop in significant ways that are related to the changes in the way children under-stand their world. Piaget's and Kohlberg's theories of moral reasoning are compared and contrasted.

- The development of memory, intelligence, and language during middle childhood is examined closely. The topics covered include mnemonic devices, rehearsal, elaboration, and external memory aids as well as the effects of race and culture on IQ tests and metacommunication.

- Childcare professionals and educators often disagree on how school can best enhance children's development. Teachers as well as parents influence how well children do in school. In addition, children with disabilities require special educational assistance. Learning disabilities and hyperactivity are examined closely, as is the topic of mainstreaming.

- Chapter 8 concludes with a discussion of giftedness, with suggestions for educating and nurturing gifted children. Bilingual speech is also covered.

CHAPTER OUTLINE

I.   PHYSICAL DEVELOPMENT

A.   GROWTH DURING MIDDLE CHILDHOOD
   1.   Growth Rates
   2.   Nutrition and Growth
      a.   Malnutrition
      b.   Obesity
B.   HEALTH, FITNESS, AND SAFETY
   1.   Children's Health
      a.   Minor medical conditions
      b.   Vision
      c.   Dental health
      d.   General fitness
      e.   Improving health and fitness
   2.   Children's Safety
C.   MOTOR DEVELOPMENT IN MIDDLE CHILDHOOD

II.   INTELLECTUAL DEVELOPMENT

A.   ASPECTS OF INTELLECTUAL DEVELOPMENT IN MIDDLE CHILDHOOD
   1.   Cognitive Development: Piaget's Stage of Concrete Operations
      a.   Operational thinking
      b.   Conservation
         (1)   How is conservation developed?
   2.   Moral Reasoning: Two Theories
      a.   Piaget and two moral stages
      b.   Kohlberg and moral reasoning
         (1)   Kohlberg's moral dilemmas
         (2)   Kohlberg's 3 levels of moral reasoning
         (3)   Evaluating Kohlberg's theory
   3.   Development of Memory: Information Processing
      a.   How memory works: encoding, storing, and retrieving
      b.   Mnemonic devices: strategies for remembering
         (1)   Rehearsal
         (2)   Organization
         (3)   Elaboration
         (4)   External memory aids
   4.   Development of Intelligence: Psychometrics
      a.   IQ tests
      b.   Norms, reliability, and validity
      c.   Race, culture, and IQ tests
         (1)   Intelligence testing of African-American children
      d.   Cultural bias
         (1)   "Culture-free" and "Culture-fair" tests
         (2)   The test situation
   5.   Development of Language: Communication
      a.   Grammar: the structure of language
      b.   Metacommunication: understanding the processes of communication
B.   CHILDREN IN SCHOOL
   1.   Educational Trends
   2.   Teachers' Characteristics and Expectations
   3.   Parents' Influence
   4.   Education for Special Needs
      a.   Children with Disabilities
         (1)   Mental retardation
         (2)   Learning disabilities
         (3)   Hyperactivity
         (4)   Educating children with disabilities
      b.   Gifted, Talented, and Creative Children
         (1)   Defining and identifying giftedness
         (2)   Educating and nurturing gifted children
   5.   Bilingualism and Bilingual Education

KEY TERMS

attention deficit hyperactivity disorder (ADHD) (page 298)
bilingual education (301)
bilingualism (301)
code-switching (302)
concrete operations (279)
conservation (279)
conventional morality (280)

convergent thinking (300)
culture-fair (289)
culture-free (289)
decenter ((279)
divergent thinking (300)
dyslexia (296)
elaboration (286)
external aids (286)
giftedness (299)
horizontal decalage (280)
learning disabilities (LDs) (296)
mainstreaming (298)
mental retardation (296)
metacommunication (292)
metamemory (286)
mnemonic devices (285)
morality of constraint (280)
morality of cooperation (280)
operational thinking (279)
organization (286)
Otis-Lennon School
  Ability Test (287)
preconventional morality (280)
rehearsal (285)
self-fulfilling prophecy (294)
Wechsler Intelligence Scale
  for Children (WISC) (286)

LEARNING OBJECTIVES

After finishing Chapter 8, students should be able to:

1. Briefly describe the growth rates of middle childhood and explain the importance of nutrition and fitness for continued healthy growth. (pp. 272-274)

2. List some medical conditions common in middle childhood that might jeopardize growth and development. (pp. 274-276)

3. Identify the most common causes of childhood accidents. (pp. 277-278)

4. Explain the typical progression of motor development in middle childhood. (p. 278)

5. Explain Piaget's stage of concrete operations and define the following terms: *operational thinking*, *conservation*, *decenter,*, *horizontal decalage* (pp. 279-280)

6. Compare and contrast Piaget's and Kohlberg's theories of the development of moral reasoning. (pp. 280-282, p. 284)

7. Explain how the memory process works and describe the following *mnemonic* strategies: rehearsal, organization, elaboration, external memory. (pp. 285-286)

8. Compare and contrast the purpose and use of the WISC-R and the Otis-Lennon School Ability Test, both of which are used to assess "intelligence." (p. 287)

9. Explain why Black American children tend to score about 15 points lower on IQ tests than white American children. (p. 288)

10. Describe the ongoing controversy over IQ scores and *culture bias* and define the following terms: *culture-free tests*, *culture-fair tests* (pp. 288-289)

11. Explain why Asian children are able to make such a strong showing on academic tasks. (pp. 290-291)

12. Describe the development of language in children of elementary school age, and explain the concept of *meta-communication*. (pp. 289, 292-293)

13. List some strategies for developing thinking and reasoning skills. (p. 294)

14. Explain how teachers' expectations can influence children's achievement. (pp. 293-295)

15. List some of the ways parents can influence their children to succeed in school. (pp. 295-296)

16. Briefly explain the ways in which children with mental retardation can benefit from mainstreamed schooling. (p. 296)

17. Describe how various disabilities, such as dyslexia and ADHD, affect children's ability to learn and provide some recommendations for educating these children. (pp. 296-299)

18.   Define giftedness, and describe what educational opportunities schools provide for children who are gifted, talented, or creative. (pp. 299-301)

19.   Briefly describe the two approaches schools use to encourage bilingualism. (pp. 301-302)

CHAPTER SUMMARY AND TEACHING RECOMMENDATIONS

The chapter opens with a discussion of physical development in middle childhood. Children's growth and nutrition are described, including differences between boys and girls and variations with race and socioeconomic level. This is a good context for pointing out the many ways in which culture and cultural expectations influence differences between males and females. Obesity in children is also reviewed.

Next, the authors discuss several aspects of health, fitness, and safety in middle childhood (and/or minor medical conditions) and note that children today are generally less fit than previous cohorts of children, in part because of decreased activity. You might want to relate this point to the discussion in Chapter 7 of the potentially negative effects of television on children. In their discussion of safety in childhood, the authors describe the most common cause of death among young children--automobile accidents. The material on physical development continues with an overview of motor development in middle childhood.

The chapter has an extensive section on aspects of intellectual development during middle childhood. Piaget's stage of concrete operations is described; this material focuses on attainment of the concept of conservation and factors that influence it. If a significant number of your students are seeking certification as teachers, you could discuss concrete operations and other cognitive advances of middle childhood in terms of their implications for education. This section continues with a review of Piaget's and Kohlberg's theories of moral development, including a critique of Kohlberg's theory on moral reasoning.

The authors next discuss improvements in memory, increasing use of memory strategies (mnemonic devices), and the development of metamemory during middle childhood. (Again, it may be appropriate to focus on the educational implications of these topics, depending on the makeup of your class.)

There is an extensive section on intelligence testing in middle childhood. The authors describe the most commonly used instruments and present fundamental psychometric concepts (norms, reliability, validity). There is a detailed discussion of problems in the use of intelligence tests, particularly for minority-group children; you may want to complement that material with a discussion of the potential value of intelligence testing (see Lecture Outlines). The authors note racial differences in mean IQ test scores, alternative explanations of those differences, and various approaches to assessing the intelligence of minority-group children.

In their section on language, the authors note limitations in children's language abilities in middle childhood but point out that language abilities increase through at least the earlier part of this period of the life span.

In the section headed "Children in School," the authors discuss how certain historical events have brought about distinct educational trends in this century. This section continues with a discussion of teachers' and parents' influence on children's educational achievement. The authors then review three of the most common educational disabilities (mental retardation, learning disability, and hyperactivity) and describe how children with such handicaps are educated. *Giftedness* is defined, and the authors present information from Terman's longitudinal study which belies stereotypes of gifted children. The educational needs of gifted children are discussed.

The chapter closes with a discussion of bilingualism and the advantages/disadvantages of providing school-aged children with a bilingual education.

Boxes in Chapter 8 are "Children's Understanding of Health and Illness," "Should IQ Tests Be Used?," "How Can Asian Children Achieve So Much?," and "Teaching Children to Think."

AUDIOVISUAL MATERIALS

Distributor, date, and running time are given for each film or video. Distributors' addresses are listed in the appendix (General Resources). If a film or video is not in color, there is a notation (BW) to that effect.

IQ testing and the school. (IM, 1991, 60 min.) This program examines different tests devised to measure intelligence and achievement, concentrating on the WISC-R and looking at whether or not these tests are valid and reliable. It explores factors affecting in-school achievement, including the expectations and style of a student's teachers, and shows how students in cooperative learning environments evidence higher achievement than those in competitive or individualistic settings.

Language. (IM, 1990, 30 min.) This video explains that language is not only a product of learning and environmental influences but is also a part of man's genetic endowment. It identifies the essential characteristics of language, evaluates research into whether or not animals can acquire language skills, details the stages of language development in children, and discusses factors influencing that development. It also shows how scientists have learned about man's ability to use and understand language by studying disorders that damage the parts of the brain that facilitate speech.

Memory. (IM, 1990, 30 min.) Biological and cognitive research findings related to how we store, encode, and retrieve memories are discussed by leading memory researchers. The program shows what memory disturbances are and how certain problems can result from accidents or disease. Memory of dramatic events is analyzed, and the practical application of memory research to witness recall in criminal trials is discussed.

The elementary mind. (IM, 1992, 30 min.) Developmental psychologist Jean Piaget's theories on the logical operational period are examined in this program, which features interviews with Robert Sternberg and Rochel Gelman. It shows experiments that demonstrate how conceptualization becomes easier in middle childhood. The importance of memory strategies in learning situations is explained, and elaboration tests that measure mental effort during interference are described. The controversy over intelligence and diagnostic testing is also discussed.

Moral development. (IM, 1978, 30 min.) This video presents four theories of moral development--the cognitive-developmental model based on the work of Lawrence Kohlberg and Jean Piaget, the social-learning approach, the Freudian or psychoanalytic approach, and Robert Hogan's framework for assessing moral thought and behavior.

Recognizing, understanding, and overcoming learning disabilities. (IM, 1990, 33 min.) Intended for the classroom teacher with mainstreamed learning-disabled students, this program explains how to recognize learning disabilities and demonstrates practical teaching strategies. Dr. Judith Birsh, Professor of Special Education at Columbia Teachers College, provides an overview of learning problems.

Mainstreaming in action. (IM, 1980, 26 min.) Filmed in several different public-school environments, this award-winning video takes viewers into both elementary and secondary classrooms to watch teachers work with handicapped students in regular classroom sessions. Interviews with teachers elucidate the underlying issue in the debate over mainstreaming and special-education--the relative values that should be placed on socialization and academic learning.

Motivation: How to encourage the learning-disabled student. (IM, 1990, 45 min.) Margaret Shepherd of the Learning Disabilities Program at Columbia Teachers College explains techniques teachers can use to motivate learning-disabled children to work for the satisfaction of learning rather than out of a desire for approval. She demonstrates how to change a feeling of learned helplessness to one of confidence and illustrates why children who struggle to learn have a fragile sense of self-worth.

Identifying gifted students. (IM, 1980, 29 min.) This program defines giftedness and explores methods for identifying gifted students. Limitations of testing procedures and the importance of flexibility in the evaluation of gifted students are emphasized. The program also explains how to involve teachers, parents, peers, and outside agencies to create a profile of "giftedness" appropriate for different educational settings.

Guest speakers

An instructor from the department of teacher education at your institution or another institution could be an excellent guest speaker. You could ask him or her to discuss, among other things, mainstreaming and its impact on teacher certification, approaches to identifying and educating gifted children, and the impact computers are having on elementary/special education. Another possible guest speaker is a clinical or school psychologist experienced in administering intelligence tests to children in elementary school and interpreting the results; you could ask this speaker to comment on the problems the textbook identifies regarding intelligence testing of schoolchildren and alternative approaches such as culture-free or culture-fair testing. Another possibility is to invite a pediatrician (a local hospital could help you find one) or a representative of a parents' support group to speak about hyperactivity (ADHD).

LECTURE OUTLINES

Lecture 1: Piaget's Stage of Concrete Operations

I. The concrete operational stage

Piaget's stage of concrete operations occurs from ages 6 or 7 years to 11 or 12 years.

A. Limitations of preoperational thought are now largely overcome.
B. The major accomplishment is the concept of conservation. Children are able to apply conservation to more and more situations as this stage goes on.
   1. Conservation of substance: 6-7 years.
   2. Conservation of weight: 9-10 years.
   3. Conservation of volume: 11-12 years.

II. Concrete operational thought

Concrete operational thought has several characteristics.

A. Thinking is now decentered: it takes account of all relevant information to reach judgments (e.g., a child considers relative length and width of pieces of clay).
B. Children now attend to processes of transformation, not just to states (the initial and final appearances of materials). Children apparently consider how materials change and use this knowledge in reasoning to solve problems.
C. Thinking is now reversible: children recognize that the process of change can be undone and that materials can be changed in compensatory ways.

III. The shift from preoperational to concrete operational thinking

For children to move from preoperations to concrete operations, two factors are important.

A. Maturation.
B. Experience. Training studies have attempted to identify specific kinds of experiences that are critical in the shift from preoperations to concrete operations.
   1. General strategy of training studies.
      a. Subjects--usually a group of preschoolers--are tested on conservation problems before training, and are then divided into a training group and a control group.
      b. Type (and duration) of training varies from study to study, but examples include these:
         (1) Children receive verbal feedback on their responses.
         (2) Children are given a general rule for solving problems.
         (3) "Conserving" children explain their judgments to "nonconserving" children in group situations.
      c. After training, all subjects are retested. If the training was successful, trained children

should now conserve but control children should not.

2. Outcome of training studies: Many such studies have been successful. Successful studies have allowed us to identify some experiences (feedback, rules, social interaction) that promote conservation, although researchers probably have not identified all such experiences.

References for Lecture 1

Ginsburg, H. P. & Opper, S. (1988). *Piaget's theory of intellectual development*. (3d ed.). Englewood Cliffs, NJ: Prentice-Hall. **Phillips, J. L (1981).** *Piaget's theory: A primer*. San Francisco: Freeman.

Lecture 2: Families and Schools

I. Congruities and incongruities between families and schools

Families and schools are both major agents of socialization. In various important ways, there is congruence between the socialization goals and processes of family and school, but there are usually also some differences.

A. Schools are a more impersonal context for socialization. The child has relatively short-term relationships with adults and other children in school.
B. Schools typically expose children to a wider diversity of values and views than the family does.
C. Schools and families may also stress different norms. Schools may place greater emphasis than families on independence, achievement, and "universalism."
   1. Independence: Children are expected to do their own work.
   2. Achievement: Children are expected to actively attempt to master specified skills.
   3. Universalism: Children are expected to interact with others on the basis of status (e.g., teacher, principal) rather than intimate knowledge.

II. Demands on schoolchildren

These incongruities affect the demands that are made on schoolchildren, who must master at least two curricula.

A. Academic curriculum. This, of course, is obvious.
B. Hidden curriculum. This may be less obvious. It involves assuming the "pupil role"--docility, orderliness, independence, achievement, responsibility, punctuality--and adopting certain conventions of communication.
   1. Mastery of the "pupil role" is an important influence on the quality of school experiences.
      a. Teachers prefer children who master the role easily, as these pupils make classroom management easier.
      b. Teachers generally expect better academic performance from these children, and this expectation may be a self-fulfilling prophecy.
   2. Mastering the "pupil role" is more difficult if there are significant incongruities between families' and schools' expectations. Some observers suggest that such incongruities may be sharper for nonwhite, non-middle-class children than for white middle-class children.
   3. Communication in school may also involve incongruities between families and schools.
      a. Communication style: Typically, a teacher asks questions and expects verbal responses from one pupil at a time. This can be difficult for a child whose family reflects a cultural emphasis on collective patterns of response (as in many nonwestern cultures).
      b. Use of language: If the vocabulary or syntax used in a child's home (e.g., black English or a foreign language) differs considerably from what is expected at school, the teacher may react negatively.

Reference for Lecture 2

Hess, R. D. & Holloway, S. D. (1984). Family and school as educational institutions. In R. D. Parke (Ed.), *Review of child development research*. Vol. 7: *The family*. Chicago: University of Chicago Press.

Lecture 3: Testing of Intelligence--Pros and Cons

I. Defining intelligence

David Wechsler--a proponent of the psychometric approach--defined *intelligence* as the capacity for acting purposefully, thinking rationally, and dealing effectively with the environment.

II. Psychometric approach

The psychometric approach to studying intelligence involves using standardized measures with demonstrated reliability and validity to determine "how much" intelligence an individual possesses.

A. Standardization.
1. Norms. An individual's performance is compared with that of a reference group. Norms provide a context for evaluation.
2. Reliability. Measures must give estimates of an individual's intelligence that are stable over time.
3. Validity. Measures must be related in logical ways to other kinds of performance thought to reflect intelligence.
B. Commonly used measures of intelligence for schoolchildren:
1. Otis-Lennon.
2. Stanford-Binet.
3. Wechsler Intelligence Scale for Children--Revised (WISC-R). This is probably the most commonly used individual measure.

III. Problems

Using intelligence tests with schoolchildren gives rise to several problems.

A. Test scores are of very limited usefulness in predicting success in careers in adulthood.
1. Most tests favor certain types of thought (e.g., analytic thought); but these skills are important for success only in some occupations.
2. Many factors other than intelligence are important influences on success in a career.
B. Test scores are limited in predicting children's performance in important nonacademic areas. Test scores provide

very little information about how well children are likely to deal with interpersonal situations, handle responsibility, etc.
C. Standardized tests do not measure processes underlying children's responses.
1. This is due at least in part to standardization. A test must be administered in the same manner to all test-takers. Examiners have little flexibility; they cannot question a child to determine why a certain (wrong) answer was given; thus, creative approaches to test items could be penalized.
2. This aspect is in contrast to Piaget's clinical method for studying children's intelligence.
D. There are problems with testing nonwhite children and children from nonwestern cultures. Penalizing unconventional responses (see above) is a factor here.
1. Test manuals specify correct responses for problems; this specification is based on the performance of reference groups; and until recently, these groups consisted almost entirely of white middle-class children.
2. The recent revision of WISC made definite efforts to represent African-American and Hispanic children in the standardization sample and to note some ways to take these children's background into account in scoring.
E. Test scores have a potential for misuse. If they are used to predict scholastic performance many years into the future (as opposed to current performance), they may be inaccurate. Testing for purposes of long-term educational tracking is probably inappropriate.

IV. Value

Intelligence testing of schoolchildren does have potential value.

A. Test scores are generally good predictors of current scholastic performance. Thus, they can be useful for short-term academic placement or tracking.
B. Test scores may have diagnostic value for children with academic problems, if certain conditions are met.
1. An IQ test should always be one

element in a "test battery," i.e, a collection of tests used to identify cognitive or emotional problems hampering school performance.
2. The examiner should be experienced in testing children generally and in administering children's intelligence tests in particular.
3. IQ (and other) test results should be interpreted in light of as much background information about the child as can be obtained.

C. Tests are usually administered because some type of decision needs to be made about a child; the child's performance can provide critical information as a basis for making a decision in the child's best interests.

References for Lecture 3

Anastasi, A. (1987). *Psychological testing* (6th ed.). New York: Macmillan.
Kaufman, A. S. (1979). *Intelligent testing with the WISC-R*. New York: Wiley.

Lecture 4: Hyperactivity

I. Definition

According to DSM III-R, hyperactivity--or attention deficit hyperactivity disorder (ADHD)--is characterized by inattention, impulsivity, hyperactivity, and onset before 7 years of age.

II. Diagnosis

Diagnosing ADHD presents difficulties. All children show the defining characteristics at some times and in some situations. The appropriate "cutoff point" for deciding when these problems are at a clinical level is uncertain.

III. Causes

There are several possible causes of ADHD. Debate has arisen over whether the cause is organic or functional.

A. Possible organic causes:
1. "Minimal brain dysfunction" (unspecified physical abnormality).
2. Disturbances of neurotransmitters (dopamine, norepinephrine).
3. Neurological immaturity.
4. Feingold suggests salicylates, artificial flavors, and food coloring. But double-blind studies of diet-based treatment have not yielded empirical support.

B. One proposed functional cause: parental maltreatment.

C. Research on causes. Results of genetic studies suggest some type of organic causal agent (rather than a functional cause).
1. Studies of biological parents of adopted children with ADHD found higher rates of alcoholism among biological fathers and higher rates of hysteria among biological mothers.
2. Concordance rates for ADHD are higher among identical twins than among fraternal twins.

IV. Treatment

Three approaches to the treatment of hyperactivity are drugs, behavior modification, and cognitive-behavioral techniques.

A. Drug treatment usually involves administration of some type of stimulant (e.g., Ritalin, Dexedrine).
1. It is effective for 60 to 90 percent of children treated but more so for children's attention (which is more adaptable to environmental demands) than for their activity level.
2. It does not always lead to improved academic progress. Children's grades may be better in school, but there is no identified effect on scores on achievement tests.
3. Social behavior is improved.
4. Side effects are a concern. Children occasionally show decreased appetite, insomnia, or a slowed growth rate.
5. Children's view of medication may not be beneficial. They tend to see it as "magic" pills that make them smart or good (an external locus of control).
6. There is no evidence of an increased risk of later substance abuse.

B. Behavior modification is often paired with drug treatment, since drug therapy increases children's attentiveness and thus makes them more amenable to operant intervention.

1. There is a positive impact on academic performance.
2. But there are problems with delivery of reinforcement. Reinforcement can distract a child and invoke impulsive reactions.

C. Cognitive-behavioral techniques. This kind of treatment works in several ways.
1. It helps children understand the nature of their problem and how behavioral training can help them.
2. It teaches the child general rules for approaching tasks.
3. It helps children label their own behavior and feelings, use verbal self-regulation, distinguish careless errors from errors of misunderstanding, and set realistic goals for themselves.

V. Help for parents

In helping parents to cope with a hyperactive child, it is important to guide them to develop appropriate expectations for the child's behavior.

Reference for Lecture 4

Kessler, J. W. (1988). *Psychopathology of childhood*. (2d ed.). Englewood Cliffs, NJ: Prentice-Hall.

TOPIC FOR DEBATE

How Should Morality be Taught?

Background

All cultures have some moral, or ethical, standards governing the behavior of their members; and virtually every culture includes practices whereby these standards are transmitted to new members. There is disagreement, however, over how morality should be taught to contemporary American children.

Some people believe that morals should be transmitted through indoctrination--either by parents, by religious organizations, or by schools. They point out that, in view of children's immaturity, there is a clear need for training and guidance in morality (just as in other areas). Furthermore, cultural stability depends on the transmission of traditional values, a process that can be achieved through deliberate instruction. There are, in addition,

a number of potentially suitable agents of deliberate instruction; the most obvious agents, as noted above, are the family, religion, and possibly the school.

Other people favor a cognitive-developmental approach to teaching morality. Kohlberg, the major proponent of the cognitive-developmental approach, maintains that children's moral development depends on their cognitive development. For that reason, according to Kohlberg, moral indoctrination is unlikely to be effective unless children are cognitively ready for it. Kohlberg believes that a more effective approach would be based on group discussions through which children would be prompted to examine their own moral reasoning and would be exposed to moral reasoning at a slightly more advanced level than their own. Cognitive developmentalists point out that this approach could, potentially, elevate the general level of morality of an entire culture. (Moral indoctrination, by contrast, can bring children's moral standards only to the same level as those of the agent of indoctrination.) Finally, advocates of this approach note that there is no clear agreement in the contemporary United States as to which morals should be taught or who should teach them.

Debate plan

Using this background, and information from additional sources (selected references appear below), student panels should debate the following positions:

Position A. Morality is best taught through deliberate instruction.

Position B. Children should be taught morality through discussion aimed at values clarification and advancement.

References for the debate

Kohlberg, L. (1975, June). The cognitive developmental approach to moral education. *Phi delta kappan*.
Wynne, E. A. (1986, December/January). The great tradition in education: Transmitting moral values. *Educational leadership*.

TOPICS FOR DISCUSSION

Topic 1: Children's Health and Fitness

1. Ask students to identify health problems of middle childhood described in the chapter. If necessary, prompt them to include obesity, dental problems, and generally poorer levels of fitness than were prevalent in the past (textbook pages 273-276).

2. For each health problem identified, ask students to list steps that parents could take to eradicate the problem in their family.

3. For each health problem identified, ask students to list steps that the public schools could take to minimize the incidence of the problem among schoolchildren.

4. Ask students to summarize the Box on page 275, "Children's Understanding of Health and Illness." Ask them to identify implications of this information; that is, what steps could children of various ages take toward optimizing their own health?

Topic 2: Development of Memory

1. Ask students to define the different mnemonic strategies described in the text (pages 285-286) and to offer concrete examples of situations in which they relied on these strategies.

2. Ask students to describe situations in which an elementary school teacher should direct students to use each of the memory strategies described in the text.

3. Ask students to suggest ways that parents and teachers could help children increase their metamemory.

Topic 3: Teachers' Influences on Children

1. Ask students to describe the best teacher they remember from elementary school. Ask them to compare elements of their description with the description of "Miss A" on pages 293-294 of the text.

2. Ask students to describe one of the worst teachers they remember from elementary school. Ask them whether their descriptions are the antithesis of "Miss A."

Topic 4: Educating Exceptional Children

1. Ask students to describe the characteristics of children who have particular educational disabilities (e.g., mental retardation, learning disability, hyperactivity) as explained in the text (pages 296-298).

2. As the text points out, many children who suffer from learning disabilities are not correctly diagnosed and thus are mislabeled. Ask students to identify reasons for these errors. Ask them to suggest procedures that could minimize misdiagnoses.

3. Ask students to note problems with the definition of *giftedness* presented in the text (pages 299-300). Ask them to suggest a more useful definition.

PROJECTS AND CLASS EXERCISES

Group Exercise: Wellness for Children

Working in groups, students should design a "wellness" program for children aged 8 to 10. The group should prepare a written description of its program which includes (1) objectives, (2) where and when the program would be offered, (3) activities included, (4) major expenses entailed, and (5) criteria and procedures for evaluating the program's effectiveness.

In planning its program, the group will probably have to select a subset of the health and fitness problems described in the chapter as "targets for improvement" (if only because of limitations of class time). The group should also prepare a rationale for its focus.

Project 1: IQ Tests and Cultural Bias

Students should examine representative items from both the verbal and the performance scales of WISC-R and from a culture-fair or culture-free intelligence measure (such as Ravens Progressive Matrices). (Sources for these examinations include textbooks on psychological testing.) Students should write a paper specifying the differences between the two approaches to assessing intelligence, and identifying problems they find with each approach. The paper should also include suggestions for an improved approach to assessing intelligence which avoids cultural bias.

Project 2: Computers in Elementary Education

Students should interview an elementary school teacher who has used educational software in the classroom. Interview topics should include types of software the teacher used, ages of the children with which the software was used, the children's apparent reaction to the software, problems that arose in using the software, advantages of using the software, and the teacher's overall reaction to educational uses of computers. Students should write a paper summarizing the interview and commenting on the teacher's responses.

Project 3: Parents' Involvement in Children's Schooling

Students should write a paper describing things their parents did to help them in school and anything their parents did that hindered them in school. Students who have young brothers and sisters could also include their parents' influences on their siblings' education. The paper should also include students' comments on their parents' actions from the standpoint of the characteristics of parents who raised high-achieving children.

ESSAY QUESTIONS

1.   Describe problems related to poor nutrition in middle childhood.

Answer guideline.   Problems related to poor nutrition include slowed growth, impaired energy for play, and decreased alertness. Impaired energy for play may further hamper children's social development; decreased alertness and decreased energy for play may also harm children's cognitive development. If poor nutrition results in obesity, children may also be rejected by their peers.

2.   Summarize age changes in children's views of illness.

Answer guideline. Preoperational children often give magical or egocentric explanations for illness. Egocentric explanations may be a way in which children defend against feelings of helplessness in the face of illness. Somewhat older children understand that germs cause illness but may overextend this concept to the notion that germs are the sole cause of illness. Adolescents understand that there are many causes of illness (including germs) and that people can take many kinds of preventive measures to increase the probability of good health.

3.   Explain steps that could be effective in enhancing schoolchildren's fitness.

Answer guideline. One of the most important steps would be to encourage children to become more physically active; this encouragement could be provided through more frequent physical education classes, although care would have to be taken not to steal time from academic programming. Community-based programs to encourage children to acquire lifetime fitness skills (e.g., running, swimming, bicycling, walking) would also be valuable; YMCAs or YWCAs, for example, could offer classes or youth competitions in these activities. Children's fitness could also be enhanced by teaching children to be more aware of the nutrients in what they eat and of the importance of good nutrition, by teaching children to monitor their own health more effectively, and by continuing and expanding current efforts to keep children from smoking, drinking, or taking drugs.

4.   Compare concrete operational children's explanations of conservation with those of preoperational children.

Answer guideline. A concrete operational child understands that the substance and weight of an object do not change when the shape changes. The child might explain this fact in terms of reversibility (the original shape can be restored), identity (the object is the same object despite the changed appearance), or compensation (changes in one dimension are compensated for by changes in another dimension).

5.   Describe each of Piaget's stages of children's conception of morality.

Answer guideline. Piaget proposed two major stages in children's development of a conception of morality; these stages correspond roughly to the preoperational and concrete operational stages of cognitive development. In the first stage, children understand the morality of constraint (or heteronomous morality); at this point, children make rigid and simplistic judgments about right and wrong. Rules are seen as fixed, and all behavior is judged as right or wrong--there is no in-between. Children also believe that all wrong behavior (no matter what the reason for the behavior) should be punished. In the next stage, children understand a morality of cooperation (or autonomous morality); at this point, children's moral judgment is more flexible and situation-oriented. Children now understand that rules are created by humans and are a product of social agreement; therefore, they understand that rules can also be changed by mutual agreement. They understand that the intention behind behavior can determine whether the behavior is right or wrong, and they believe that punishment should be in accordance with the "rightness" or "wrongness" of the behavior.

6.   Describe each of Kohlberg's stages of moral reasoning, and explain how children move from one stage to the next.

Answer guideline. According to Kohlberg, children's level of moral reasoning is related to their level of cognitive development; as children's cognitive skills become more sophisticated, they also become capable of more advanced levels of moral reasoning. The first level is preconventional morality: at this level, children are guided by their desire to obtain rewards or avoid punishment. The second level is conventional role conformity: at this level, children obey rules in order to be a "good boy" or a "good girl." The third level (which may never be attained) is morality of autonomous moral principles: at this point, the individual realizes that there are many possible definitions of right and wrong and that definitions may conflict with one another. The definition of right and wrong then becomes a personal decision.

7.   Define *metamemory* and describe changes in metamemory during childhood.

Answer guideline.   Metamemory is knowledge of how memory works, including awareness of the demands of various kinds of memory tasks and awareness of one's own memory abilities. Children at ages 5 or 6 know that studying and external aids help people to remember and that forgetting increases with time. By age 8 or 9, children are aware of individual differences in memory and recognize that memory tasks vary in difficulty.

8.   Define *metacommunication* and describe advances in metacommunication in middle childhood.

Answer guideline. Metacommunication is knowledge of the process of communication. Young children's metacommunication is poor: they often give incomplete, ambiguous, or incomplete messages and are unaware of these problems in their communication. Also, they are often not aware of not understanding other people's communications, or they are ineffective in indicating their misunderstanding. Older children are better at communicating, partly because they are better able to monitor the quality of their own messages and better able to detect and express their own confusion over other people's messages.

9.   Summarize various explanations for racial differences in IQ test scores.

Answer guideline. One explanation is environmental: African Americans may not do as well as white Americans on IQ tests because of cultural differences or differences in educational opportunities. Another explanation is that IQ tests are culturally biased in content or that the testing situation itself is "stacked" against black children. A third explanation is that genetic differences between blacks and whites account for differences in their mean IQ test scores.

10. Define *self-fulfilling prophecy* and explain how it can apply to minority group children in particular.

Answer guideline. The concept of a self-fulfilling prophecy implies that students live up or down to their teachers' expectations regarding their achievements. This principle could be especially important for minority-group children because teachers are often more likely to develop low expectations for these students' performance. Expectations are likely to be unrealistically low because most teachers are white and middle-class, and many may be racist even if they are not aware of it.

11.   Identify ways in which parents can help children to do well in school, and ways in which teachers can encourage parents' involvement.

Answer guideline. Parents can help their children do well in school by becoming involved in their children's education. Ways of becoming involved include creating a "home curriculum" (e.g., reading, talking and playing with children), providing a place for children to study, providing materials for children to use in studying, seeing that children do their homework and meet deadlines, monitoring the time children spend on television and work, and talking with children about school and school-related problems. Teachers can encourage parents' involvement by urging parents to do all these things, by sending home more specific suggestions for helping children (e.g., schoolwork-related games and other activities), and by inviting parents to visit the school.

12.   Explain *mainstreaming*. What are positive and negative aspects of mainstreaming?

Answer guideline. Mainstreaming requires that handicapped children be educated in the "least restrictive" environment in which they can learn. Advocates of mainstreaming stress that handicapped children need to learn to relate to nonhandicapped peers and that the nonhandicapped need to become accustomed to people with handicaps. Another positive aspect is enhanced academic achievement for retarded children. Negative aspects of mainstreaming are that it will not necessarily diminish the stigma that may be associated with handicaps and the concerns of teachers who lack training in special education.

CHAPTER 9

PERSONALITY AND SOCIAL DEVELOPMENT IN MIDDLE CHILDHOOD

INTRODUCTION

Cognitive changes of middle childhood were described in Chapter 8. As **Chapter 9** explains, these are accompanied by personality and social changes. From the ages of 6 to 12, children's lives expand socially through greater interaction with peers, friends, neighbors, and families. Personal awareness of individual capabilities also expands as children enter school and other activities. Through these interactions, children can explore and develop their attitudes, values, and skills.

- Three major accomplishments during this stage are development of the self-concept, a centering of control from outside the child to within the child, and the development of self-esteem. Even though the family remains a vital influence, children during this stage become more independent of their parents.

- The peer group is an important arena for the building of self-concept and self-esteem. Both positive and negative effects of the peer group are discussed. Popularity also influences self-esteem. Children who are ignored and rejected by

their peers are at risk of emotional and behavioral problems. Guidelines for helping unpopular children are provided.

- Because family structures have changed considerably over the past few generations (there are more divorces, more single parents, more working mothers, more children in day care, etc.), some children fail to develop healthy self-esteem and may be more susceptible to stress, child abuse, depression, and emotional disorders.

- Children of middle years often develop emotional disturbances. These include acting-out behavior, anxiety disorders, and depression. A variety of ways to treat these emotional problems are discussed.

- Some psychologists are concerned about the "hurried" child of our society. Yet some "resilient" children are able to cope with stress. A variety of techniques are described to help children develop a healthy self-concept before entering the next stage of development, adolescence.

CHAPTER OUTLINE

I. THE SELF-CONCEPT

A. DEVELOPING A SELF-CONCEPT
1. Beginnings: Self-Recognition and Self-Definition
2. Coordination of Self-Regulation and Social-Regulation
B. SELF-ESTEEM
1. Industry and Self-Esteem
2. Sources of Self-Esteem

II. ASPECTS OF PERSONALITY DEVELOPMENT IN MIDDLE CHILDHOOD

A. EVERYDAY LIFE
1. How Do Children Spend Their Time?
2. With Whom Do Children Spend Their Time?
B. THE CHILD IN THE PEER GROUP
1. Functions and Influence of the Peer Group
   a. Positive effects
   b. Negative effects--conformity
2. Makeup of the Peer Group
3. Friendship
4. Popularity
   a. The popular child
   b. The unpopular child
   c. Family influences on popularity
   d. How Can unpopular children be helped?
C. THE CHILD IN THE FAMILY
1. Parent-Child Relationships
   a. Issues between parents and children
   b. Discipline
   c. Control and coregulation
2. Parents' Work: How It Affects Their Children
   a. Mothers' work
   (1) The mother's psychological state
   (2) Interactions in working-mother families
   (3) Working mothers and children's values
   (4) Children's reactions to mothers' work

   b. Fathers' work
3. Children of Divorce
   a. Children's adjustment to divorce
   (1) Tasks of adjustment
   b. Influences on children's adjustment to divorce
   (1) Parenting styles and parents' satisfaction
   (2) Remarriage of the mother
   (3) Remarriage of the father
   (4) Accessibility of both parents
   c. Long-term effects of divorce on children
   d. The One-Parent Family
   (1) Current trends
   (2) Effects on children
   (3) Effects on schooling
   (4) Long-term effects
   (5) Stepfamilies
   e. Sibling relationships

III. CHILDHOOD EMOTIONAL DISTURBANCES

A. TYPES OF EMOTIONAL PROBLEMS
1. Acting-Out Behavior
   a. Anxiety disorders
   (1) Separation anxiety disorder
   b. School phobia
2. Childhood Depression
B. TREATMENT FOR EMOTIONAL PROBLEMS
1. Therapies
2. Effectiveness of Therapy

IV. STRESS AND RESILIENCE

A. SOURCES OF STRESS: LIFE EVENTS, FEARS, AND THE "HURRIED" CHILD
B. COPING WITH STRESS: THE RESILIENT CHILD

KEY TERMS

acting-out behavior (page 331)
affective disorder (332)
behavior therapy (333)
childhood depression (332)
coregulation (320)
discipline (319)
drug therapy (333)
family therapy (333)
global self-worth (310)
ideal self (309)
individual psychotherapy (333)
industry versus inferiority (310)
prejudice (315)
psychological maltreatment (334)
real self (309)
school phobia (331)
self-care children (323)
self-concept (308)
self-definition (308)
self-esteem (309)
separation anxiety disorder (331)

LEARNING OBJECTIVES

After finishing Chapter 9, students should be able to:

1. Explain what is meant by a person's sense of self, or *self-concept*, which begins to develop during middle childhood. (pp. 308-309)

2. List some of the tasks children must fulfill toward the development of self-concept, as they strive to become functioning members of society. (p. 309)

3. Describe the development and importance of healthy *self-esteem*. (pp. 309-310)

4. Describe Erikson's middle childhood crisis of *industry vs. inferiority* and its successful resolution. (p. 310)

5. Explain the term *global self-worth*, and list some of the sources of *self-esteem*. (pp. 310-311)

6. Briefly discuss how, and with whom, middle-aged children spend their time. (pp. 311-313)

7. Explain some positive and negative effects of the peer group. (pp. 313-314)

8. Define *prejudice* and its effect on the peer group. (p. 315)

9. Differentiate between how a young child views a friend and how a child in the middle years views a friend. (pp. 315-316)

10. Explain some personality characteristics of popular children and unpopular children. (pp. 316-317)

11. List some ways in which adults can help unpopular children. (pp. 317-318)

12. Briefly describe the kinds of issues that arise between children in middle childhood and their parents concerning the following: discipline, control and coregulation (pp. 319-320)

13. Explain some research findings concerning mothers' work and its effects on the following: the mother's psychological state, the father's involvement with the children, the children's development (pp. 321-322)

14. Discuss the topic of *self-care* children, and explain how parents can tell when a child is ready for *self-care*. (p. 323)

15. Briefly describe the research on how men's work (or unemployment) affects their families. (p. 322)

16. Describe some common reactions of children to parent's divorce. (pp. 322, 324)

17. List 5 suggestions for helping children adjust to divorce. (pp. 330)

18. Identify how each of the following factors influence a child's adjustment to divorce (based on research findings): parenting styles, the mother's remarriage, relationship with the father, accessibility of both parents (pp. 324-325)

19. List some of the long-term effects of divorce on children. (pp. 325-326)

20. Briefly explain the current trend of one-parent families in the U.S., and list some of the common stressors for children

from these families. (pp. 326-327)

21. Describe some research findings concerning stepfamilies. (p. 328)

22. Explain some research findings concerning sibling relationships. (pp. 328-329)

23. Describe the following nonphysical disturbances and list some possible treatments: acting-out behavior, separation anxiety disorder, school phobia, childhood depression (pp. 331-332)

24. Name and explain the treatment techniques for these emotional disturbances: psychological therapies (3 forms), drug therapy (p. 333)

25. Explain the term psychological maltreatment and its relationship to child abuse. (p. 334)

26. Explain what David Elkind and other psychologists mean by the term "hurried" child. (p. 334)

27. List some ways that help a child cope with and become more resilient to stress. (pp. 334, 336)

CHAPTER SUMMARY AND TEACHING RECOMMENDATIONS

The chapter begins with a section on the self-concept. The authors distinguish aspects of the self-concept (self-awareness, self-definition, and self-regulation) and note both cognitive and social influences of the developing self-concept. The authors also discuss the importance of children's self-esteem and factors which influence self-esteem; in this context, they explain Erikson's fourth crisis, industry versus inferiority, which occurs during middle childhood. An important point (which deserves reinforcement during a class session) is that there may be reciprocal influences between parenting style and children's self-esteem.

The next section discusses various aspects of personality development in middle childhood. The authors describe children's everyday lives in terms of time spent on

various activities and the increasing importance of the peer group. In discussing the peer group, the authors note both positive effects on children's social and cognitive development and the potentially negative consequences of conformity to undesirable peer-group norms. The authors also discuss friendship and popularity among schoolchildren; they note factors associated with both popularity and unpopularity and describe efforts to teach unpopular children social skills.

The chapter goes on to describe relationships between parents and children at this age; among the prominent issues covered are the approaches to discipline and the regulation of children's behavior.

The authors next describe several "emergent" family experiences and their effects on children's development. These topics include mothers' and fathers' employment, children's reaction to divorce, children in one-parent families, and children in stepfamilies. As the authors point out, each of these circumstances can be associated with negative consequences for children. Students who represent any (or all) of these family situations may find this part of the chapter upsetting, and you might point out that later in the chapter the authors also emphasize children's resilience.

The authors close this section by discussing both direct and indirect ways in which siblings influence one another. They do not, however, discuss the only child; given the varied effects ascribed to sibling influences, you may wish to address this topic.

The chapter continues with a summary of emotional disorders appearing during middle childhood, including acting-out behavior, separation anxiety disorder, school phobia, and childhood depression. In addition, the authors present a variety of approaches for treating these disorders.

The final section of the chapter describes sources of stress in middle childhood and factors related to children's ability to withstand the negative consequences of stress.

Boxes in Chapter 9 are "Family Ecologies of Children from Ethnic Minority Groups," "After-School Care: What Kind Is Best?," "Helping Children Adjust to Divorce," and "Children Who Live in Chronic Danger."

AUDIOVISUAL MATERIALS

Distributor, date, and running time are given for each film or video. Distributors' addresses are listed in the appendix (General Resources). If a film or video is not in color, there is a notation (BW) to that effect.

Family influences. (IM, 1992, 30 min.) This program illustrates how family background influences the way people view themselves and others. It defines four types of parents--authoritative, permissive, authoritarian, and uninvolved--and compares the characteristics of children raised by each. How parents can promote a sense of responsibility in children is discussed, and the role of siblings in a child's development is explored. The program examines the role of older siblings and presents opposing views on the influence of birth order on personality. It also considers nontraditional families and discusses recent findings on the effects of divorce on children.

Self-esteem in school age children. (IM, 1990, 25 min.) Self-esteem affects mental health, motivation, and behavior. This video explores the components of the self: self-concept, self-control, and self-esteem. It outlines five criteria for self-perception and relates the way an individual ranks these five criteria to the individual's feelings of self-worth. It concludes with an exploration of how adults can enhance self-esteem in children.

Helping your child succeed. (IM, 1990, 50 min.) This presents six steps for anticipating and preventing problems and demonstrates how to use these steps to help children succeed. It shows how to instill self-esteem in a child, give effective praise, teach problem-solving techniques, and prepare a child to resist peer pressure.

Teaching responsible behavior. (IM, 1992, 54 min.) This video shows parents how to correct children's misbehavior and get them to accept responsibility. It teaches how to reinforce positive changes in behavior and how to help children set and achieve realistic goals.

Single parenting. (IM, 1988, 20 min.) This program teaches single parents how to respond effectively to the difficulties of raising children alone. It details a four-step plan for raising children after a divorce. Vignettes illustrate ways to minimize the adverse effects on a child of the loss of a parent. The video also suggests ways to handle discipline, financial problems, and family crises.

Peers in development. (IM, 1991, 60 min.) Probing the importance of peer relationships in social and emotional development, this program examines the growth of peer relationships from the social interest of infants through the groupings of adolescence. It considers the importance of play in cognitive development, as explained by Piaget and Vygotsky, and describes Parten's six categories of social participation. Commentary from children of different ages provides insights into how the idea of friendship changes with age.

Me and my friends. (IM, 1992, 30 min.) Noted psychologists consider how children during the middle years prove their competence and how they develop durable, vital friendships. The program discusses children's perceptions of competence and identifies two patterns of how children deal with failure: the helpless pattern and the mastery pattern. What makes a child popular in his or her peer group and why certain children are rejected is examined.

Guest speakers

For this chapter, your best resources for guest speakers are likely to be psychologists or social workers who provide services to children and their families; your local community mental health center, a city or county department of child and family services, or a local hospital would probably be able to put you in touch with a suitable speaker. You could ask such a professional to address any one of several topics covered in the chapter, including emotional disturbances of childhood, the impact of divorce on children, or children's reactions to stress.

LECTURE OUTLINES

Lecture 1: Children's Reaction to Divorce

I. Age as a factor in children's reactions

Even young children are aware of--and react to--parents' emotions. All children share in the emotional turmoil of a divorce, but their specific reaction depends on their age.

A. Infancy.
  1. Reactions often seen in infants include the following.
     a. General symptoms of upset: fussiness; changes in patterns of sleeping, eating, and elimination.
     b. Occasional temporary delays in early motor development (e.g., crawling or walking later than is typical).
  2. However, infants are typically resilient: normal behavior and development resume when the immediate crisis has passed and new routines are established.
B. Early childhood.
  1. Reactions observed in preschoolers include these.
     a. Anger at "desertion" by the noncustodial parent.
     b. Guilt--a belief that the parent "left" because of the child's misbehavior.
     c. Regression to infantile behaviors (e.g., relapses in toilet training; clinging to or overdependency on the remaining parent.)
     d. Nightmares.
     e. Tantrums.
  2. There are ways to minimize these negative reactions.
     a. Establish new routines.
     b. Provide opportunities to visit the noncustodial parent (if this is feasible).
     c. Demonstrate to the child that both parents still love him or her, that the child's relationship with the noncustodial parent will continue, and that both parents will cooperate in the child's care (if this is the case).

C. Middle childhood.
  1. Reactions of school-age children often reflect problems in adapting, which can be signaled in various ways.
     a. Problems at school (academic, behavioral).
     b. Excessive (for age) dependency on the custodial parent.
     c. Taking sides with a parent or attempting to manipulate the parents.
  2. Following are ways to minimize these negative reactions.
     a. Establish new routines.
     b. Provide an explanation of divorce appropriate for the child's level of cognitive maturity. Concrete operational children are better able to understand divorce than preoperational (egocentric) children.
     c. Give the child clear messages that both parents still love him or her, both will cooperate in the child's care, and the child's relationship with both will continue (if these things are true).

II. Other factors

Factors other than the child's age also influence children's reaction to divorce.

A. Child's gender.
B. Custody arrangements (mother, father, joint).
C. Circumstances preceding the divorce.
D. Changes in household income after the divorce.
E. Support network available to the custodial parent after the divorce.
F. Probably, other factors yet to be identified.

References for Lecture 1

Black, A. & Pedro-Carroll, J. (1993). Role of parent-child relationships in mediating the effects of marital disruption. *Journal of the American academy of child and adolescent psychiatry, 32,* 1019-1027.
Farmer, S. & Galaris, D. (1993). Support groups for children of divorce. *The American journal of family therapy, 21,* 40-50.

Mazur, E., Wolchik, S., & Sandler, I. (1992). Negative cognitive errors and positive illusions for negative divorce elements: Predictions of children's psychological adjustment. *Journal of abnormal child psychology, 20,* 523-542.

Shaw, D., Emery, R., & Tuer, M. (1993). Paternal functioning and children's adjustment in families of divorce: A prospective study. *Journal of abnormal child psychology, 21,* 119-134.

Wallerstein, J. S. & Kelley, J. B. (1980). *Surviving the breakup: How children and parents cope with divorce.* New York: Basic Books.

Warshak, R. A. & Santrock, J. A. (1983). Children of divorce: Impact of custody disposition on social development. In E. J. Callahan & K. A. McCluskey (Eds.), *Life-span developmental psychology: Nonnormative life crises.* New York: Academic, 241-262.

Lecture 2: Children in Single-Parent Families

I. The single-parent family: Statistics

As of the mid-1990s, nearly half of all children could be expected to spend some time in a single-parent home before age 18. This is a dramatic increase: as of 1980, 20 percent of children would spend some time in a single-parent home before age 18; as of 1970, this figure was only 12 percent. Most single-parent homes are single-mother homes.

II. Single mothers

Certain problems confront all (or nearly all) single mothers; other problems are faced only (or mostly) by specific categories of single mothers.

A. Common problems.
   1. Financial difficulties. Their own income (if any) may be low, and child support payments are often delinquent.
   2. Role conflict and role overload. Single mothers must be both mother and father to their children; they also have roles as employees, daughters, girlfriends, etc.
   3. Role shift. If the mother remarries, she must relinquish her role as "father"; this role will be assumed by her children's new stepfather.

   4. Social stigma. Though this is a common problem, it does vary, depending on the reason for single motherhood.
      a. Widows experience the least stigma.
      b. Greater stigma is experienced by never-married mothers and divorced mothers.
   5. Loneliness. Single mothers often lack adult companionship.
   6. Inadequate institutional support. This problem has been less severe since the 1980s than it was in the 1970s and earlier. We now see more support groups (e.g., Parents without Partners) and a better response from school systems (e.g., before- and after-school programs). However, such supports are still inadequate.

B. Special situations. Some problems vary according to different circumstances of single motherhood.
   1. Deserted mothers. This status is usually involuntary and unexpected.
      a. There is no court supervision or regulation (at least initially); thus, no support is established or enforced, and visitation is unregulated.
      b. Deserted mothers are not free to remarry.
   2. Separated mothers.
      a. Agreements are often, but not invariably, made about support and visitation.
      b. These mothers are also not free to remarry.
   3. Divorced mothers. These women have some advantages in comparison with deserted and separated mothers.
      a. Courts are involved in support and visitation arrangements.
      b. They are free to remarry.
   4. Widowed mothers. In some ways, widows may be in the most advantageous position.
      a. They usually have the most sympathy and support from friends and relatives of any "type" of single mother.
      b. They are usually older than other single mothers and thus may be more financially secure; their children also tend to be older and therefore more independent.
      c. They are free to remarry.

5. Never-married mothers.
   a. Never-married mothers typically have the lowest incomes of any "type" of single mother.
   b. They face considerable social stigma (although it is much less severe than it was in the past).
   c. They are typically younger than other single mothers, and thus, they may not have completed high school.

III. Single fathers

According to the census of 1980, 13 percent of single-parent families are single-father families.

A. Single fathers have advantages over single mothers.
   1. They rarely need to relocate in order to find work (typically, they are already working when they gain custody).
   2. They generally have higher incomes.
B. However, there are similarities between single fathers and single mothers.
   1. They have similar views of the divorce process and the stresses it entails.
   2. They have similar views of the stresses of being a single parent (although fathers generally experience less financial stress).
   3. They have similar values and child-rearing practices.
   4. They have a similar interest in remarriage.

IV. Joint custody

One recent study compared children whose mothers had sole custody, children whose fathers had sole custody, and children whose parents shared custody. Parents of these children responded to questionnaires about their own and their children's adjustment.

A. Impact on children.
   1. No group differences were found in children's adjustment.
   2. Children's adjustment was found to be positively related to the parents' adjustment.
B. Impact on parents.
   1. Parents with joint custody were less

likely than those with sole custody to feel burdened or overwhelmed.
   2. Parents in joint custody arrangements had more positive feelings toward the ex-spouse and believed that their children maintained stronger relationships with the ex-spouse.
   3. Parents in joint custody arrangements were more satisfied with their social lives and had more free time.

References for Lecture 2

Jackson, A. (1993). Black, single, working mothers in poverty: Preferences for employment, well-being, and perceptions of pre-school-age children. *Social work, 38,* 26-34.
Kennedy, M. (1994). *The single-parent family: Living happily in a changing world.* New York: Crown.
LeMasters, E. E. & DeFrain, J. (1983). *Parents in contemporary America: A sympathetic view.* Homewood, IL: Dorsey.
Olson, M. (1993). Successful single parents. *Families in society, 74*(5), 259-267.

TOPIC FOR DEBATE

Are the Costs of Mothers' Employment Worth the Benefits?

Background

Since the 1980s, more mothers have been employed outside the home than ever before. Employment undoubtedly has a number of substantial benefits for these women themselves and for their families. However, most mothers employed outside the home also find that working entails a number of costs-- tangible and less tangible. Some people doubt that the benefits of mothers' employment outweigh these costs.

In Chapter 9 of the textbook, the authors note some of the costs to children of employed mothers. Sons, in particular, may experience academic problems, and babies whose mothers are employed outside the home may become insecurely attached. Furthermore, an employed mother nearly always incurs some expense for after-school supervision of her children. If adequate supervision cannot be arranged, the parents (as well as society) may experience long-term costs in the form of children's behavioral problems or adolescents' involvement in delinquency or substance abuse.

Even assuming that these costs to children can be avoided--and many employed mothers do an admirable job of avoiding them--the mother herself faces costs. School policies and practices tend to be unresponsive to these mothers' needs and schedules: for instance, parent-teacher conferences and special programs are nearly always set for weekday hours. Many employed mothers report "innuendos" and subtle criticisms from homemakers who imply that they lack love and concern for their families; other employed mothers say that they feel pushed away from their communities and excluded from formal and informal support networks available to full-time homemakers.

It would be foolish to deny, however, that employed mothers provide a number of benefits to themselves and their families. Obviously, family income will benefit from the mother's employment. Many employed mothers also feel that their self-esteem is higher than it would be if they did not work outside the home. And, despite evidence that children of employed mothers may suffer slightly, there is also ample evidence that children of employed mothers may benefit in several ways. These children tend to be more independent and to have more egalitarian views of gender roles than children of nonemployed mothers, and daughters tend to have more ambitious career goals than do children of nonemployed mothers.

Furthermore, employed mothers may escape certain costs borne by many full-time homemakers. Full-time homemakers some-times complain about being burdened with demands for planning school trips and community projects, and they experience their share of insensitivity from school systems, which do attempt to meet the needs of dual-career families. Perhaps most important, many full-time homemakers find themselves intellectually isolated and virtually starved for adult companionship. Many report feeling devalued or humiliated by professional, career-oriented friends.

Debate plan

Using this background, and information from additional sources (selected references appear below), student panels should debate the following positions:

Position A. The costs of mothers' full-time employment overshadow any benefits that may be obtained.

Position B. Mothers' full-time employment provides benefits that more than compensate for any costs that are entailed.

References for the debate

Berg, B. (1985, December). Women at odds. *Savvy*, 24-29.
Greenstein, T. (1993). Maternal employment and child behavioral outcomes: A household economic analysis. *Journal of family issues, 14*, 323-354.
Hong, G. (1993). Do working mothers have healthy children? *Journal of family and economic issues, 14*(2), 163-186.
Shuster, C. (1993). Employed first-time mothers: A typology of maternal responses to integrating parenting and employment. *Family relations, 42*, 13-20.

TOPICS FOR DISCUSSION

Topic 1: Development of Self-Esteem

1. Ask students to identify ways in which children's self-esteem depends on their self-concept (textbook pages 308-311).

2. Ask students to list some characteristics of children with high self-esteem as well as children with low self-esteem (pages 309-310).

3. The authors discuss how a child's sense of global self-worth is related to self-esteem. Ask students to summarize Harter's findings on sources of low and high self-esteem during middle childhood (pages 310-311).

Topic 2: The Peer Group

1. Ask students to summarize the positive and negative influences that peers can have in middle childhood (pages 313-314). Ask them to suggest steps that parents can take to maximize the positive influence of peers and minimize the negative influence.

2. Ask students whether a parent can or should take steps to help children increase their popularity (pages 317-318).

Topic 3: Children and Divorce

1. On pages 324-325 (and in the Box on page 330), the authors outline steps that can help children adjust to their parents' divorce. Ask students which of these steps seems most important and why.

2. Ask students to explain some of the factors that could either facilitate or impede a child's adjustment to divorce (pages 324-326).

Topic 4: Stress in Childhood

1. Ask students to list as many sources of stress in children's lives as they can think of (page 334). Ask them to rank the resulting list, roughly, from "most severe" to "least severe." Ask them to identify sources over which parents or teachers could reasonably be expected to exert some control. Ask them to identify sources of stress over which children themselves could reasonably be expected to exert some control.

2. On pages 334-335, the authors list factors which seem to be related to children's ability to "bounce back" from stress. Ask students which they think would be of greatest importance, and why. Ask them which of these factors would seem to be potentially most controllable (by parents, by other significant adults in a child's life, or by children themselves), and why.

PROJECTS AND CLASS EXERCISES

Group Exercise: Designing a Children's Support Group

Working in groups, students should plan a "self-help" group for children whose parents have divorced within the last year. The students should describe and justify the general format of the self-help group, including such factors as (1) whether the group would be "segregated" by children's age, gender, custody arrangements, or other factors, and why; (2) where the group would meet (e.g., at a school, at a community center, at a religious center, or somewhere else); (3) how often the group would meet.
The students should also select a set of five topics for discussion at meetings of the self-help group and justify each topic.

Project 1: The Self-Concept

Students should ask 5 to 10 children between the ages of 8 and 12 about the five domains in life used by Harter to measure self-esteem: how well they do in school, how good they are in sports, how accepted they feel by other children, how they behave, and what they look like (page 311). Based upon these responses, the students should prepare papers stating their findings; comparing them with Harter's findings; and defending their own choice of the factor they believe has the most impact on a child's self-esteem.

Project 2: Children's Everyday Lives

Students should interview two or more school-children of different ages (preferably, both boys and girls). The interview should focus on how each child spends a "typical" school day and a "typical" weekend day. Students should write a paper commenting on age and gender differences; similarities in the children's use of time; and how their findings correspond with the information presented in the text.

Project 3: Emotional Disturbances and Treatments

Students should select one of the emotional disturbances described in the text and write a research paper summarizing and documenting current research on its cause or causes and prognosis, as well as the various approaches to treating it.

ESSAY QUESTIONS

1. Distinguish self-concept, self-recognition, and self-definition.

Answer guideline. Self-concept: sense of self; knowledge of who we were, are, and may become. The self-concept includes ideas of the real self and the ideal self.   Self-recognition: toddlers' ability to identify themselves in the mirror--an early step toward formation of the self-concept. Self-definition: identification of the inner and outer character-istics important in describing ourselves to others. Preschoolers tend to define themselves in terms of concrete physical characteristics (e.g., appearance, neighborhood), whereas most older children include psychological terms in their self-definition.

2. Identify consequences of low self-esteem in childhood, and describe the factors which contribute to a child's sense of self-worth.

Answer guideline. Consequences of low self-esteem for children include decreased motivation, increased anxiety, undesirable levels of conformity to the wishes of others, and difficulty in getting along with other children. According to Susan Harter, the most vital contributor to a child's self-worth is the degree to which a child feels valued by the most important people in his or her life. These figures include parents, classmates, friends, and teachers. Unfortunately, children's self-worth is especially shaped by their physical appearance and others' approval of their "looks." Social acceptance also contributes highly toward a child's overall self-worth.

3. Discuss positive and negative effects of peer groups.

Answer guideline. Positive influences of the peer group include giving children a standard for comparing themselves (in terms of abilities and skills) with others, exposing children to new values and attitudes (in addition to those that they have been exposed to at home), providing children with a type of support that adults cannot give, and helping children learn interpersonal skills. The primary negative influence that the peer group may have is promoting conformity. At worst, children may be pressured by their peers into behaviors such as shoplifting or experimenting with cigarettes, alcohol, drugs, or sex.

4. Describe the popular child and factors associated with unpopularity.

Answer guideline. Typically, popular children are healthy, physically attractive, poised, assertive, and able to adapt and conform when appropriate. These children also tend to be responsible, sensitive to others, and able to express affection. They have moderate levels of self-esteem, are able to seek help when they need it from children or adults, and are generally enjoyable to be with. Unpopular children are often belligerent, aggressive, or hostile; they may act in immature ways or show excessive uncertainty about how they should speak or behave. Unpopular children may also be obese, extremely unattractive, or retarded, or may display bizarre behavior.

5. Contrast the disciplinary methods of parents of a toddler with those of parents of a child of elementary-school age.

Answer guideline. Parents of a toddler would probably discipline their child by using distraction or physical separation to keep the child away from forbidden but tempting objects. Parents of an older child would attempt to control his or her behavior by restricting privileges, by reasoning with the child, by praising the child for good behavior, and by appealing to the child's self-esteem or conscience.

6. Discuss the importance of sibling relationships during middle childhood.

Answer guideline. Sibling relationships can be important as a resource in developing the self-concept, since siblings provide opportunities for comparing oneself with others. Sibling relationships also provide opportunities for learning to resolve conflicts and for learning how to handle dependency in peer relationships.

7. What types of treatments for emotional disorders of childhood are available, and how well do they seem to work?

Answer guideline. Treatment techniques for emotional disorders of childhood include individual psychotherapy, family therapy, behavior therapy (or behavior modification), and drug therapy. The effectiveness of any therapy varies according to what problem is being treated and who is administering treatment. However, research shows that most therapies are generally effective for children.

8. Identify factors that contribute to children's resilience to stress.

Answer guideline. Factors contributing to children's resilience to stress include characteristics of the child's family, such as the extent of parental support or the presence of at least one caring older relative. Experience in solving social problems--often, finding positive models by observing how parents or siblings deal with challenges or frustrations--is important. Finally, the fewer stressors to which a child has been exposed, and the more compensating factors are present, the more resilient the child is likely to be.

CHAPTER 10

PHYSICAL AND INTELLECTUAL DEVELOPMENT IN ADOLESCENCE

INTRODUCTION

Chapter 10 examines the dramatic physical and intellectual development that occurs in adolescence. Physically, adolescence is a time of moving from pubescence to puberty, toward sexual and physical maturation; while intellectually this period is marked by the attainment of the ability to think abstractly.

- The chapter begins by examining the physiological changes of adolescence and the psychological impact of those changes.

- Health and nutrition are discussed, with special attention being paid to various nutrition and eating disorders.

- Current trends and various problems associated with drug use and abuse are discussed, as are sexually transmitted diseases, as they impact adolescents.

- Intellectual development is examined from the perspective of Piaget's theory, and adolescent egocentrism is discussed

in detail.

- The development of moral reasoning is explored using Kohlberg's theory.

- The transition to secondary school is examined, including a discussion of some of the factors that influence that transition.

- The nature of the high school today is discussed, including an examination of home influences on high school achievement.

- The phenomenon of school drop outs is examined, culminating with a discussion of preventing dropping out.

- Finally, career planning in late adolescence is considered, with a description of the stages of vocational planning and a discussion of the influence of parents and gender on vocational planning.

CHAPTER OUTLINE

I. **ADOLESCENCE: A DEVELOPMENTAL TRANSITION**

PHYSICAL DEVELOPMENT

II. **MATURATION IN ADOLESCENCE**

    A.   **PHYSICAL CHANGES**
        1.   Puberty and the Secular Trend
        2.   The Adolescent Growth Spurt
        3.   Primary Sex Characteristics
        4.   Secondary Sex Characteristics
        5.   Menarche
    B.   **PSYCHOLOGICAL ISSUES RELATED TO PHYSICAL CHANGES**
        1.   Effects of Early and Late Maturation
          a.   Early and late maturation in boys
          b.   Early and late maturation in girls
        2.   The Relationship between Stress and the Timing of Puberty
        3.   Reactions to Menarche and Menstruation
        4.   Feelings about Physical Appearance

III.   **HEALTH CONCERNS OF ADOLESCENCE**

    A.   **NUTRITION AND EATING DISORDERS**
        1.   Nutritional Needs
        2.   Obesity
        3.   Anorexia Nervosa and Bulimia Nervosa
          a.   Anorexia
          b.   Bulimia
          c.   Treatment for anorexia and bulimia
    B.   **USE AND ABUSE OF DRUGS**
        1.   Current Trends
        2.   Alcohol
        3.   Marijuana
        4.   Tobacco
    C.   **SEXUALLY TRANSMITTED DISEASES (STDs)**
        1.   What Are STDs?
        2.   STDs and Adolescents

INTELLECTUAL DEVELOPMENT

IV.   **ASPECTS OF INTELLECTUAL DEVELOPMENT IN ADOLESCENCE**

    A.   **COGNITIVE DEVELOPMENT: PIAGET'S STAGE OF FORMAL OPERATIONS**
        1.   Cognitive Maturity: The Nature of Formal Operations
        2.   Tracing Cognitive Development: The Pendulum Problem
        3.   What Brings About Cognitive Maturity?
        4.   Assessing Piaget's Theory
    B.   **ADOLESCENT EGOCENTRISM**
        1.   Finding Fault with Authority Figures
        2.   Argumentativeness
        3.   Self-Consciousness
        4.   Self-Centeredness
        5.   Indecisiveness
        6.   Apparent Hypocrisy
    C.   **MORAL REASONING: KOHLBERG'S LEVELS OF MORALITY**
        1.   How Adolescents at Different Levels React to Kohlberg's Dilemmas
          a.   Preconventional Level. Stage 1
          b.   Stage 2
          c.   Conventional Level. Stage 3
          d.   Stage 4
          e.   Postconventional Level. Stage 5
          f.   Stage 6

V.   **SECONDARY SCHOOL**

    A.   **THE TRANSITION TO JUNIOR HIGH OR HIGH SCHOOL**
        1.   Patterns of Transition
        2.   Effects of the Transition
          a.   Gender-related Causes
          b.   School-related Causes
          c.   Home-related Causes
    B.   **HIGH SCHOOL TODAY**
    C.   **HOME INFLUENCES ON ACHIEVEMENT IN HIGH SCHOOL**
        1.   Parent's Interest
        2.   Parenting Styles
        3.   Socioeconomic Status

D.   DROPPING OUT OF HIGH
     SCHOOL
     1.   Who Drops Out?
     2.   Why Do They Drop Out?
     3.   What Happens to Drop
          Outs?
     4.   How Can Dropping Out Be
          Prevented?

VI. **DEVELOPING A CAREER**

     A.   STAGES IN VOCATIONAL
          TRAINING
     B.   INFLUENCES ON
          VOCATIONAL PLANNING
          1.   Parents
          2.   Gender

KEY TERMS

adolescence (page 342)
adolescent growth spurt (346)
anorexia nervosa (353)
bulimia nervosa (354)
ecological approach (367)
formal operations (360)
imaginary audience (363)
menarche (347)
obesity (352)
personal fable (363)
primary sex characteristics (347)
puberty (342)
secondary sex characteristics (347)
secular trend (346)
sexually transmitted diseases (STDs) (357)

LEARNING OBJECTIVES

After finishing Chapter 10, students should be
able to:

1.   Describe the process and characteristics
     of physical maturation in *adolescence*.
     (pp. 344-348)

2.   List the *primary sex characteristics* and
     secondary sex characteristics of both
     boys and girls. (pp. 347)

3.   Understand *menarche* and menstruation
     and their psychological effect. (pp. 347-
     348, pp. 349-350)

4.   Discuss the psychological impact of
     physical changes and the effects of early

and late maturation. (pp. 348-349)

5.   Describe adolescents' concerns about
     physical appearance. (p. 350)

6.   List the major health concerns during
     adolescence. (p. 351)

7.   Explain the difference between various
     nutrition problems and eating disorders
     and describe their effect on teenagers:
     obesity, *anorexia nervosa*, *bulimia
     nervosa* (p. 352-354)

8.   List the drugs most commonly used by
     adolescents and discuss the problems of
     abuse for this age group. (pp. 354-357)

9.   List the most common *sexually
     transmitted diseases* (STDs) and their
     effects, and describe how they are
     transmitted. (pp. 357-360)

10. From the list in item 9, identify which
     STDs are curable, which are not, and
     which are life-threatening. (pp. 357-
     360)

11. Discuss Piaget's stage of *formal
     operations* in cognitive development.
     (p. 360)

12. Describe how the solutions to the
     "pendulum problem" at different ages
     illustrate the changes in thinking
     associated with maturation. (pp. 360-
     361)

13. Describe egocentrism in the adolescent
     and give examples. (pp. 362-364)

14. List Kohlberg's levels of morality and
     provide a brief explanation of moral
     reasoning at each level. (pp. 364-365)

15. Describe the transition from elementary
     to secondary school and discuss some of
     the problems associated with that
     transition. (pp. 367-368)

16. Discuss the effects of high school on
     adolescents' development, and describe
     the influence of home and of
     socioeconomic status on achievement.
     (pp. 368-371)

17. Explain how different parenting styles
     may influence the school achievement of
     adolescents. (pp. 369-370)

18. Discuss the phenomenon of high school dropouts. (pp. 371-372)

19. Discuss career development, and the stages and influence of vocational planning. (pp. 372-375)

CHAPTER SUMMARY AND TEACHING RECOMMENDATIONS

The authors describe the physical changes of puberty and the sequence in which these changes occur. A "Window on the World" box describes an Apache rite of passage formally marking a young girl's coming of age, and the authors note that contemporary American culture lacks such universal rites of passage. In class, you might want to reiterate this point and note that the lack of clear demarcation of the beginning and end of adolescence may make identity development (to be discussed in Chapter 11) particularly challenging. The secular trend in sexual maturation and the adolescent growth spurt are described; you might want to ask students to consider the impact of this trend on adolescents' sexuality. The authors also describe changes in primary sex characteristics and secondary sex characteristics.

Next, the authors describe psychological reactions to these physical changes, including the positive and negative effects of early and late maturation for boys and girls. This is another context in which you might want to point out the associations between physical development and identity development (see Lecture Outlines, below), as well as the importance of teaching positive attitudes toward all signs and phases of sexual maturity in boys and girls.

In the next section, the authors note that adolescents are generally healthy. But they describe health problems such as obesity and eating disorders, substance abuse, and sexually transmitted diseases.

In the section on aspects of intellectual development, the authors describe Piaget's stage of formal operations. They note that, with formal operations, adolescents acquire the ability to engage in hypothetical-deductive reasoning, think in terms of hypotheses contrary to fact, consider problems flexibly, and test hypotheses. The authors point out that experience seems to be a critical factor in

the attainment of formal operations, and they note that some individuals apparently never attain formal operations. You might want to add that cross-cultural research suggests that some nonwestern cultures do not seem to foster formal operational thinking, and Piaget himself suggested that formal operations may be used only for problems with which individuals are particularly familiar and in which they are particularly interested.

Adolescent egocentrism is described and distinguished from the egocentrism characteristic of young children. Implications of finding fault with authority figures, argumentativeness, self-consciousness, self-centeredness, indecisiveness, and apparent hypocrisy are considered. The authors describe Kohlberg's levels of moral reasoning and note that most adolescents are at the middle level, although there is great variation in adolescents' (and adults') levels of moral reasoning.

The next section begins by clarifying factors which impede the adolescent's transition from elementary to junior high school. Subsequently, the authors describe current efforts to improve the quality of high schools and point out characteristics of an effective high school. Also detailed are the ways in which parents and the family's socioeconomic status can affect high school students' scholastic achievement. Students who drop out of high school, their reasons for dropping out, and vital preventive measures are also discussed.

The chapter closes with a brief section on vocational planning. The authors point out that part-time employment in adolescence is rarely beneficial for vocational planning. Parents and gender are identified as important influences on the career-planning process. You might note that most adolescents could benefit substantially from professional guidance in choosing a career.

Boxes in this chapter are "An Apache Girl Comes of Age," "Female Genital Mutilation," "Protecting Against Sexually Transmitted Diseases," "Gender Differences in Moral Development," and "Should Teenagers Hold Part-Time Jobs?"

AUDIOVISUAL MATERIALS

Distributor, date, and running time are given for each film or video. Distributors' addresses are listed in the appendix (General Resources). If a film or video is not in color, there is a notation (BW) to that effect.

Piaget's developmental theory: Formal thought. (DAV, early 1970s, approximately 30 minutes.) Presents tasks used to assess formal operational thinking, and the responses of concrete operational and formal operational thinkers to these tasks.

Adolescent development. (IM, 1990, video, 30 min.) This program describes the physical, social, and psychological changes that force individuals to make the transition from childhood to adulthood.

Teenage drinking: Hey, how about another one? (CRM, 1975, approximately 15 min.) Topics include motivations for drinking in adolescence and consequences of teenage drinking.

Moral development. (IM, 1978, video, 30 min.) This video presents four theories of moral development: the cognitive-development model based on the works of Lawrence Kohlberg and Jean Piaget, the social-learning approach, the Freudian or psychoanalytic approach, and Robert Hogan's framework for assessing moral thought and behavior.

Teenage suicide. (FFHS, 1994, video, 19 min.) This documentary explores some of the reasons teens commit suicide and the recent increase in suicide and describes some of the behavior patterns of which family and friends should be aware.

Eating disorders. (FFHS, 1994, video, 19 min.) This program covers the personality profiles of the likeliest anorexic people and shows how anorexia develops and can be cured.

Teenage mind and body. (IM, 1992, video, 30 min.) Focusing on cognitive and physical development in adolescence, this program probes the differences between teenagers' abilities and interests and parents' expectations.

Rich kids on drugs. (FFHS, 1994, video, 28 min.) In this specially adapted Phil Donahue program, a teenager tells his story about how he got hooked on drugs.

Shortchanging girls, shortchanging America. (IM, 1992, video, 19 min.) This program interviews educators and business leaders to illuminate the devastating effects of gender bias in schools. It calls upon educators to encourage girls to develop math and science skills.

Guest speakers

Many of the topics of this chapter may be of special relevance to young college students, and there are probably professionals on your campus who are potential resources. You could ask a representative from the student health service or student counseling service to speak to the class on sexually transmitted diseases or substance abuse. Another campus resource is a representative from the career planning and placement office, who could talk about the career-planning process, common errors in career planning, common influences on career planning, and resources available on campus to students who are currently planning careers. (Chances are, most of the students in your class are in the process of career planning.)

LECTURE OUTLINES

Lecture 1: Formal Operations

I.   **Piaget's stage of formal operations**

Formal operations is Piaget's highest level of cognitive development. When does it occur?

A.   Piaget originally said that this stage begins at age 11 or 12 and continues until death.
B.   But he later revised this because research showed that many adolescents and even many adults do not reason at the formal level. There are at least two possible reasons:
1.   Formal operations may not be universal.
2.   Or, if all people do attain formal operations, it may be that some people use these skills (the most sophisticated abstract reasoning skills ever attained) only for familiar problems or situations

(e.g., a chef might use them for revising or adapting a recipe but not for planning the route of a cross-country trip). With familiar problems, one knows all the factors to be considered and how these factors interact.

II.   Formal operational thought

There are significant differences between formal operational and concrete operational thought.

A.   Abstractions. A person who has attained formal operations can think about the abstract: thought, emotions, ideals, social issues, values, beliefs, etc.

B.   Adolescent egocentrism. This trait is closely associated with the individual's developing capacity for abstraction (described by David Elkind). The various signs of this adolescent tendency include the "imaginary audience" and the "personal fable.

1.   Imaginary audience. Adolescents can think about thought itself and can try to analyze other people's thoughts. This can lead to egocentrism because teenagers imagine that other people's thoughts are focused on them (their appearance, behavior, etc.) and so feel constantly "on stage."

2.   Personal fable. Adolescents believe that they have a unique and dramatic origin and destiny. They are fascinated with their own emotions and believe these emotions to be uniquely intense (parents "don't understand" how it feels to be so in love, depressed, angry, etc.).

C.   Analyses. Formal operations involves combinatorial analysis--a more sophisticated approach to reasoning and problem solving than is seen in earlier stages.

1.   The individual can now approach a problem by identifying many possible solutions and evaluating alternative solutions to determine the best or most promising.

2.   According to Piaget, this change was based on experiments with children and adolescents involving specific kinds of problems; many of these problems involved principles of mathematics, physics, or both. An example is the pendulum problem described in the text.

III.   Postformal stages

Piaget did not discuss possible stages following formal operations. He believed that formal operations lasted until death or until disease impaired cognitive functioning. Later theorists were dissatisfied with this position and discussed ways in which intelligence might change during adulthood. Two of the best known are Riegel and Arlin.

A.   Riegel: Dialectical operations.
1.   Riegel proposed that adults are not constantly seeking a "single best" solution to relatively clear-cut problems and that many adult problems do not have a "single best" solution.
2.   Adult intelligence is the ability to identify a solution with the awareness that alternative solutions may exist.

B.   Arlin: Problem finding.
1.   Defining a problem to be solved represents a step beyond solving clearly identified or defined problems.
2.   Arlin provided some evidence that such a stage exists, but other researchers have been unable to replicate her findings.

References for Lecture 1

Arlin, P. (1985). Adolescent and adult thought: A structural interpretation. In N. Commons & S. Benack (Eds.), *Post-formal operations*. New York: Basil Blackwell.
Beilin, H. & Pufall, P. (Eds.) (1992). *Piaget's theory : Prospects and possibilities.* Hillsdale, NJ: Erlbaum.
Ginsburg, H. P. & Opper, S. (1988). *Piaget's theory of intellectual development* (3rd ed.). Englewood Cliffs, NJ: Prentice-Hall.

Lecture 2: Early and Late Maturation

I.   Girls

We look first at early and late maturation in girls.

A.   Early maturation.
  1.   Research. A longitudinal study of early-maturing girls revealed both positive and negative consequences.
    a.   Positive effects. In sixth and seventh grades, compared with later-maturing girls, early maturers:
      (1)   Felt better about their figures.
      (2)   Were more popular with boys.
      (3)   Dated more frequently.
      (4)   Were more independent.
    b.   Negative effects. Compared with later-maturing girls, early maturers:
      (1)   Were less likely to get good grades.
      (2)   Were more likely to get into trouble at school.
    c.   Follow-up. By tenth grade, many of these differences between early and later maturers had disappeared.
  2.   General conclusions regarding early maturation for girls.
    a.   Potential advantages:
      (1)   Early-maturing girls are treated as more mature by adults and peers (and thus are more likely to show mature behavior).
      (2)   They have more social sophistication, owing to their more active social life.
      (3)   They have high levels of cognitive maturity and coping skills, owing to their richer experiences during puberty.
    b.   Potential disadvantage: Shorter period of preparation for puberty may lead to a greater sense of crisis and to more confusion over these changes.
B.   Late maturation.
  1.   Potential advantages:
    a.   Late-maturing girls are under less social pressure while growing up.
    b.   Emergence from puberty at approximately the same time as boys of the same age means that they may develop emotionally and socially at the same rate as boys.
    c.   Late maturers tend to be gregarious, socially poised, and assertive.
  2.   Potential disadvantages:
    a.   Late maturers may experience anxiety and doubt regarding their physique.
    b.   Late maturers' relatively safe adolescence may lead to development of lower levels of cognitive sophistication and coping skills than are seen in early maturers.

II.   Boys

The consequences of early or late maturation are generally more marked for boys than for girls. Early maturation tends to have more advantages, and late maturation more disadvantages for boys than for girls.

A.   Early maturation.
  1.   Potential advantages:
    a.   Early-maturing boys have a competitive edge in athletics (generally a valued area of accomplishment for adolescent boys).
    b.   Early maturers are more often viewed as leaders by their peers.
    c.   Adults expect more mature behavior from early maturers.
    d.   Early maturers are more attractive to girls of their own age than are boys who mature on time or late.
    e.   Early maturation is associated with more positive personality traits (poise, self-confidence, etc.).
  2.   Potential disadvantages:
    a.   The period of adolescent experimentation may be curtailed for early maturers because adults expect more

mature, "settled" behavior from them.
   b.   There is less time to adjust to physical maturity; this may result in social immaturity.
B.   Late maturation.
   1.   Potential advantage: A longer period of pubertal adjustment may permit development of a wider range of cognitive abilities and coping skills.
   2.   Potential disadvantages:
      a.   Late-maturing boys may be at a competitive disadvantage in athletics and boy-girl relationships.
      b.   Late maturers are often less popular with their peers and are less frequently chosen as leaders.
      c.   Boys may react to late maturation by developing a negative self-concept: feelings of inadequacy, dependency, and rejection.

III.   Individual differences

Individual adolescents vary in rates of various physiological changes of puberty (e.g., growth spurt, breast development, menarche). Adolescents with an athletic build are most likely to be early maturers; those with a slight build are most likely to be late maturers.

References for Lecture 2

Alasker, F. (1992, November). Pubertal timing, overweight, and psychological adjustment. *Journal of early adolescence, 12*(4), 396-419.
Flannery, D. (1993, January). Impact of pubertal status, timing, and age on adolescent sexual experience and delinquency. *Journal of adolescent research, 8*(1), 21-40.
Richards, M. (1993). Pubertal development and the daily subjective states of young adolescents. *Journal of research on adolescence, 3*(2), 145-169.

Lecture 3: Improving High Schools

I.   Public Opinion: A Gallup Poll

What does the public think of the public schools? Results of the 1986 Annual Gallup Poll of the Public's Attitudes toward the Public Schools give a picture.

A.   Methodology. The Gallup poll reflects interviews with a representative national sample of 1,552 adults:
   1.   Parents of students attending public, parochial, and private high schools.
   2.   High school teachers and administrators.
B.   Findings.
   1.   Overall rating of schools. Most respondents gave schools an "A" or "B."
      a.   Parents rated schools more favorably than nonparents.
      b.   Parents whose children had above-average grades rated schools most favorably of all groups of parents.
      c.   Teachers rated schools more favorably than nonteachers.
   2.   Parents' views of ways to improve schools.
      a.   Nearly all parents supported competency testing for teachers; many supported merit pay for teachers.
      b.   Most parents supported increased academic rigor in the curriculum.
         (1)   They favored more required courses in English, mathematics, science, American government, history, and computer literacy.
         (2)   They also wanted more elective courses in business, health, career preparation, physical education, and sex education.
   3.   Parents' views of problems facing schools. Most parents saw problems as less serious in their own children's schools than in high schools in general. They cited two problems as most serious.
      a.   Drugs.
      b.   Lack of discipline.
         (1)   Parents believed that discipline problems be handled by the least harsh method possible.

(2) They supported special training for teachers in dealing with problem students.

(3) They were also in favor of classes for parents of problem students.

II. Educators' recommendations: Report of a national commission

Educators' recommendations for improving high schools appeared in the 1983 report of the National Commission on Excellence in Education.

A. Raising standards.
   1. Educators recommended adding courses in language, mathematics, and sciences.
   2. They also recommended increasing rigor throughout the curriculum.
B. Using time more effectively.
   1. The educators recommended that students spend more time in school:
      a. Longer school day.
      b. Longer school year.
   2. They also recommended more efficient use of time in school.
C. Improving teaching. The educators recommended:
   1. Higher standards for teacher certification.
   2. Better salaries for teachers.
   3. Involving personnel from outside education as consultants to schools.
   4. Greater involvement of teachers in decision making.

III. Students' views: A study of teenagers

A study by Poole (1984) examined teenagers' views of the schools.

A. Overall rating. Most teenagers were satisfied with their schools.
B. Teenagers' views about ways to improve schools.
   1. Discipline. The teenagers opposed an authoritarian approach to school governance; they wanted a more democratic approach and greater freedom and flexibility for individual students.

2. Curriculum. The teenagers wanted:
   a. More diverse subjects.
   b. A curriculum more directly oriented toward vocational concerns.
   c. Greater attention to practical experience and practical applications in the curriculum.
3. Teachers. Teenagers wanted:
   a. Greater competence, as reflected in formal qualifications, knowledge, experience, and classroom management skills.
   b. Better teacher-student communication.

References for Lecture 3

Bell, T. (1993, April). Reflections one decade after *A Nation at Risk*. *Phi delta kappan, 74*, 592-597.

Clinton, B. (1992, October). The Clinton plan for excellence in education. *Phi delta kappan, 74*. 131+

Cunningham, W. (1993). *Cultural leadership: The culture of excellence in education.* Boston: Allyn & Bacon.

Lynch, J., Modgil, C., & Modgil, S. (Eds.) (1992) *Cultural diversity and the schools.* London, Washington, DC: Falmer.

Poole, M. E. (1984, Summer). The schools adolescents would like. *Adolescence.* 447-458.

TOPIC FOR DEBATE

Should High School Students Be Allowed to Work?

Background

Many people assume that part-time jobs are a valuable experience for high school students; in fact, this belief is something of a tradition. Virtually any job, it is said, can be a valuable learning experience for teenagers. Even if the work itself is not terribly challenging, it provides an opportunity to learn how to manage time, how to deal with the public, how to become poised and present oneself effectively, and how to manage money. Many jobs can, in addition, provide experience that teenagers will later find valuable when they are seeking full-time employment.

Furthermore, work is a financial necessity for many teenagers and their families. Some adolescents are able to attend college, for example, only because of the money that they have earned at part-time jobs during their high school years.

Finally, many would argue that teenagers enjoy the same civil liberties as adults, including the right to work.

Recently, however, serious questions have been raised regarding the value of work for teenagers. The part-time jobs generally available to teenagers are best described as menial, dead-end work with little potential for learning the skills useful in adult careers or any other sphere of life. Recent research shows, further, that part-time employment is of virtually no value in helping adolescents to develop the skills needed for managing time or money or for interpersonal relations.

One can even argue that employment in adolescence is harmful both to teenagers and to society. Not surprisingly, teenagers who work more than 15 to 20 hours per week tend to have more problems in school than those who do not work; working students also spend less time with their families. Furthermore, the money teenagers earn at work is more often spent on short-term luxuries (e.g., drugs, clothes, cars) than on necessities or on long-term goals such as college.

Finally, some people would maintain that, in a recessionary economy, jobs should be reserved for adult men and women who are responsible for supporting themselves or their families.

Debate plan

Using this background, and information from other sources (selected references appear below), student panels should debate the following positions:

Position A. Adolescents should be encouraged to have a part-time job.

Position B. Adolescents should be forbidden to work.

References for the debate

Greenberger, E. & Steinberg, L. (1986). *When teenagers work.* New York: Basic Books.
Lennings, C. (1993, Fall) The role of activity in adolescent development: A study of employment. *Adolescence, 28,* 701-710.
Silbereisen, R. & Todt, E. (1994). *Adolescence in context: The interplay of family, school, peers, and work in adjustment.* New York: Springer, Verlag.

TOPICS FOR DISCUSSION

Topic 1: Physiological Changes in Adolescence

1. Ask students to list the physiological changes that occur during puberty and adolescence. Ask them to identify the changes that have the greatest psychological impact on boys and on girls. Ask them to discuss how parents and teachers could best prepare schoolchildren for these coming changes (textbook pages 342-348).

2. Ask students to suggest which physiological changes have the greatest potential to affect parents' perceptions of adolescent children. Ask them to discuss the potential impact of these changes on parent-child relationships.

3. Ask students to describe the secular trend (page 346) and discuss its implications for sex education; for adolescent sexuality; and for sex-related problems, including teenage pregnancy and STDs.

Topic 2: Adolescent Egocentrism

1. Ask students to describe the aspects of adolescent egocentrism discussed in the chapter. Ask them to identify the ways in which these forms of egocentrism reflect cognitive growth during adolescence (page 362)

2. Ask students to discuss the impact of adolescent egocentrism on teenagers' relationships with parents and peers. Ask them to suggest what advice parents might give teenagers about coping with adolescent egocentrism.

Topic 3: High School

1. Ask students to consider their own experiences when they made the transition from elementary school to junior high or high school and to compare their own experiences with the

information on this topic presented on page 367 of the text.

2. Ask students what they consider the most serious problems facing high schools today and what they think should be done to improve the quality of American high schools.

3. Ask students to identify the steps recommended in the text for preventing high school students from dropping out (page 371). Ask them which step they consider most important and why. Ask them which step they consider most feasible, and why.

Topic 4: Career Development

1. Ask students to identify the stages in career planning and influences on career planning discussed in the chapter (pages 372-373). Ask them to describe how parents and gender have--or have not--affected their own career plans.

2. Ask students to describe the types of services or programs that could help adolescents make wise decisions about careers.

PROJECTS AND CLASS EXERCISES

Group Exercise: Designing a Drug Prevention Program for Teenagers

Working in groups, students should plan a program to educate teenagers about the dangers of substance abuse. The plan for the program should reflect not only information about adolescents' use of drugs and the consequences of drug abuse in adolescence, but also information on adolescent egocentrism.

Specifically, the group's plan should include statements about how information on substance abuse would be presented so as to have the greatest impact, given such factors as adolescents' self-centeredness, their apparent hypocrisy, and the personal fable. The group's plan should also include a list of specific drug-related topics that would be covered in the program.

Project 1: Physiological Changes of Adolescence

Students should write autobiographical papers in which they describe their own experience of the physical changes of puberty and adolescence. Papers should include memories of their psychological reaction to these changes and the impact of these changes on their family and peer relationships. Students should also note in their papers whether they were early or late maturers and discuss the impact of early or later maturation. Finally, students should identify the cultural taboos, social attitudes, or stereotypes which made their sexual maturation most difficult.

Project 2: Eating Disorders

Students should read a recent novel, watch a recent movie about anorexia nervosa or bulimia. They should then write a paper describing the fictional account of the eating disorder and evaluating the accuracy of its portrayal of the problem.

Project 3: Moral Development

Students should interview two or more adolescents of different ages. Interview topics should include moral choices or dilemmas that each adolescent has faced and factors that the adolescent considered in making a decision. Students should then write a paper describing each interview and characterizing each adolescent's level of moral reasoning in terms of Kohlberg's framework.

Project 4: Influences on School Achievement

Students should write a paper describing ways in which their parents and their family background affected their own performance in high school and how these factors are now affecting their performance in college.

Project 5: Transition to Junior High School

Students should write a position paper in which they take and defend their stand on the current 6-3-3 educational sequence, a pattern which involves two disruptive transitions for adolescents. They may use their own experience to support their position and/or interview students who underwent a similar sequence. Students may focus on the emotional and psychological effects of especially the junior high school transition.

Factors to consider include changes in peer pressure, self-directedness, self-esteem, scholastic achievement, friends and family relationships.

ESSAY QUESTIONS

1.   Describe the timing of sexual maturation, and explain the term *secular trend*.

Answer guideline. Although there is a great deal of individual variation, the average age for the beginning of sexual maturation is 10 for girls and 12 for boys. Even though the age at which these changes begin varies, the sequence of the changes bringing sexual maturation is fairly constant. For girls, the sequence is growth of breasts, growth of pubic hair, and growth of the body; menarche; growth of underarm hair; and increased output of sweat- and oil-producing glands. For boys, the sequence is growth of testes and the scrotal sac, growth of pubic hair, and body growth; growth of penis, prostate gland, and seminal vesicles; change in voice; first ejaculation; growth of facial and underarm hair; and increased output of sweat- and oil-producing glands. The secular trend is a trend toward sexual maturation at younger and younger ages in many countries.

2.   Discuss the impact of early and late maturation on boys and girls.

Answer guideline. In some studies, early-maturing boys have been found to be more poised, popular, relaxed, and easygoing; less affected; and more likely to be leaders than later-maturing boys. However, other studies have found early-maturing boys to be more worried about other people's opinion of them and more cautious and rule-oriented than later-maturing boys. Various characteristics have also been identified for late-maturing boys. Some studies find these boys to be more insecure, rejected, dominated, dependent, aggressive, and rebellious and to have a poorer self-concept than earlier maturing boys; in other studies, however, late-maturing boys were among the most flexible and adaptable. For girls, early maturation seems to be associated with decreased sociability, expressiveness, and poise as well as with high levels of introversion and shyness.

3.   Describe anorexia nervosa and bulimia, and identify possible causes of these disorders.

Answer guideline. Anorexia nervosa is an eating disorder characterized by self-starvation. Anorexics are preoccupied with food, although they eat very little; they have a distorted body image and seem not to be aware of their emaciation; they tend to be withdrawn, depressed, and obsessed with repetitive, ritualistic, perfectionistic behavior. Victims of anorexia nervosa are almost always female; they are usually between the ages of 12 and 25; they tend to be from stable, affluent families; they are typically white. The cause of anorexia is unknown, but it is now thought that the disorder may be caused by neurophysiological factors, depression, fear of growing up, family disturbances, and societal pressures on women to be slender. Bulimia is an eating disorder characterized by regular eating binges followed by self-induced vomiting or use of laxatives. Victims of bulimia are also usually white, female, and young. Proposed causes of bulimia include family disturbances and depression.

4.   Describe the known extent of adolescents' use of alcohol and signs of problems related to adolescents' use of alcohol.

Answer guideline. Drinking appears to be fairly common among teenagers: 85 percent of high school seniors in a recent survey had drunk alcohol within the past year, 65 percent had drunk within the past month, and 37 percent had had two or more drinks in a row within the last 2 weeks. A recent survey identified approximately 30 percent of teenagers as problem drinkers: these adolescents had been drunk at least 4 times in the last year or had gotten into trouble of some kind because of drinking.

5.   Discuss the implications of STDs for adolescents.

Answer guideline. STDs are sexually transmitted diseases; they include chlamydia, gonorrhea, genital or venereal warts, herpes simplex, syphilis, and AIDS. The rate of STDs among teenagers is high for a number of reasons, including increased sexual activity among adolescents, the use of oral contraceptives rather than condoms, and adolescent egocentrism. The long-term physical consequences of STDs are at least as serious for adolescents as for adults, but adolescents are less likely than adults to seek prompt treatment for these diseases.

6.   Describe Piaget's stage of formal operations.

Answer guideline. In Piaget's formal operations stage, individuals are able to approach complex problems in an organized manner. The individual can carefully identify possible solutions to a problem and systematically evaluate and test each possibility. At this stage, the individual is also capable of thinking about hypothetical or contrary-to-fact conditions, and can use hypothetical-deductive reasoning.

7.   According to Elkind, how are adolescents egocentric?

Answer guideline. Elkind identified several reflections of egocentrism in adolescence; he believed that these aspects of egocentrism stem from cognitive growth. Adolescents typically find fault with authority figures, as a result of their new capacity to imagine an ideal state of affairs. Because of their new capacity to identify possible alternatives, teenagers are often argumentative or indecisive. Adolescents' self-consciousness may be described in terms of an "imaginary audience"; adolescents attempt to imagine other people's thoughts but egocentrically assume that they themselves are the objects of those thoughts. Elkind also noted that self-centeredness is common in adolescence; he termed this aspect of egocentrism the personal fable. The teenager imagines himself or herself to be special, unique, and unaffected by the forces which govern the rest of the universe. Finally, Elkind noted that adolescents may display apparent hypocrisy because they fail to distinguish between simply expressing an ideal and actually working toward it.

8.   How does the home influence high school students' scholastic achievement?

Answer guideline. Recent surveys show that parents' involvement can be an important influence on high school students' achievement. Students who got the best grades tended to come from homes in which the parents, particularly the father, monitored students' homework and grades and knew what their children were doing outside of school. Socioeconomic status has relatively little relationship to achievement in high school, although the home atmosphere (amount of reading material available, parents' attitude toward education, parents' goals for children, quality of language and conversation at home, family stability, and participation in cultural activities) is closely related to students' scholastic achievement.

9.   Describe typical stages in career planning.

Answer guideline. There are three classic stages in career planning. In the fantasy stage (elementary school years), children tend to plan to enter active, exciting, glamorous careers; these plans tend not to be realistic or practical. In the tentative period (approximately at the time of puberty), youngsters make somewhat more realistic efforts to select a career in accordance with their own interests and abilities. The realistic stage begins by the end of high school; in this stage, adolescents are much more capable of selecting a career and planning for the appropriate training. Even in this stage, however, many teenagers do not make wise choices based on their own capabilities or interests; moreover, many teenagers are ill-informed about career requirements, current employment trends and job statistics.

CHAPTER 11
PERSONALITY AND
SOCIAL DEVELOPMENT
IN ADOLESCENCE

INTRODUCTION

The search for one's identity is a major theme of adolescence, a time at which a person's physical, cognitive, emotional, and social development reach a peak. In **Chapter 11** we learn that adolescence is a period of both struggle and triumph. During this eventful period, the young person's quest for individualism is influenced by several factors; in particular, the adolescent peer group and family play significant roles.

• The chapter begins with an examination of the major task of adolescence--the quest for identity, including sexual identity.

• The psychosocial task of defining identity is contrasted with the problem of identity (or role) confusion.

• The findings of recent research, which indicate that adolescence is a period during which people can be said to

possess one of four identity states, are explained.

• The changing relationships between adolescents and their families and peers are described.

• Some current sexual practices and attitudes among adolescents are described, including a discussion of two persistent problems associated with adolescence: pregnancy and delinquency. Various preventive measures used by families affected by these problems are presented as well as how society, in general, tries to decrease the high rates of teenage pregnancy and juvenile delinquency.

• The chapter concludes with a discussion of the many special personality strengths possessed by adolescents. Three cohort studies are used to provide a positive view of adolescence.

CHAPTER OUTLINE

I. THE SEARCH FOR IDENTITY

A. IDENTITY VERSUS IDENTITY CONFUSION
B. RESEARCH ON IDENTITY
   1. Identity States: Crisis and Commitment
      a. Identity achievement
      b. Foreclosure
      c. Identity confusion
      d. Moratorium
   2. Gender Differences in Identity Formation
      a. Research on female identity formation
      b. Research on female self-esteem
   3. Ethnic factors in Identity Formation
C. ACHIEVING SEXUAL IDENTITY
   1. Studying Adolescents' Sexuality
   2. Sexual Attitudes and Behavior
      a. Masturbation
      b. Sexual orientation
         (1) What determines sexual orientation?
         (2) Homosexuality
         (3) Attitudes, behavior, and the "sexual evolution"

II. SOCIAL ASPECTS OF PERSONALITY DEVELOPMENT IN ADOLESCENCE

A. RELATIONSHIPS WITH PARENTS
   1. An Ambivalent Relationship
   2. Conflict with Parents
   3. What Adolescents Need from Their Parents
   4. How Adolescents Are Affected by Their Parents' Life Situation
      a. Parents' employment
      b. "Self-care" adolescents
      c. Adolescents with single parents
B. SIBLING RELATIONSHIPS
C. RELATIONSHIPS WITH PEERS
   1. How Adolescents Spend Their Time--and with Whom
   2. Friendships in Adolescence
   3. Peer Pressure versus Parents' Influence
   4. Parents' Influence over Adolescents' Choice of Friends

III. TWO PROBLEMS OF ADOLESCENCE

A. TEENAGE PREGNANCY
   1. Consequences of Teenage Pregnancy
   2. Why Teenagers Get Pregnant
   3. Who Is Likely to Get Pregnant?
   4. Preventing Teenage Pregnancy
   5. Helping Pregnant Teenagers and Teenage Parents
B. JUVENILE DELINQUENCY
   1. Personal Characteristics of Delinquents
   2. The Delinquent's Family
   3. The Influence of the Peer Group
   4. Dealing with Delinquency

IV. A POSITIVE VIEW OF ADOLESCENCE: THREE COHORT STUDIES

KEY TERMS

adolescent rebellion (page 390)
commitment (382)
crisis (382)
foreclosure (383)
heterosexual (386)
homosexual (386)
identity achievement (383)
identity diffusion (383)
identity versus identity confusion (380)
masturbation (385)
moratorium (383)
sexual orientation (386)
status offender (402)

LEARNING OBJECTIVES

After finishing Chapter 11, students should be able to:

1. Describe the psychosocial conflict of *identity versus identity confusion*. (pp. 380-381)

2. Discuss some of the ways that adolescents resolve the conflict of *identity versus identity confusion*. (pp. 380-381)

3. Describe the dangers of not being able to resolve the conflict of *identity versus identity confusion*. (p. 381)

4. Explain what is meant by the virtue of fidelity. (p. 381)

5. Name and explain the main characteristics of each of the 4 specific identity states described by James Marcia. (p. 383)

6. Describe some of the differences between males and females in the formation of identity. (pp. 383-384)

7. Describe how ethnic factors influence the formation of identity. (p. 385)

8. Discuss some of the current sexual practices and attitudes among adolescents. (pp. 385-389)

9. Briefly explain how adolescents' attitudes regarding sex differ from their actual sexual practices. (pp. 387-389)

10. Describe how the relationship between children and parents changes during adolescence. (pp. 390-391)

11. Explain how adolescents are affected by their parents' life situation. (pp. 392-394)

12. Discuss the changes in relationships with siblings during adolescence. (pp. 394-395)

13. Compare the importance of an adolescent's peer group to that of his/her family, and describe how each influences adolescents' attitudes and behaviors. (pp. 395-398)

14. Describe some of the reasons why teenagers become pregnant. (pp. 399-400)

15. Describe some of the consequences of teenage pregnancy. (p. 399)

16. Identify some of the disadvantages of being the child of a teenage parent? (p. 399)

17. Describe some of the factors that are related to the problem of juvenile delinquency. (pp. 402-404)

18. List some of the special personality strengths of adolescents. (pp. 404-405)

CHAPTER SUMMARY AND TEACHING RECOMMENDATIONS

The chapter begins with a lengthy summary of Erik Erikson's psychosocial adolescent crisis, the conflict of "identity versus identity confusion." You may wish to elaborate on the text's presentation through a lecture, discussion, or project (see below). Carol Gilligan's findings that girls seem to value intimate relationships while males value achievement are also discussed. The authors present James E. Marcia's research on identity states, or statuses. Students often view the four statuses as a developmental progression; for that reason, you may want to call their attention to the authors' statement that the statuses are not such a progression, but rather are contingent on distinct personality changes.

The research on adolescent identity continues with a discussion of the views of Sigmund Freud and Gilligan. The authors outline recent feminist criticisms (particularly Gilligan's) of the classic work on identity development; they also note the growing awareness of ethnic factors on identity.

The next section of the chapter ("Social Aspects of Personality Development in Adolescence") begins with a detailed discussion of how adolescents and parents communicate and handle conflicts. The authors note that some conflict with parents is normal, although severe and prolonged conflict would be cause for concern; furthermore, they give suggestions for improving communication and clarify important adolescent needs parents should fulfill. The effects of parental lifestyles on adolescents are also discussed, especially the effects of working and single parents. The authors then examine the changes in sibling relationships.

The major aspects of peer relationships impacting identity, particularly how and with whom adolescents spend their time, are emphasized. Factors that influence people's ability to make and keep friends are presented; the section ends with a brief discussion of the relative influence of peers and parents on adolescents.

The chapter continues with a discussion of adolescent sexuality. The authors explain problems with the scientific study of sexuality, in general, and adolescents' sexuality in particular; their points are quite well taken and well expressed and could be a basis for discussion in class. In discussing teenagers' sexuality, the authors review current information about adolescents' sexual attitudes and sexual orientation. Finally, the authors describe what they call a <u>sexual evolution</u> (rather than a "revolution") from the early 1920s through the late 1970s and summarize recent studies and findings on adolescents' sexual behavior.

In a section on problems of adolescence, the authors discuss teenage pregnancy and juvenile delinquency. Again, you could consider these topics in terms of how they may be related to cognitive functioning, personality development, and family relationships in adolescence.

The final section of the chapter presents findings from three cohort studies of adolescents.

Boxes in Chapter 11 are "Gender Differences in Personality Development," "Communicating with Adolescents about Sex," and "Preventing Teenage Pregnancy."

AUDIOVISUAL MATERIALS

Distributor, date, and running time are given for each film or video. Distributors' addresses are listed in the appendix (General Resources). If a film or video is not in color, there is a notation (BW) to that effect.

Teenage shoplifting. (CRM, 1981, approximately 10 min.) CBS News film describing one community's approaches to controlling shoplifting by teenagers. Includes interviews with teenagers, parents, and shop owners.
Hope is not a method. (PER, 1984, approximately 20 min.) Available as a film or video. Reasonably current overview of birth control methods and discussion of possible methods for the future.
Street gangs of Los Angeles. (FFHS, 1994, video, 44 min.) This program looks at the thrills and dangers of life for black and Hispanic gang members and their parents.

Coping with peer pressure. (FFHS, 1994, video, 15 min.) Viewers learn to cope with peer pressure by looking ahead to the consequences of their actions and being honest with themselves.
Ignoring the risks: Teenage pregnancy and AIDS. (FFHS, 1994, video, 28 min.) In this specially adapted Phil Donahue program, teens themselves explain why they ignore the warning that unprotected sex can cost them their lives.
Parents' views and teenagers' rights. (FFHS, 1994, video, 28 min.) In this program, teens tell of their battles with their parents. Young women tell how they feel they must lie to their parents to stand up for their own rights. Muslim girls, in particular, are unhappy when their parents try to prevent them from becoming part of western culture.
Educating pregnant teens. (FFHS, 1994, video, 25 min.) This program takes a candid look at teenage pregnancy and attitudes toward it through the forthright views of a young group of women.
Teens, sex, and AIDS. (FFHS, 1994, video, 28 min.) This program combines an open discussion among teens about their AIDS concerns, with dramatizations of teens dealing with decisions about sex.
AIDS, teens, and Latinos. (FFHS, 1994, video, 28 min.) This program profiles a Cuban-American teenager with AIDS who is dedicating his life to public awareness efforts and the education of Miami Latinos.

Guest Speakers

Teenage pregnancy and juvenile delinquency are topics in this chapter that guest speakers could effectively address. You could probably locate a speaker on teenage pregnancy through your city or county department of human services; that department should be able to help you locate some sort of program directed at preventing teenage pregnancy, meeting the needs of teenage mothers, or both. Other sources that can help you locate such programs are hospitals and childbirth education organizations (in some communities, special childbirth preparation classes for teenagers are offered) or high schools. You should be able to locate a speaker on juvenile delinquency through the local police department.

LECTURE OUTLINES

Lecture 1: Development of Identity

I. Erikson's theory: Identity versus identity confusion

Erikson's psychosocial crisis of adolescence is ego identity versus identity confusion. The approximate ages are 11 or 12 to 18 or 19.

A. Challenge. To develop consistent ideas about who you are and how you can potentially fit into your culture and society as an adult (as opposed to conflict and doubt about who you are and what you can be).

B. Issues. Several issues are especially important in resolving this crisis.
1. Choice of values. ("What do I believe in?")
2. Choice of vocation or career. ("What will I be?")
3. Choices concerning sexuality and sex roles. ("What kind of man or woman am I? How can I best relate to people of the other sex?")

C. Processes. Several processes are important in resolving these issues.
1. Introspection: Looking inward, considering alternatives for oneself.
    a. Evaluation of various beliefs, religions, and value systems.
    b. Consideration of various possibilities for career and lifestyle.
    c. Consideration of one's own masculinity or femininity, and of different types of relationships.
2. Role experimentation: actually trying out possible values, careers, forms of sexuality, and sex roles. Young people experiment with roles in several ways.
    a. They may endorse specific religions (for instance, cults) and political beliefs (this can take the form of political protest).
    b. Part-time employment, summer jobs, internships, and externships are a way of experimenting with possibilities for careers.
    c. Young people also experiment with different types and degrees of intimacy and with different

ways of expressing masculinity and femininity.

D. Outcomes. The crisis can be resolved in various ways.
1. Identity foreclosure. Decisions on basic issues are reached without consideration of alternatives. The processes of introspection and role experimentation are prevented for some reason.
2. Negative identity. Issues are resolved in socially unacceptable ways. Erikson could explain delinquency this way; he would warn against labeling an adolescent as "delinquent" (because of the danger that the label would be a self-fulfilling prophecy).
3. Role confusion. The adolescent is unable to form a single, clear, consistent view of himself or herself.
    a. In this case, the adolescent remains confused and uncommitted concerning issues of values, vocation, and sexuality.
    b. This may occur because the adolescent is confronted with contradictory value systems and expectations (e.g., parents may simultaneously expect adult and childlike behaviors, such as being responsible and being unquestioningly obedient).
4. Ego identity. This is the most positive outcome of the crisis. Adolescents integrate their self-image with options available in their society and form a consistent picture of who they are and how they can fit into their society and culture.

II. Marcia's research: Identity statuses

One major criticism of Erikson's theory is the difficulty of testing his ideas through research. However, fairly extensive research on the identity crisis has been done by James Marcia.

A. Methodology: Research on identity states. Marcia measured identity statuses of college students and compared the personality characteristics of students with

different statuses.
1. To measure identity, he used a questionnaire to see if the respondent had experienced a crisis and reached any commitment concerning central issues.
2. He also measured students' attitudes toward authority, their self-esteem, their levels of anxiety, and their levels of moral reasoning.
B. Findings: Identity achievement.
1. "Identity achieved" students had experienced crises and had made commitments.
2. Other characteristics of "identity achieved" students:
   a. Less inclination to submit unquestioningly to authority.
   b. Less anxiety.
   c. Higher self-esteem.
   d. More mature moral reasoning.

References for Lecture 1

Erikson, E. H. (1963). *Childhood and society* (2nd ed.). New York: Norton.
Hughes, D. & Brand, M. (1993, September). Myths or truths of adolescence? *Journal of the American academy of child and adolescent psychiatry, 32*, 1077.
Steinberg, L. (1993). *Adolescence* (3d ed.), New York: McGraw-Hill.
Terrell, F., Terrell, S., & Miller, F. (1993, Fall). Level of cultural mistrust as a function of educational and occupational expectations among black students. *Adolescence, 28*, 573-578.

Lecture 2: Friendship in Adolescence

I. Importance of friendship

Friendship is important in adolescence for two major reasons.

A. Adolescence is a transitional period (physically, emotionally, intellectually, and socially). Thus, support from others who are undergoing similar transitions is important.
B. There is also a gradual loosening of emotional ties to parents. Most adolescents question adult authority and attempt to decrease their dependence on parents. Again, support from peers is significant.

II. Changes in friendship

The significance and nature of friendship change during adolescence. Research has identified differences in friendships at three phases of adolescence.

A. Early adolescence: Ages 11 to 13.
1. Friendship is centered on shared activities, not on less tangible aspects of the relationship (e.g., shared interests or mutual affection).
2. There is relatively little notion of reciprocity or mutuality in friendship.
B. Middle adolescence: Ages 14 to 16. Friendship is centered on feelings of security; friends are defined as people who can be expected to show loyalty and maintain trust.
C. Later adolescence: Ages 17 to 19.
1. There is continued stress on exchanges of confidence, trust, and sharing.
2. There is greater interest in friends' personalities and interests.
3. There is greater appreciation of differences between oneself and one's friends; more positive value is placed on individuality.
4. There is greater interest in cross-sex friendships.

III. Expectations concerning friendships

There are sex differences in adolescents' expectations about friends.

A. Adolescent boys.
1. Friends are expected to share activities.
2. Friends are also expected to provide practical help when necessary.
B. Adolescent girls.
1. Friends are expected to maintain trust and to be loyal.
2. Girls expressed more anxiety about friendship at all age levels studied (11 through 19). Their anxiety centered on the possibility of being rejected or excluded by their friends. (Boys expressed anxiety only over the possibility of quarrels about property, activities, or girlfriends.)

IV. Family and friendships: Absent fathers

One aspect of family influences on adolescents' friendships is the effect of an absent father.

A. An absent father may affect teenage boys' experiences with peers: boys' gender-role development or development of self-control may be adversely affected.

B. An absent father may affect teenage girls' ability to interact appropriately with boys; it could also affect friendships in later adolescence (when the importance of cross-sex friendships increases).
   1. Girls who have lost their fathers through divorce may spend more time than other girls in boys' company.
   2. Girls who have lost their fathers through death may avoid contact with boys.

References for Lecture 2

Adelson, J. (1980). *Handbook of adolescent psychology.* New York: Wiley.
Fuligni, A. & Eccles, J. (1993,July). Perceived parent-child relationships and early adolescents' orientation toward peers. *Developmental psychology, 29,* 622-623.
VanHasselt, V. (1994). *Handbook of adolescent psychopathology.* New York: Lexington Books.
Wentzel, K. & Erdley, C. (1993, September).   Strategies for making friends: Relations to social behavior and peer acceptance in early adolescence. *Developmental psychology, 29,* 819-826.

Lecture 3: Teenage Pregnancy

I.   Medical considerations

Pregnancy during adolescence is often considered high risk (to both mothers and infants).

A. Poor nutrition is more common among adolescent pregnant women than among older pregnant women.
B. Complications during pregnancy are more common for adolescents.
C. There are also likely to be complications of labor and delivery.

II. Choices and decisions

Several factors influence the resolution of adolescent pregnancies.

A. Choices.
   1. Carry the pregnancy to term. In this case there are several possibilities, including the following:
      a. The mother may raise the baby (married to the father or as a single mother).
      b. The baby's grandparents may take over as caregivers.
      c. The baby may be given up for adoption.
   2. Abortion.
B. Factors influencing the decision to carry the pregnancy to term or to abort.
   1. Family and peer relationships.
      a. Abortion is more likely for adolescents with an active, supportive family network.
      b. Abortion is more likely when the relationship with the baby's father has been of relatively short duration and has involved relatively little intimacy.
   2. Economic and demographic considerations.
      a. Abortion is more likely for adolescents from families of higher socioeconomic status.
      b. Abortion is more likely for adolescents with better-educated parents.
   3. Educational factors.
      a. Abortion is more likely for adolescents with previously good records of school attendance and performance.
      b. Adolescents who abort are more likely to continue their education.
   4. Age. The youngest and oldest adolescent mothers are most likely to choose abortion.
C. Abortion and its aftermath. Support from the family is critical for teenagers who choose abortion. Studies of teenagers who aborted and had family support found that:
   1. They expressed no regret 2 years later.
   2. Most were in school or working 2 years later.
   3. Most maintained good relationships with their parents.

4. Substantial changes in the relationship with the baby's father were typical; many had terminated the relationship.

III. Adolescent fathers

There has been little research on adolescent fathers; this is attributable partly to neglect of research on fathers in general and partly to social prejudice against adolescent fathers. However, the available research does provide some findings.

A. Psychological profiles.
   1. Many adolescent fathers show signs of maladjustment shortly after the pregnancy is detected.
   2. When adolescent fathers are compared with similar adolescent boys who are not fathers, no differences in IQ or personality have been identified.
B. Reactions to fatherhood.
   1. These fathers often express concern for the girlfriend and the infant and a desire to assume responsibility for them.
   2. Levels of actual involvement after the baby's birth vary.
C. Fathers' involvement. Several advantages are associated with involvement and support by the father during teenage pregnancies and births.
   1. For the father: increased self-esteem.
   2. For the mother: a sense of security; greater self-assurance.
   3. For the infant: a positive impact on cognitive and emotional development; also, greater financial resources are likely to be available for child rearing.

References for Lecture 3

Freeman, E. W. (1993) *Early childbearing: Perspectives of black adolescents on pregnancy, abortion and contraception.* Newbury, Park, CA: Sage.
Kiselica, M. (1993, June). Is society giving teenage fathers a mixed message? *Youth & society, 24*(4), 487-501.
Trad, P. (1993, September). Abortion and pregnant adolescents. *Families in society, 74,* 397-409.
Zabin, L. (1993). *Adolescent sexual behavior and childbearing.* Newbury Park, CA: Sage.

TOPIC FOR DEBATE

What Is the Best Approach for Dealing with Juvenile Delinquency?

Background

Juvenile delinquency--like crime in general--is widely regarded as one of the most serious problems facing our society today. There is disagreement, however, as to how this problem can most effectively be solved. Currently, juvenile delinquents are "processed" by the juvenile justice system, with the intention of rehabilitation taking precedence over restitution for crimes committed.

The juvenile justice system includes the police (usually the first authorities to come into contact with youthful offenders), juvenile courts, and correctional institutions. There is considerable diversity in how the juvenile court system deals with juveniles, depending on the young person, the offense, previous offenses, and the judge. Charges may be dismissed outright; or the youngster may be referred to a social agency, placed on probation, or--after a formal hearing--sent to a correctional facility. These facilities, unfortunately, tend to be unsuccessful at either correction or rehabilitation. Many juveniles sent to correctional facilities develop lowered self-esteem, and they come into contact with more experienced, "hardened" offenders. Not surprisingly, most facilities have high rates of recidivism.

Many people believe that the time has come for serious consideration of alternative approaches to dealing with delinquency. Some believe that youthful offenders should be treated as adult criminals--not only in terms of protection of their civil rights but also in terms of how legal proceedings are conducted and what sentences are imposed. Such an approach would actually represent a return to early legal traditions which predated modern knowledge of human development and recognition of childhood and adolescence as special periods of the life cycle. Others advocate a therapeutically based approach to intervention. Already, behavior therapy programs have been used successfully with some juvenile offenders; in these programs, appropriate behavior is defined and rewarded, positive social skills are taught, and deviant behavior is extinguished. Family therapy has also proved effective for some young people; apparently, family pathology can be an important contributing factor in some cases of delinquency. In still other treatment efforts, the focus is on attempting to enhance the troubled youngster's self-concept, in the belief that success will also lead to positive change in his or her behavior. Thus, even though there is agreement that delinquency is an urgent problem that must be faced, there is little agreement over the best steps to take in facing the challenge.

Debate plan

Using this background, and information from additional sources (selected references appear below), student panels should debate the following positions:

Position A. Juvenile delinquency should be handled simply as a form of crime: youthful offenders should be treated the same as adult criminals.

Position B. Juvenile delinquency should be regarded as a cry for help by troubled youngsters; therapeutic approaches are the best way to deal with the problem.

References for the debate

Agnew, R. (1993, August). Why do they do it? An examination of the intervening mechanisms between "social control" variables and delinquency. *Journal of research in crime and delinquency, 30,* 245-266.
Hollin, C. (1993, June). Social functions and delinquency: A return to basics. *Journal of adolescence, 16*(2), 205-210.
Huizinga, D., Loeber, R., & Thornberry, T. (1993). Longitudinal study of delinquency, drug use, sexual activity and pregnancy among children and youth in three cities. *Public health reports, 108,* 90-96.

TOPICS FOR DISCUSSION

Topic 1: Theoretical Perspectives on Identity

1. Ask students to summarize the four different statuses of identity presented in the chapter (textbook pages 382-383). Ask them to identify the perspective they find most acceptable and to justify their choice.

2. Ask students to identify an implication of each of the four perspectives for relationships with parents during adolescence and for relationships with peers during adolescence.

3. Ask students to consider the suggestions in the "Practically Speaking" Box (page 389) concerning communication between parents and adolescents regarding sex. Ask them to evaluate the validity of the suggestions in light of their own development in adolescence.

Topic 2: Ethnic and Peer Influences on "Vulnerable" Teenagers

1. Ask students to discuss what the text says about how ethnic factors affect identify formation (page 385).

2. Ask students to identify steps that the extended family (e.g., grandparents, uncles, etc.) could take to minimize the negative influence of peers on adolescents. Also ask students to identify steps that communities could take (e.g., programs that could be established, services that could be offered) to minimize peers' negative influence.

Topic 3: Teenage Sexuality

1. The text points out that--often despite the best of intentions--many parents and teenagers have trouble talking about sex (page 389). Ask students to identify possible sources of these difficulties, to identify the source that is likely to be the greatest barrier to communication, and to explain their choice.

2. Ask students to develop a list of suggestions for parents and teenagers for improving their communication about sex.

3. The text describes a number of possible programs designed to meet the needs of teenage parents (page 401-402); ask students to identify the program they believe would be most important, and to justify their choice.

PROJECTS AND CLASS EXERCISES

Project 1: Women's Identity Development

As the text notes, Erikson's treatment of identity development in women has recently been criticized. Students should read Erikson's original statement and then the more recent approaches of Gilligan, Marcia, or both. Students should then write a paper specifying how these more recent considerations depart from Erikson's original views and expressing their own reactions to these departures.

Project 2: Peers and Friends in Adolescence

Students should write a paper in which they recall ways in which they were influenced (both positively and negatively) by peers during their teenage years. The paper should also identify a friend who was particularly important during adolescence: students should explain why this friend was so important and how the friendship was similar to or different from friendships during childhood.

Project 3: Media Portrayals of Adolescent Sexuality

Students should select a recent book, television program, or movie in which adolescent sexuality is a primary topic. Students should write a paper summarizing the treatment of adolescent sexuality and evaluating the accuracy of this treatment from the standpoint of the information presented in the text.

Project 4: Teenage Pregnancy

Students should interview a professional who works with pregnant teenagers; the professional might be a nurse, childbirth educator, social worker, teacher, physician, etc. Interview topics should include the professional's experience with pregnant teenagers and his or her view of the causes of teenage pregnancy, its most serious consequences, and the steps needed to reduce its incidence. Students should write a paper summarizing the interview.

ESSAY QUESTIONS

1. According to Erikson, what crisis is experienced during adolescence? What is its resolution?

Answer guideline. Erikson's theory proposes that teenagers experience the conflict of identity versus identity confusion; the desired outcome of this conflict is coming to an understanding of oneself as a unique individual with a meaningful contribution to make to one's culture. Erikson identified the search for a career as one important element in this effort, and he believed that a period of confusion over future vocation is both normal and desirable. Erikson also identified cliquishness and intolerance of differences as typical adolescent behaviors that reflect the search for identity.

2. Describe the four identity states specified in Marcia's research.

Answer guideline. Identity achievement-- people in this state have experienced a period of crisis and have made commitments; they are characterized by flexible strength (they are thoughtful, have a sense of humor, cope well with stress, are capable of intimacy, and are open to new ideas but also maintain their own beliefs). Foreclosure--people in this state have made commitments but have not experienced crisis; they are characterized by rigid strength (they are smug and self-satisfied, have a strong sense of family ties, have an orientation toward "law and order," are followers, may be dogmatic if challenged). Identity diffusion--people in this state may have experienced crisis, but they have not yet made commitments; they may seem carefree or aimless, superficial, unhappy, and lonely. Moratorium--people in this state are currently experiencing crisis but have not yet made commitments; they are lively, talkative, conflicted, competitive, and anxious.

3. Summarize Carol Gilligan's findings on how gender differences influence identity formation.

Answer guideline. Gilligan's studies indicate that males and females achieve identity in different ways. For the female adolescent, relationships are the most powerful factor which shape and define the self; her identity evolves more within a context of social interaction and responsibility. For the male adolescent, on the other hand, identity strongly correlates with personal success and achievement. Girls, moreover, are far more likely to suppress genuine feelings and individual interests and to conform to stereotyped images of femaleness.

4. According to the text, what is "normal" in parent-adolescent conflict?

Answer guideline. Usually, both teenagers and their parents have mixed feelings for one another. Teenagers often want to establish an identity separate from their parents but to retain at least some dependency on them, while parents want more independence on the part of their teenage children but also some continued dependence. Research suggests that many aspects of parent-adolescent communication are thus characterized by "double messages." Research also shows, however, that in most families there is more minor, short-lived conflict between teenagers and their parents than long-drawn-out, hostile battles.

5. What does research show about adolescents' use of time?

Answer guideline. In a recent study of suburban teenagers, adolescents spent most of their time with friends and classmates and relatively little time with either or both parents. Even though teenagers were at home nearly half of the time, they spent most of their time at home in their rooms rather than with the rest of the family. Teenagers reported that they were happy most of the time and that the time they spent with friends tended to be most enjoyable.

6. How do peers tend to influence self-care ("latchkey") adolescents?

Answer guideline. Peers may have no more influence over self-care ("latchkey") adolescents--those whose parents both work and who thus spend a considerable period of time at home without direct adult supervision--than they do over other adolescents. When teenagers spend their unsupervised time at home, when they check in with a parent by phone, and when there is an agreed-upon schedule for completing homework and other responsibilities, peer influence is comparable to that of adolescents who have adults or siblings at home. However, if the teenager spends the

unsupervised hours away from home, if there are few provisions for checking with parents, or if parents make few efforts to keep track of what their teenager is doing, peer influence may be greater.

7. According to the text, what do contemporary teenagers report about their experience with masturbation?

Answer guideline. Teenagers in recent surveys more often report masturbating than respondents in research conducted in the 1960s. Most teenagers who report that they have masturbated also report feeling guilty about this behavior.

8. Discuss consequences of teenage pregnancy.

Answer guideline. Medical consequences include higher-than-normal susceptibility to complications of pregnancy and birth, increased likelihood of having a low-birthweight or premature baby, and increased likelihood of having a baby with serious medical problems. For the mother herself, other consequences include the following: many do not finish high school and therefore become unemployable and dependent on welfare, and the rate of suicide is higher for teenage mothers than for other teenage girls. Teenage fathers are also at risk of not completing high school. The children of teenage parents are more likely to have low IQs and problems at school (including behavior problems) and to become teenage parents themselves.

9. Describe the two types of juvenile delinquents and some factors underlying these behaviors.

Answer guideline. Juvenile delinquents fall into two categories. Status offenders are young people who commit acts not normally considered criminal except when done by a minor. A second type includes youths under age 16 or 18 who have been convicted of an offense punishable by law. Emotional turmoil is far more likely than socioeconomic status to trigger delinquency. Other possible catalysts include physical and sexual abuse and neuro-logical and psychiatric problems. Delinquents, moreover, often lack adequate parental supervision and effective discipline.

CHAPTER 12
PHYSICAL AND INTELLECTUAL DEVELOPMENT IN YOUNG ADULTHOOD

INTRODUCTION

Chapter 12 examines the physical and intellectual development which occurs in young adulthood, from about 20 to 40 years of age.

- The chapter begins with a discussion of the general physical condition of young adults and how sensory and psychomotor functioning reach their peak in this period.

- Health issues especially pertinent to young adults are addressed, with emphasis on factors that influence the health and fitness of people in this age category.

- Aspects of intellectual development are reviewed, with an explanation of how

intellectual functioning continues to develop into the adult years.

- Theoretical approaches useful in describing cognitive development during this period are discussed, and the development of morality during young adulthood is examined.

- The college experience as a part of the life of many young adults is considered, and the relationship between college and career decisions and intellectual functioning is explored.

- The chapter concludes with an exploration of career development and how age and gender influence a person's satisfaction with work.

CHAPTER OUTLINE

PHYSICAL DEVELOPMENT

I. SENSORY AND PSYCHOMOTOR FUNCTIONING

II. HEALTH AND FITNESS IN YOUNG ADULTHOOD

    A.   HEALTH STATUS
    B.   INFLUENCES ON HEALTH AND FITNESS
       1.   Diet
          a.   Diet and weight
          b.   Diet and cholesterol
          c.   Diet and cancer
       2.   Exercise
       3.   Smoking
       4.   Alcohol
       5.   Indirect Influences on Health
          a.   Socioeconomic factors
          b.   Education
          c.   Gender
             (1) Biological differences
             (2) Behavioral and attitudinal differences
          d.   Marital status

INTELLECTUAL DEVELOPMENT

III. ADULT THOUGHT: THEORETICAL APPROACHES

    A.   K. WARNER SCHAIE: STAGES OF COGNITIVE DEVELOPMENT
    B.   ROBERT STERNBERG: THREE ASPECTS OF INTELLIGENCE
    C.   BEYOND JEAN PIAGET: POSTFORMAL THOUGHT

IV. ADULT MORAL DEVELOPMENT

    A.   HOW DOES EXPERIENCE AFFECT MORAL JUDGMENTS?
    B.   ARE THERE GENDER DIFFERENCES IN MORAL DEVELOPMENT?

V. COLLEGE

    A.   WHO GOES TO COLLEGE?
    B.   INTELLECTUAL GROWTH IN COLLEGE
    C.   GENDER DIFFERENCES IN ACHIEVEMENT IN COLLEGE
    D.   LEAVING COLLEGE

VI. STARTING A CAREER

    A.   WORK AND AGE
       1.   How Young Adults Feel about Their Jobs
       2.   How Young Adults Perform on the Job
    B.   WORK AND GENDER

KEY TERMS

achieving stage (page 420)
acquisitive stage (420)
componential element (421)
contextual element (421-422)
executive stage (420)
experiential element (421)
postformal thought (422-423)
premenstrual syndrome (419)
reintegrative stage (420)
responsible stage (420)
tacit knowledge (422)

LEARNING OBJECTIVES

After finishing Chapter 12, students should be able to:

1. Describe the sensory and psychomotor functioning of a typical young adult. (pp. 410-411)

2. Discuss health during young adulthood, including the factors that influence health and fitness. (pp. 411-420)

3. List some of the factors that indirectly influence young adult health. (pp. 417-420)

4. Describe the specific things an individual can do to improve his or her health. (pp. 411-420)

5. Describe the relationship between socioeconomic factors and health. (pp. 417-418)

6. Explain how good health is related to an individual's level of education. (p. 418)

7. Discuss some of the factors that account for health and death rate differences in men and women. (p. 418)

8. Describe the intellectual development and functioning of young adults. (pp. 420-423)

9. Describe Schaie's five stages of cognitive development. (pp. 420-421)

10. Describe the three aspects of intelligence formulated by Sternberg. (pp. 421-422)

11. Describe the characteristics of mature, or *postformal thought*. (pp. 422-423)

12. Describe Kohlberg's theory of moral development as it applies to young adults. (pp. 423-424)

13. Discuss the issue of possible gender differences in moral development. (pp. 424-425)

14. Explain who goes, and who does not go, to college. (p. 426)

15. Describe how the college experience affects intellectual growth. (pp. 426-427)

16. Discuss how the college experience differs for men and women. (p. 427)

17. Summarize some of the implications of leaving college, both permanently and temporarily. (p. 428)

18. Describe how a person's age, or stage of life, affects the way he or she thinks about work. (pp. 428-430)

19. Discuss the relationship between work and gender. (pp. 430-431)

CHAPTER SUMMARY AND TEACHING RECOMMENDATIONS

In the opening section, "Sensory and Psychomotor Functioning," the authors note that young adulthood tends to be a period of optimal functioning of sensory and physical abilities, a time when general health is excellent. They then consider health issues of young adulthood at greater length. The focus here is on demographic correlates of health and the impact of lifestyle and health-related choices (e.g., diet, smoking, drinking, exercising). The authors describe gender differences in health and attitudes toward health and offer possible explanations for these differences.

In the section on intellectual development, the authors first present an overview of three approaches to conceptualizing adult intelligence (Schaie's, Sternberg's, and Labouvie-Vief's). In addressing this material in class, you might want to comment that valid and reliable means of assessing intelligence according to these models have not yet been developed, although performance on currently available measures of intelligence could be regarded as reflecting Schaie's stages or Sternberg's components.

Next, the authors again review Kohlberg's view of moral reasoning, noting the ties between moral reasoning and the individual's general level of cognitive development. The authors also describe Gilligan's recent research on women's moral judgment. Given the critical importance of Gilligan's work, we would suggest addressing this topic in class in some way; in so doing, however, you may want to point out that Gilligan's research involved a very small, selective sample (both of subjects and of the moral issues these subjects considered).

The chapter continues with a discussion of college. The authors give a very brief summary of the changes in thinking which occur during the college years and identify gender differences in achievement in college. They also discuss reasons for leaving college without completing a degree program. This section obviously addresses issues of immediate relevance to students, and it would be an excellent starting point for a lecture or discussion.

The final section of the chapter describes career development. The authors compare young adults' and older workers' feelings about work and performance on the job, and they contrast the career paths and employment conditions of women and men.

Boxes in Chapter 12 are "What You Can Do to Improve Your Health," "A Chinese Perspective on Moral Development," and "How Dual-Earner Couples Cope."

AUDIOVISUAL MATERIALS

Distributor, date, and running time are given for each film or video. Distributors' addresses are listed in the appendix (General Resources). If a film or video is not in color, there is a notation (BW) to that effect.

The causes of individuality. (FFHS, 1994, video, 28 min.) This program looks at the principal identifying elements of men and women and explains the biological facts responsible for them.

Woman and man. (FFHS, 1994, video, 52 min.) This program looks at differences between men and women and presents the notion that role-differences between men and women is beginning to fade.

Recognizing gender differences. (FFHS, 1994, video, 24 min.) This program examines the many ways men and women are attracted to each other.

Don't call me stupid. (BCN, 1983, approximately 25 min.) Available as film or video. Topics include adult illiteracy, effects of illiteracy in adulthood, and literacy programs for adults.

Driving drunk. (WK, 1983, approximately 30 min.) Available as a film or video. Topics include statistics and related information on drunk driving.

Progressive Relaxation Training. (RP, 1990, 20 min.) Available as a film or video. Topics include relaxation techniques for stress management, tension reduction, or problem solving.

Guest speakers

A representative from a "wellness" program--either on your campus or in the community (e.g., YMCA, YWCA, local hospitals)--would be a valuable guest speaker for this chapter. You could ask the speaker to address some of the points covered in the text regarding the effects of lifestyle on health and to give interested students information about how to get involved in a wellness program. Another possible guest speaker is a representative from the American Civil Liberties Union, who could talk about sex or race discrimination in the context of the text material on career development. As with Chapter 10, you could also ask a representative from your institution's career planning or placement office to give a more general talk about career development.

LECTURE OUTLINES

Lecture 1: Stress and Health

I.   Physical and psychological factors in illness

There is a long-standing controversy over the extent to which illness stems from physical or from psychological factors. Rahe (a leading researcher on stress) proposes that most illnesses are caused by both physical and psychological factors in varying degrees.

A.   Some illnesses are due almost entirely to physical factors. Example: botulism.

B.   Some illnesses are due almost entirely to psychological factors. Example: conversion hysteria.
   1.   Definition. Conversion hysteria has clear physical symptoms (e.g., blindness, paralysis) with no known physical cause.
   2.   Situation. Usually, the patient is suffering from some type of intolerable psychic conflict and the illness provides a "legitimate" escape from it.
      a.   These patients are not malingering: the symptoms are apparently created unconsciously and the individual is not aware of any link between the illness and the psychic conflict. According to Freud, a patient can gain awareness of this link--and thus be cured of the symptoms--through psychoanalysis.
      b.   Studies of conversion symptoms in servicemen during World War II found that the symptoms were often related to their military duties (e.g., combat pilots developed eye or ear problems; paratroopers developed paralysis).

C.   Most illnesses have a greater "mix" of physical and psychological factors than either of these examples.

II. Stress-related illnesses

There are several illnesses for which a link to stress is fairly well established.

A. Headaches and backaches following prolonged contraction of muscles.
B. Ulcers.
C. Cardiovascular disease. This group of illnesses, identified as a leading cause of death (especially for men), may develop with repeated exposure to stress.
  1. Stress--such as a threat--produces physiological reactions, including a rise in blood pressure. (Normally, blood pressure drops when the threatening situation passes; but with repeated exposure to stress, blood pressure may rise and remain at a high level.)
  2. There is some evidence that stress may also increase cholesterol levels in the blood and that this increase may be associated with cardio-vascular disease.

III. Research on stress and illness

Friedman and Rosen studied effects of behavior patterns; Holmes and Rahe examined effects of life changes.

A. Friedman and Rosen: Stress, behavior patterns, and illness.
  1. Methodology and findings. These researchers conducted a long-term study of patients with cardiovascular disease.
    a. Concrete causes of the disease-- smoking, drinking, diet, activity level, etc.--could be identified in only about half of these patients.
    b. In the other patients, a specific pattern of behavior-- "Type A behavior"--was apparently a cause of the illness.
  2. Type A behavior.
    a. Definition. Type A behavior is a pattern characterized by impatience and aggressiveness. Type A people try to accomplish a great deal in any given time span, create deadlines for themselves, tend to think of success in terms of quantitative measures, have

few hobbies, and feel guilty if they try to relax.
    b. Type A behavior can be contrasted with Type B behavior. Type B people are more relaxed and less competitive; they are easygoing and generally "mellow."
    c. Incidence. In Friedman and Rosenman's research, approximately 60 percent of the sample were more or less Type A's; this behavior pattern seems to be more frequent in urban dwellers.
B. Holmes and Rahe: Stress, life changes, and illness.
  1. Theory. Holmes and Rahe propose that adaptation to any change entails some stress and that major adaptations entail more stress than minor adaptations.
  2. Methodology. These researchers identified and ranked common major life changes (e.g., death of a spouse, divorce, marriage) and minor life changes (e.g., vacations, changes in eating habits). Their set of life changes included positive or welcome events (e.g., marriage, vacations) as well as negative or unwelcome events (e.g., divorce, parking tickets).
  3. Findings. Holmes and Rahe found that subjects who had experienced a great deal of change within a year's time were likely to experience illness as well. There are at least three possible explanations for this finding:
    a. Experiencing a great deal of change may be physically stressful and may thus weaken the body.
    b. People who are in poor health may be less capable of avoiding unnecessary changes in their lives.
    c. Experiencing a great deal of change may so disorganize one's life that good health habits are neglected.

References for Lecture 1

Aseltine, R. (1993). Mental health and social

adaptation following the transition from high school. *Special Issue: Late adolescence and the transition to adulthood, 3*(3), 247-270.

Goldberger, L. (1993). *Handbook of stress: Theoretical and clinical aspects.* New York: Free Press; Toronto: Maxwell MacMillan.

Loehr, J. (1993). *Toughness training for life: A revolutionary program for maximizing health, happiness, and productivity.* New York: Dutton.

Vilnamaki, H. (1993, April-June). Unemployment: financial stress and mental well-being: A factory closure study. *European journal of psychiatry,* 7(2), 95-102.

Lecture 2: Higher Education

I.　Students

What are some characteristics of students seeking higher education? The current cohort differs from recent cohorts in at least two respects: diversity and goals.

A.　Diversity. There is a new diversity in today's college students. Since the 1960s, a spirit of egalitarianism has dominated higher education, and college enrollments increased dramatically in the 1970s and early 1980s.
    1.　Of students in postsecondary education in the fall of 1980: 31 percent were at 4-year colleges, 18 percent at 2-year colleges, and the rest at other types of postsecondary institutions.
    2.　Greatest increases in percentages attending college were for women, black and other nonwhite students, students over age 25, part-time students, and students at 2-year colleges.
B.　Goals. Today's college students are generally career-oriented.
    1.　Survey of college-bound high school seniors in 1984-1985 examined their reasons for wanting to attend college.
       a.　Ninety percent said that a primary reason was "to have a more satisfying career."
       b.　Approximately 90 percent said that college would prepare them for a specific occupation and help them get a better job.
    2.　These goals are different from parents' goals for their children's college education. Parents stressed college as a means of becoming well-rounded and more interesting and as an opportunity to clarify values and beliefs.

II.　Outcomes

What impact does college have on students? There has been considerable research on this since the 1960s, and several broad areas of impact--generally positive--have been identified.

A.　Increased knowledge and cognitive development. College seems to provide more substantive knowledge, a greater intellectual disposition, increased verbal skills, and a greater aesthetic sense.
    1.　This is the primary purpose of colleges.
    2.　It is the benefit that has been most consistently demonstrated.
    3.　This impact has been identified through a variety of research strategies.
       a.　Comparing freshmen with seniors.
       b.　Comparing college students with matched controls.
       c.　Comparing alumni with matched controls.
B.　Career development and income. Despite problems of unemployment and underemployment among college graduates, figures on job opportunities and income consistently favor college graduates over people with less education.
C.　Practical competence. In many ways, college seems to provide skills in getting things done and solving practical problems. This has been demonstrated in several areas.
    1.　Family life: College attendance is associated with later ages of marriage and childbearing, with having fewer children, with family planning, with more investment (of time, thought, effort, and money) in child rearing, and with a slightly lower divorce rate.
    2.　Financial and consumer affairs: College is associated with saving more, making wiser investments, and spending a relatively high percentage of one's income on cultural and educational pursuits.

It is also associated with greater skill in dealing with various kinds of bureaucracies and the legal system, and with greater skepticism regarding false or misleading advertising.

3. Health care: College graduates are better informed and more highly motivated with regard to preventive health care (as opposed to treatment of illness). They tend to have a more healthful diet, better exercise habits, and greater ability to manage stress.

References for Lecture 2

Altonji, J. (1991). *The demand for and return to education when education outcomes are uncertain.* Cambridge, MA: National Bureau of Economic Research.
Belth, M. (1993). *Metaphor and thinking: The college experience.* Lanham, MD: University of America.
Boyer, E. L. (1987). *College: The undergraduate experience in America.* New York: Harper & Row.
Hannan, D. (1991). *The quality of their education: school leavers' views of educational objectives and outcomes.* Dublin: Economic and Social Research Institute.

Lecture 3: Gilligan's Research on Women's Concepts of Self and Morality

I. **Earlier research**

There was some research, before Gilligan's, on women and morality.

A. Findings. Previous research on women's concepts of morality identified two major differences between types of moral judgments made by women and by men.
 1. Women's judgments were more tied to feelings of empathy and compassion.
 2. Women were more concerned with resolution of real (as opposed to hypothetical) issues and dilemmas. Women thus showed more tendency to request (or invent) additional information about hypothetical people and these people's circumstances.
B. Interpretation. Interpreting these differences in terms of categories derived from research on men was problematic. Divergence from the masculine standard

could appear only as "inadequacy." Thus, women's responses to moral dilemmas were seen as inadequate, and women's thinking was often equated with moral immaturity.

II. **Gilligan's Abortion Study**

The context of Gilligan's landmark research on women and morality was a study of abortion.

A. Basis. Gilligan's study was based on a belief that conflict between "self" and "others" is a central moral problem for women and that birth control and abortion (and thus effective control of fertility) present women with an issue or dilemma involving this conflict in a central arena of life.
B. Subjects. Gilligan's subjects were 29 women (ages 15 to 33), diverse in ethnicity and social class.
 1. All had been referred by pregnancy or abortion counseling services but were participating in the study for various reasons (e.g., a desire for greater insight into their own thinking, a desire to contribute to research, a counselor's concern about repeated abortions).
 2. Circumstances in which the subjects' pregnancies had occurred also varied.
 3. These women may have experienced greater-than-normal conflict over the abortion decision. However, the significance of the findings has to do with proposed schemata--general ways in which women think about issues and dilemmas in their lives--rather than with abortion per se.
C. Methodology.
 1. Two interviews were conducted: the first when the subject was making the abortion decision (during the first trimester of a confirmed pregnancy); the second at the end of the following year.
 2. Topics for the initial interview.
  a. Decision faced, how the subject was confronting the decision, alternatives under consideration, reasons for and against each alternative, people involved in the decision, conflicts entailed in

the decision, and how the
decision affected the subject's
self-concept and relationships.
b.   Three hypothetical moral
dilemmas (including "Heinz's
dilemma" from Kohlberg's
research).
D.   Results and conclusions. The abortion
decision revealed a distinct moral
language in these women, reflecting a
distinct set of transitions in moral
reasoning. A sequence of three
perspectives was identified, each
representing a more complex understanding of the relationship between self
and others.
1.   Initial perspective: concern with
survival.
2.   Intermediate perspective: focus on
"goodness." (Traditional
femininity equates goodness with
self-sacrifice.)
3.   Final perspective: care is seen as
the most adequate guide for
resolving conflicts in human
relationships. Care is directed
toward the self as well as toward
others.

References for Lecture 3

Brown, L., & Gilligan, C. (1992). *Meeting
at the crossroads: Women's psychology and
girls' development.* Cambridge, MA: Harvard
University Press.
Gilligan, C. (1982). *In a different voice.*
Cambridge, MA: Harvard University Press.
Held, V. (1993). *Feminist morality:
Transforming culture, society, and politics.*
Chicago: University of Chicago Press.
Meilander, G. (1989, November/December).
Abortion: The right to an argument. *The
Hastings center report, 19,* 13-16.
Olsen, F. (1991, Summer). A finger to the
devil: Abortion, privacy, and equality.
Dissent, 38, 377-382.

Lecture 4: Work and Adult Development

I.   Significance of work in development

There are several reasons for studying work as
an aspect of adult development.

A.   Adult life is particularly structured by
work-related experiences.
1.   Phases of career preparation,
training, or apprenticeship.

2.   Phases of full involvement in a
career.
3.   Milestones: promotions, transfers,
career changes, etc.
4.   Phases of preparation for
retirement and retirement itself.
B.   Work affects adults' lifestyle:
residence, friends, leisure activities, etc.
(For instance, these aspects of a
professional musician's life would be
very different from the aspects of a coal
miner's life.)
C.   There are associations between work
and the self-concept: adults' identity is
defined partially in occupational terms.

II.   Super's model of career entry and progression

Donald E. Super proposed a five-stage model
of career development which was subsequently
tested by researchers.

A.   Super suggested five stages of career
development.
1.   Crystallization (early adolescence):
Concrete awareness of the eventual
need to decide on a career.
2.   Specification (later adolescence):
Career is chosen and preparatory
education or training is begun.
3.   Implementation (early adulthood):
Career is entered. The individual
learns what expectations are
associated with the "worker" role,
establishes work-related friendships and evaluates the lifestyle
associated with the chosen career.
4.   Stabilization (early and middle
adulthood): Focus is on
advancement within the career; the
worker is concerned with
productivity, initiative, and
recognition. Further training may
be required during this stage.
5.   Consolidation (middle and later
adulthood): Decreased
involvement with career and
preparation for retirement.
B.   Super's model was tested through a
longitudinal study. Little
correspondence was found between the
model and actual careers of most of the
subjects. Possible reasons are:
1.   The model has no provision for
career changes, although such
changes are a fairly common
experience for contemporary
adults.

2. Social and historical changes are not incorporated into the model. For example, the model does not take into account the role of technology in creating new careers and making some careers obsolete, or the role of changes in available energy resources. The study is particularly inapplicable given the major socioeconomic crises of the 1990's, widespread unemployment and the increase in single-parent families. These two problems alone weaken the validity of a career development paradigm.

References for Lecture 4

Bowman, S. (1993, September). Career intervention strategies for ethnic minorities. Special section: A symposium of multicultural career counseling. *Career development quarterly, 42*(1), 14-25.

Cunningham, J. (1992, August). Fostering advancement for women and minorities' cultural diversity in the 1990's. *Public management, 74,* 20-22+.

Neugarten, B. L. (1968). *Middle age and aging.* Chicago: University of Chicago Press. (This reader--a classic in the field--includes several articles that could be used to supplement or enhance the lecture outline).

Super, D. E. (1957). *The psychology of careers.* New York: Harper.

Zimmerman, J. (1992, June). Alignment of family and work roles. *Career development quarterly, 4*(4), 344-349.

TOPIC FOR DEBATE

Is a College Education a Worthwhile Investment?

Background

Not only has the American system of public education come under close scrutiny in recent years; many people today also have serious doubts about the value of a college education. These critics point to dramatic increases in the cost of a college education and claim that the price increases do not reflect any corresponding growth in the market value of a college degree. In fact, one could argue that a college degree is actually worth less today than it was a generation ago, since a greater percentage of the population now attends college. As college degrees have become more and more common, they have also become less distinctive and far less indicative of outstanding achievement.

Those who question the value of a college education also say that much college coursework lacks relevance. For many college graduates, the curriculum studied in college has little, if any, bearing on the jobs they take after graduation. In essence, a college education seems to be relatively poor vocational preparation; most graduates are expected to go through an apprenticeship or training period when they take their first entry-level job.

Furthermore, the quality of teaching at many colleges has also been criticized. At many institutions, there are few rewards for teaching well and few penalties for teaching poorly. Rather, research and publishing are the surest routes to professional recognition, and these pursuits only draw the faculty away from teaching.

Finally, a college degree is certainly no guarantee of personal satisfaction.

There are still many people, however, who are firmly convinced of the value of a college education. They point out, first of all, that colleges seem to be effective in imparting knowledge and fostering cognitive growth-- which are, after all, their primary purposes. A number of studies show that college graduates have a greater fund of substantive knowledge, a stronger intellectual disposition, and a deeper sense of aesthetics than comparable people who have not attended college. Many of these studies also identify other benefits of a college education: college graduates seem to be more adept at financial management, for example, and seem to make choices concerning family life that many would view as advantageous. While these characteristics are no guarantee of personal satisfaction, they undoubtedly increase the probability of living a satisfying life after college.

Defenders of a college degree would also point out that college curricula are not intended as vocational training. The curriculum of many liberal arts colleges, at least, would be more accurately described as "education for life." As a whole, the curriculum should give students an understanding of their own culture and other cultures, including arts, sciences, humanities, and other aspects of cultural heritage. While this may not be of tremendous benefit at the entry level in many careers, it is probably essential for attaining positions of leadership in most of them.

Finally, many people would maintain that problems with college teaching are greatly overstated. Although there are undoubtedly poor teachers at almost every college, most college administrators, faculty members, and students can also identify outstanding teachers at their institution. Involvement in research and publishing should by no means be regarded as antithetical to effective teaching: many of the best college teachers are also vitally involved in scholarship through conducting and disseminating research.

Debate plan

Using this background, and information from other sources (selected references appear below), student panels should debate the following positions:

Position A. A college education has almost no value today.

Position B. A college education is still one of the best investments in the future.

References for the debate

Boyer, E. L. (1987). *College: The undergraduate experience in America.* New York: Harper & Row.

Carter, M. & Carter, C. (1992, Spring/Summer). The value of an education: Two 92-year-olds reminisce. *Phylon, 49,* 84-98.

Leslie, L. (1988). *The economic value of higher education.* American Council on Education. New York: Macmillan; London: Collier Macmillan.

Psacharopoulos, G. (1993). *Returns to investment in education: A global update.* Washington, DC: Office of the Director, Latin America and the Caribbean Region, World Bank.

TOPICS FOR DISCUSSION

Topic 1: Influences on Health and Fitness

1. Ask students to summarize the health-related behaviors described in the chapter (pages 412-420). Ask them what type of behavior they believe is most commonly neglected in young adulthood and have them explain the basis for their choice.

2. Ask students to consider the box on page 413 of the textbook, describing steps that can be taken to enhance health. Ask students to identify the step that they think would be most <u>important</u> for people like themselves to take, the step that would be most <u>difficult</u> for people like themselves, and the step that would be most <u>likely</u> for people like themselves.

3. Ask students to identify current programs on campus or in the community that promote wellness. If they are unable to identify any such programs, ask them to suggest types of programs that could be developed.

Topic 2: Intelligence and Moral Development

1. Ask students to summarize Schaie's and Sternberg's theoretical models of adult intelligence (pages 420-422). Ask them which viewpoint they consider a better description of intelligence in adulthood, and why.

2. Have students explain the differences between Kohlberg's and Gilligan's approaches to moral development and identify the major concerns and conflicts that Gilligan attributes to women (page 425).

Topic 3: College

1. The text notes contemporary diversity in both colleges and college students (page 426). Ask students to describe some of the other colleges that they considered attending and ways in which each was similar to or different from your institution. Ask them to identify the factors that were important in their selection of your institution. Ask them to identify aspects of diversity in the students attending your institution.

2. According to the text, one way in which people typically change in college is movement away from polarized thinking toward more relativistic thinking and finally toward commitment to intellectual and moral stances (pages 426-427). Ask students to identify aspects of college life (the curriculum, other students, the faculty, extra-curricular activities, etc.) that encourage

this pattern of development. Ask them also to identify possible negative consequences of this pattern of development.

3. Ask students to think of someone they know who has left college, or is thinking of leaving, without attaining a degree. Ask them to identify the factors they are aware of that motivated the decision and to consider the possible advantages or disadvantages of this decision.

Topic 4: Career Development

1. In the section "How Young Adults Feel about Their Jobs" (page 428-430), the authors identify several negative reactions to work that are common in young adulthood. On this basis, ask students to suggest steps that employers could take to promote more positive feelings about jobs among young adult employees. Ask students also to evaluate the feasibility and probable success of the steps that they suggest.

2. Ask students to discuss the extent to which they have ever confronted sex discrimination or racial discrimination in the workplace.

PROJECTS AND CLASS EXERCISES

Group Exercise: "Selling" a College Education

Working in groups, students should design a recruitment brochure for your institution. The brochure should include information on what benefits are attained from college in general, what unique advantages your institution offers, and what types of students are most likely to be satisfied and successful at your institution. The groups should also describe categories of prospective students targeted to receive the brochure (e.g., honors students in high schools, reentering or nontraditional students, minority students). They should also note when and where the brochure would be made available.

Project 1: Influences on Health and Fitness

Students should evaluate their current health-related behaviors, using the behaviors identified in the text (pages 411-420) as a

framework. They should identify the area in which they currently engage in the least healthful behavior and do further reading on the health impacts of this behavior. Students should write a paper describing their current behaviors, the results of their reading, and a plan for incorporating more healthful behaviors in the area they selected.

Project 2: Gender Differences in Moral Development

Students should read and evaluate Gilligan's original research on women's concepts of morality. Their criticism should include a summary of the distinctions between Gilligan's model of women's moral judgment and Kohlberg's model of moral development and a discussion of the soundness of the evidence on which Gilligan's model is based.

Project 3: Career Development

Students should select a career in which they are interested and interview two people--one a relatively young adult and the other middle-aged or elderly--who work in that field. Interview topics should include feelings each worker has about his or her job. Students should write a paper describing age differences and similarities in these people's reactions to their work, comparing this information with the material presented in the chapter.

ESSAY QUESTIONS

---

1. Describe sensory and psychomotor functioning in young adulthood.

Answer guideline. Most young adults are in good physical condition, and declines in physical functioning usually do not become noticeable until later middle adulthood. For physical strength, manual dexterity, and all the sensory systems, young adulthood tends to be the point of peak functioning in the life span.

2. Explain the associations between diet and health problems discussed in this chapter.

Answer guideline. Not only can being overweight cause emotional problems in a fitness-conscious culture, it can also increase a person's risk of suffering from gout and diabetes as well as certain cancers, high blood pressure, and heart disease. Dieters, however, need to avoid fad diets and to adopt a slower but balanced rate of weight loss to prevent dangerous "cycling." A diet in which the LDL (bad) cholesterol level exceeds the HCL (good) cholesterol level has been definitely linked with heart disease. A healthier diet involves greatly reduced salt and fat and increased complex carbohydrates and fiber. Perhaps the most unquestionable link exists between unhealthy diet and certain cancers such as colon, stomach, and esophageal.

3.   How is gender associated with health?

Answer guideline. Gender differences in health include differences in death rates, frequency of illnesses, and use of health care services. Throughout adulthood, women have lower death rates than men. However, women are also ill more often than men, and women tend to make greater use of health care services than men. Women's lower death rates seem to reflect hormonal factors and may also reflect the greater use of health care resources (including health care related to the reproductive system). Women's greater frequency of illness and greater use of health care services may reflect still other gender differences, including sensitivity to the body, knowledge of health and illness, and gender-role stereotypes regarding illness and dependency.

4.   Describe the elements of intelligence in Sternberg's triarchic model, and give an example of a situation in which each element would be particularly significant.

Answer guideline. Componential element: efficiency in processing and using information, skill in approaching and solving problems, and skill in monitoring and evaluating problem solutions. This element would be critical to success in winning a legal case. Experiential element: means of approaching new tasks, ability to compare new with familiar information and to combine information in novel ways. This element would be critical to success in creating a work of art. Contextual element: "practical" intelligence, ability to evaluate a situation and determine a course of action. This element would be critical to success in finding a new job.

5.   Describe major areas of intellectual and personality development during college.

Answer guideline. One area of personal change in college, for many students, is moral reasoning: the diversity of the student body and the diverse views of the faculty prompt many students to reevaluate their moral standards. According to Kohlberg, two experiences common to young adults--values conflicts away from home and increased responsibilities for others' welfare--help generate moral development. Many students also experience intellectual development in college. According to Perry's research on Harvard and Radcliffe students, there was a developmental progression from (1) thinking in terms of polarities, to (2) acceptance of diverse viewpoints and of one's own uncertainty, to (3) awareness that knowledge and values are relative, to (4) choices of values and commitments leading to a personal identity.

6.   What are some reasons the text offers to account for gender-based differences in students' career preferences?

Answer guideline. These patterns may have resulted from gender socialization, since during adolescence girls become more focused on relationships and boys become more focused on careers. Society gives girls messages that emphasize the roles of wife and mother and stress the difficulty of combining personal success with love and family. Young men are given no reason to feel that their roles as future husbands and fathers interfere with developing their career potential. This may help to explain why the great majority of engineering, architecture, and science students are boys, whereas girls account for most students of teaching, foreign languages, and home economics.

7.   According to the text, how do young adults and older adults differ in job performance?

Answer guideline. Younger workers tend to have less job satisfaction and more "avoidable" absences from work, while older workers have more job satisfaction and more "unavoidable" absences. It is difficult to characterize age differences in actual job performance, since the effects of age are virtually inseparable from the effects of experience.

CHAPTER 13

PERSONALITY AND SOCIAL DEVELOPMENT IN YOUNG ADULTHOOD

INTRODUCTION

Following the critical period of adolescence, during which all aspects of development proceed at an alarming rate, most young adults have reached the point where physical growth has stabilized. However, development of the adult personality continues throughout life. Young adults are at the stage where they are just learning to maximize their physical and intellectual capabilities and realize that social and emotional development is a life-long process. **Chapter 13** looks specifically at how the major events of young adulthood influence an individual's personality and social development.

- Two models of personality development in young adulthood are discussed: the normative-crisis model and the timing-of-events model. The normative-crisis model describes human development in terms of a predictable sequence of chronological changes. The timing-of-events model suggests that adult development proceeds according to

individual experiences in relation to the time in a person's life when they occur.

- The chapter then focuses on the desire of young adults to form intimate, sexual relationships with each other. This need to develop intimate relationships is discussed from the perspective of the influence it will have on future social and emotional development.

- The advantages and disadvantages of various specific lifestyles (marriage, divorce, cohabitation, or single) are discussed.

- The text discusses parenthood as a developmental experience for both the parent and the child. The alternative of remaining childless is also examined.

- The chapter concludes with a discussion of the characteristics of friendships in young adulthood.

CHAPTER OUTLINE

I. **PERSONALITY DEVELOPMENT IN YOUNG ADULTHOOD: TWO MODELS**

    A. NORMATIVE-CRISIS MODEL
      1. Erik Erikson: Crisis--Intimacy versus Isolation
      2. George Vaillant: Adaptation to Life
        a. Vaillant's adaptive mechanisms
        b. Career consolidation and stages of development
      3. Daniel Levinson: Life Structure
        a. Levinson's life eras
        b. Women and Levinson's theory
          (1) The dream
          (2) The love relationship
          (3) The mentor
          (4) Forming an occupation
      4. Evaluation of the Normative-Crisis Approach
    B. TIMING-OF-EVENTS MODEL
      1. Types and Timing of Life Events
        a. Normative versus nonnormative events
        b. Individual versus cultural events
        c. The decline of age consciousness
      2. Responding to Life Events

II. **INTIMATE RELATIONSHIPS AND PERSONAL LIFESTYLES**

    A. LOVE
    B. MARRIAGE
      1. Benefits of Marriage
      2. Marriage and Happiness
      3. Marriage and Health
      4. Predicting Success in Marriage
      5. Domestic Violence
    C. DIVORCE
      1. Why Divorce Has Increased
      2. Reactions to Divorce
      3. Remarriage after Divorce
    D. SINGLE LIFE
    E. COHABITATION
    F. SEXUALITY
      1. Sexual Activity among Unmarried People
      2. Sexual Activity in Marriage
      3. Extramarital Sex
    G. PARENTHOOD
      1. Why People Have Children
      2. When People Have Children
      3. Finding Alternative Ways to Parenthood
        a. Infertility
          (1) Psychological effects of infertility
          (2) Causes of infertility
        b. Adoption
        c. New methods of becoming a parent
          (1) Artificial insemination
          (2) In vitro fertilization
          (3) Ovum transfer
          (4) Surrogate motherhood
          (5) Technology and conception: Ethical issues
      4. The Transition to Parenthood
      5. Parenthood as a Developmental Experience
      6. Blended Families
    H. REMAINING CHILDLESS
    I. FRIENDSHIP
      1. Characteristics of Adult Friendship
      2. Benefits of Friendship

KEY TERMS

adaptive mechanisms (page 438)
artificial insemination (458)
cohabitation (453)
in vitro fertilization (459)
infertility (456)
intimacy versus isolation (436)
life structure (439)
nonnormative life events (442)
normative life events (442)
normative-crisis model (436)
ovum transfer (459)
surrogate motherhood (459)
timing-of-events model (442)
triangular theory of love (444)

LEARNING OBJECTIVES

After finishing Chapter 13, students should be able to:

1. Describe personality development in young adulthood according to the *normative-crisis model* and the *timing-of-events* model. (pp. 436-443)

2. Describe the crisis of young adulthood according to Erikson. (pp. 436-438)

3. Explain Vaillant's formulation of the mechanisms by which people adapt to life circumstances. (pp. 438-439)

4. Discuss the developmental changes that occur during each phase of young adulthood, according to Levinson. (pp. 439-441)

5. Explain how the adult development of women is different from that of men, according to Levinson's theory. (pp. 441-442)

6. Evaluate the *normative-crisis* approach to adult development. (p. 442)

7. Explain the differences between *normative life events* and *nonnormative life events*, and give an example of each. (pp. 442-443)

8. Distinguish between individual and cultural events. (p. 443)

9. Explain the *triangular theory of love*. (pp. 444-445)

10. List some of the advantages of married life. (p. 446)

11. Discuss the relationship between marriage and each of the following: happiness, health (pp. 446-448)

12. List some of the factors related to success in marriage. (pp. 448-449)

13. Discuss the problem of domestic violence. (p. 449)

14. Discuss the phenomenon of divorce, including its causes and consequences. (pp. 449-452)

15. Discuss being single and *cohabitation* as alternatives to marriage. (pp. 452-453)

16. Discuss sexuality and sexual activity during young adulthood. (pp. 453-455)

17. List the reasons why people become parents. (p. 455)

18. Discuss the trend toward delayed parenthood and identify the advantages and disadvantages of this trend. (pp. 455-456)

19. Define infertility, discuss the psychological effects of infertility, and explain some of the common causes of infertility. (pp. 456-458)

20. List and describe the various alternative methods for becoming a parent. (pp. 458-459)

21. Discuss some of the ethical issues related to the alternative methods for becoming a parent. (p. 459)

22. Describe the transition to parenthood and explain the process of becoming a parent in developmental terms. (pp. 459-461)

23. Explain what is meant by a blended family and discuss the various strategies for coping with the stress associated with blended families. (pp. 461-464)

24. Discuss various aspects of the choice to remain childless. (p. 464)

25. Explain some of the characteristics and benefits of friendship during young adulthood. (pp. 464-465)

CHAPTER SUMMARY AND TEACHING RECOMMENDATIONS

The first section of the chapter describes the normative-crisis model and the timing-of-events model of adult development. In discussing the normative-crisis model, the authors first describe Erikson's crisis of intimacy versus isolation. They note the limitations of Erikson's view of this stage (e.g., he equates normal development with heterosexual intimacy), and this point could certainly bear repetition in class. Next, the authors describe Vaillant's Grant Study of Harvard university men; in discussing this research, you may wish to note the unrepresentative sample involved. Finally, Levinson's work on life structures is presented; again, the small and unrepresentative sample should be called to the students' attention. In addition, if possible, the work of Levinson et al. on women's life structures should be discussed and evaluated in class. The authors review recent research on women's adult development and then offer an evaluation of the normative-crisis model.

In discussing the timing-of-events model, the authors identify major "types" of life events and note consequences of being "off-time" for major life events. The authors also emphasize the diversity and individuality of each adult's response to a life event.

The next major section of the chapter deals with various types of intimate relationships. The authors review recent research on love and on marriage. Factors predicting success in marriage are identified, as well as associations among marital status, health, and happiness. The authors also briefly discuss violence between spouses and options available to abused spouses.

This section continues with an overview of the increasing divorce rate and the reactions to divorce. The authors next discuss research on single life, noting that, for the most part, the common stereotypes are inaccurate. Cohabitation and the diverse ways in which adults react to it are discussed. In our experience, single life and cohabitation are topics especially relevant to many college students, and we would recommend addressing these topics in class in some way.

Research on sexual activity in various contexts (before marriage, in marriage, extramarital sexual activity) is considered next. In dealing with this topic, you may want to point out the difficulties of research on sexuality.

The authors provide an extensive discussion of parenthood and related topics. Motivations for having children are detailed; this material is followed by a discussion of the timing of first birth and correlates of that timing. You might want to direct students' attention to the material on motivation in particular, noting that not all reasons for having children are necessarily good ones.

The discussion of parenthood continues with a description of the reactions to infertility and the causes of infertility, as well as alternative means of becoming a parent. The authors describe adoption and much of the "emerging technology" of conception (artificial insemination, in vitro fertilization, ovum transfer, and surrogate motherhood). They also discuss the ethical implications of these new alternatives. Students in our classes sometimes have quite heated reactions to these new approaches, and the topic could be treated effectively as a debate. "Parenthood" closes with a discussion of parenthood as a developmental experience and the problems faced specifically by blended families.

The text then presents some reasons why couples may be childless.

Friendship is the final topic of the chapter. The authors describe the characteristics of adult friendship and the benefits of friendship in general.

Boxes in Chapter 13 are "Establishing Mature Relationships with Parents," "Marriage and Divorce Patterns," "Advantages of Having Children Early or Late," "The Hassles of Raising Young Children," and "Both Job and Family Roles Affect Men's Psychological Well-Being."

AUDIOVISUAL MATERIALS

Distributor, date, and running time are given for each film or video. Distributors' addresses are listed in the appendix (General Resources). If a film or video is not in color, there is a notation (BW) to that effect.

Male and female infertility. (FFHS, 1994, video, 19 min.) The causes of and treatments for infertility in men and women are explained.

Second thoughts on being single. (FI, 1984, video, approximately 50 min.) Topics include factors influencing the choice to remain single as well as advantages and disadvantages resulting from that choice.

Psychology of parenting. (FFHS, 1994, video, 19 min.) This video presents how parents can communicate more effectively with their children.

Life with baby. (FML, 1984, approximately 25 min.) Available as a film or video. Topics include single parenthood and stresses involved in parenting.

Working pregnant. (FFHS, 1994, video, 19 min.) This video presents some of the problems experienced by pregnant women in the workplace, including fatigue and stress and on-the-job hazards.

An American stepfamily. (FFHS, 1994, video, 26 min.) This program discusses the problems of conflicting loyalties and rivalries, dealing with former spouses and the three categories of kids: his, hers, and theirs.

New fathers. (FFHS, 1994, video, 28 min.) Four hundred fathers and their infants get together with Phil Donahue and swap advice.

Problems of working women. (FFHS, 1994, video, 24 min.) This analyzes the pressures facing women with small children.

Nanny care. (FFHS, 1994, video, 26 min.) How to find a nanny and keep the cost of finding one within reason; the obligations of parents as employers.

Interracial marriage. (FFHS, 1994, video, 52 min.) This program examines how and why couples of different colors, religions, and ethnic roots are drawn to one another, how their differences affect their marriage, and how they deal with their friends and families.

Guest speakers

This chapter includes many topics of personal relevance to college students, most of whom are young adults. A marriage counselor or family therapist could be an excellent choice for a speaker; such a professional could talk to the class about common problems in marriage, factors important to success in marriage, when a married couple would be wise to seek counseling, what can and cannot be expected from marriage counseling, and when divorce may be the best decision. Another possible guest speaker is a representative from a support group for people who are recently divorced; you might be able to locate such a group in your area through a community mental health center, a city or county department of human services, or local religious organizations. Similarly, a representative from a support group for parents could talk to the class about the stresses and satisfactions of parenting and the impact of parenthood on work, marriage, and other aspects of life.

LECTURE OUTLINES

Lecture 1: Erikson--Intimacy versus Isolation

I. **What is "intimacy"?**

Erikson's sixth psychosocial crisis is intimacy versus isolation. Erikson proposed that this crisis is normally confronted in early adulthood. He had a very specific concept of "intimacy."

A. Definition. Erikson defined intimacy (in <u>Childhood and Society</u>) as a close heterosexual relationship within which procreation could be accomplished.

B. There are problems with this definition.
   1. It excludes the possibility of intimacy in homosexual relationships.
   2. It excludes the possibility of intimacy in platonic friendships.
   3. It excludes the possibility of intimacy in childless marriages.

C. Intimacy as a threat. Erikson believed that intimacy preceding identity achievement is threatening: a person loses the tenuous sense of self through closeness with another.

D. Intimacy and development. Erikson sees intimacy as a necessary step in optimal personal growth, provided that identity formation is completed (except for reworking during the crisis of ego identity versus identity confusion). By implication, he might also see marriage (or commitment to a stable relationship) as an important step in psychosocial development.

II. **What is "isolation"?**

For Erikson, a negative outcome of this crisis entails isolation. As with intimacy, he meant by "isolation" something quite specific.

A. Definition. Erikson defined isolation in terms of its consequences. Isolation, for Erikson, means that the individual does not develop a capacity for sharing or for caring about others. For such a person, relationships will be superficial, competitive, antagonistic, or all three.

B. There are problems with this definition of isolation.
    1. Consequences of isolation cannot be distinguished readily (or at all) from its causes.
    2. Isolation may exist even in the context of a stable relationship. (Consider "isolation à deux": each partner is self-absorbed rather than intimately involved with the other.)

Reference for Lecture 1

Erikson, E. H. (1963). *Childhood and society*. New York: Norton.

Lecture 2: Single Life

I. Statistics

The number of single people has increased. Striking contrasts emerged between the 1950s and the 1980s.

A. There has been an increase in absolute numbers of single adults during the twentieth century, partly as a result of population growth.
B. The percentage of adult population remaining single has also increased (e.g, approximately 33 percent in 1960 and approximately 40 percent today).
    1. The greatest increase is in the percentage of divorced and never-married people.
    2. There is little change in the percentage of widowed people.
C. There is an increased tendency to postpone marriage. Median age at first marriage has risen since the 1960s (from 20 to 22 for women and from 22 to 24 for men).

II. Historical trends

The tendency to postpone marriage has actually been apparent during most of the twentieth century except for the 1950s.

A. At the turn of the century, the percentage of never-married young adults was approximately the same as it is today.
B. During the great depression of the 1930s, there was extensive unemployment and poverty; also, the pattern of "breadwinner husband, homemaker wife, and medium to large family" became more difficult to attain and maintain. As a result, this pattern became idealized and romanticized.
C. The children of the depression, who reached adulthood in the 1950s, acted on this idealized concept. They tended to marry early and to have large families, and the economy of the 1950s allowed this (there were many jobs for men, who could thus support a wife not employed outside the home).
D. From the 1960s to the present, there has been a later age at marriage; thus, there have been more never-married young adults than there were during the 1950s. This represents a return to a pattern more typical of most of the twentieth century.

III. Social factors

At least four social factors encourage singlehood and postponement of marriage.

A. Increased job and career opportunities for women.
B. Improved contraception (which means that there are fewer "shotgun" marriages).
C. Demographics: the "marriage squeeze."
    1. The "marriage squeeze" results from two conditions.
        a. The baby boom peaked in the mid-1950s and diminished in the early 1960s.
        b. There is a tendency for women to marry slightly older men. Thus, women born during the "baby boom" reached the average age for marriage 2 to 3 years earlier than men of the same age, and there were generally fewer men born 2 to 3 years earlier than these women. In other words, a bumper crop of women were looking for mates among fewer men.
    2. The "marriage squeeze" should reverse in the next few years, as women born after the "boom" look for mates among men born during it.
D. Changes in attitudes.
    1. Attitudes toward marriage have changed, although there is disagreement among sociologists

about how to interpret this.

a. Singlehood may be increasingly chosen simply as a lifelong option.

b. Or marriage may be postponed in order to pursue other goals first. More data support this second interpretation; apparently, most single people want to marry eventually, and most divorced people want to remarry eventually.

2. Attitudes toward being single have also changed. Generally, there is a more positive view, although many negative myths about single people persist.

a. Changed attitudes are reflected in public opinion polls.

(1) In the 1950s, singles were characterized as neurotic, immoral, and unattractive.

(2) In current polls, 75 percent of the respondents considered singles "normal."

b. Changed attitudes are also reflected in the media. A content analysis of articles in the Reader's Digest from 1900 on provides an example.

(1) Earlier themes in articles on single people: "Why am I single?" "How is my name to live on?"

(2) Recent themes: singlehood as a normal option, the variety of singles, changes in the image of single people, money, loneliness, freedom and responsibility, attitudes toward singles, personal safety.

IV. Typologies

Single people vary along many dimensions.

A. Reason for being single. Single people can be never married, annulled, divorced, or widowed.

B. Demographic characteristics. Many demographic characteristics have important implications for lifestyles and for a person's satisfaction with his or her lifestyle; these include race, sex, age, rural or urban residence, religion, and income. Thus, generalizations about "singles" are often unwarranted (such generalizations imply that, say, a 30-year-old yuppie, a 40-year-old nun, a 50-year-old who was recently divorced, and a 72-year-old widow can be grouped together).

C. Choice and stability. One effort to develop a "typology" of singles considers whether the status is voluntary or involuntary and whether it is likely to be temporary or permanent.

1. "Voluntary temporary." Younger never-married people and divorced people who are postponing marriage or remarriage. These people expect to marry but are currently more interested in other pursuits (e.g., career).

2. "Involuntary temporary." Singles who want and expect to marry or remarry and are actively seeking mates.

3. "Voluntary stable." Singles who do not want to marry or remarry. This category includes cohabitants and people whose lifestyles preclude marriage (e.g., priests and nuns).

4. "Involuntary stable." Generally older people who wanted to marry or remarry but have not found a mate. These people have accepted being single as probably permanent.

V. Common concerns

Despite these variations among single people, they do have some common concerns.

A. Discrimination in employment, income, or both.

B. Sex and sexually transmitted diseases.

C. Loneliness.

References for Lecture 2

Exter, T. (1992, September). Home alone in 2000. *American demographics, 14,*67.
Goldscheider, F. (1993). *Leaving home before marriage: Ethnicity, familism, and generational relationships.* Madison, Wis.: University of Wisconsin Press.
Keith, P. (1989). *The unmarried in later life.* New York: Praegen.

Lecture 3: Cohabitation

I.   Statistics

There has been a national increase in cohabitation--unmarried couples living together--since the 1970s.

A.   There are 3 to 4 times as many cohabitants today as there were in the 1970s.
B.   The extent of this change varies depending on region of the country (the incidence of cohabitation is generally higher in western states), age group, race, and previous marital status.

II.   Has cohabitation become institutionalized?

Posing the question. This increase gives rise to a question: Has cohabitation become institutionalized in the United States as part of the process of selecting a mate? This question can be phrased in at least two ways.

A.   One way to ask the question is: To what extent do cohabiting couples eventually marry? But there are problems with attempting to answer this question.
    1.   It could, in theory, be answered by prospective or longitudinal data, but in practice this approach is not easily accomplished.
    2.   Previous studies of unmarried cohabitants cannot answer the question with any certainty, for two reasons.
        a.   The samples are usually college students and thus are unrepresentative.
        b.   In most cases, data are retrospective (as opposed to longitudinal), and retrospective data are subject to memory bias.

B.   Another way to ask the question is: To what extent have contemporary married couples cohabited, as compared with couples in the past?
    1.   This phrasing makes the question more answerable.
    2.   In fact, this was the approach taken in a recent "case study" of a single Oregon county.

III.   HAS COHABITATION BECOME INSTITUTIONALIZED?-- ANSWERING THE QUESTION

The case study of a county in Oregon was one attempt to answer the question.

A.   Methodology. This study used archival data: marriage license applications completed in 1970 and 1980. Prospective bride and groom giving the same home address were counted as cohabitants. (The researchers also noted applicants' ages, race and ethnicity, previous marital status, and occupations.) This use of marriage license applications as a data base had both pros and cons.
    1.   One advantage: Since these are official, legal documents, the information reported is more likely to be accurate than survey or interview responses.
    2.   Two problems with the use of marriage license applications:
        a.   Couples may report their future joint residence as their address, for convenience (such couples would be inaccurately counted as cohabitants).
        b.   Couples may report different addresses--e.g., they might give their parents' home addresses--if they want to conceal cohabitation (such couples would be inaccurately counted as noncohabitants).
B.   Findings. The data were used to provide information about several points.
    1.   The researchers wanted to identify changes over time in the extent of premarital cohabitation.
        a.   They found many more cohabitants in 1980 (53 percent of the couples) than in 1970 (13 percent).

b. This increase for the Oregon county parallels available national data.

2. The researchers also wanted to identify changes over time in characteristics of cohabitants. They found somewhat more diversity among cohabitants in 1980 than in 1970.

a. There was more variation in age, previous marital status, race, and occupation. (In 1970, young, previously married, nonwhite, unemployed people, and people not in the labor force were more likely to cohabit than older, never-married, white, employed people.)

b. There are some differences between these Oregon data and recent analyses of census data: in census data, the greatest increases are seen in young people and previously married people.

3. The researchers also looked for changes over time in the similarity or dissimilarity of cohabiting partners.

a. Findings here would indicate whether cohabitation was being used as "trial marriage" by people statistically likely to divorce (that is, heterogeneous couples).

b. In this regard, no change over time was found. In both 1970 and 1980, cohabiting couples were more likely than noncohabitants to differ in age, previous marital status, and race.

4. The researchers also tried to determine if cohabitants delayed marriage longer than noncohabitants.

a. There was no sign of this in 1970, but ages at marriage were significantly higher for cohabitants in 1980. This case study is the first evidence for such a tendency.

b. There was also some general rise in age at first marriage over this time period. This allows speculation that the greater acceptance of cohabitation may be a factor contributing to later age at first marriage.

C. Conclusion. The tentative conclusion of this study is that there is a new normative pattern of courtship now including premarital cohabitation as a step between dating and marriage. Bases for this conclusion:

1. Extent of premarital cohabitation: More than half the marriage license applicants had apparently cohabited.

2. Greater diversity of cohabitants in 1980 than 1970: Cohabitation was apparently chosen by more types of people (not just by more of one or two types of people).

References for Lecture 3

American households: The 1990 census reveals dramatic changes in the American family. Here's what you need to know about married parents, single parents, childless couples, singles, and more.

(1992, July). *American Demographics, 14, Supplement 24.*

Cargan, L. & Melko, M. (1982). *Singles: Myths and realities.* Beverly Hills: Sage.

Cargan, L. (1991). *Marriages and families: Changing relationships.* New York: Harper Collins.

Lamanna, M. (1991). *Marriages and families: Making choices and facing change.* Belmont, CA: Wadsworth Publishing Co.

Schonpflug, W. (1993, January). Practical and theoretical psychology: Singles with wedding rings? *Applied psychology: An international review, 42*(1), 58-66.

Lecture 4: Transition to Parenthood

I.   Background: Rossi's work

Alice Rossi, a sociologist, wrote in the mid-1960s about the experience of becoming a parent and why this experience is especially difficult. Today, we need to consider two points about Rossi's work.

A. To what extent does her view still apply, and to whom does it apply (men, women, younger new parents, older new parents, etc.)?

B.   If the transition is so hard, what could be done to make it easier? How could parents be better prepared for parenting?

II.   Stages of transition

Four stages of transition to a role, such as parenthood, can be described.

A.   Anticipation. This first stage is a period of training, preparation, and socialization. An individual learns about the demands of the role and may acquire special skills or knowledge needed for it.
    1.   In the case of the parental role, the anticipatory period coincides with pregnancy.
    2.   It typically involves reading about infant and child care, talking with other parents, gathering supplies, attending courses, etc.
B.   Honeymoon. This second stage occurs immediately after the role is assumed. How long it lasts depends on individuals and situations.
    1.   For the parental role, the honeymoon stage begins when the child is born; its duration is different for different parents.
    2.   This is a period of intimacy, prolonged contact, and formation of mother-infant bonds.
    3.   It is also a period of learning for new parents. Only now can they learn about the unique characteristics of their infant and how these mesh with their own characteristics and expectations. (During pregnancy, by contrast, the child is mostly a fantasy.)
C.   Plateau. This third stage occurs when the role is being fully exercised.
    1.   For parents, it is a time when the child is dependent and they themselves are actively, intensively involved in being parents.
    2.   This stage could be subdivided, since a child's dependency (and thus the responses needed from parents) will change as the child matures.
D.   Termination. This fourth stage occurs when involvement in the role ends. One feature of the parental role is that

there is no clear termination, or perhaps no termination at all.

III.   Why the transition to parenthood is stressful

The parental role has certain unique--or at any rate distinctive--features which explain why the transition is stressful.

A.   Culture. There are cultural pressures to assume the role of parent, particularly for women: maternity is often equated with maturity.
B.   Inception. How the role is taken on is also a factor.
    1.   It may be involuntary (an unplanned pregnancy).
    2.   It is, under some circumstances, irrevocable. Once a pregnancy is begun, it may not be terminable. (When Rossi originally wrote, abortion was illegal; even today, many people do not consider it an option.) And once an infant is born, the parent is (typically) committed to the role for life (you cannot be an ex-parent while you and your child are both alive).
C.   Preparation. Often, preparation for the role of parent is deficient.
    1.   The educational system makes no attempt to provide parenting skills.
    2.   The transition is abrupt. Most preparation takes place "on the job." Parents immediately assume full responsibility for a completely dependent infant; there is no time to ease into the role, gradually taking on more and more challenging responsibilities.
    3.   Only limited learning is possible during pregnancy. Parents-to-be can learn some concrete skills but cannot prepare for a specific relationship with an individual infant.

References for Lecture 4

Belsky, J. (1994). *Transition to parenthood: How a first child changes a marriage: Which couples grow closer or apart, and why* (based on a landmark study). New York: Delacorte Press.
Crawford, D. & Husten, T. (1993, February). The impact of the transition to

parenthood on marital leisure. *Personality and social psychology bulletin, 19*, 39-46.

Emerson, J. (1992, December). Goodness of temperamental fit between infant and mother and maternal distress in the transition to parenthood. *Dissertation abstracts international, 53*(6-B), 3197.

Rossi, A. (1968). Transition to parenthood. *Journal of marriage and the family*, 30, 26-39.

Squire, S. (1993). *For better or worse: A candid chronicle of five couples adjusting to parenthood.* New York: Doubleday.

TOPIC FOR DEBATE

Should Training for Parenthood Be Mandatory?

Background

Most people would agree that being a good parent is a tremendously demanding undertaking. Surprisingly, however, it is one major challenge that is usually taken on with little or no formal, systematic training. Many people would argue that training for parenthood should be as much a part of contemporary American education as driver's education courses.

Parenting requires a diversity of skills and capacities, including knowledge of child development, basic first aid, home safety, and financial management; the ability to interact effectively with children; and the ability to give and receive affection. Just as the abilities needed for effective parenting can be identified, many (if not all) of them can be taught. In fact, many courses in effective parenting are already being offered throughout the country. Usually, the people enrolled in these courses are either exceptionally interested in children and parenting or considered "high-risk" parents on the basis of their age, education, or income. In both instances, parent effectiveness training seems to have proved its worth.

Advocates of mandatory parenthood training also point out that training (and often licensure) are required for many occupations which are far less critical than the "occupation" of parenthood. Hairdressers, electricians, and truck drivers, to give just a few examples, all take special courses of training. Surely, children have a right to the assurance that their parents will have received at least as much preparation.

Other people would argue, however, that training for parenthood is likely at best to be ineffective, and at worst to have negative consequences for parents and for society in general. Some believe that the "right stuff" needed for effective parenting cannot be specified, let alone taught. They would argue that parental love, the maternal instinct, or even the desire to be a parent cannot be taught. Others worry about who will decide what skills and standards of effective parenting would be taught and who would teach parenting courses. Choices regarding child rearing, like all important life decisions, stem from personal values and cultural background. In this context, systematic instruction in how to bring up children could be regarded as a step toward creating "Big Brother."

Finally, many people would point out that children are known to be resilient. If parents make mistakes in child rearing--and even the best-prepared parents are bound to make mistakes--their children still have every chance of developing into happy, productive adults.

Debate plan

Using the above background, and information from other sources (selected references appear below), student panels should debate the following positions:

Position A. Courses designed to prepare people to be effective parents should be a mandatory part of public, private, and parochial schooling.

Position B. Courses designed to prepare people to be effective parents should be available, but no one should be required to take them.

References for the debate

Berry, M. (1993). *The politics of parenthood: Childcare, women's rights, and the myth of the good mother.* New York: Viking.

Frankel, F. & Simmons, J. (1992, December). Parent behavioral training: Why and when some parents drop out. *Journal of clinical child psychology, 21*, 322-330.

Lovell, M. & Richey, C. (1991, November). Implementing agency-based social-support skill training. *Families in society, 72*, 563-572.

Rosier, K. (1993, July). Competent parents, complex lives: Managing parenthood in poverty. *Journal of contemporary* *ethnography,* 22, 171-204.

TOPICS FOR DISCUSSION

Topic 1: Two Models of Adult Development

1.   Ask students to state the general thesis of the normative-crisis model and to identify theorists associated with it (pages 436-442).

2.   Ask students to state the general thesis of the timing-of-events model and to identify major categories of life events considered in it and theorists associated with it (pages 442-443).

3.   Ask students which model-- normative-crisis or timing-of-events-- they consider the more adequate representation of personal change during adulthood, and why.

4.   As the authors note, much of the research on adult development has been concerned with <u>men's</u> development. Ask students to identify the implications of this limitation and ways in which models of adult development could change as researchers give more attention to women's patterns of development.

Topic 2: Marriage, Divorce, and Remarriage

1.   The authors describe associations between marriage and health and between marriage and happiness. Ask students to consider married couples they know and, on that basis, to suggest additional benefits of marriage. Also ask them to suggest personal costs or liabilities of marriage (or, alternatively, benefits of remaining single).

2.   In the section on divorce, the authors identify a number of possible reasons for the increased divorce rate in recent decades (pages 449-450). Ask students which of these reasons they consider most important and why. Also explore the liabilities of marriage and the benefits of remaining single that students identified previously as possible contributors to the divorce rate.

3.   Ask students to suggest ways in which a first marriage is likely to be different from and similar to subsequent marriages (page 451-452).

Topic 3: Parenthood

1.   In the section on parenthood, the authors identify several reasons for having children (pages 455). Ask students to evaluate each reason mentioned ("Is this a wise or an unwise basis for having a child?") and to explain their evaluation of each reason.

2.   Using the section "When People Have Children" (pages 455-456) as a basis, ask students to suggest the ideal age for having a first child. Also, ask them whether this age is different for men and for women; if so, why. You might also ask them to consider their responses to these questions in the context of the text material on the timing-of-events model.

3.   The last issue in the section "Finding Alternative Ways to Parenthood" deals with ethical questions concerning these alternatives (pages 456-459). Ask students if they find any of these alternatives ethically troublesome; if so, why.

Topic 4: Friendship in Adulthood

1.   Ask students to identify the factors that are now most important in their own choice of friends and maintenance of friendships. You might want to comment on differences and similarities between the factors identified by men and women in the class or by older and younger students. Ask them to identify differences between these factors and factors that they believe they would have identified when they were 5 or 10 years younger.

PROJECTS AND CLASS EXERCISES

Group Exercise: Choices in Adult Life

Working in groups, students should complete a "tree diagram" representing the alternatives which unfold from a decision that is critical for most young adults: to marry or not to marry. The group's diagram should specify two or more alternatives confronted following a decision to marry (e.g., to have children or not to have children) and two or more alternatives confronted following a decision not to marry (e.g., to remain celibate or to enter a sexual relationship). The diagram should continue as far as the group's imagination (and class time) allows, again showing two or more alternatives confronted following each subsequent decision of adult life. At the outset of this exercise, students should identify personal characteristics (e.g., gender, social class) which would affect the particular alternatives that unfold and explain their selection of these characteristics.

Project 1: Women's Development in Adulthood

Students should read primary source material discussing women's development in adulthood and write a paper comparing this material with the authors' discussion of women's adult development on pages 441-442.

Project 2: The Decline of Age-Consciousness

Students should interview several relatives or acquaintances of various ages regarding the "right" ages to do certain things. Table 13-2 on page 444 should provide a basis for constructing an interview schedule. Students should write a paper summarizing the interviews and supporting whether or not the responses reflect a decline in age-consciousness.

Project 3: Violence between Spouses

Students should locate a shelter for battered women in the community and interview a worker there. Interview topics should include the worker's views on factors contributing to spouse abuse as well as how society could most effectively respond to the problem. Students should write a paper summarizing the interview.

Project 4: Alternative Ways of Becoming a Parent

Students should select one of the alternatives described in the text and write a paper summarizing its medical, psychological, and ethical implications.

ESSAY QUESTIONS

1.   Discuss the thesis of the normative-crisis model and identify theorists associated with it.

Answer guideline. According to the normative-crisis model, human development occurs in a definite sequence of age-related social and emotional transitions. Erikson is one theorist associated with this position; he believes that the transition which normatively occurs in early adulthood is intimacy versus isolation. Other theorists associated with the normative-crisis model are Vaillant and Levinson. Levinson believes that a life structure with age-related periods of transition and reformation is the normative pattern.

2.   Discuss the thesis of the timing-of-events model and describe the types of events considered in it.

Answer guideline. According to the timing-of-events model, adult development is shaped by which events one experiences and when those events occur. This model includes consideration of normative life events (those that people expect, since most people experience them), nonnormative life events (those that people normally do not expect), individual events (those that affect one person or one family), and cultural events (those that affect the social context in which development takes place).

3.   According to the text, what are the benefits of marriage?

Answer guideline. Marriage ideally provides friendship, affection, and companionship. Studies conducted before the 1980s found that married people (particularly those without children) tended to report greater happiness, although more recent studies have found little difference in the happiness reported by married and unmarried respondents. Marriage is also associated with better health, although it is unclear why this association exists.

4.   What are the "pulls" and "pushes" promoting a decision to remain single?

Answer guideline. In a recent interview study, single young adults described both incentives to remain single and disincentives to getting married. The incentives for the single

life included career opportunities,
self-sufficiency, sexual freedom, and mobility
and personal freedom. The disincentives of
marriage included the restrictions of
monogamy, limited mobility and personal
freedom, and the threats of poor
communication, sexual frustration, and
restrictions on friendships.

5.   According to the text, how has sexual
      activity in marriage changed over the
      past several decades?

Answer guideline. Husbands and wives have
sex more frequently today than they did in
previous decades, engage in a wider variety of
sexual practices, and report more pleasure
from their sexual relations. These changes
seem to reflect more open attitudes toward
sexuality, a generally higher level of sexual
knowledge, the wider availability of
contraceptives (including more effective
contraceptives) and abortion, and changes in
women's attitudes toward their sexuality.

6.   Identify factors which distinguish
      marriages that deteriorate after
      parenthood from those that improve.

Answer guideline. The study conducted by
Belsky and Rovine revealed that, in
deteriorating marriages, the partners were
more likely to be younger and less educated,
to earn less money, and to have been married
for fewer years.

7.   Discuss the psychological effects of
      infertility.

Answer guideline. Infertility is difficult for
most people to accept, and it can put a severe
strain on the marital relationship. People who
are infertile may become angry with themselves, their partners, and their doctors; they
may also feel worthless and depressed. For
many couples, the sexual relationship suffers
as well.

8.   What are the characteristics of
      friendship in adulthood?

Answer guideline. In a recent interview
study, young adults identified respect, trust,
mutual enjoyment, mutual understanding and
acceptance, willingness to help one another,
and a feeling of freedom of self-expression as
characteristic of their friendships. Most often,
adults' "best" friendships are same-sex
relationships.

CHAPTER 14

PHYSICAL AND INTELLECTUAL DEVELOPMENT IN MIDDLE ADULTHOOD

INTRODUCTION

Chapter 14 examines physical and intellectual development in middle adulthood, the period between the ages of 40 and 65 years.

- The physical changes which occur during this period are discussed, including: changes in reproductive and sexual capacity, appearance, and loss of reserve capacity.

- The general status of health of middle adults is described, and various health concerns and problems of this age group are also discussed.

- In the area of intellectual development, the chapter examines intelligence and cognition in adults and discusses various aspects of the adult learner.

- Occupational patterns are described and factors related to work in middle adulthood, such as occupational stress and career changes, are considered.

CHAPTER OUTLINE

PHYSICAL DEVELOPMENT

I. PHYSICAL CHANGES OF MIDDLE AGE

A. SENSORY AND PSYCHOMOTOR FUNCTIONING
  1. Vision, Hearing, Taste, and Smell
  2. Strength, Coordination, and Reaction Time
  3. Physiological Changes
B. SEXUALITY
  1. Sexual Activity
  2. Reproductive and Sexual Capacity
    a. Menopause
      (1) Physical effects of menopause
      (2) Psychological effects of menopause
    b. The male climacteric
C. APPEARANCE: THE DOUBLE STANDARD OF AGING

II. HEALTH IN MIDDLE AGE

A. HEALTH STATUS
B. HEALTH PROBLEMS
  1. Diseases and Disorders
  2. The Impact of Stress on Health
    a. Can stressful life events lead to illness?
    b. Why does stress affect some people more than others?
      (1) Control and stress
      (2) Personality and stress: Behavioral patterns and heart disease
  3. Death Rates and Causes of Death
C. THE IMPACT OF RACE AND SOCIOECONOMICS ON HEALTH

INTELLECTUAL DEVELOPMENT

III. ASPECTS OF INTELLECTUAL DEVELOPMENT IN MIDDLE ADULTHOOD

A. INTELLIGENCE AND COGNITION
  1. Psychometrics: Does Intelligence Change in Adulthood
  2. Mature Thinkers: Does Cognition Change in Adulthood
    a. Integrative thinking
    b. Practical problem solving
B. THE ADULT LEARNER

IV. WORK IN MIDDLE ADULTHOOD

A. OCCUPATIONAL PATTERNS
  1. Pattern 1: Stable Careers
  2. Pattern 2: Changing Careers
B. OCCUPATIONAL STRESS
C. UNEMPLOYMENT
D. WORK AND INTELLECTUAL GROWTH

KEY TERMS

burnout (page 492)
climacteric (475)
crystallized intelligence (485)
fluid intelligence (485)
hypertension (480)
male climacteric (478)
menopause (475)
osteoporosis (475)
presbycusis (473)
presbyopia (473)
stress (480)
substantive complexity (493)

LEARNING OBJECTIVES

After finishing Chapter 14, students should be able to:

1. Identify the period known as middle age and the markers that denote it. (p. 472)

2. List some common physical abilities which decline in middle adulthood. (pp. 473-474)

3. Describe the compensations that can be made for the changes listed in Item 2. (pp. 473-474)

4. Discuss sexuality in midlife. (pp. 474-475)

5. Describe *menopause* and its effects, both physical and psychological. (pp. 475-477)

6. Describe the *male climacteric* and its effects, both physical and psychological. (pp. 477-478)

7. Describe the "double standard of aging" in the United States. (pp. 478-479)

8. List the major health problems of middle age. (pp. 479-480)

9. Describe the impact of stress on health. (pp. 480-482)

10. Discuss the impact of race and socioeconomics on health. (pp. 482-484)

11. Discuss the results and appropriateness of standardized intelligence testing on middle-aged adults. (pp. 484-486)

12. Explain the term "fluid intelligence." (p. 485)

13. Explain the term "crystallized intelligence." (p. 485)

14. Compare and contrast fluid intelligence and crystallized intelligence. (pp. 485-486)

15. Describe the processes of integrative thinking and problem solving in middle age. (pp. 486-489)

16. Identify the characteristics and attitudes of adults who attend school. (p. 489)

17. Describe different occupational patterns of middle-aged people. (pp. 490-491)

18. Describe how occupational stress can affect physical and emotional well-being. (pp. 491-492)

19. Discuss the effects of unemployment on middle-aged people. (pp. 492-493)

20. Discuss how the work people do affects their intellectual growth. (pp. 493-495)

CHAPTER SUMMARY AND TEACHING RECOMMENDATIONS

In the first section of the chapter, covering physical development in middle adulthood, the authors describe changes in sensory functioning and in strength, coordination, and reaction time. They also note that these changes are gradual and that most middle-aged people compensate for them without realizing that they are doing so. The latter point is especially important to stress in class: students sometimes overreact to information on physical "decline" in middle age.

The section continues with a discussion of changes in reproductive and sexual capacity. In another medical breakthrough, some women who have already experienced menopause are choosing to become pregnant through donor eggs and the in vitro fertilization process (women in their late forties, fifties and early sixties). This has created quite a controversy around the world. The authors describe menopause and associated physiological and psychological changes, including the possible development of osteoporosis. Given the current interest in and concern about osteoporosis, you may want to supplement the information in the text with a lecture, a film, or a guest speaker.

The section also includes a brief description of the male climacteric.

The authors discuss the "double standard of aging" with regard to physical appearance; you may want to address this topic together with age changes in reproductive and sexual functioning. In discussing menopause in class, you could stress that, for most women, the psychological effects are minimal and that age changes in appearance are likely to have far greater psychological and sexual impact.

The section on physical development closes with a discussion of health in middle adulthood. The authors take up common diseases and disorders, the connection between stress and illness, and causes of death. You may want to add that a general and important change is a shift from experiencing mostly acute illnesses during childhood, adolescence, and early adulthood to experiencing mostly chronic illnesses during middle adulthood and old age.

The next section of the chapter deals with intellectual development in middle adulthood. The authors review findings from psychometric studies of intelligence, noting that performance in most areas is stable or even increases through middle adulthood. The authors also raise questions about the appropriateness of widely used measures of intelligence for middle-aged adults. Later in the course, you may want to refer back to this point when you are discussing psychometric performance in old age; potential problems with test content and testing practices (e.g., timed testing) are also apparent in that context. The authors also review research on problem solving in adulthood, emphasizing that middle-aged people are often particularly adept at solving practical problems; you may want to discuss the latter point in terms of job performance and family life for adults of various ages.

The authors next consider "adult learners," describing adults' motivations for returning to school and common problems middle-aged people face in school. If your class includes older students, this topic could be an excellent starting point for a discussion.

The final section of the chapter deals with various work-related issues. The authors outline typical career patterns in the United States today and identify common sources of occupational stress and burnout. They also note consequences of unemployment, and they describe how work can contribute to continued intellectual and personal growth throughout adulthood.

Boxes in Chapter 14 are "Preventing Osteoporosis," "Japanese Women's Experience of Menopause," "Moral Leadership in Middle and Late Adulthood," and "Creativity Takes Hard Work."

AUDIOVISUAL MATERIALS

Distributor, date, and running time are given for each film or video. Distributors' addresses are listed in the appendix (General Resources). If a film or video is not in color, there is a notation (BW) to that effect.

Menopause. (CORT, 1983, video, 19 min.) A detailed, animated explanation of the menopause process is given.
Age-related sensory losses. (UFV, 1975, video, approximately 15 min.) Topics include normal age-related changes in vision, when they typically begin, and how they affect daily functioning.
Slowing the clock. (FFHS, 1994, video, 26 min.) This program shows how the aging process can be slowed down.
Sex, lies, and toupee tape. (FFHS, 1994, video, 60 min.) This NOVA program discusses why hair loss occurs, whom it affects most, and what treatments are available.
The middle years. (UFV, 1976, 20 min. approximately) Topics include psychological and emotional challenges of midlife.
How to live longer...better. (FFHS, 1994, video, 25 min.) Discusses the life-style changes that are playing an important part in extending the life span of Americans.
Pregnancy after 35. (FFHS, 1994, video, 19 min.) The risks of pregnancy after age 35 and the medical technology used to minimize these risks are discussed.
Getting a handle on stress. (FFHS, 1994, video, 26 min.) This program explains the effects of stress and how stress can be managed and visits a stress management course that teaches stress reduction techniques.
Women and stress. (FFHS, 1994, video, 28 min.) Women of various age groups discuss stress.

Guest speakers

Osteoporosis is arousing a great deal of interest and concern; you could probably locate a speaker on this topic (most likely, a nurse) through a local hospital or women's health center. Work-related issues are another set of topics that could be effectively addressed by a guest speaker; you might try to locate a counselor, social worker, or industrial psychologist who works with clients experiencing occupational stress or burnout, or with workers who have been laid off or are unemployed.

LECTURE OUTLINES

Lecture 1: Some Age Changes in Sensory Functioning

I.   Vision

Changes in the physical structure of the eye during adulthood result in changes in visual perception. For middle-aged adults, these changes are detectable (e.g., during an eye examination or in laboratory studies) but rarely impair daily functioning. Changes continue to progress and become more noticeable in later adulthood.

A. Lens.
  1. Functioning of the lens. Light passes through the lens, which changes shape to focus visual images onto sensory cells in the retina.
  2. Changes in the lens.
     a. Lens becomes less flexible as dead cells shed and accumulate on and within it.
     b. Later in adulthood (usually), the lens becomes clouded and opaque. Extreme clouding of the lens is called <u>cataracts</u>.
  3. Effects of changes in the lens.
     a. With decreasing flexibility:
        (1) The lens is less able to focus, and farsightedness (presbyopia) results.
        (2) Flexibility begins to decrease in childhood, but farsightedness is usually not noticed until the forties or fifties.
     b. With increasing cloudiness and opacity:
        (1) Color discrimination is decreased; blues and greens become particularly hard to distinguish.
        (2) Susceptibility to glare is increased (since light is scattered differently within the eye by a clouded as opposed to a clear lens).
        (3) Cataracts, which are much more common in old age (the seventies and eighties), impair vision, but may be surgically correctable.
B. Iris, pupil, and retina.
  1. Functioning of the iris, pupil, and retina.
     a. The iris contracts in response to light, thus controlling the size of the pupil; the rods and cones are located in the retina.
     b. Normally, when the level of light decreases, the iris expands; thus, the pupil becomes larger, and more of the available light is focused (by the lens) on the rods (which are primarily involved in low-level vision).
  2. Changes in the iris, pupil, and retina.
     a. In adulthood, the iris reacts more slowly and with less magnitude to changes in light.
     b. Maximum size of the pupil decreases as the reaction of the iris decreases, and so less of the available light can potentially reach the retina.
     c. With aging, the retina loses rods.
  3. Effects of changes in the iris, pupil, and retina.
     a. These changes are important to the process of dark adaptation.
     b. Overall impact: Dark adaptation takes longer for middle-aged and older adults and occurs to a lesser extent. That is, vision takes longer to adjust, and the adjustment is not as complete as it was earlier in life.

II. Hearing

There are also changes in hearing during adulthood.

A. Presbycusis. Older adults typically cannot hear sounds of higher frequency (this is the range of conversational speech) at the same volume as young adults. However, the condition is rarely noticeable under normal conditions until later adulthood.
B. By age 70, there is some loss in hearing throughout the human frequency range. (Most of the loss is in the higher frequencies.)

References for Lecture 1

Hampton, J. (1991). *The biology of human aging*. Dubuque, IA: William C. Brown.
Jackson, J., Chatters, L., & Taylor, R. (Eds.). (1993). *Aging in black America*. Newbury Park, CA: Sage.
Walk, R. D. (1981). *Perceptual development*. Monterey, CA: Brooks/Cole.

Lecture 2: Neugarten's Research on Menopause

I. Methodology

Bernice Neugarten conducted a classic study of women's attitudes toward menopause, with interviews and the development of a checklist.

A. Neugarten used unstructured interviews with women in their forties and fifties who varied in self-assessed menopausal status.

1. Most women were eager, or at least willing, to discuss menopause.
2. Many wanted more information about menopause.
3. Most were aware of "folk wisdom" about menopause, even if they did not believe it.

B. Checklist. On the basis of these interviews, Neugarten developed an "Attitudes toward Menopause (ATM) Checklist": statements about menopause to which women responded by indicating agreement or disagreement.
   1. ATM checklist was administered to 100 young (21-44) women, 100 middle-aged (45-55) women, and 65 older (56-65) women.
      a. All were married and living with their husbands, all had children, and all were in good health.
      b. Few of the young women, but most of the older women, had experienced menopause at the time of the interview.
   2. Objective of the ATM checklist was to see if attitudes toward menopause differed depending on women's age or menopausal status.

II. Findings

Differences in attitudes toward menopause were identified in Neugarten's sample.

A. Generally, more positive attitudes toward menopause were associated with greater age, greater experience with menopause, or both.
   1. Middle-aged and older women (but not younger women) recognized a definite postmenopausal "recovery" (they generally felt better, were more confident, were calmer, and felt freer than before).
   2. Middle-aged and older women were less likely than younger women to see menopause as a major change in their lives.
   3. Middle-aged and older women were less likely than younger women to believe that suffering (physical or psychological) related to menopause is inevitable.
B. For other aspects of attitudes toward menopause, either no age differences or inconsistent age differences were identified.

III. Conclusions

Neugarten drew some general conclusions.

A. Menopause was not seen as a major or serious loss by middle-aged or older women. Thus, the psychoanalytic view of menopause as a "closing of the gates" would be inaccurate for these women; furthermore, reproductive capacity was not supremely valued by them.
B. There seemed to be two reasons why young, premenopausal women generally had a more negative view of menopause.
   1. They saw menopause as a far-off, vague event, not differentiated from the aging process.
   2. Middle-aged and older women's greater experience with menopause allowed them to separate fact from folklore.

References for Lecture 2

Braus, P. (1993, March). Facing menopause. *American demographics, 15*, 44-48.
Chira, S. (January 2, 1994). Of a certain age and in a family way. *New York Times*.
Neugarten, B. L., Wood, V., Kraines, R. J., & Loomis, B. (1963). Women's attitudes toward the menopause. *Vita humana, 6*, 140-151.
Pavelka, M. & Fedigan, L. (1991). Menopause: A comparative life history perspective. *American journal of physical anthropology, Supplement 13,* 13-38.
Riding, A. (January 4, 1994). French government proposes ban on pregnancies after menopause. *New York Times*.
Schneider, K. (1992, May). Birth at 52. *People weekly, 37,* 101-102.

Lecture 3: Health Changes in Middle Adulthood

I.   Subjects

Longitudinal data on changes in health and physical functioning during adulthood can be found in a study reported by L. M. Bayer and others.

A. Characteristics of subjects.
   1. Subjects were mostly white.
   2. Subjects were mostly middle-class.
   3. Number of males and females was approximately equal.

B. How the subjects were studied.
1. Collection of data on physical, intellectual, and personality development began in the late 1920s, when the subjects were very young children; data collection continued until about 1980, when the remaining subjects were very elderly.
2. Data on health in middle adulthood were based on interviews conducted when the subjects were in their forties and fifties.

II. Findings

Data on health were obtained from physicians' assessments of the subjects and from the subjects' self-assessments.

A. Physicians' assessments included medical records of illnesses and physicians' overall ratings of subjects' health at various ages.
1. Illnesses (medical records).
    a. Percentages of men and women reporting many types of illnesses increased during middle adulthood.
    b. There was a shift from mostly acute illnesses (e.g., broken arm or sprained ankle impairing mobility) to mostly chronic illnesses (e.g., arthritis impairing mobility).
2. Physicians' overall ratings of health.
    a. Overall ratings were made when the subjects were 34, 42, and 50 years old and were based on frequency, severity, and duration of illnesses and on the impact of physical problems on daily activity.
    b. Between adolescence and the fifties, the average rating for men and women declined from "good" to "fair." Note that this could be cohort-specific, since data were gathered from the 1940s to 1960s. (Today's increased health consciousness and increased information about how lifestyle affects health may mean that similar changes would not appear in future cohorts.)
B. Self-assessments by the subjects.
1. In interviews conducted when they were in their thirties, forties, and fifties, the subjects were questioned about their view of their own health and about changes in their health.
2. Most (more than 80 percent) rated their own health as "excellent" or "good."
3. These percentages were similar to those for national samples studied at approximately the same times.

III. Conclusions

Certain characteristics are apparently related to health status in middle adulthood.

A. Health habits.
1. Two health habits associated with health status were smoking and drinking.
2. The strength of this association increased throughout adulthood. Thus, these factors evidently have a cumulative impact on health.
B. Socioeconomic status: education.
1. For males, the subjects' own educational level was positively related to health status.
2. For females, a subject's health status was positively related to her husband's educational level.

References for Lecture 3

Bayer, L., Whissell-Buechy, D., & Honzik, M. (1981). Health in the middle years. In D. Eichorn, J. Clausen, N. Haan, M. Honzig, & P. Mussen (Eds.), *Present and past in middle life.* New York: Academic.
Davis, N., Cole, E., & Rothblum, E. (Eds.). *Faces of women and aging.* New York: Haworth.
Julian, T. (1992, October-December). Components of mens' well-being at mid-life. *Issues in mental health nursing, 13*(4), 285-299.

Lecture 4: Careers in Middle Adulthood

I. Subjects

Longitudinal data on changes in men's and women's careers during adulthood can be found in studies reported by Clausen and Stroud. With regard to work and careers, the experiences of the cohort in this research are different from contemporary experience, but examining them is still important; there are few longitudinal data sets of this scope describing life-span development.

A. Characteristics of subjects.
1. Subjects were mostly white.
2. Subjects were mostly middle-class.
3. Number of males and females was approximately equal.
B. How the subjects were studied.
1. Collection of data on physical, intellectual, and personality development began in the late 1920s, when the subjects were very young children; data collection continued until about 1980, when the remaining subjects were very elderly.
2. Different analytic approaches were used for men's and women's careers, since for this cohort, men's and women's experiences with the labor market were quite different.

II. Career development for men

It is useful to consider the male subjects in terms of their work profiles as a group and in terms of their satisfaction with work.

A. Occupational profile.
1. The sample represented a wide range of occupations but was slanted toward administrative, business, and professional positions.
2. Upward occupational mobility was typical of the sample: Most held more prestigious jobs than their fathers had held at the same age. At least three factors contributed to this trend.
   a. There were historical changes in types of careers available.
   b. This sample was somewhat elite (participants lived near a major university).
   c. Attrition had an effect: More downwardly mobile subjects dropped out of the study more often than other subjects.
B. Men's feelings about their careers.
1. Job satisfaction.
   a. Most of the male subjects were satisfied with their current jobs and with their career progress to this point in their lives.
   b. Factors in job satisfaction for these men:
      (1) Intrinsic features were most important--extent to which a job reflected their personal interests, made use of their talents, and gave them freedom to develop their own ideas.
      (2) Extrinsic features (e.g., salary, fringe benefits, hours, working conditions) were less important: income was the only extrinsic feature related to job satisfaction.
2. Aspirations.
   a. Most male subjects expected to stay with the same type of work and with the same employer.
   b. Most male subjects in their early forties hoped for further advancement, but few in their fifties expected or hoped to advance.
3. Commitment to careers.
   a. Most male subjects exhibited moderate to high investment in their careers (they worked 48 hours a week).
   b. Investment decreased between the forties and the fifties for most workers; but professionals and top executives showed increased commitment over this age span.

III. Career development for women

For women, it is useful to consider career patterns and their association with psychological functioning.

A. Career patterns for women. In this sample, four patterns were identified on the basis of employment status (work outside the home) and subjective "career involvement" (assessed in interviews) at middle age:
1. "Work committed." The first pattern was shown by women who were working and deeply involved in their careers.
2. "Double track." The second pattern was shown by women who were working but had lower levels of career involvement.
3. "Homemakers." Women in pattern 3 were not working at middle age and had never worked since having children.
4. "Unstable." Women in pattern 4 had irregular work histories and relatively low levels of career involvement. ("Off-time" career transitions for this cohort would

involve working while their children were young and leaving the labor force when the children were older.)

B.   Career patterns and psychological functioning in middle adulthood. The following associations were found:

1.   "Homemakers" had the highest levels of morale and self-esteem.

2.   "Work committed" women had somewhat lower, but still above-average, levels of morale and self-esteem. They had satisfying relationships with others and were more independent than homemakers.

3.   "Double track" women had low levels of morale and self-esteem but high levels of assertiveness and independence.

4.   "Unstable" women showed poor psychological functioning at midlife. They were hostile and dissatisfied with themselves, their work, and their family roles.

References for Lecture 4

Coleman, M. & Pencavel, J. (1993, July). Trends in market work behavior of women since 1940. *Industrial and labor relations review, 46,* 653-676.

Elder, G. & Pavalko, E. (1993, July). Work careers in men's later years: Transitions and historical change. *Journal of gerontology, 48,* 180-191.

Herrig, C. & Wilson-Sadberry, K. (1993, May). Preference or necessity? Changing work roles of black and white women. *Journal of marriage and the family, 55,* 314-325.

Huck, C. (1992, November). Midlife career changes of men and women. *Dissertation abstracts international, 53*(5-A), 1401.

Shelton, B. A. (1992). *Women, men, and time: Gender differences in paid work.* New York: Greenwood Press.

Stroud, J. G. (1981). Women's careers: Work, family, and personality. In D. H. Eichorn, J. A. Clausen, N. Haan, M. P. Honzik, & P. H. Mussen (Eds.), *Present and past in middle life.* New York: Academic.

TOPIC FOR DEBATE

Should the "Three Boxes" of Life Be Reorganized?

Background

In a book called *The Three Boxes of Life,* Richard Bolles argues that the "traditional" pattern of life--with education concentrated in the early years, work in the middle portion, and leisure in the final years--may be maladaptive and thus unwise. He argues that people should, instead, intersperse periods of education, work, and leisure throughout the life cycle. Arguments can be offered both for and against Bolles's proposition.

One of Bolles's strongest arguments has to do with personal growth and fulfillment. He asserts that most people will simply enjoy life more and develop more fully as complex individuals, if they experience education, work, and leisure in all periods of their lives. One could further argue that individual experiences of each of these three basic "boxes" of life--education, work, and leisure--would be enhanced. For example, students could be expected to show greater motivation for learning if their education were tied to concurrent work experience; work performance, similarly, might be improved if workers were allowed periodic "sabbaticals" for leisure. One could also argue that, given these benefits to individuals, our culture and nation as a whole would benefit from redesign of the life cycle.

However, one can certainly argue against Bolles's proposal. First, balancing education, work, and leisure over the life span would not guarantee greater fulfillment. In fact, some people might argue that such a plan would be unnecessarily stressful: it would defy the traditional ""social clock" and thus entail repeated "off-time" life transitions. It is also possible that our experiences of each of the three basic "boxes" would be impaired, not enhanced by this redesign. Specialized education, as well as career advancement and recognition, may well require a continuous, long-term investment of time; and leisure may be most enjoyable as an uninterrupted respite from such time investments.

Finally, many people would say that social institutions would be more likely to suffer than to benefit. Certainly, Bolles's plan would make it more difficult for society to predict and prepare for demands on its educational institutions, or for the size and composition of the labor force.

Debate plan

Using this background, and information from additional sources (selected references appear below), student panels should debate the following positions:

Position A. Individuals should intersperse education, work, and leisure throughout their lifetimes.

Position B. Individuals should continue to devote the early part of life to education, the middle part to work, and the final part to leisure.

Reference for the debate

Bartalus, M. (1993). Work, health, and recreation: Aspects of the total person. *Loss, grief, and care, 6*(4), 7-14.
Bolles, R. N. (1979). *The three boxes of life.* Berkeley, CA: Ten Speed.
Bolles, R. N. (1981). *The three boxes of life and how to get out of them: An introduction to life/work planning.* Berkeley, CA: Ten Speed Press.

TOPICS FOR DISCUSSION

Topic 1: The Double Standard of Aging

1.   Ask students to explain what the authors mean by the "double standard" of aging (pages 478-479). Ask them if they agree a double standard exists.

2.   Ask students to describe portrayals of middle-aged and elderly men and women in the popular media (television, movies, magazines, etc.). Ask them how these portrayals reflect and contribute to a double standard of aging.

3.   Ask students to speculate on how society would have to change in order to eradicate the double standard of aging (on the assumption that such a phenomenon does exist). Ask them to speculate also on how the eradication of the double standard would affect individual men and women of all ages.

Topic 2: Cognitive Changes in Middle Adulthood

1.   Ask students to identify characteristics of mature thinkers, and middle-aged people's performance in solving practical problems (pages 486-489).

2.   Ask students to discuss the implications of these aspects of adult cognition for family relationships and performance at work during middle adulthood.

3.   Ask students to summarize the problems commonly experienced by adult learners that the authors identify (page 489). If your class includes some older students, ask them to comment on the accuracy of the authors' discussion and to suggest additional problems or concerns. Ask students how colleges and universities could adapt to minimize these problems for older students, and what costs would be entailed in making such adaptations.

Topic 3: Unemployment

1.   Some people maintain that unemployment is most stressful for white males. Present this idea to the students, and ask them to generate arguments for and against it.

2.   Ask students to suggest intervention or support programs that could be offered to help unemployed people cope with this crisis. Also, ask students to identify costs (financial and other) that would be entailed in implementing such programs.

PROJECTS AND CLASS EXERCISES

Group Exercise: Sex Education for Adults

The text describes reproductive changes that middle-aged men and women experience. These changes are at least as extensive as those experienced at puberty, but there have been relatively few efforts to educate adults about them (in comparison with the intensive efforts to provide sex education for teenagers).

Working in groups, students should design a sex education program for middle-aged people. The group should describe (1) what topics would be included in the program, (2) how the program would be "marketed" to convince middle-aged adults that it would be useful to them, and (3) what positive and negative consequences program participants could expect to experience.

Project 1: Double Standard of Aging

Students should find portrayals of middle-aged men and women in popular magazines and identify recurring themes, images, and gender roles in the portrayal of each sex. They should write a paper presenting their findings and discussing them in light of the text material on the double standard of aging.

Project 2: Nontraditional Students

Students should research the experiences of nontraditional students at your institution. The resulting papers should include statistics on the number of nontraditional students at the institution, describe efforts to recruit and retain nontraditional students and support services available specifically for them, and report on an interview with a nontraditional student.

Project 3: Midlife Career Changes

Students should interview a middle-aged person who has recently changed careers or is in the process of making such a change. Interview topics should include the motivation for making the change; problems encountered in the process of change; how these problems are being dealt with; finally, the interviewee's expectations for the future, including intellectual and social benefits (or drawbacks) of the career change. Students should write a paper describing the interview.

ESSAY QUESTIONS

1. How do vision and hearing change during middle adulthood?

Answer guideline. One of the most common changes in vision is development of farsightedness, or presbyopia; this occurs because the lens of the eye becomes less flexible with age and thus less able to focus readily. Other changes in vision are a slight loss in the sharpness of vision and a need for more light in order to see well. Presbycusis is a common change in hearing; this is a gradual loss in hearing, particularly for sounds of higher frequencies.

2. Describe the physical and psychological changes that women experience at menopause.

Answer guideline. As a result of declining production of estrogen, women experience physical symptoms which may include hot flashes, thinning of the vaginal lining, urinary dysfunction, and osteoporosis. Most women experience few psychological effects of menopause.

3. Describe the health status of most middle-aged adults.

Answer guideline. Most middle-aged adults are in very good health. Most rate their health quite positively, and few suffer from conditions which impair their activities.

4. What are the findings of psychometric studies of middle-aged adults' cognitive abilities, and what are reasons for being skeptical of these findings?

Answer guideline. In psychometric studies, performance on measures of different abilities peaks at different points in adulthood. Fluid intelligence (the ability to solve novel problems) seems to decline after early adulthood, but crystallized intelligence (the ability to apply previously learned material) seems to increase throughout adulthood. It is important to be skeptical of these findings because traditional intelligence tests may not be valid measures of adults' intelligence; such tests were originally designed for children.

5. Describe the performance of middle-aged adults in studies of practical problem solving.

Answer guideline. Although middle-aged adults do not perform as well as young adults on "twenty questions" types of tasks, they usually perform much better than young adults in studies designed to measure the ability to solve practical problems (e.g., "Your basement is flooded"; "You are stranded in a car during a blizzard"; "Your 8-year-old child is late coming home from school"). In these studies, middle-aged adults had a greater fund of actual problem-solving experiences on which to draw.

6.   Identify common sources of occupational
     stress.

Answer guideline. Sources of occupational
stress include insufficient promotions or
raises, low salaries, dull work, lack of
authority, a heavy work load, problems with a
boss or supervisor, ambiguous guidelines
regarding job performance, barriers to
expressing frustration or anger, and difficulties
in coordinating work and family
responsibilities. Workers in certain
occupations, including low-status health care
occupations and personal service jobs, have
particularly high rates of admission to
community mental health centers.

7.   What are common motivations for
     changing careers in midlife?

Answer guideline. One reason for changing
careers in midlife is today's life expectancy:
many people realistically conclude that there is
time during life for more than one career.
Others change careers involuntarily when they
are unemployed or divorced, or when
technology makes their initial career obsolete.
Many women change careers when their
children reach adolescence or adulthood and
no longer need as much day-to-day care and
supervision. Still others change careers out of
boredom or frustration or because they face
fewer financial burdens at this point in their
lives and are anxious to take on the challenge
of a new career.

CHAPTER 15

PERSONALITY AND SOCIAL DEVELOPMENT IN MIDDLE ADULTHOOD

INTRODUCTION

Midlife is a time to search for meaning in one's life with respect to the achievement of earlier goals and ambitions (particularly in the areas of careers and intimate relationships), often with a recognition that if there are changes to be made, one will need to act quickly.

- **Chapter 15** begins with a discussion of the stressful period during the middle to early forties which supposedly accounts for the common changes in personality and lifestyle during middle adulthood. This period is referred to as the midlife crisis.

- The chapter then examines middle adulthood (ages 40 to 65) from several theoretical perspectives: those of Carl Jung, Erik Erikson, and Robert Peck.

- Men's development in middle adulthood is discussed in light of the research of George Vaillant and Daniel Levinson, and women's development is discussed

from the viewpoint of research on a variety of themes.

- A discussion of the pervasiveness of the midlife crisis forms the basis for an evaluation of the normative-crisis model for development in middle adulthood.

- The text discusses several important relationships from the perspective of the timing-of-events model, including a variety of important events such as changes in: marriages (which often end in divorce at this time), sexual relationships, relationships with siblings, friendships, relationships with one's own maturing children, and relationships with parents.

- The chapter concludes with a discussion of the changes brought about as a result of the strain that accompanies the demands of caring for aging and often infirm parents.

CHAPTER OUTLINE

KEY TERMS

emotional flexibility versus emotional impoverishment (page 503)
"empty nest" (515)
generativity versus stagnation (503)
interiority (504)
mental flexibility versus mental rigidity (503)
midlife crisis (500)
socializing versus sexualizing in human relationships (503)
valuing wisdom versus valuing physical powers (503)

LEARNING OBJECTIVES

After finishing Chapter 15, students should be able to:

1. Describe the characteristics of what is known as the *midlife crisis*. (p. 500)

2. Summarize the major elements of development in middle adulthood according to Carl Jung's theory. (p. 501)

3. Explain Jung's notion of balancing the personality in midlife. (p. 501)

4. Summarize the major elements of development in middle adulthood according to Erik Erikson's theory. (p. 503)

5. Explain Erikson's seventh crisis-- *generativity versus stagnation*. (p. 503)

6. Identify the virtue of Erikson's seventh stage. (p. 503)

7. Summarize the major elements of development in middle adulthood according to Robert Peck's theory. (pp. 503-504)

8. Describe the four psychological developments that Peck views as critical to successful adjustment to middle age. (p. 503)

9. Describe the findings relevant to middle adulthood of Vaillant's longitudinal Grant Study. (p. 504)

10. Describe the changes in life structures that characterize midlife according to the view of Levinson. (p. 504)

11. Describe how mastery and pleasure combine to influence women's adjustment in the middle adult years. (pp. 504-506)

12. Identify and describe the typical crisis themes that characterize women's development in the middle years. (pp. 506-508)

13. Discuss the proposition that middle age is the "prime of life" for women. (p. 508)

14. Identify and discuss the major criticisms of the research on middle age, particularly of the normative-crisis model. (pp. 508-510)

15. Describe the pattern of marital satisfaction through adulthood. (pp. 511-512)

16. Discuss the factors that influence whether a couple remains married or gets divorced. (pp. 512-513)

17. Describe the status of relationships with siblings in middle age. (pp. 513-514)

18. Discuss friendship in middle age. (p. 514)

19. Explain some of the research findings about relationships between maturing children and their middle-aged parent(s). (pp. 514-517)

20. Explain what is meant by the terms:
    a. *"empty nest"* (p. 515)
    b. "not-so-empty nest" (pp. 515-516)

21. Explain the phenomenon of lifelong parenting. (pp. 516-517)

22. Describe how relationships with older parents often change during middle age and how those changes affect the development of the middle aged adult. (pp. 517-519)

23. Discuss how the relationship between aging parents and middle aged children is affected when a parent becomes infirm. (pp. 518-519)

CHAPTER SUMMARY AND TEACHING RECOMMENDATIONS

The first section of the chapter summarizes the major changes attributed to the midlife transition as well as the inadequacies of the label "crisis" for this phase. Eliciting student discussion of the pros and cons of using this arbitrary label would provide a stimulating way to launch this chapter's material. In reviewing the normative-crisis theory and research, the authors begin with Carl Jung's discussion of midlife transition as a necessary aspect of psychological development.

The next perspective discussed is Erikson's crisis 7: generativity versus stagnation. In presenting this section of the chapter in class, you may want to comment on significant differences between Erikson's means of achieving generativity and those he envisions for achieving intimacy. According to Erikson, a homosexual or a celibate could not attain mature intimacy, but each could--through productive or creative work--express generativity. The authors next describe Peck's expansion of Erikson's theory into the four crucial adjustments of midlife.

Key changes and conflicts experienced by middle-aged men, based on Vaillant's and Levinson's studies, are then reviewed. By contrast, the authors then present recent important studies describing women's development and change in middle adulthood from the perspective of normative-crisis theory; they emphatically focus on the emerging need of these women to balance individual achievements with traditional caregiving. At this point, you could most likely invite lively student discussion of the changing socioeconomic roles of men and women during midlife.

This section concludes with a look at several issues generated from an overall evaluation of the normative-crisis model of adult development.

The next section, discussing the timing-of-events model, considers personal relationships that are important in middle adulthood. The authors first consider research on marriage and divorce in middle adulthood; their points concerning the problems of researching these topics are worth reiterating in class. In discussing marriage and sexual relationships, you may want to refer back to the discussion of extramarital sexual activity in Chapter 13. The authors next describe research on sibling bonds, as well as research on friendships in middle adulthood.

Intergenerational relationships are the next type of relationship considered. The authors identify issues important in relationships between middle-aged parents and adolescent children, the experience of the "empty nest," and problems related to "nests" which fail to empty. In discussing these issues of parent-child relationships, you might want to also consider their impact on the middle-aged parents' marriage (and vice versa).

Finally, relationships between middle-aged adults and their aging parents are examined. The authors note that frequent parent-child contact and varied exchanges of help are the norm; they also explain the problems and conflicts that ensue with the middle-aged adult's new role as caregiver for aging parents. The latter topic is certainly worthy of additional activities in class, given the increasing frequency of this experience in society today and problems inherent in it.

The authors close this chapter by analyzing how a parent's death can affect an adult's handling of midlife issues.

Boxes in Chapter 15 are "Does Personality Change in Middle Age?" "A Society without Middle Age?" "Enhancing Marriage at Midlife," and "Reacting to a Parent's Death."

AUDIOVISUAL MATERIALS

Distributor, date, and running time are given for each film or video. Distributors' addresses are listed in the appendix (General Resources). If a film or video is not in color, there is a notation (BW) to that effect.

Family and survival. (FFHS, 1994, video, 52 min.) This program investigates the state of the American family.

Women in management: Threat or opportunity. (CRM, no date available, approximately 25 min.) Topics include problems and satisfactions for women in business; although this chapter does not discuss work roles at any great length, you may want to use this film in connection with normative-crisis research on women's development.

Divorce: For better or worse. (CRM, no date available, approximately 45 min.) Topics include the period between separation and divorce, from the perspectives of attorneys, judges, members of the clergy, and marriage counselors.

Factors in healthy aging. (FFHS, 1994, video, 28 min.) The impacts of diet, smoking, drinking, family history, personality and their effects on aging are discussed.

Caring for your parents. (FFHS, 1994, video, 24 min.) This program deals with the problems of caring for elderly parents while attempting to maintain one's own family and career.

Parenting our parents. (FFHS, 1994, video, 26 min.) More middle-aged people are facing the prospect of having both growing kids and ill or disabled parents. As the size of the elderly population increases, the forecast is a society of the old caring for the very old. This program examines various ways of coping with the stress of caring for aging parents and suggests personal and political remedies.

Divorced and sorry. (FFHS, 1994, video, 28 min.) This specially adapted Phil Donahue program is devoted to the stories of some divorced persons who regret having ended their marriage--and to an examination of those marital difficulties that could have been resolved.

Guest speakers

One topic which is especially likely to arouse students' interest--and which may be of personal relevance or concern to some students--is family caregiving for aged relatives. You could probably locate a speaker on family caregiving by contacting a local hospital, a senior center, the local Agency on Aging, a community mental health center, or the state Office on Aging. Also, in many communities religious organizations offer support to caregivers of dependent elderly people.

LECTURE OUTLINES

Lecture 1: Three Studies of Personality Development in Middle Adulthood

I. Erikson

Erik Erikson saw "generativity versus stagnation" as the psychosocial crisis of middle adulthood.

A. Generativity.
1. Definition. Erikson defined generativity as concern for the establishment and welfare of succeeding generations and a desire to leave a legacy, prompted by the awareness of one's own mortality.
2. Expression. Generativity is expressed through child rearing, making scientific or artistic contributions, being a mentor, or having a career involving work with the young (e.g., teaching).
3. Research support. Erikson's concept of generativity is supported by interviews with middle-aged people eliciting their feelings about themselves, their work, and their families. Characteristics consistent with the concept of generativity:

a. Sense of responsibility for the younger generation (giving advice and guidance).
b. Commitment to humanitarian goals (support for charities and social causes).

B. Stagnation
1. Definition. Erikson defined stagnation as a primary concern for oneself.
2. Expression. Stagnation is expressed through obsessive self-indulgence.

II. Peck

Robert Peck gives a more detailed description of four personality changes ideally occurring in middle adulthood.

A. Shift from valuing physical powers to valuing wisdom. Physical strength and stamina decline after young adulthood, but experience provides increased wisdom and insight for problem solving.
B. Transition from sexualizing to socializing in human relationships. After the climacteric (male and female), people have greater ability to appreciate members of the opposite sex as complex individuals rather than sex objects.
C. Development of cathectic (emotional) flexibility. People develop a greater ability to shift emotional attachments from one person or activity to another. There are at least two factors operating in this transition:
1. Many earlier bonds are likely to be disrupted at this time: parents die, children leave the "nest," etc.
2. People are likely to be involved in wider variety of social roles at this point than earlier in adulthood: they become parents-in-law and grandparents, are more involved in religious or civic activities, etc. (Failure to take advantage of such involvements, Peck believes, will cause emotional impoverishment.)
D. Development of mental flexibility. People are increasingly able to consider past experiences as a set of tentative guidelines for dealing with new problems. (A potential danger is mental rigidity--using past experiences as absolute rules for new situations, without considering how well or poorly past experience applies to a problem at hand.)

III. Neugarten

Bernice Neugarten conducted a classic study of personality development in middle adulthood.

A. Goal. Neugarten's goal was to identify outstanding characteristics of midlife from a subjective viewpoint.
B. Sample. Neugarten studied an elite sample, which included alumni of the University of Chicago, business and professional leaders, American Men of Science, and people selected from *Who's Who in America*.
  1. An obvious disadvantage of this sample is that the findings might not be widely generalizable.
  2. An advantage of this sample is that the subjects were likely to be introspective, reflective, and articulate.
C. Findings.
  1. Some outstanding characteristics of middle adulthood were reported by both men and women.
    a. Delineation of middle age.
      (1) Middle age was seen as a distinct part of the life cycle.
      (2) This delineation was based not on age but on accomplishments, events in various spheres of life, changes in physical functioning, etc.
    b. Attitudes toward younger and older adults. The subjects thought of themselves as a bridge between generations in the family and the community.
      (1) They had a new feeling of distance from young people, with more awareness of young people's naiveté, inexperience, and even arrogance.
      (2) They had a feeling of greater closeness and empathy with older adults.
    c. Time perspective. Subjects had begun thinking in terms of time left to live rather than time since birth.
    d. Sense of competence. Subjects felt more capable of dealing with problems than ever before and capable of exercising better judgment (having learned from experience).
  2. Some gender differences in perceptions were found.
    a. Events delineating middle age.
      (1) For men, middle age was delineated primarily by career-related events.
      (2) For women, middle age was delineated primarily by family events. This could be a cohort effect, since it characterized even single women (who thought of the family they might have had).
    b. Physical changes. Physical changes of midlife were perceived as more important by men than by women.
      (1) Women generally did not consider menopause tremendously important; they were often more concerned with the physical changes their husbands experienced than with their own menopause.
      (2) Men were acutely aware of changes in their health and of their own physical functioning in comparison with that of younger men.
    c. Freedom versus constraint.
      (1) Women saw middle age as a time of increased freedom. Since child rearing was less time-consuming, they had more time and energy for other activities.
      (2) Men saw middle age as a time of increased constraints. This was the period of greatest occupational pressures and responsibilities.

References for Lecture 1

Krueger, J. (1993, May). Personality development across the adult life span: Subjective conceptions vs. cross-sectional contrasts. *Journal of gerontology, 48*(3), 100-108.
Neugarten, B. L. (1968). *Middle age and aging.* Chicago: University of Chicago Press.

Silverstein, M. & Waite, L. (1993, July). Are blacks more likely than whites to receive and provide social support in middle and old age? Yes, no, and maybe so. *Journal of gerontology, 48,* 212-222.

Lecture 2: Marriage at Midlife

I.   Research approaches

In studies of marriage, the most common variable of interest is some measure of the emotional quality of marriages. But any such research involves problems.

A. The concepts involved are vague and are used with little explicit differentiation. They include <u>marital satisfaction</u>, <u>marital adjustment</u>, and <u>marital success</u>.
B. There are the usual problems associated with self-report measures: subjects may consciously or unconsciously distort their reports to give "right" or "desirable" responses.
C. One spouse's rating of a marriage will rarely be checked against other criteria (e.g., the other spouse's rating, the interviewer's rating, or ratings by other people who know the couple well).

II.   A longitudinal study

One longitudinal study examined changes in marital satisfaction during adulthood.

A. Subjects.
  1. Subjects were white, mostly middle-class residents of northern California.
  2. Most were in their first marriage and had been married approximately 20 years when they were interviewed in middle age.
B. Methodology. Spouses were interviewed (separately) in early adulthood and middle adulthood. Data on marital satisfaction were collected:
  1. Each spouse rated his or her own satisfaction with the marriage.
  2. Interviewers rated each couple on apparent marital adjustment, closeness, hostility, satisfaction, and agreement over child rearing.
C. Goals. The researchers wanted to identify:
  1. Personal characteristics associated with various degrees of marital satisfaction.

2. Differences between satisfying and unsatisfying marriages.
3. Changes over time in marital satisfaction.
D. Findings.
  1. Personal characteristics and marital satisfaction. In this regard, the researchers considered similarity versus complementarity of spouses' personalities. Correlations between husbands' and wives' responses to personality measures indicated that similarity was more typical than complementarity.
    a. Positive correlations were generally found between husbands' and wives' scores.
    b. Comparisons of spouses' ratings of marital satisfaction for "most similar" and "least similar" personalities indicated that "most similar" personalities showed significantly greater satisfaction than "least similar" personalities.
  2. Differences between satisfying and unsatisfying marriages. The sample was divided into "highly satisfying" marriages and "nonsatisfying" marriages, and the spouses' statements about the marriage were compared.
    a. "Highly satisfying" marriages:
      (1) These were characterized by affectionate and enjoyable relationships between spouses. They were close relationships, although not all activities were shared. Subjects' statements were characterized as "likes spouse," "admires and respects spouse," "enjoys spouse's company."
      (2) These marriages were not free of conflict, but conflict was handled openly and adaptively and was outweighed by positive features.
    b. "Nonsatisfying" marriages:
      (1) These were characterized either by avoidance of conflict or by handling of conflict in ways that led to hostility and tension.
      (2) Subjects' statements were characterized as "critical of

spouse," "serious conflicts with spouse," "spouses have discordant personalities," "avoids conflict with spouse," "marriage is utilitarian."

3. Changes in marital satisfaction between early and middle adulthood. The researchers compared ratings of marital satisfaction at the early-adulthood and middle-adulthood interviews.
    a. No change was found in _average_ scores.
    b. But the researchers did identify drastic changes (both increases and decreases) in satisfaction within _individual_ marriages. These changes were generally associated with changes in situational factors (e.g., financial resources, child-rearing problems, health, easing or worsening of problems with in-laws).

References for Lecture 2

Cargan, L. (1991). _Marriages and families: Changing relationships_. New York: Harper Collins.

Levenson, R. (1993, June). Long-term marriage: Age, gender, and satisfaction. _Psychology and aging, 8_(2), 301-313.

Skolnick, A. (1981). Married lives: Longitudinal perspectives on marriage. In D. H. Eichorn, J. A. Clausen, N. Haan, M. P. Honzik, & P. H. Mussen (Eds.), _Present and past in middle life_. New York: Academic.

Lecture 3: Family Caregiving for Frail Elderly People

I. Significance

Why is it important to study family caregiving?

A. The population of the United States is aging (the "graying of America").
    1. The percentage of the population aged 65 and older is increasing.
    2. The most rapid increase is in the percentage of very old people (aged 85 and older): these are the elderly people most likely to need supportive care.
B. Today, most care of frail elderly people is provided by family members. One recent estimate is that families provide 80 to 90 percent of such care.
C. Family caregivers for the "oldest old" (people aged 85 and older) are likely to be caught in a "generation squeeze." They must meet the challenges of their own aging while providing care to still older parents. This is likely to result in stress or an inordinate burden.

II. A study of caregivers

What kinds of care do family members provide, and what kinds of stress are encountered? One study of a nonrandom sample of 104 caregivers for frail elderly people in shared households examined these questions.

A. Subjects.
    1. Most of the respondents were the daughters or daughters-in-law of the elderly people for whom they provided care.
    2. About 66 percent of the caregivers were in their fifties or sixties.
    3. Most caregivers also had children living at home.
B. Findings. Caregivers described their tasks and identified those that were most stressful.
    1. Tasks included household management (e.g., cooking, laundry, errands); transportation; grooming (e.g., dressing, bathing, diapering); health care (e.g., giving medications, changing dressings); help with rising from chairs or walking; financial management (e.g., financial support, writing checks, managing money); social and emotional support (taking the elderly person visiting, making phone calls and writing letters for him or her); mental health support (help with decision making, remembering, and protection).
    2. Most stressful tasks were those involving social-emotional support and mental health (these were time-consuming); household management (shared households entailed a lack of privacy and disrupted family lifestyles); health care and grooming (these tasks were physically or financially stressful or distasteful).

III. Support available for caregivers

Three general kinds of support are available for caregivers.

A. Educational and support groups.
   1. These provide information about normal and pathological aging and about formal services available in the community.
   2. They may also provide instruction in practical skills needed in caregiving (e.g., lifting a patient).
   3. They represent an opportunity to share concerns and strategies with other caregivers.
B. Adult day care. This is care in a congregate setting during the day for the elderly person; it may include "reality orientation." It is especially important for caregivers employed outside the home.
C. Respite care. In this arrangement, the elderly person is cared for by professionals (in his or her own home or in an institution) temporarily, while family caregivers are unavailable (e.g., on vacation or themselves hospitalized).

References for Lecture 3

Adams, T. (1993). *When parents age: What children can do.* New York: Berkley Books.
Anderson-Ellis, E. (1992). *Aging parents and you.* New York: Mastermedia.
Nelson, M. (1993). Race, gender, and the effect of social supports on the use of health services by elderly individuals. *International journal of aging and human development, 37*(3), 227-246.
Springer, D. & Brubaker, T. H. (1984). *Family caregivers and dependent elderly.* Beverly Hills, CA: Sage.

TOPIC FOR DEBATE

Should Adult Children Be Required by Law to Care for Their Aging Parents?

Background

Most people have heard of the "graying of America," the rapid growth of the older segments of the population. The population group growing most rapidly is the "old old": people aged 85 and older. Generally, it is recognized that these demographic changes bring the need for supportive services so that the quality, as well as the quantity, of life continues to expand. However, there is disagreement over whether these services should be provided by the families of aged people or through formal bureaucratic programs.

Some people believe that adult children should be held legally responsible for the care of their aging parents. Current gerontological research informs us that, in fact, the family already provides a great deal of the care given to the elderly. Research also shows that most adult children genuinely want to do all they can for their elderly parents. In addition, family caregiving could promote inter-generational continuity of affection and values in a society that many believe is growing more fragmented each day.

Many people would argue that, issues of affection aside, family care is almost certain to be superior to care provided by other agents. Supportive services by the family, in the home, are likely to provide more cognitive and social stimulation to a frail elderly person than institutional care. Institutional care, furthermore, often involves problems far more serious than lack of stimulation. Privacy in general is usually minimal, and residents' expressions of sexuality in particular are typically restricted. In some institutions, residents are abused. Institutional care which is free of such obvious problems tends to be quite costly.

Other people argue, however, that requiring adult children to care for their aging parents is unreasonable and unworkable. Some older people have no children, and any solution based fundamentally on families could result in neglect of these individuals. Also, today most family care that is provided to the elderly is provided by women; yet, women's increasing participation in the labor force can make the support of aging parents highly stressful or even unbearable. Furthermore, some families have a history of antagonism between parents and children, which would make family caregiving a burdensome situation for all concerned. Mandatory family care could very well sow the seeds of abuse in overburdened families.

Another argument against mandatory family care has to do with society's responsibility to its aging members. A call for adult children to take greater responsibility for care of their aging parents could be an attempt to mask irresponsibility on the part of government and social agencies. Many people would argue that the state has a deep obligation to those who helped to build our

society through paid employment, child
rearing, and fulfilling the duties of citizenship.

Debate plan

Using this background, and information from
additional sources (selected references appear
below), student panels should debate the
following positions:

Position A. Adult children should be required
by law to provide any necessary support for
their aging parents.

Position B. Government and social agencies
should provide care to the aged, and families
should provide, at most, supplements to this
care.

References for the debate

Greenburg, V. (1994). *Children of a certain
age: Adults and their aging parents.* New
York: Lexington Books.
Hendricks, J. & Rosenthal, C. (1993). *The
remainder of their days: Domestic policy and
older families in the United States and
Canada.* New York: Garland.
Springer, D. & Brubaker, T. H. (1984).
Family caregivers and dependent elderly.
Beverly Hills,CA: Sage.
Zarit, S., Pearlin, L., & Schaie, K. (1993).
*Caregiving systems: Informal and formal
helpers.* Hillsdale, NJ: Erlbaum.

TOPICS FOR DISCUSSION

Topic 1: The Normative-Crisis Model

1. Ask students to summarize the
    normative-crisis model as it addresses
    development in middle adulthood. Ask
    them to identify some of the researchers
    using this model whose work is reviewed
    in the chapter (pages 500-508).

2. Ask students to list and briefly explain the
    questions the authors raise about the
    normative-crisis model (pages 508-511).
    Ask students which questions they feel
    cast the greatest doubt on the validity of
    the model as an explanation of midlife
    development and to justify their choice.

**Topic 2: Relationships with Children in
Middle Adulthood**

1. The authors describe issues that are often
    difficult for middle-aged parents in their
    relationships with adolescent children
    (page 514-515). Ask students to suggest
    and describe resources that middle-aged
    parents might draw on in dealing with
    these issues.

2. Ask students to summarize the material
    on parents who are distressed by the
    "empty nest" (page 515) and to suggest
    interventions that could help these parents
    adapt to the transition. Also, ask students
    to identify problems that can arise in
    families in which the "nest" does not
    empty and the kinds of help that could
    ease these problems (pages 515-516).

Topic 3: Relationships with Aging Parents

1. According to the authors, most
    middle-aged people have a more objective
    view of their aging parents than they ever
    had before (page 517). Ask students to
    suggest reasons why middle-aged people
    might develop such objectivity. Also, ask
    them to identify events in their own
    families which could illustrate this.

2. Ask students to summarize some of the
    things middle-aged people do to help and
    care for their aging parents (pages 517-
    519). Also ask students to identify
    potential strains that these forms of
    support might create for a middle-aged
    person and his or her family. Ask
    students to identify ways in which our
    society could provide greater support to
    middle-aged people caring for elderly
    parents.

PROJECTS AND CLASS EXERCISES

Group Exercise: Family Caregiving

The basis for this discussion exercise is the
following case history:

A case study. Julie is a 40-year-old
homemaker. Besides chauffeuring her very
active 13-year-old son and 15-year-old
daughter to school activities, maintaining the
household, and providing emotional support to
her husband (who is facing a stressful job

situation), Julie cares for her 70-year-old widowed father. Her father had a stroke last year. After her father's stroke, Julie dropped the two college courses she had been taking, so that she could visit him regularly in the hospital and help with his rehabilitation there. When he was released from the hospital, he moved into her home for an indefinite period. That seemed to be the only option other than a nursing home. Julie's brother and sister live out of town and are unable to provide physical care for their father. It has now been several months since Julie's father moved into her home. Julie is feeling overwhelmed as she tries to meet the needs of her father, her husband, and her children.

In groups, students should discuss steps that could be taken to solve or prevent problems for Julie and possible pitfalls in taking these steps. Dimensions of the situation that the group should consider are (1) finances, (2) health, (3) emotional functioning of individuals, and (4) relationships between family members.

Project 1: Evaluating the Normative-Crisis Model

Students should read at least one primary source describing Erikson's, Vaillant's, Peck's, or Levinson's work on development in middle adulthood. Students should write a paper summarizing this material and criticizing it in terms of the four questions the authors raise on pages 508-510 of the text.

Project 2: Marriage at Midlife

Students should interview a couple they consider very happily married--both the husband and the wife. Interview topics should include ways in which the marriage has or has not changed over the years, the biggest problems that the couple has faced, and the experiences that have brought them the greatest satisfaction. Students should write a paper describing the interview and commenting on the couple's responses in the context of the text's discussion of marriage in midlife (pages 511-514).

Note: Remind the students to protect the respondents' anonymity by using pseudonyms or initials and omitting or disguising any other identifying information. They should make it clear to the respondents that their privacy will be respected.

Project 3: Reducing the Strain of Caregiving

Students should locate a program in the community which provides services to family caregivers of the aged. Students should write a paper describing the program. The description should include what kinds of services are provided, how many caregivers are served, what the services cost the clients, how the program is funded, and how the program might be improved; these descriptions should be based on interviews by the students with one or more employees or administrators and (if possible) one or more clients of the program.

ESSAY QUESTIONS

1. How do Erikson and Peck describe personality development during middle adulthood?

Answer guideline. According to Erikson, the middle-aged adult faces the crisis of generativity versus stagnation. Ideally, the individual attains generativity or a concern with establishing and guiding the next generation; this concern may be expressed through child rearing, work with young people, creativity, or productivity. An individual who does not attain generativity experiences stagnation, expressed through self-concern and self-indulgence. Peck elaborated on Erikson's description of middle age; he described four developmental crises faced in this period: (1) valuing wisdom versus valuing physical powers, (2) socializing versus sexualizing in human relationships, (3) emotional flexibility versus emotional impoverishment, and (4) mental flexibility versus mental rigidity.

2. Describe indications of well-being for middle-aged women.

Answer guideline. In a study of middle-aged women from varied social backgrounds, two factors--mastery and pleasure--were the most important indicators of psychological well-being. Mastery referred to how much control the women felt they had over their lives, and pleasure was simply the enjoyment that the women derived from their lives. In this sample, neither mastery nor pleasure was related to age. Women experiencing the greatest mastery and pleasure (and the greatest sense of well-being) were employed married women with children; those experiencing the least mastery and pleasure (and the least sense of well-being) were unemployed, childless married women.

3. According to the text, what questions can be raised about the adequacy of the normative-crisis model?

Answer guideline. One question is to what extent the findings of research based on this model can be generalized to other populations. This research was conducted, for the most part, on samples of white middle-class and upper-class men born in the 1920s or 1930s; thus the results may not apply to women, nonwhites, the very poor, or members of other cohorts. Another question is how typical a "crisis" is in middle age. Much evidence shows that crises are not unique to middle adulthood, and that there are few regularities in the content or resolution of crises which do occur in middle age. A third question is to what extent adult development is age-linked; this question is particularly serious, given the characteristics of the samples used in research based on this model. Finally, some people question how healthy the "normal" adult male model is for adult development. Again, the appropriateness of this model for the development of women (and also for the development of many men) has been questioned.

4. How does marital satisfaction typically change during adulthood?

Answer guideline. Several studies show that marital satisfaction follows a U-shaped curve during adulthood. Positive aspects of marriage (such as discussion, cooperation, shared laughter, and satisfaction with the marriage) are at a high point early in the marriage and then decline in middle age; after middle age, these aspects of the marriage increase again. Negative aspects of the marriage (e.g., sarcasm, anger, disagreements over important matters) seem to decline from the early years of marriage through old age, at least in marriages that survive.

5. How is friendship in middle age different from and similar to friendship earlier in adulthood?

Answer guideline. One difference between friendship in middle adulthood and in early adulthood is that middle-aged people usually have fewer friends than younger or older adults. Furthermore, friendships in middle age may be less complex, since middle-aged people give less elaborate descriptions of their friends than adults of other age groups. A similarity between friendships of middle-aged people and those of older and younger adults is the function of friendship as a source of emotional support and well-being.

6. How do men and women typically react to the "empty nest"?

Answer guideline. Most women react positively to the "empty nest," unless they have been exclusively invested in their roles as mothers. Some men, however, have more negative reactions; these reactions may stem from regrets at not having spent much time with their children when the children were younger.

7. Describe problems that may be experienced by middle-aged adults caring for aging parents.

Answer guideline. Usually, it is daughters who provide care for elderly parents; these women may experience numerous sources of stress. Some experience stress because the parent seems impossible to satisfy, some are anxious about the parent's impending death, and some resent having to be a source of strength for the parent rather than vice versa. Furthermore, many family caregivers experience financial strain and time constraints (including lack of time for rest and personal enjoyment) and feel caught between the needs of their spouse and children and those of their parent.

CHAPTER 16

PHYSICAL AND INTELLECTUAL DEVELOPMENT IN LATE ADULTHOOD

INTRODUCTION

Many developmental changes and challenges still lie ahead for people after the age of 65. **Chapter 16** examines physical and intellectual development in late adulthood, the last age-defined group discussed in the text.

- The chapter begins with an examination of some common myths about aging and a discussion of how people can make the most of their later years.

- Longevity and the aging process are discussed from two theoretical perspectives, and the physical changes in late adulthood and health problems and concerns of older adults are described.

- Changes in intelligence and intellectual functioning in late adulthood are discussed, as are changes in the functioning of memory.

- The relationship between intellectual activity and intellectual functioning are discussed in the context of lifelong learning.

- Finally, the chapter closes with an examination of the influence of work and the transition to retirement.

CHAPTER OUTLINE

I. **OLD AGE TODAY**

   A. WHAT IS OUR ATTITUDE TOWARD OLD AGE?
   B. WHO ARE THE ELDERLY?
     1. "Young Old" and "Old Old"
     2. The Graying of the Population
     3. The Oldest Old
       a. Gender differences
       b. Health
       c. Life circumstances
   C. HOW CAN WE MAKE THE MOST OF THE LATER YEARS?

PHYSICAL DEVELOPMENT

II. **LONGEVITY AND THE AGING PROCESS**

   A. LIFE EXPECTANCY
     1. Trends in Life Expectancy
     2. Death Rates and Causes of Death
     3. Race, Gender, and Life Expectancy
       a. Racial differences
       b. Gender differences
   B. WHY PEOPLE AGE: TWO THEORIES
     1. Programmed Aging
     2. Aging as Wear and Tear

III. **PHYSICAL CHANGES OF OLD AGE**
   A. SENSORY AND PSYCHOMOTOR FUNCTIONING
     1. Vision
     2. Hearing
     3. Taste and Smell
     4. Strength, Coordination, and Reaction Time
   B. THE BRAIN IN LATE ADULTHOOD
   C. OTHER PHYSICAL CHANGES
   D. RESERVE CAPACITY

IV. **HEALTH IN OLD AGE**

   A. HEALTH CARE AND HEALTH PROBLEMS
     1. Medical Conditions
     2. Dental Health

   B. INFLUENCES ON HEALTH AND FITNESS
     1. Exercise and Diet
   C. MENTAL AND BEHAVIORAL DISORDERS
     1. Reversible Mental Health Problems
       a. Depression
       b. Overmedication
     2. Irreversible Mental Problems
       a. Alzheimer's disease
         (1) Causes of Alzheimer's disease
         (2) Symptoms and diagnosis
         (3) Treatment
       b. Other irreversible conditions

INTELLECTUAL DEVELOPMENT

V. **ASPECTS OF INTELLECTUAL DEVELOPMENT**

   A. DOES INTELLIGENCE DECLINE IN LATE ADULTHOOD?
     1. Two Views of Intelligence
       a. Fluid and crystallized intelligence: Which is more important?
       b. Fluid and crystallized intelligence: How are they tested?
         (1) Sequential testing
         (2) Helping older people improve their intellectual performance
     2. A New View: Mechanics and Pragmatics of Intelligence
   B. HOW DOES MEMORY CHANGE IN LATE ADULTHOOD?
     1. The Three Memory Systems
       a. Sensory memory
       b. Short-term (or working) memory
       c. Long-term memory
     2. Why Does Memory Decline?
       a. Biological hypotheses
       b. Processing hypotheses
       c. Contextual considerations
       d. Memory training

VI. **LIFELONG LEARNING: ADULT EDUCATION**

VII. **WORK AND RETIREMENT**

    A. WHY PEOPLE RETIRE
    B. HOW PEOPLE FEEL ABOUT RETIREMENT
    C. MAKING THE MOST OF RETIREMENT
       1. Planning Ahead
       2. Using Leisure Time Well

KEY TERMS

ageism (page 526)
Alzheimer's disease (541)
dementia (540)
dual-process model (547)
free radicals (533)
gerontology (526)
life expectancy (531)
long-term memory (547)
mechanics of intelligence (547)
plasticity (546)
pragmatics of intelligence (547)
primary aging (534)
programmed-aging theory (533)
reserve capacity (537)
secondary aging (534)
selective optimization with
   compensation (547)
senescence (530)
sensory memory (547)
short-term memory (547)
terminal drop (545)
wear-and-tear theory (533)

LEARNING OBJECTIVES

After finishing Chapter 16, students should be able to:

1. Describe common attitudes toward old age and the elderly. (p. 526)

2. Identify various categories of elderly people. (pp. 526-528)

3. Explain several specific steps that an older people can take in order to make the most of their later years. (p. 529)

4. Define *senescence* and explain why changes in life expectancy in this century have focused attention on it. (p. 530)

5. Describe current trends in life expectancy. (p. 531)

6. List the major causes of death among older people. (pp. 531-532)

7. Describe the differences in life expectancy attributable to race. (p. 532)

8. Describe the differences in life expectancy attributable to gender. (pp. 532-533)

9. Summarize the main points of the *programmed-aging theory*. (p. 533)

10. Summarize the main points of the *wear-and-tear theory* of aging. (p. 533)

11. Distinguish between *primary aging* and *secondary aging*. (p. 534)

12. Describe the changes in vision associated with old age. (p. 534)

13. Describe the changes in hearing associated with old age. (pp. 534-535)

14. Describe the changes in taste and smell associated with old age. (p. 535)

15. Describe the changes in strength, coordination, and reaction time associated with old age. (pp. 535-536)

16. Describe the physical changes to the skin and bones that are associated with old age. (p. 537)

17. Define *reserve capacity* and explain its relevance to aging. (p. 537)

18. Describe the general health of older people, and list the health problems that commonly affect older people. (pp. 537-539)

19. List and describe the factors that influence health and fitness among the elderly. (pp. 539-540)

20. List and describe some of the reversible mental health problems that afflict older people. (pp. 540-541)

21. Discuss the causes, symptoms, and treatment of *Alzheimer's* disease. (pp. 541-543)

22. Describe some techniques for measuring changes in intellectual functioning. (pp. 543-544)

23. List some physical and psychological factors that can influence older adults' performance on intelligence tests, and how older people continue to learn. (pp. 545-546)

24. Discuss the *dual-process model* of intellectual functioning, which helps explain how some aspects of intelligence seem to increase with age. (p. 547)

25. Describe differences between young people and old people in *sensory*, *short-term*, and *long-term memory*. (pp. 547-548)

26. Summarize the various theories that seek to explain these differences. (pp. 548-550)

27. Discuss the importance of continued mental activity and explain how learning and memory are interrelated. (pp. 550-551)

28. Describe the effect of work and retirement on the older person. (pp. 551-552)

29. List and describe some of the things that can be done to insure a fulfilling retirement. (pp. 552-553)

CHAPTER SUMMARY AND TEACHING RECOMMENDATIONS

The chapter opens with a discussion of negative attitudes toward aging. The authors then describe important demographic trends-- the overall "graying of America" and the particularly rapid increase in the number of people over age 85. This section concludes with a discussion of how society can better serve the older population and describes the diversity found within older cohorts in the contemporary United States.

In the section on physical development, the authors define <u>life expectancy</u> and point out how life expectancy has increased in the twentieth century; causes of death and racial and gender differences in life expectancy are outlined. Next, the authors explain two theories of aging: "programmed" aging and aging as wear and tear. The authors also distinguish the processes of primary aging and secondary aging. In this context, you might want to reiterate the authors' point that aging need involve only minimal decrements in many areas of physical and intellectual functioning, if wise choices regarding health practices and lifestyle have been made earlier in adulthood.

The next section of the chapter deals with age-related changes in physical functioning. The authors describe typical changes in vision, hearing, taste, smell, and temperature sensitivity; they also outline changes in coordination, reaction time, sleep patterns, and reserve capacity. Changes in physical "structures" (e.g., skin, muscles, bones) are described; the authors also call students' attention to Box 14-1 on osteoporosis (that appeared in Chapter 14). In discussing these aging changes, you could emphasize the decline in the reserve capacity of the heart and other organs as well as encourage student discussion of the effects this change could have on specific activities.

Age-related changes in health are discussed in the next section. The authors describe the increased frequency of chronic illness in old age and note the importance of diet and exercise for maintaining health into old age. In treating the topic of health in class, you may want to emphasize (as the authors do) that most older people are in excellent or good physical health. The authors also point out that most older people enjoy good mental health. They describe dementia in this section but point out that its symptoms can be caused by several reversible factors; in this context, they discuss the effects of overmedication and depression. In concluding this section, they consider the symptoms, diagnosis, and treatment of Alzheimer's disease and--more briefly--other forms of irreversible dementia.

The chapter continues with a section on age changes in normal processes of intellectual functioning. The authors review the controversy over the supposed age-related decline in intelligence. They describe the different patterns of change for fluid and crystallized intelligence, noting the different patterns documented in sequential research. The authors also note factors other than ability which can influence performance on measures of intelligence, and they review recent research documenting and explaining the variability of older adults' test performance. This material closes with a discussion of the dual-process model of intelligence in which mechanics of intelligence are believed to decline with age but pragmatics of intelligence are believed to increase.

The next aspect of intellectual functioning discussed is memory. The authors distinguish sensory, short-term, and long-term memory and note that age differences are most pronounced for recall from recent long-term memory. The authors also offer several hypotheses to explain age differences in memory, including biological, processing, and contextual influences on long-term memory for recent events.

The next section focuses on adult education in old age; it discusses motivations for education in late life and recent programs and approaches designed in response to the steady demand for educational opportunities.

The chapter closes with a discussion of work and retirement. The authors note the trend toward early retirement and also note that many retired people do part-time or volunteer work. The authors describe attitudes toward retirement held by different types of workers, pointing out the importance of planning for the financial changes and changes in lifestyle entailed by retirement.

Boxes in Chapter 16 are "Aging in Asia," "You and the Older People in Your Life," and "Wisdom in Late Adulthood."

AUDIOVISUAL MATERIALS

Distributor, date, and running time are given for each film or video. Distributors' addresses are listed in the appendix (General Resources). If a film or video is not in color, there is a notation (BW) to that effect.

Growing old in a new age. (CPB, 1993, video, 60 min. each) This is a 13-part series that covers the following aspects of aging:
Pt. 1: Myths and Realities of Aging
Pt. 2: How the Body Ages

Pt. 3: Maximizing the Physical Potential of Older Adults
Pt. 4: Love, Intimacy, and Sexuality
Pt. 5: Learning, Memory, and Speed of Behavior
Pt. 6: Intellect, Personality, and Mental Health
Pt. 7: Social Roles and Relationships in Old Age
Pt. 8: Family and Intergenerational Relationships in Old Age
Pt. 9: Work, Retirement, and Economic Status
Pt. 10: Illness and Disability
Pt. 11: Dying, Death and Bereavement
Pt. 12: Societal and Political Aspects of Aging
Pt. 13: The Future of Aging

Alzheimer's disease. (FFHS, 1994, video, 28 min.) This specially adapted Phil Donahue program shows the ravages of Alzheimer's disease on patient and family.

How to live longer...better (FFHS, 1994, video, 25 min.) This program focuses on the lifestyle changes, with emphasis on exercise, that are playing an important role in extending the life span of Americans.

The aging process (FFHS, 1994, video, 19 min.) Part of the aging process is inevitable, but only part. This program explains the effects of aging on the human mind and body.

Factors in healthy aging. (FFHS, 1994, video, 28 min.)

Ageless America. (FFHS, 1994, video, 52 min.) Why women live longer than men, the "sandwich" generation of adults with responsibilities for aging parents, young children, and the process and problems of aging itself.

Slowing the clock. (FFHS, 1994, video, 26 min.) We can't stop the aging process, but this program shows how we can at least slow down its effects.

Guest speakers

In our experience, students show great interest in Alzheimer's disease: most have heard of it through the popular media or other sources, and some may have a friend or relative suffering from the disease. You may be able to locate a speaker on the problems involved in diagnosing Alzheimer's disease if your institution is near a fairly large hospital or medical center. Many of the sources for speakers on family caregiving (see

Chapter 15) would probably also be helpful for locating speakers on services available to caregivers of Alzheimer's patients.

Other topics which might be effectively addressed by guest speakers are adult education and retirement. If Elderhostel is held at your institution, you could ask the campus Elderhostel director to speak about the program, its implementation on your campus, and its participants. You may be able to locate a speaker on retirement through your institution's personnel office, the personnel office of a local business or industry, or the local social security office.

LECTURE OUTLINES

Lecture 1: Aging and Cognition

I. Learning and memory

One area in which aging and cognition can be examined is learning and memory.

A. Learning, memory, and performance: Important distinctions.
  1. Learning versus memory. This is an arbitrary distinction: one must first learn in order to remember; and one can remember only what has previously been learned.
  2. Learning and memory versus performance.
      a. Learning and memory are both internal, unobservable processes.
      b. To estimate the extent to which learning and memory have occurred, some type of performance is necessary. Performance is always an estimate of learning and memory, and may be biased.
B. Research: An overview. There have been countless studies of age differences in learning and memory.
  1. Findings. In general, elderly subjects (usually in their sixties or older) do not perform as well as young and middle-aged subjects in such studies.
  2. Possible conclusions:
      a. There may in fact be age differences in people's ability to learn and remember.
      b. On the other hand, apparent age differences in learning and memory may reflect situational

factors--circumstances of the task--that have an especially strong impact on older learners.
C. Research: Situational factors. At least three circumstances seem to impair the performance of older people more than younger people: the pacing of tasks, the meaningfulness of tasks, and the use of memory strategies (mnemonics).
  1. Pacing of tasks.
      a. In most studies, the time allotted for studying material to be learned and for remembering it was limited.
      b. It has been demonstrated that both of these limitations affect older subjects' performance more than younger subjects' performance.
        (1) Smallest age differences are found when one or both periods are relatively long or when subjects are allowed to pace themselves.
        (2) Largest age differences are found when one or both periods are relatively short.
  2. Meaningfulness of tasks.
      a. Typical experimental tasks may be seen as meaningless and thus as a waste of time. Older subjects seem to be less willing than younger subjects to exert their best efforts in learning tasks of this nature.
      b. An example is Hulicka's paired-associates study.
        (1) Original task: Subjects had to remember arbitrary word pairs (e.g., window--dog; table--card). With this task, the dropout rate for older subjects was 80 percent; this, and the relatively poor performance of the remaining older subjects (relative to younger subjects), prompted a redesign.
        (2) Redesigned task: Word pairs consisted of occupations and surnames (e.g., banker--Smith; lawyer--Jones). With this task, older subjects stayed in the experiment, and age differences in performance were smaller than with the original task.
  3. Mnemonics. Elderly subjects tend not to use mnemonics spontaneously but can improve their performance if instructed to use them.

a. "No instruction" condition. In many studies, subjects are questioned afterwards to determine what memory strategies (if any) they used.
   (1) College students (young adults) almost always use some mnemonics. (These are typical subjects in most studies.)
   (2) Older subjects (nearly always nonstudents) rarely report using any strategy or system to remember experimental material.
b. "Instruction" condition. However, in several studies, subjects have been instructed to use some sort of mnemonic device (visual imagery, rhymes, etc.).
   (1) Young subjects' performance in such studies differs very little from their performance in the "no instruction" condition. It is likely that young subjects use mnemonics whether or not they are instructed to.
   (2) Older subjects' performance is usually much better in the "instruction" condition than in the "no instruction" condition. Older subjects can use mnemonics to their benefit but usually do not do so spontaneously.

D. Research: Implications for older people. For elderly people to perform at their best, learning and memory tasks should:
   1. Allow plenty of time for learning and remembering.
   2. Have some apparent practical value.
   3. Include instructions or suggestions about strategies for organizing efforts to learn and remember.

II. Problem solving

There have been many studies comparing the performance of older and younger subjects in problem solving. Results have varied.

A. Recent research. Denney's research used "real-life" practical problems.
   1. Middle-aged subjects generally performed best.
   2. Older subjects' performance was often similar to that of young adults.

B. Earlier research. Earlier studies used more "laboratory-experimental" problems (e.g., subjects had to discover what combination of switches would turn on a light; or they had to deal with problems involving "concept attainment"; or they had to answer questions about jars of water.).
   1. Older subjects generally performed substantially worse than young or middle-aged subjects in studies like these.
   2. Possible explanations.
      a. Older subjects' approach to these tasks was usually unsystematic. They often failed to record the results of their initial, unsuccessful efforts and so repeated some false starts.
      b. Older subjects took longer to reach a solution (at least in part as a result of their unsystematic approach); thus, they had to remember more during their efforts to solve problems.
      c. The nature of the problems may also have an effect. These types of problems are rarely encountered anywhere but in laboratory situations. The impact on older subjects' motivation and their interest in performing well may be like that in studies of learning and memory (such as Hulicka's, described above).

III. Conservation

Older people's performance on Piagetian conservation tasks is another area of study. Papalia (1972) was among the first to examine age differences in these tasks across the entire life span.

A. Papalia's research.
   1. Subjects.
      a. Subjects were children (aged 8), adolescents (13), college students (late teens to early twenties), middle- aged people (in their forties), and elderly people (in their sixties).
      b. According to Piagetian theory, the children should have been in the stage of concrete operations, and all the other age groups should have been in formal operations.
   2. Tasks. Several conservation tasks were given.

        a. Conservation of number, mass, and weight--all concrete operational tasks.
        b. Conservation of volume--a formal operational task.
    3. Results.
        a. Oldest subjects: Most could not conserve volume; some could conserve weight and mass; all could conserve number.
        b. Middle-aged subjects could solve all the conservation problems.
        c. College students could solve all the problems except conservation of volume (most could not solve that).
        d. Adolescents and children: Virtually all could solve all the problems except conservation of weight and volume.
B. Implications of Papalia's findings. Middle-aged people performed best overall; the oldest subjects were most similar to college students; all the adults performed better than adolescents and children. The fact that middle-aged people performed best has several possible interpretations.
    1. It may reflect an actual decrease in cognitive ability with age. That is, the older subjects might have performed as well as the middle-aged subjects in the past. Such a decrease could be due to:
        a. Neurological changes.
        b. Environmental changes. Older people may encounter less intellectual stimulation and fewer problem-solving situations than middle-aged people.
    2. It may reflect age differences in subjects' reactions to conservation tasks. Again, such tasks may be seen as meaningless and may thus fail to motivate older subjects.
    3. It may reflect age differences in educational background. The older subjects were functioning essentially at the concrete operational level. Attainment of formal operations (needed for conservation of volume) is associated with higher educational levels.

References for Lecture 1

Erber, J. (1993). Age and forgetfulness: Young perceivers' impressions of young and older adults. *International journal of aging*

and human development, 37(2), 91-103.
Rabbitt, P. (1993, August). Does it all go together when it goes? The Nineteenth Bartlett Memorial Lecture in *Quarterly journal of experimental psychology: Human experimental psychology, 46A*(3), 385-434.
Rybash, J. M., Hoyer, W. J., & Roodin, P. A. (1986). *Adult cognition and aging.* New York: Pergamon.
Salthouse, T. (1991). *Theoretical perspectives on cognitive aging.* Hillsdale, NJ: Erlbaum.
West, R. & Sinnott, J. (Eds.). (1992). *Everyday memory and aging: Current research and methodology.* New York: Springer-Verlag.

Lecture 2: Dementia

I. Definition

Dementia is a general term referring to a set of symptoms, not a single disease. These symptoms are produced by any of several diseases affecting the brain or brain functioning.

II. Symptoms

Symptoms of dementia are generally progressive--that is, increasing in severity. They can affect cognitive, emotional, and motor functioning.

A. Impact on cognitive functioning.
    1. Loss of recent memory for virtually all kinds of information.
    2. Decreased efficiency in learning new material.
    3. Impaired concentration.
    4. Impaired judgment.
    5. Decreased capacity for abstract thinking (e.g., identifying themes in prose, interpreting proverbs, distinguishing important from trivial points).
B. Impact on emotional functioning.
    1. Initial symptoms: apathy, flattened affect.
    2. Later symptoms: increased emotional lability, less emotional control.
C. Impact on motor functioning (these symptoms may appear relatively late).
    1. Impaired coordination.
    2. Impaired muscular control.

III. Primary versus secondary dementia

It is important to distinguish primary dementias from secondary dementias. Primary dementias are (at present) irreversible, but secondary dementias often can be reversed (at least partially) if the cause is identified and eliminated early enough.

A. Primary dementias are diseases which affect the physical structure of the brain. Each disease in this group is associated with a unique neurological impact.
  1. Alzheimer's disease is the best known and most common primary dementia. Approximately 50 percent of cases of dementia are diagnosed as Alzheimer's disease.
      a. Neurological impact: Neurofibrillary tangles and senile plaques. These changes are identified primarily in the hippocampus.
      b. Age of onset is difficult to determine because the symptoms develop gradually. Operationally, age of onset is defined as the age when impaired functioning is undeniable to the victim or the victim's family. This age ranges from the forties to the eighties, but most cases begin after age 60.
      c. Cause: Not yet identified, but Alzheimer's disease is believed to have some type of genetic basis and to be related to disturbances (possibly inherited) of neurotransmitter production or action.
      d. Diagnosis: Currently made by a process of excluding other potential causes of symptoms through neurological and psychiatric evaluation; certain diagnosis is possible only through brain autopsy after death.
  2. Other forms of primary dementia: Pick's disease, Huntington's disease.
B. Secondary dementias are conditions that do not affect brain structure (as far as is known at this time) but do affect the functioning of the brain to produce symptoms of dementia. Sources of secondary dementia include overmedication (over-the-counter drugs as well as prescription medication), use or abuse of alcohol, depression, vascular diseases, infections, and malnutrition.

IV. Treatment

Treatment for primary and secondary dementias differs.

A. Primary dementias. Treatment usually focuses on helping victims, caregivers, and families adapt to changes in functioning.
B. Secondary dementias. Treatment involves elimination of the cause (e.g., depression, nutrition).

References for Lecture 2

Davis, K. (1993, August). Strategies for the treatment of Alzheimer's disease. *Neurology, 43*(8), Suppl. 4, 52-55.
Henderson, J., Gutierrez-Mayka, M., & Garcia, J. (1993, June). A model for Alzheimer's disease support group development in African-American and Hispanic populations. *The gerontologist, 33,* 409-414.
Heston, L. L. & White, J. A. (1983). *Dementia: A practical guide to Alzheimer's disease and related illnesses.* New York: Freeman.
Meier-Ruge, W. (Ed.) (1993). *Dementing brain disease in old age.* New York: Karger.

Lecture 3: Age Discrimination in Employment

I. Definition

The Age Discrimination in Employment Act of 1967 (with more recent amendments) defines age discrimination as failure to hire individuals between ages 40 and 70 because of their age, firing these individuals because of their age, discrimination in pay or benefits based on age, limiting or classifying workers (to their disadvantage) because of age, or instructing an employment agency to limit referrals on the basis of age.

II. Incidence

Age discrimination is experienced by men and women in diverse occupations; it has been documented in both industrial and professional work (including engineering and science). Older job seekers must usually look for work longer.

III. Sources of age discrimination

There are at least two fundamental reasons for age discrimination.

A. Characteristics (or supposed characteristics) of younger workers.
1. Younger workers are usually cheaper to hire.
2. Younger workers are believed to have more years of potential service to offer employers.
B. Characteristics--or stereotypes--of older workers.
1. Older workers are believed to be less productive, to have substantially less strength or endurance, to be rigid, to be grumpy and unable to mix with other workers or the public, to learn slowly, and to lack motivation.
2. Although some older workers may show some of these characteristics, the stereotype is grossly inaccurate for the vast majority of middle-aged and older employees. Available data suggest that older workers are at least as good an investment as younger workers and can offer far greater experience, reliability, and commitment.

IV. Legal aspects

Although age discrimination is prohibited by law for many employers, some employers are not covered: the federal government, small companies, and jobs in which age is a bona fide occupational qualification (e.g., modeling maternity clothes).

A. What can workers do about age discrimination?
1. Filing a charge. Within 6 months, the worker must file a charge with EEOC and with the relevant state agency.
2. Providing evidence to support a charge. The employee must give evidence that the employer relied on age in making a personnel decision, but gathering such evidence is difficult.
a. Overt evidence.
(1) Examples of overt evidence include personnel manuals and other written guidelines, and reported reasons for firing or not hiring in this instance or similar circumstances.
(2) Such evidence is rarely available.
b. Statistical evidence.
(1) Statistics are used to support a logical argument. For example, one might describe a pool of workers qualified for promotion, the age distribution of this pool, the percentage of promotions of relatively young workers, and the percentage of promotions of workers who are the same age as the complainant (or older).
(2) Usually, an employer can present an effective counterargument also using statistics. For example, the employer can point out that more younger workers are fired.
c. "Covert" evidence.
(1) The worker may attempt to show that stated reasons for a personnel decision were actually a "cover" for the real reason--age. The cited reason for a decision may be a "neutral" factor (a factor unrelated to age), such as strength, speed, or education. Such factors usually put older people at a disadvantage.
(2) "Cover" factors may constitute evidence of discrimination if it can be shown that they are arbitrary, that is, irrelevant to the job in question (e.g., strength for an accountant).
(3) However, if the cited factor is genuinely relevant to the ability to perform a job (e.g., strength for a firefighter), then it does not constitute evidence of age discrimination.
B. When may employers base personnel decisions on age?
1. Employers can legally use age as a consideration in personnel decisions if they can show that age is a "bona fide occupational qualification" (BFOQ).

2. To establish age as a BFOQ, employers must be able to show that:
   a. All or virtually all older workers are deficient in certain abilities.
   b. These abilities are involved in activities that are the essence (not a peripheral function) of the employer's business.
3. Example. The courts upheld a bus company's refusal to hire new workers over age 40.
   a. The company argued that "new hires" drew the most rigorous schedules, that there are age-related changes in stamina and reaction time, and that stamina and reaction time are relevant to adequate job performance.
   b. Providing safe transportation was presented as the essence of the company's business.

References for Lecture 3

Brown, R. (1989). *The rights of older persons* (complete rev.). Carbondale: Southern Illinois University Press.
Greene, R. (1993). Ethical decision making with the aged: A teaching model. *Gerontology and geriatrics education, 13*(4), 37-52.

Lecture 4: Retirement

I. Retirement as a social trend

Retirement is a relatively recent social phenomenon. Before the early twentieth century, fewer people survived to old age, and those who did survive generally continued to work as long as they were physically able. As society became more urban and more industrialized, at least two social trends contributed to the "rise" of retirement.

A. Fewer people are self-employed (and thus fewer people are free to work as long as they can or want to).
B. Fewer worker-hours are needed to produce most goods and services.

II. Adjusting to retirement

Retirement is usually seen as demanding some adjustment.

A. Miller proposes two alternatives for adapting to a leisure-oriented lifestyle.

1. Introduce elements of work into leisure by choosing leisure activities which not only are meaningful and enjoyable but also can be perceived as productive in some sense (e.g., collecting stamps or coins, restoring antiques, making and selling handicrafts).
2. Use leisure time in the service of other people or in support of workers (e.g., volunteer work for hospitals, religious organizations, and schools).

B. Atchley questions Miller's approach.
1. Atchley does not agree that a leisure-oriented lifestyle necessarily requires major adaptation or psychological justification. For those who are not highly work-oriented, it may be entirely possible to assume a leisure-dominated lifestyle with only minor adaptations.
2. Atchley has proposed that retirement be viewed as a life-span process comprising seven phases.
   a. Remote. The first phase begins with the beginning of working life; the individual has a vague but positive view of retirement and might (unsystematically and even unintentionally) gather some information about retirement.
   b. Near. In the second phase, retirement is only a few years off; the individual develops fantasies of retirement and may make formal preparations for the transition. Examples:
      (1) Retirement planning courses or workshops.
      (2) Financial planning.
   c. Honeymoon. The third phase begins immediately after retirement and lasts varying lengths of time for different people; the individual lives out his or her fantasies of retirement to the extent that time, health, and finances permit.
   d. Disenchantment. Phase four begins when serious discrepancies appear between fantasies of retirement and the demands of reality.
   e. Reorientation. Phase five centers on the need to develop more realistic expectations about retirement and a new lifestyle.
   f. Stability. In phase six, a retirement lifestyle providing at

least a minimal level of
satisfaction has been developed
or evolved.
g.   Termination. The seventh and
final phase ends the role of
retirement; this phase may be
signaled by a number of events.
Examples:
(1) Return to the work force.
(2) Failing health or death.

References for Lecture 4

Foner, A. & Schwab, K. (1983). *Aging and
retirement*. Monterey, CA: Brooks/Cole.
Harper, D. (1993). Remembered work
importance, satisfaction, reminiscence, and
adjustment in retirement: A case study.
Counseling psychology quarterly, 6(2), 155-
164.
Krause, N. (1993, September). Race
differences in life satisfaction among aged men
and women. *Journal of gerontology, 48*, 235-
244.
Manchester, J. (1993). *Baby boomers in
retirement: An early perspective*. Washington
DC: Congress of the United States,
Congressional Budget Office.
Neugarten, B. L. (1968). *Middle age and
aging*. Chicago: University of Chicago Press.
Walker, J. (1994). *Changing concepts of
retirement and their educational implications*.
Aldershot; Brookfield: Avebury.

TOPIC FOR DEBATE

**Should Driving Privileges Be Revoked or
Restricted after a Specified Maximum Age?**

Background

Virtually all Americans are concerned about
safety on our roads and highways. Recent
legislation dealing with restraints for children,
the use of seat belts, and penalties for driving
while intoxicated reflect this widespread
concern. Evidence documenting age-related
changes in sensory and physical functioning
has raised some questions about older drivers'
own safety and that of other motorists.
Some people believe that driving
privileges should be revoked or restricted after
a maximum age. They point out that
decrements in visual perception and in hearing
are an inevitable part of the normal aging
process. When these decrements progress
beyond a certain point in old age, driving

ability is bound to be impaired. Similarly,
reaction time lengthens as part of normal
aging. The consequences of this age-related
change could be disastrous in a traffic
situation requiring a quick decision and
response. Some experts also assert that such
factors as medication, stress, and fatigue may
have a more pronounced impact on
performance for older drivers than for
younger drivers.
There is evidence that these normal
changes do affect older drivers' performance.
Recent statistics show that, with appropriate
statistical controls for numbers of miles
driven, drivers over age 65 have accident and
traffic fatality rates similar to those of teenage
drivers. Although the younger drivers can be
expected to improve with experience and
maturity, older drivers' performance is more
likely to decline than improve.
However, other people are opposed to
restricting or revoking the privileges of older
drivers. They point out that there are large
individual differences in virtually all
age-related changes, including vision, hearing,
and reaction time. Any overall age cutoff for
driving privileges would be arbitrary in that it
would not take these differences into account.
Furthermore, the changes in vision, hearing,
and reaction time that any individual driver
does experience may well be outweighed (at
least in normal daytime traffic situations) by
years of driving experience and by caution.
Moreover, older drivers have been shown
to benefit substantially from driver training or
refresher courses aimed especially at their
needs. It can be argued that such training
would be a more humane response to
problems of older drivers than restriction or
revocation of privileges. Finally, it is
undeniable that the public transportation
systems of most American communities would
be nowhere near adequate to meet the needs of
a growing elderly population suddenly
confined by denial of driving privileges.

Debate plan

Using this background, and information from
additional sources (selected references appear
below), student panels should debate the
following positions:

Position A. Driving privileges should be
revoked or restricted after age 80.

Position B. Older people's driving privileges,
like younger people's, should be based on
driving performance.

References for the debate

Driving skills decline. **(1988, August).** *Milwaukee journal*, pp. 1A, 12A.
Harrell, W. (1992-93). Older motorists yielding to pedestrians: Are older drivers inattentive and unwilling to stop? *International journal of aging and human development, 36*(2), 115-127.
O'Neill, D. (1992, April). The doctor's dilemma: The aging driver and dementia. *International journal of geriatric psychiatry, 7*(4), 297-301.

TOPICS FOR DISCUSSION

Topic 1: Trends in Life Expectancy

1. Ask students to speculate on the changes in society that will result from the growing proportion of elderly members of the population. Ask them, for example, how health care, education, and employment are likely to differ as this demographic trend continues.

2. Ask students to summarize the gender and racial differences in life expectancy presented in the chapter (pages 532-533). Ask them what social changes would have to occur if these differences were to be eliminated.

Topic 2: Age Changes in Sensation

1. Ask students to summarize the changes in vision that occur as a part of normal aging (page 534). Ask them to identify ways in which these changes would affect everyday activities for an older person, and environmental interventions that could minimize the impact of these changes.

2. Ask students to summarize the changes in hearing that occur as a part of normal aging (pages 534-535). Ask them to identify ways in which these changes would affect everyday activities for an older person, and environmental interventions that could minimize the impact of these changes.

Topic 3: Intellectual Functioning

1. Ask students to summarize the findings of the sequential study of performance on intelligence measures for older people.

Ask them what conclusions can be drawn from each type of data (pages 543-546).

2. Ask students to identify factors other than ability which could impair an older person's performance in a testing situation. Ask them to suggest steps that could be taken to optimize older test-takers' performances (pages 545-546).

3. Ask students to identify ways in which the material in your course would have to be presented differently for optimal learning if the students were all elderly, given the age differences in learning and memory that the text summarizes (pages 546-548).

PROJECTS AND CLASS EXERCISES

Group Exercise: Adapting to the Needs of Older Students

Many colleges and universities allow older people to audit courses tuition-free. But-- perhaps because the arrangement does not generate tuition--most institutions do not actively promote this option or encourage people to take advantage of it; the number of old people who actually enroll in such courses tends to be fairly low.

Suppose that your institution began taking aggressive and effective measures to encourage elderly people to enroll in courses, with the eventual result that around half of the students in most classes were 65 or older. The group should discuss two issues:

(1) First, how should instructors modify their teaching and their evaluation and testing procedures in response to this change in the student population, given the material in the text describing older adults' cognitive performance and abilities?

(2) Second, how would classes be enriched by an increase in the proportion of older students, and how would classes suffer through such an increase?

Project 1: The Aging Process

Students should select one of the theories of physical aging described in the text and read some primary research based on that theory. Students should then write a paper summarizing the research and evaluating the extent to which it provides support for the theory.

Project 2: Community Support for Victims of Dementia and Their Caregivers

Students should identify a program in the community aimed at meeting the needs of caregivers for dementia victims. Students should write a paper describing the program; the description should include what services are provided, how many caregivers are served, what the services cost clients, how the program is funded, and how the program might be improved. Students' descriptions should be based on interviews with one or more employees or administrators and (if possible) one or more clients of the program.

Project 3: "Task Influences" on Cognitive Performance

Students should review primary research on age differences in learning, memory, problem solving, or all three; the review should focus on interventions and task designs which optimize the performance of older subjects. Students should write a paper summarizing these approaches to optimization and discussing their practical application in education and training.

Project 4: Planning for Retirement

Students should contact the personnel department of a local business or industry and obtain information about services available to help employees prepare for retirement. They should also interview one employee who is currently engaged in retirement planning and one former employee who has recently retired. They should then write a paper describing these services and their interviews.

ESSAY QUESTIONS

---

1. Explain the programmed-aging and the wear-and-tear theories of aging.

Answer guideline. According to programmed-aging theory, the body ages in accordance with a normal developmental pattern unique to each species; and human cells are genetically programmed to divide a finite number of times and then stop. According to the wear-and-tear theory of aging, humans age because organs and organ systems simply wear out.

2. What is reserve capacity, and how does it change in old age?

Answer guideline. Reserve capacity is a kind of "backup" capacity which allows the body to function under stress and maintain homeostasis. With aging, reserve capacity decreases. The change is not noticeable under normal everyday circumstances but may be apparent when an older person is fatigued, under stress, or ill.

3. Identify two reversible causes of dementia.

Answer guideline. The symptoms of dementia may be caused by depression; depression is widespread among the elderly as a result of changes in health, bereavement, the death of friends, and financial worries (among other factors). The symptoms of dementia may also be caused by overmedication. Because older people tend to take several kinds of medication, it is possible for these chemicals to interact and have unintended side effects on behavior, including confusion, forgetfulness, and disorientation.

4. Describe the symptoms and diagnosis of Alzheimer's disease.

Answer guideline. The most pronounced symptom of Alzheimer's disease is a progressive deterioration in cognitive functions, including memory, judgment, concentration, orientation, and use of language. Other symptoms include irritability, restlessness, and agitation. At present, Alzheimer's disease can be diagnosed with certainty only by brain autopsy after death, when plaques and tangles in the hippocampus can be detected. A diagnosis made while the patient is still alive is the result of a long process of excluding other possible causes of the symptoms.

5. Describe terminal drop, and explain its importance in considering the findings of cross-sectional studies of intelligence.

Answer guideline. Terminal drop is a sudden decline in cognitive functioning occurring shortly before death. Although terminal drop can occur at all ages, it tends to lower mean scores of older age groups in cross-sectional studies of intellectual functioning, since more older than younger adults are likely to be near death.

6. Distinguish between the mechanics and pragmatics of intelligence.

Answer guideline. Mechanics of intelligence are processes such as information processing and problem solving; content is not a part of the mechanics of intelligence. Mechanics of intelligence, like fluid intelligence, are believed to decline with age. Pragmatics of intelligence include practical thinking skills, the ability to apply experience and wisdom, specialized professional insight, and general "street smarts. Pragmatics of intelligence may increase through late adulthood.

7. Summarize three explanations presented in the text for memory declines in late adulthood.

Answer guideline. According to one explanation, age changes in memory result from physiological aging: changes in neurological structures cause changes in performance. According to processing hypotheses, older people are less adept than the young at encoding information to be remembered, storing that information, and retrieving it. Finally, contextual hypotheses propose that background factors (e.g., motivation, familiarity with a task, learning habits) are the source of age differences in memory.

8. Describe factors which influence feelings about retirement.

Answer guideline. Demographic factors are one correlate of feelings about retirement: generally, better-educated and higher-status workers tend to be less eager to retire. Health and income are important correlates of reactions to actual retirement: healthier people with a relatively adequate retirement income tend to be relatively well satisfied with retirement. Finally, the ability to find meaningful uses of leisure time is an important correlate of satisfaction with retirement.

CHAPTER 17

PERSONALITY AND
SOCIAL DEVELOPMENT
IN LATE ADULTHOOD

INTRODUCTION

How people adapt to aging depends, to a large extent, on their personalities and on how they have adapted to situations throughout life. They can experience the last stage of life positively and may even experience it as a time of growth and fulfillment.

- **Chapter 17** begins with an examination of two theories of psychological development in late adulthood: Erikson's eighth crisis, integrity versus despair, and Peck's three crises of late adulthood.

- The chapter then describes the results of several research studies pertaining to emotional health and the stability of the personality in late adulthood.

- Several approaches to successful aging are discussed, including activity theory and disengagement theory.

- The relationship between personality and

patterns of aging are discussed, and four major personality types, with associated patterns of aging, are described.

- The chapter examines several social issues related to aging, such as changes in income, choices of living arrangements (including nursing homes), and the shocking problem of abuse of the elderly.

- A discussion of personal relationships in late life is provided, including such topics as: marriage and marital happiness, divorce, surviving a spouse's death, remarriage, sexual relationships, relationships with siblings, and friendships.

- The chapter concludes with an exploration of relationships with adult children, with a discussion of childlessness, and with the benefits of grandparenthood.

CHAPTER OUTLINE

I. THEORY AND RESEARCH ON PERSONALITY DEVELOPMENT

A. ERIK ERIKSON: CRISIS 8: INTEGRITY VERSUS DESPAIR
B. ROBERT PECK: THREE ADJUSTMENTS OF LATE ADULTHOOD
C. GEORGE VAILLANT: FACTORS IN EMOTIONAL HEALTH
D. RESEARCH ON STABILITY AND CHANGE IN PERSONALITY
E. APPROACHES TO "SUCCESSFUL AGING"
   1. Disengagement Theory
   2. Activity Theory
   3. Personal Definitions of Aging Successfully
F. PERSONALITY AND PATTERNS OF AGING

II. SOCIAL ISSUES RELATED TO AGING

A. INCOME
B. LIVING ARRANGEMENTS
   1. Living Independently
   2. Living in Institutions
      a. Who lives in nursing homes?
      b. What makes a good nursing home?
      c. Problems in nursing homes
C. ABUSE OF THE ELDERLY

III. PERSONAL RELATIONSHIPS IN LATE LIFE

A. MARRIAGE
   1. Marital Happiness
   2. Strengths and Strains in Late-Life Marriage
B. BEING SINGLE AGAIN: DIVORCE AND WIDOWHOOD
C. REMARRIAGE
D. SINGLE LIFE: THE "NEVER MARRIEDS"
E. SEXUAL RELATIONSHIPS
F. RELATIONSHIPS WITH ADULT CHILDREN
G. FRIENDSHIPS
H. RELATIONSHIPS WITH ADULT CHILDREN
   1. How Parents Help Children
   2. How Children Help Parents
I. CHILDLESSNESS
J. GRANDPARENTHOOD AND GREAT-GRANDPARENTHOOD

KEY TERMS

activity theory (page 562)
disengagement theory (562)
elder abuse (570)
integrity versus despair (558)

LEARNING OBJECTIVES

After finishing Chapter 17, students should be able to:

1. Explain Erikson's eighth crisis--*integrity versus despair*--and the virtue that results from its successful resolution. (pp. 558-559)

2. Describe the three psychological adjustments of late adulthood according to Peck.
   a. broader self-definition versus preoccupation with work roles (p. 559)
   b. transcendence of the body versus preoccupation with the body (pp. 559-560)
   c. transcendence of the ego versus preoccupation with the ego (p. 560)

3. Describe some of the factors that have been found to be associated with emotional health in late adulthood. (pp. 560-561)

4. List and discuss some of the research findings on stability and change in personality in late adulthood. (p. 561)

5. Summarize the main ideas of the following two theories of successful aging: *disengagement theory* and *activity theory* (pp. 562-563)

6. Describe the four major personality types found in elderly people: integrated, armor-defended, passive dependent, unintegrated (p. 564-566)

7. Explain how income affects the way people adjust to aging. (p. 566)

8. Discuss the relationship between one's living arrangements and the way one adjusts to aging. (pp. 566-570)

9. Describe each of the following independent living arrangements: Retirement and life-care communities, Sharing a house, Group homes, and Accessory housing (p. 569)

10. Describe those elderly who live in nursing homes. (pp. 569-570)

11. Describe the characteristics of a good nursing home. (p. 570)

12. List and discuss some problems sometimes found in nursing homes. (p. 570)

13. Discuss the problem of abuse of the elderly. (pp. 570-572)

14. Describe some research findings about marital happiness in long-term marriages. (pp. 572-573)

15. Discuss some of the strengths and strains in late-life marriage. (p. 573)

16. Discuss the issue of divorce among the elderly. (p. 574)

17. Discuss remarriage in late adulthood. (p. 574)

18. Explain how being single and never married is related to growing old. (pp. 574-575)

19. Describe how sexual relationships develop in old age. (pp. 575-576)

20. Explain the significance and quality of relationships between elderly people and the following: siblings, friends, and adult children (pp. 576-578)

21. Describe what life is like for the elderly who are childless. (pp. 578-580)

22. Discuss how the elderly adapt in roles as grandparents and great-grandparents. (pp. 580-581)

CHAPTER SUMMARY AND TEACHING RECOMMENDATIONS

The chapter begins with a section called "Theory and Research on Personality Development." Erikson's final stage of psychosocial development, Peck's three adjustments of old age, and Vaillant's study on factors contributing to emotional health in late adulthood are reviewed. Following is a brief discussion of research on personality development in old age, in which the authors note both stability and change.

The authors then discuss disengagement theory and activity theory. They present findings from two studies--one reporting middle-aged and older people's personal definitions of "successful aging" and the second indicating that various lifestyle patterns are associated with aging successfully.

The next section, "Social Issues Related to Aging," examines three social issues related to aging: income, living arrangements, and abuse of the elderly. The authors note that although the economic situation of the elderly has generally improved in recent years, many older people experience financial problems. In discussing living arrangements, the authors point out that most older people live more or less independently in their communities, rather than in institutions, and they describe a variety of options which could make it possible for still more older individuals to remain in the community.

The authors next discuss institutional-ization, describing both the features of high-quality care and the typical problems in nursing homes. The section closes with a discussion of "elder abuse." The authors point out that such abuse can be inflicted in different ways and discuss treatments available for both victims and abusers.

The next section of the chapter is "Personal Relationships in Late Life." The authors first take up marriage, pointing out that marital satisfaction tends to be high in old age, although age-related adjustments (e.g., retirement and changes in health) may strain a marriage. There is a brief section on divorce, in which the authors note that divorce is uncommon in later life. The authors then present findings from several studies on widowhood, indicating how people adjust to the death of a spouse and identifying factors which contribute to resolution of grief. They next take up remarriage, identifying correlates of the probability of remarriage and discussing satisfaction with remarriage. They also examine the situation of older people who have never married: these people are presented as relatively independent and satisfied in old age.

Age-related changes in sexual functioning are considered next; the authors stress that despite physiological changes, we remain sexual beings throughout the life span.

The next topic in this section is sibling relationships in old age. The authors note that, although there has been little empirical work on this topic, the available evidence suggests that these bonds remain important throughout life and may become especially important in old age.

The authors continue with a discussion of friendships in old age. They describe recent research on contact with friends and on how such contact is related to psychological well-being; they also discuss the importance of friends as resources in coping with age-related stresses.

Closing the chapter is a discussion of parenthood in old age; the authors note that frequent contact and exchanges of assistance are typical for older parents and adult children. The authors also discuss the consequences of childlessness in old age, pointing out that there is no evidence of long-term negative consequences of childlessness.

The chapter closes with a discussion of grandparenthood. Here, the authors note that most grandparents see at least some of their grandchildren often, but that few grandparents take an active role in everyday tasks of their grandchildren's upbringing. They emphasize, however, that grandparents can be an important family resource during times of crisis.

Boxes in Chapter 17 are "Religion and Emotional Well-Being in Late Life," "Aging among African Americans, Hispanic Americans, and Other American Minority Groups," "Visiting Someone in a Nursing Home," and "Extended Family Living in Latin America."

AUDIOVISUAL MATERIALS

Distributor, date, and running time are given for each film or video. Distributors' addresses are listed in the appendix (General Resources). If a film or video is not in color, there is a notation (BW) to that effect.

Caring for the elderly. (FFHS, 1994, video, 19 min.) An overview of the various methods of care available for the aging, from day care centers and group housing to nursing homes.

To be old, black, and poor. (FFHS, 1994, video, 58 min.) This a gritty and painfully real exposition of what it means to be black, poor, and elderly in the United States.

Over 100. (FFHS, 1994, video, 28 min.) Three men and three women explain what life is like after 100.

How to live past 100. (FFHS, 1994, video, 19 min.) This program examines the lives of some centenarians in seeking clues to longevity and to determining the reasons for the increasing numbers of people over 100 in America today.

Aging in Japan: When traditional mechanisms vanish. (FFHS, 1994, video, 45 min.) A record of a society in flux in which the traditional mechanisms for looking after old people are breaking down.

Grandma didn't wave back. (FFHS, 1994, video, 24 min.) A "Young People's Special," this is the story of the love between an aging grandmother and 11-year-old Debbie.

Growing older and better. (FFHS, 1994, video, 28 min.) This specially adapted Phil Donahue program features experts and ordinary people who discuss ways to stay healthy and active.

Nursing home care. (FFHS, 1994, video, 19 min.) What constitutes a well-run nursing home and criteria for evaluating them.

The search for intimacy: Love, sex, and relationships in the later years. (UFV, 1986, approximately 25 min.) Includes discussions of sexuality by Dr. Alex Comfort and by older people, whose marital status varies.

Guest speakers

Of the topics in this chapter, three that could be effectively addressed by guest speakers are institutionalization, abuse of the elderly, and crime. You could contact a nursing home in your area (preferably, of course, one that is well regarded in the community) to see if an administrator, the social services director, or the activities director would be willing to talk to the class. Topics for such a speaker include the circumstances which usually bring an older person into a nursing home, ways in which the family and community can maintain involvement with residents of nursing homes, and social or emotional needs that are particularly pressing for people in nursing homes.

A speaker on elder abuse may be somewhat more difficult to locate, as the problem is being openly recognized very slowly. However, possible sources would include a local hospital, a senior center, the local Agency on Aging, a community mental health center, the state Office on Aging, and community religious organizations offering support programs for family caregivers.

Your state or local police force, or the district attorney's office, would probably be the best sources for a speaker on crime as it affects the elderly. A few communities have police officers specially trained to work with older victims of crime; if this service is available in your community, one of the officers might be able to speak to the class. Similarly, some communities have victims' assistance programs (usually operated from the district attorney's office) whose clients include elderly victims.

LECTURE OUTLINES

Lecture 1: Patterns of "Successful Aging"

I. Disengagement theory

Disengagement theory is a major theory of "successful aging"--that is, of what circumstances lead to or contribute to satisfaction and morale in old age.

A. Thesis. Older people's "adjustment" is typically judged by middle-aged standards and found wanting. To the contrary, aging involves a natural withdrawal of old people from the social world (relationships and activities) and of the social world from old people; this withdrawal brings increased relaxation and contentment.

1. Withdrawal is beneficial to older people. They no longer want to or can behave like young people (because of decreased strength, stamina, etc.); withdrawal spares them from any need to do so.

2. Withdrawal is beneficial to society. Since older people's capacities decrease, old people (and their contributions) must be replaced with newer, younger people (and their contributions).

B. Research on disengagement theory. Disengagement theory is based on the Kansas City Study of Adult Life, which began in 1955.

1. Subjects and methodology. The Kansas City Study involved interviews with two samples.

   a. Relatively young people: 172 subjects aged 48-68. These subjects were interviewed five times over the next 3 years. They were relatively well educated and had moderate incomes.

   b. Older people: 107 subjects in their seventies and eighties. These subjects were interviewed three times over the next 2 years.

   c. Interview topics: demographic background; recent changes in subjects' lives; TAT; recent changes in patterns of social interaction; F scale, morale scale, and anomie scale; outlook on life and on family.

2. Findings.

   a. For many subjects, the researchers identified decreased social interaction with age, except with family members. This pattern emerged even among the youngest subjects (who were in their late forties when first interviewed and their early fifties when last interviewed).

b. Oldest subjects viewed themselves as taking less initiative in social relationships, thought that others also saw them that way, and wanted others to see them that way.
c. Disengagement was a gradual process. For some subjects, life satisfaction and morale decreased at the beginning of the disengagement process, but this seemed to indicate a period of transition and adjustment. When these subjects were completely disengaged, their life satisfaction and morale were higher.
C. Problems with disengagement theory. Questions have been raised about disengagement theory, although the Kansas City study supports it.
1. Is disengagement voluntary on the part of older people? Some data from other research indicate lower levels of life satisfaction and morale among "disengaged" elderly people.
2. Is disengagement necessary for "successful aging"? Some data, from still other studies, indicate high levels of life satisfaction and morale without disengagement; this suggests that identifying disengagement as the means of adjustment to aging is probably an oversimplification.

II. Activity and satisfaction with life

Neugarten's research provides another perspective on "successful aging."

A. Neugarten found various relationships between levels of activity and satisfaction with life. That is, high levels of life satisfaction were correlated with several patterns of activity and lifestyles. Various "styles" of aging in this sample included the following:
1. Some responsibilities and involvements were dropped with aging, while high satisfaction was maintained.
2. Responsibilities and involvements were decreased, and life satisfaction decreased.
3. A lifelong pattern of low levels of responsibility and involvement was paired with high satisfaction.
4. A lifelong pattern of high levels of responsibility and involvement was paired with high satisfaction.
B. Neugarten proposed that personality determines what level of activity and involvement leads to successful aging, and that (given enough options in the environment) older people choose the activity levels and types of involvement most compatible with their self-concept.

References for Lecture 1

Neugarten, B. L. (1968). *Middle age and aging.* Chicago: University of Chicago Press.
Neugarten, B. L. (1972). *Middle age and aging: A reader in social psychology.* Chicago: University of Chicago Press.

Lecture 2: Institutionalization

I. Statistics

Despite a widespread belief that most old people live in nursing homes, relatively few elderly people are institutionalized.

A. About 4 to 5 percent of people over age 65 are living in nursing homes at any one time.
B. The "typical" resident of a nursing home is:
1. Quite old (nationwide, the average age of residents is 82, and 70 percent of residents are over 70).
2. Female.
3. Unmarried (that is, with no living spouse).
4. Admitted to the nursing home after a period of hospitalization.

II. Nursing homes

Nursing homes can be considered in terms of care and personnel.

A. Care. There are several levels of nursing home care. The major distinction is between skilled and intermediate care; these levels of care may be provided in different institutions or in different parts of the same institution.
1. Skilled nursing care includes:
a. Fairly extensive medical and rehabilitative services (e.g., emergency and regularly available physician services, pharmaceutical services,

laboratory services, radiology services, dental services) which are either available within the institution or formally contracted for an outside agency or agencies.

b. Regular physician visits for each patient, development and periodic revision of patient care plans, and a moderately high ratio of staff to patients (7 employees for every 10 patients).

2. Intermediate care is designed for people who need some health supervision and access to health and rehabilitative services, but who do not need full-time professional health care. In intermediate care, at least as much attention is given to social and recreational services as to medical services.

B. Personnel. Many people who are concerned about the situation of patients in nursing homes focus on the staffs of these homes.

1. Nationwide, only about 7 percent of nursing home staff members are RNs, and only about 8 percent are LPNs. Most of the remaining staff members are nurses' aides and orderlies.

a. Nurses' aides and orderlies receive only the most minimal training (if any), and over half of them have had no previous experience working either with older people or in a medical setting.

b. Nationally, there is a 75 percent turnover rate in nurses' aides and orderlies employed in nursing homes, and it is easy to see why: their salaries are at the minimum-wage level or only slightly above it, they are not trained (as noted above), and burnout is a common experience.

III. Legislation

There is considerable legislation concerning nursing homes.

A. Both state and federal legislation has been enacted in an effort to ensure high-quality care in nursing homes, and facilities are inspected by fire and safety authorities.

B. However, there are many problems, particularly with regard to inspections.

1. First, inspections primarily evaluate the physical plant (e.g., exits, fire-prevention systems, cleanliness), as opposed to other things that might influence the quality of care.

2. Second, there are few penalties that officials can levy against institutions not complying with regulations. Legally, the institution's license can be revoked. However, this step takes a long time and is probably unnecessary for minor violations. Closing a facility may cause the residents greater suffering than the violations themselves did.

3. Third, although inspections are in theory unannounced, they are rarely a surprise to administrators.

References for Lecture 2

Bartlett, H. (1993). *Nursing homes for early questions of quality and policy.* Philadelphia, PA: Harwood.

Belgrave, L., Wykle, M., & Choi, J. (1993, June). Health, double jeopardy, and culture: The use of institutionalization by African-Americans. *The gerontologist, 33,* 379-385.

Gelfand, D. E. & Olsen, J. K. (1980). *The aging network: Programs and services.* New York: Springer.

Sixsmith, A. (1993, May). Delivering "positive care" in nursing homes. *International journal of geriatric psychiatry, 8*(5), 407-412.

Lecture 3: Aging Parents and Their Children

I. Myths and misconceptions

There are some widespread misconceptions about the family relationships of older people.

A. Isolation. It is often believed that elderly people rarely see their children or grandchildren, are geographically isolated from relatives, rarely visit family members, and have little contact with their families by telephone or mail.

B. Neglect. It is believed that when older people need help of some kind (practical, affective, or financial), the family is not the usual source of help; also, that adult children are concerned only with the needs of their own nuclear families and do not try to meet the needs of parents or grandparents.

II. Facts

Gerontological research indicates that very few elderly people are isolated from their families: only orphans and those who do not want close ties tend not to have regular contact with family members. Research on family relationships in old age describes residential proximity and visiting patterns (rather than isolation) and exchanges of help (rather than neglect).

A. Proximity. Typically, older people and their adult children prefer to live near one another but not in the same household. A common goal, "intimacy at a distance," is attained by most families.
1. Today there are few multigenerational households, and those that do exist are typically set up out of necessity rather than desire (as far as we can tell, this was also the case in earlier times).
2. However, most elderly people live within a short drive of at least one of their children. An international study (which collected data in the United States, England, and Denmark) found that nearly two-thirds (60 percent) of people over age 65 lived within walking distance of one or more of their children.
3. Children most likely to live near older parents are daughters and married children.
B. Visiting. Patterns of visiting parallel those of proximity. Most older people see at least some of their children often.
1. Recent surveys of older people in the United States (and earlier surveys of older people in several other countries) have found that about 75 percent see at least some of their children weekly, and about 50 percent see at least some of their children daily.
2. For most families, visiting is more frequent and more regular when it involves female lineage (mother-daughter). This has led to a designation of women as "kin keepers."

3. Some husbands have more contact with their wife's parents than with their own.
4. Widowed men sometimes have problems maintaining earlier patterns of family contact because their wives took the initiative.
C. Exchanging help. Exchanges of help seem to be common in most families.
1. Young adults (newly married couples, families with young children) typically receive various forms of help from middle-aged parents (financial help, child care, advice, practical help).
2. Elderly adults typically receive various forms of help from middle-aged children (financial aid, care during illness, home repairs and maintenance, transportation, etc.).
3. Therefore, the middle-aged are usually helping both their young adult children and their elderly parents. Usually, they also receive some help from the older and younger generations, but they tend to receive less help than they provide.
4. Most help within families is provided by women (except for strenuous home and yard work, financial help, and advice).

References for Lecture 3

Adams, T. (1993). *When parents age: What children can do.* New York: Berkley.
Hendricks, J. & Rosenthal, C. (Eds.) (1993). *The Remainder of their days: Domestic policy and older families in the United States and Canada.* New York: Garland.
Levitt, M. (1993, September). Convoys of Social support: An intergenerational analysis. *Psychology and aging,* 8(3), 323-326.
Troll, L. (1986). *Family issues in current gerontology.* New York: Springer.

Lecture 4: Abuse of the elderly

I. Definition

Abuse of the elderly--or <u>elder abuse,</u> as it is often called--can be defined in terms of types of abuse.

A. Physical abuse: beatings; lack of personal care, food, medical care, or needed supervision; restraint (e.g., being tied to a bed or chair); sexual abuse.

B.   Psychological abuse: verbal assaults, threats, isolation, inducing fear.
C.   Material abuse: theft or misuse of money or property, exploitation.

II.   Victims

"Typical victims" of abuse can be identified, although no racial, socioeconomic, or other social characteristics have been found to distinguish victims from other elderly people.

A.   They are the most vulnerable elderly people: of advanced age, frail, and with chronic diseases or physical or mental impairments. They usually have two or more physical disabilities.
B.   They are less aware than others in their age cohort of alternative living arrangements or alternative means of support.
C.   They are more often women than men.

III.   Explanations

No single explanation is likely to apply in all cases of elder abuse. In most cases, there is probably some combination of the following explanations.

A.   Revenge. Abusers were (or perceived themselves to be) mistreated by the elderly victim in the past.
B.   Incapacity. The caregiver may be incapable of performing required tasks.
C.   Pathology. Personality disorders may explain aggressive behavior in an intimate relationship.
D.   Economic exploitation. The caregiver misuses the victim's economic and material resources to gain control of the victim and the resources.
E.   Generational transmission. Violent behavior may be transmitted from one generation to the next as a learned response to stress.
F.   Behavior of the victim. Dependent elderly people may seek control in maladaptive ways (e.g., pouting, withdrawal, manipulation, pitting family members against one another, imposing guilt on caregivers).
G.   Lack of community resources. If community support for caregivers is lacking, their frustration may be expressed through violence.

IV.   Legislation

Protective service laws have been developed in at least 26 states; mandatory reporting laws have been enacted in 16 states.

V.   Treatment

At least two treatment approaches can be noted.

A.   Teaching caregivers more effective ways to provide care and to use available community resources.
B.   Teaching caregivers how to control anger.

References for Lecture 4

Burton, R. (1992). A comparative analysis of abuse of senior citizens in urban and rural areas by their spouse, children, grandchildren, and caretakers. *Dissertation abstracts international, 52*(12-A), 4438.
Coyne, A. (1993, April). The relationship between dementia and elder abuse. *American journal of psychiatry, 150*(4), 643-646.
Kosberg, J. (1983). *Abuse and maltreatment of the elderly: Causes and interventions.* Boston: Wright.
Lucas, E. (1991). *Elder abuse and its recognition among health service professionals.* New York: Garland.

Lecture 5: Gender Differences in Grandparenthood

I.   Meaning and styles of grandparenthood

In Neugarten and Weinstein's classic study of the "changing American grandparent" (1964), interviews were conducted with 70 grandparent couples in the Chicago area to identify the subjects' "personal meaning" of grandparenthood and their styles of grandparenting.

A.   Sources of "personal meaning" in grandparenthood.
   1.   General findings. Five types of "meaning" were identified in the sample, although each subject was classified as endorsing one primary source of meaning.
   2.   Gender differences in "meaning." Women (more often than men) found a sense of biological renewal or continuity in

grandparenthood. The researchers suggested that this finding may be explained by the fact that most of the couples were maternal grandparents.

B.   Styles of grandparenting. When and for what purposes did these grandparents see their grandchildren? What kinds of activities did they share with their grandchildren?
1.   General findings. Five styles of grandparenting were identified in the sample.
2.   Gender differences in styles.
    a.   "Parent surrogate" style (in which the grandparent regularly cared for the grandchild while the mother worked outside of the home) was found only in grandmothers.
    b.   "Reservoir of family wisdom" style (in which the grandparent passed on special knowledge and skills to grandchildren) was infrequent; but when it occurred, it was found primarily in grandfathers.

II.   Mental health and the meaning of grandparenthood

In Helen Kivnick's more recent study of mental health and the "meaning" of grandparenthood (1982), over 200 grandparents in northern California were interviewed. They discussed the personal significance of grandparenthood and completed measures of life satisfaction and morale.

A.   Findings for women. For grandmothers in Kivnick's study, the "meaning" of grandparenthood was related to mental health (life satisfaction and morale) in two ways.
1.   In general, "meaning" had a compensatory function; it "buffered" age-related deprivations (such as widowhood and changes in health) and thus decreased their impact on mental health.
2.   Women experiencing the greatest deprivations, in particular, tended to make grandparenthood a central aspect of their lives and to use it as a "prompt" for reminiscence; reactions minimized the impact of deprivation on mental health.

B.   Findings for men. For grandfathers, the relationship between "meaning" and mental health was more direct than it was for grandmothers, in that high levels of life satisfaction and morale were associated with strong endorsement of at least some aspects of "meaning."

III.   Responsibilities and satisfaction in grandparenthood

Thomas's study of satisfaction with grandparenting and perceived responsibilities of grandparenthood (1986) used a mail survey of more than 200 grandparents in southeastern Wisconsin (the return rate was over 80 percent). Survey items asked to what extent respondents enjoyed being grandparents and to what extent they felt they should carry out four types of responsibilities (giving advice on child rearing, taking care of grandchildren, disciplining grandchildren, and helping grandchildren).

A.   Gender differences in levels of satisfaction and perceived responsibility.
1.   Grandmothers expressed greater satisfaction with grandparenthood.
2.   Grandfathers expressed a greater sense of responsibility for taking care of grandchildren and giving advice on child rearing.
B.   Gender differences in associations between feelings about grandparenthood.
1.   For grandmothers, endorsing responsibility for caretaking and helping predicted high levels of satisfaction with grandparenthood.
2.   For grandfathers, being older, having relatively young grandchildren, and endorsing responsibility for caretaking and helping predicted high levels of satisfaction with grandparenthood.

References for Lecture 5

Kivnick, H. (1988). Grandparenthood, life review, and psychosocial development. Special issue: Twenty-five years of the life review: Theoretical and practical considerations. *Journal of gerontological social work, 12*(3-4), 63-81.
Storm, R. (1991). *Becoming a better grandparent. Viewpoints on strengthening the family.* Newbury Park, CA: Sage.
Thomas, J. (1986a). Age and sex differences in perceptions of grandparenting. *Journal of gerontology,* 41, 417-423.

Thomas, J. (1986b). Gender differences in satisfaction with grandparenting. *Psychology and aging*, 1, 215-219.

Thomas, J. (1990). The grandparent role: A double bind. *International journal of aging and human development, 31*(3), 169-177.

TOPIC FOR DEBATE

Should National Legislation be Enacted to Protect Grandparents' Access to Grandchildren Following Parents' Divorce?

Background

As divorce has become a more prominent feature of American society, we can identify more and more ways in which disruption of a marriage affects all members of the family. There has long been great concern, on the part of professionals as well as divorcing parents, about how children are affected by their parents' divorce. More recently, attention has turned to how grandparents may be affected when their children are divorced.

In some cases, grandparents lose the opportunity to have any contact at all with their grandchildren after their children's divorce. Individual case histories and recent research indicate that this causes deep psychic pain to grandparents. Some states have recognized these grandparents' plight by enacting laws providing for "grandparental visitation" rights following divorce.

Some people feel that these laws should be enacted on a broader, national level. They argue that relationships with grandchildren are typically of great importance to grandparents: most grandparents express enjoyment of their family status, and most make a point of seeing their grandchildren often. Furthermore, some research shows that feelings about grandparenthood are associated with grandparents' mental health.

It can also be argued that grandparents can be of enormous importance to grandchildren. Grandparents can be significant links to family heritage, as well as to cultural or ethnic heritage. Particularly for children whose parents are divorced, grandparents may also represent a source of security and stability. Children who have frequent contact with their grandparents have been shown to hold less stereotyped and less negative views of older people than children who see their grandparents less often.

However, there are also strong arguments against legislation ensuring grandparental visitation. After divorce, the first priority is to stabilize the parent-child relationship, and grandparental visitation rights could complicate this process even under the best of circumstances. Under the worst of circumstances, grandparents may even be a disruptive influence. Grandparents may use grandchildren as pawns in their own efforts to express hostility and resentment toward their children or their former children-in-law.

More generally, opponents of grandparental visitation rights argue that parents have the ultimate right to decide what values and behaviors they wish to instill in their children. If parents believe that grandparents represent values and behavior that they, as parents, cannot condone, then they should have the right to isolate their children from the grandparents.

Debate plan

Using this background, and information from additional sources (selected references appear below), student panels should debate the following positions:

Position A. National legislation should be enacted to ensure that grandparents maintain the rights to see their grandchildren after parental divorce.

Position B. After a divorce, parents should have the right to decide what contact between grandparents and grandchildren is appropriate.

References for the debate

Cherlin, A. J. & Furstenberg, F. F. (1986). *The new American grandparent: A place in the family, a life apart.* New York: Basic Books.

O'Reilly, E. (1993, Spring). Grandparent-headed families: New therapeutic challenges. *Child psychiatry and human development, 23*(3), 147-159.

Oyserman, D. (1993, May). Dynamics in a three-generational family: Teens, grandparents, and babies. *Developmental psychology, 29*(3), 564-572.

Purnell, M. & Bagby, B. (1993, April). Grandparents' rights: Implications for family specialists. *Family relations, 42*, 173-178.

TOPICS FOR DISCUSSION

Topic 1: Successful Aging

1. Ask students to summarize the disengagement and activity theories of aging (pages 562-563). Ask them to evaluate the extent to which research has or has not supported each theory. Ask them which theory seems to provide the best explanation for patterns of aging among older people they know personally.

2. Ask students to summarize the findings of the study on styles of aging, as presented in the text (pages 563-566). Ask them what this implies about disengagement theory and activity theory.

Topic 2: Social Issues Related to Aging

1. The text discusses three social issues: income, living arrangements, and abuse (pages 566-572). Ask students which of these issues seem to pose the greatest problems for older people, and why.

2. Ask students how contemporary society could go further to ensure an adequate income for all older people. Ask them to suggest steps that older individuals themselves could take to ensure an adequate income.

3. The text describes several alternatives for older people who want to live independently (pages 568-569). Ask students to suggest additional types of individual living arrangements. Ask them what alternative they would prefer for their own parents or grandparents, and why. You might also ask them what alternative they would prefer for themselves.

4. Ask students to suggest steps that might be effective in minimizing older people's vulnerability to abuse.

Topic 3: Marriage and Widowhood

1. Ask students to identify the greatest potential satisfaction in, and the most difficult aspect of, a long-term marriage, and to explain their selection.

2. The text identifies several important relationships outside of marriage which can enrich late life (pages 574-578). Ask students to list these relationships and to explain some of the psychological and emotional benefits of these continued bonds.

PROJECTS AND CLASS EXERCISES

Group Exercise: Optimizing Nursing Home Environments

Although most older people prefer to live independently in the community, and most are successful in doing so, institutional care is an essential option for an aging population. Some facilities are excellent, providing high-quality care, comfort, and intellectual and social stimulation. However, even in these excellent settings, there is probably some room for improvement.

Working in groups, students should develop a description of an ideal nursing home. Their description should include the approximate number of residents, the approximate number of staff members, the qualifications of the staff, the physical design of the facility, provisions for promoting contact between residents and the community, and activities offered within the facility.

Project 1: Aging in Minority Cultures

Students should read an ethnographical study of a nonwestern culture. They should then write a paper describing the situation of older people in the culture, including older peoples' participation in the economy, in government, in religion, and in the family.

Project 2: Personal Relationships in Old Age

Students should select one of the personal relationships discussed in the chapter (e.g., marriage, remarriage, friendships) and read one or more recent review articles or research reports discussing it. They should also interview one or more elderly people who have experience with that type of relationship. Students should write a paper discussing the interview in the context of the research.

ESSAY QUESTIONS

1. Describe personality development in old age, according to Erik Erikson and Robert Peck.

Answer guideline. According to Erikson, people experience the crisis of integrity versus despair in old age. Ideally, the person can look back over his or her life and see a pattern of coherence and wholeness; if not, the person is likely to experience profound regret and fear of death. Peck proposes that older people confront three crises. The first is ego differentiation versus work-role preoccupation, which necessitates redefining personal worth on a basis broader than work performed. The second crisis is body transcendence versus body preoccupation; in this case, the older person must come to value relationships and activities more than optimal health (which is unlikely to be attained or maintained at this point in life). The final crisis is ego transcendence versus ego preoccupation. In resolving this crisis, the older person must move beyond self-concern and accept his or her own mortality.

2. Contrast disengagement theory and activity theory.

Answer guideline. According to disengagement theory, aging is characterized by withdrawal of the older person from society and of society from the older person. Withdrawal benefits older people by decreasing responsibilities and demands just as their strength and stamina are waning. Withdrawal also benefits society, as its younger members are recruited to fulfill the functions formerly carried out by older people. This process of mutual withdrawal is held to maximize "life satisfaction" in old age. According to activity theory, life satisfaction in old age is attained through continued involvement and responsibility rather than withdrawal. Thus, involvements inevitably lost through aging (e.g., through retirement and widowhood) are replaced with new sources of involvement (e.g., volunteer work and grandparenthood).

3. Describe elements of high-quality nursing home care.

Answer guideline. One important element of high-quality nursing home care is the opportunity for residents to make decisions and exert control over their daily lives. When such opportunities are present, residents tend to be more alert, more active, happier, and healthier, and even to live longer. Other elements of high-quality care are a staff with specialized training in care of the aged, adequate government insurance programs, an attractive and hygienic physical plant, a structure permitting various levels of care within a single facility, varied and stimulating activities, and as much privacy as possible.

4. Discuss sources of strain in marriage in old age.

Answer guideline. Strains in older peoples' marriages include differences in values, interests, and philosophies. These factors would cause problems in marriage at any age but may emerge late in marriages if one or both spouses experience personal change to which the other is unable or unwilling to adapt. Ill health may also strain marriages in old age; the caregiving spouse is likely to experience anger and resentment toward the frailer spouse, as well as fatigue and financial strain.

5. Identify factors which contribute to satisfying sexual relationships in old age.

Answer guideline. Although sexual functioning undergoes physiological change with aging, we remain sexual beings throughout the life span. Sexual functioning is likely to remain most satisfying for those who have been sexually active and have enjoyed sex earlier in life and for those who recognize sexual feelings as normal and pleasurable throughout life. It is also likelier to remain satisfying if younger adults show an open and welcoming attitude toward sexuality among the aged.

6. What functions does friendship serve in old age?

Answer guideline. Older people report that they derive greater enjoyment from time spent with friends than from time spent with family, perhaps because friendships are relationships that are voluntarily chosen and because contact with friends is often initiated for the purposes of leisure and enjoyment. Friendships are also an important source of intimacy for older people, particularly for those without family living nearby.

CHAPTER 18
DEATH AND BEREAVEMENT

INTRODUCTION

Chapter 18, the final chapter of the text, examines the final chapter of life--death and bereavement.

- The chapter begins with a discussion of three aspects of death: biological, social, and psychological.

- Attitudes, at different ages, toward death and dying are discussed, as are the idea of confronting one's own death and dealing with bereavement, mourning, and grief.

- Coping with the death of a spouse is discussed, as are various aspects of living as a widow or widower.

- Several important controversial issues related to death and dying are examined, namely, euthanasia and suicide.

- Finally, the chapter concludes with an examination of finding a purpose in life and death, which includes a discussion of the meaning of death.

CHAPTER OUTLINE

I. THREE ASPECTS OF DEATH

II. FACING DEATH

 A.   ATTITUDES TOWARD DEATH AND DYING ACROSS THE LIFE SPAN
  1.   Childhood
  2.   Adolescence
  3.   Young Adulthood
  4.   Middle Adulthood
  5.   Late Adulthood
 B.   CONFRONTING ONE'S OWN DEATH
  1.   Changes Preceding Death
   a.   Personality changes
   b.   Near-death experiences
  2.   "Stages of Dying": Elisabeth Kübler-Ross
 C.   BEREAVEMENT, MOURNING, AND GRIEF
  1.   A Multicultural Perspective on Mourning
  2.   Forms of Grief
   a.   Anticipatory grief
   b.   "Grief work": A three-phase pattern
   c.   Other patterns of grieving
  3.   How Children Cope with Bereavement
  4.   Helping People Deal with Dying and Bereavement
   a.   Implications of research
   b.   Grief therapy
   c.   Hospices
   d.   Support groups and services
   e.   Death education
    (1)   Goals of death education
    (2)   Teaching children about death
 D.   WIDOWHOOD: SURVIVING A SPOUSE
  1.   Adjusting to the Death of a Spouse
  2.   Living as a Widow or Widower

III. CONTROVERSIAL ISSUES OF DEATH AND DYING

 A.   EUTHANASIA AND THE RIGHT TO DIE
 B.   SUICIDE
  1.   Patterns of Suicide
   a.   Suicide among children
   b.   Suicide among adolescents
   c.   Suicide among adults
  2.   Preventing Suicide
   a.   What society can do
   b.   What family and friends can do
    (1)   Warning signs of suicide
    (2)   Actions that might avert suicide

IV. FINDING A PURPOSE IN LIFE AND DEATH

 A.   THE MEANING OF DEATH
 B.   REVIEWING A LIFE

KEY TERMS

active euthanasia (page 603)
anticipatory grief (596)
bereavement (593)
death education (600)
grief (593)
grief therapy (599)
hospice care (599)
life review (611)
living will (605)
medical durable power of attorney (609)
mourning (593)
near-death experience (592)
passive euthanasia (604)
thanatology (588)

LEARNING OBJECTIVES

After finishing Chapter 18, students should be able to:

1.   Define *thanatology*. (p. 588)

2.   Describe recent developments in the field of *thanatology*. (p. 588)

3. List and define three aspects of death. (p. 589)

4. Describe young children's attitudes toward death. (pp. 589-590)

5. Describe adolescents' attitudes toward death. (p. 590)

6. Describe how attitudes toward death develop from early to late adulthood. (pp. 590-592)

7. Discuss attitudes of people of different ages as they confront the approach of their own death. (pp. 592-593)

8. Identify some intellectual and personality changes which people often undergo shortly before death. (pp. 592-593)

9. Describe the results of studies of *near-death experiences*. (p. 593)

10. Explain Kübler-Ross's five stages of coming to terms with death. (p. 593)
    denial   depression
    anger   acceptance
    bargaining

11. Compare and contrast the concepts of *bereavement*, *mourning*, and *grief*. (p. 593)

12. Describe how *mourning* attitudes and practices vary in different cultures. (pp. 594-596)

13. Describe the various forms of *grief*. (pp. 596-598)

14. Describe the three phases that characterize the pattern of "grief work." (p. 597)

15. Summarize the five common beliefs about loss and the findings that these beliefs may not be valid. (pp. 597-598)

16. Describe the special aspects of mourning associated with grieving and mourning by children. (pp. 598-599)

17. Explain how the following are ways of helping people deal with dying and bereavement: *grief therapy*, *hospice*, support groups and services, *death education* (pp. 599-600)

18. Discuss the problem of adjusting to the death of a spouse. (pp. 601-602)

19. Describe living as a widow or widower. (p. 602-603)

20. Discuss the following controversial issues regarding death and dying: *euthanasia* and the right to die, suicide (pp. 603-605)

21. Differentiate between *active euthanasia* and *passive euthanasia*. (p. 603-605)

22. Outline the common provisions of a *"living will."* (p. 605)

23. Describe patterns of suicide among different age groups. (pp. 605-608)

24. Describe some actions that can be taken to help prevent suicide. (pp. 608-610)

25. Discuss the challenge of finding a purpose in life and death and factors which most influence attitudes. (pp. 610-611)

26. Discuss the *life review* and its benefits. (pp. 611-612)

CHAPTER SUMMARY AND TEACHING RECOMMENDATIONS

The first section of the chapter distinguishes three aspects of death--the biological (cessation of physiological functioning), the social (mourning customs and legal procedures), and the psychological (emotional reactions). In this section, the authors also note the interrelationships among these aspects and the growing complexity of the biological dimension as a result of advances in medical technology.

The next section describes attitudes toward death across the life span. The authors review studies documenting age changes in children's awareness of death; they discuss adolescents' views of death in the context of adolescents' cognitive functioning. Finally, reactions to death typical of early adulthood, middle adulthood, and later adulthood are described.

The authors describe personality changes that occur shortly before death and present research on "near-death experiences." Kübler-Ross's work on emotional reactions to dying is described, together with cautions about viewing her "stages" as a sequential progression. As the authors note, it is important to emphasize that acceptance is not always the ideal or healthiest reaction to impending death.

Next, the authors describe and distinguish bereavement, mourning, and grief. They also discuss the different ways in which people express grief, noting that many common beliefs about loss have not been validated through research. This section includes a discussion of support programs available to grieving people, including grief therapy, death education, and hospices.

Controversial issues related to death and dying are addressed in the next section. The authors discuss euthanasia and distinguish active from passive euthanasia. The implications of advances in medical technology for terminal care are addressed, and the authors describe "living wills" in this context. The authors then discuss suicide among children, adolescents, and adults, and outline the steps which society can take to prevent suicides.

The final section of the chapter is entitled "Finding a Purpose in Life and Death." The authors note the importance of finding meaning in one's life and explain the "life review" as an effort to find such meaning.

Boxes in Chapter 18 are "Postponing Death," "Mourning Customs among Traditional Jews," "Should Anencephalic Babies Be Used as Organ Donors?" "The Living Will and Medical Durable Power of Attorney," and "Evoking Memories for a 'Life Review.'"

AUDIOVISUAL MATERIALS

Distributor, date, and running time are given for each film or video. Distributors' addresses are listed in the appendix (General Resources). If a film or video is not in color, there is a notation (BW) to that effect.

Living with death: Unfinished business. (NIT, 1983, approximately 30 min.) Presents Kübler-Ross's views on death and dying.

Saying good-bye. (FFHS, 1994, video, 26 min.) Almost no one will escape the pain of surviving a loved one. This program talks to people who have gone through this difficult time to find out how they dealt with their grief.

Medicine and mercy. (FFHS, 1994, video, 26 min.) This program looks at the interplay among technology, ethics, and the quality of human life.

Family caregivers. (FFHS, 1994, video, 30 min.) This program steps into the lives of caregivers and their families and offers ideas for dealing with these stresses.

Living wills. (FFHS, 1994, video, 30 min.) This program examines the concept of living wills and advanced directives.

"Doctor Death": Medical ethics and doctor-assisted suicide. (FFHS, 1994, video, 28 min.) In this specially adapted Phil Donahue program, the man dubbed "Dr. Death" offers an in-depth explanation of his beliefs about incurable illness and the ethics of doctor-assisted suicide.

Last rites: A child's reaction to death. (FL, 1979, approximately 45 min.) Describes a young child's reaction to his mother's death.

Childhood's end: A look at adolescent suicide. (FML, 1981, approximately 25 min.) Topics include interviews with adolescents who have attempted suicide and with relatives and parents of teenagers who have committed suicide.

Suicide: Teenage crisis. (CRM, 1981, approximately 10 min.) An examination of teenage suicide and a discussion of possible preventive approaches.

Guest speakers

If there is a hospice in your community, try to arrange for one of its administrators, practitioners, or volunteers to visit the class. This person could describe the unique aspects of hospice care, including family involvement and approaches to controlling pain. Another possible guest speaker is a professional involved in death education or grief therapy; your most likely starting point for locating such a speaker would be a community mental health center or a hospice. You might also consider asking a funeral director to speak to the class on the various ways in which grief is expressed and the growing trend toward planning funerals before the actual need arises.

LECTURE OUTLINES

Lecture 1: Widowhood

I. Death of a spouse

The death of a spouse is among the most traumatic life events for men and women of any age, but it is a normative event of later life (at least for women). Some gerontologists have contrasted the experiences of widows and widowers.

II. Women's adjustment to widowhood

Some observers believe that adjusting to the death of a spouse is more difficult for women than for men, because women experience changes in social interactions, typically experience loneliness, and must adapt to a new identity.

A. Social interactions. Widowed women typically experience major changes in their patterns of social interaction.
   1. These changes include decreased contact with their in-laws. (Even if this change is welcome to a widowed woman, it still means that she has a more restricted range of social interaction than she had before her husband's death.)
   2. Other people may expect the widow to "keep her husband's memory alive" by associating only with other widows or with her family (certainly not with potential dating partners).
   3. Many women find that their friendship patterns are disrupted when their husbands die.
      a. This experience is most likely for women who are relatively young when they are widowed. For these women, friendships and social activities are often "couple-centered," and few of their women friends are likely to be widowed yet.
      b. Women who are widowed when they are older, however, may find that their widowed friends provide a "ready-made" close, informal support group.
B. Loneliness. Related to disrupted social interactions is another typical experience for widowed women: loneliness. Not only has the woman lost the companionship of her spouse, but she must also adapt to changes in other sources of companionship.
C. Identity. Another important part of a woman's adjustment to the death of her husband is adapting her identity to her new status of widow, as opposed to wife.
   1. How difficult this adaptation is varies from one woman to another.
   2. Adaptation depends partly on how central the role of "wife" was to the woman's self-concept or identity. A woman with many important adult roles (e.g., wife, mother, daughter, career woman, member of a religious group, community volunteer, grandmother, friend) would be expected to adjust her identity more easily than a woman with fewer important roles.

III. Men's adjustment

Some gerontologists maintain that adjusting to the death of a spouse is more difficult for men than for women. However, others point out that men typically have certain advantages over women in adapting.

A. Disadvantages for men include practical matters, loss of intimacy, and lack of "peers," though it is possible that changes in gender roles will lessen these disadvantages for future cohorts of men.
   1. Older men are often unprepared to deal with the practical tasks of managing a household. This can create various problems.
      a. Frustration becomes likely.
      b. Finances may become a problem for a widower who must hire a housekeeper.
      c. Health problems may arise for a widower who does not learn to cook or hire someone to cook for him.
   2. Loss of intimacy. Older men often have no confidant other than their wives, so that they may lose all intimacy following the death of their spouse.
   3. Lack of a support group. One other problem that many gerontologists consider greater for widowed men than for women is unavailability of "peers"--that is, a support group of people in the same situation. Because there are fewer widowers than widows (at any age), men are

unlikely to be able to turn to same-sex peers for information, sympathy, or assistance.

B. Widowed men do have some advantages over widowed women.
1. Men's identity is often disrupted less.
2. Men tend to have more adequate incomes and to be more skilled at financial management.
3. Men who want to remarry have far more opportunities to do so.

References for Lecture 1

Burgess, L. (1993). 20 years serving all generations. *Modern maturity, 36*(5), 6-7.
Connidis, Ingrid. (1992). Life transitions and the adult sibling tie: a qualitative study. *Journal of marriage & the family.* 1992, 54(4), 972-982.
Demo, Dr. (1994). Stuck at home. *American demographics*, 16(2), 6.
Gallagher, S. & Gerstel, N. (1993). Kinkeeping and friend keeping among older women: The effect of marriage. *Gerontologist*, 33(5), 675-681.
Rosenblum, C. & Whittington, F. (1994). The effects of bereavement on eating behaviors and nutrient intakes in elderly widowed persons. *Journal of gerontology, 48*(4), 223-229.
Umberson, D., Wortman, C., and Kessler, R. C. (1992). Widowhood and depression: Explaining long-term gender differences in vulnerability. *Journal of health & social behavior, 33*(1), 10-24.
Wolinsky, F. D. & Johnson, R. J. (1992). Widowhood, health status, and the use of health services by older adults: A cross-sectional and prospective approach. *Journal of gerontology, 47*(1), 8-16.

Lecture 2: Dying and Perceiving Death

I. The dying person

An assumption underlying most research on death and dying is that fear, denial, or both are universal and normal reactions to one's own impending death.

A. Early research. In early studies examining people's attitudes toward their own death, all reactions were classified as reflecting either "overt fear" or "latent fear."

B. More recent research: Kübler-Ross's model. Elisabeth Kübler-Ross developed a model of "stages" of reaction to impending death. In her model, the first stage is characterized by denial and fear. She theorized that impending death elicits a complex emotional reaction and that acceptance is not possible unless it is preceded by emotional turmoil.

1. Kübler-Ross's stages.
   a. Stage 1: Denial.
      (1) Kübler-Ross believed that fear of death is inescapable and is manifested initially by denial.
      (2) This reflects the psychoanalytic view that the unconscious cannot conceive of death or of a finite personal future.
   b. Stage 2: Anger.
   c. Stage 3: Bargaining.
   d. Stage 4: Depression.
   e. Stage 5: Acceptance.
2. Critique. Questions can be raised about Kübler-Ross's conclusions.
   a. With regard to denial: It is not certain that all the patients interviewed as the basis for this model had been given an unambiguous diagnosis of their condition; their reaction should in some cases be described as uncertainty rather than denial.
   b. With regard to anger and bargaining: The prevalence of these reactions may have reflected the youth of many of Kübler-Ross's subjects. These reactions are easily understandable in young people but might be much less common in a sample of older patients.

II. Attitudes toward death: Effects of age

Kalish and Reynolds (1976) studied effects of age, gender, and ethnicity on perceptions of death. They found no effects of gender or ethnicity, but did find age differences.

A. Methodology. Approximately 500 subjects in Los Angeles, representing four ethnic groups (African Americans, Asians, Hispanics, and "Anglos"), were asked to respond to this question: "Some say that they are afraid to die, some say that they're not. How do you feel?"

B. Findings. Relatively few respondents of any age reported a fear of dying.

1. The percentage reporting fear was highest in the youngest age group (ages 20 to 39); 40 percent described their reaction as afraid or terrified.
2. Of the middle-aged subjects (aged 40-59), 52 percent said that they were unafraid or eager; 26 percent said that they were afraid or terrified.
3. Of the oldest subjects (aged 60 and older), 71 percent said that they were unafraid or eager; only 10 percent said that they were afraid or terrified.

C. Interpreting the results. There are at least three possible reasons why elderly people apparently have less fear of death.
   1. Elderly people are less likely to be concerned about unfinished plans or projects; they are more likely to have made preparations for death (e.g., a will) and to have attained "closure" wherever possible.
   2. Elderly people have stronger grounds for viewing their death as "timely."
   3. They have had more practice in confronting death (death of spouses, parents, and friends).

References for Lecture 2

Greyson, B. (1985, August). A typology of near-death experiences. *American journal of psychiatry, 142*, 967-969.

Kalish, R. A. & Reynolds, D. K. (1976). *Death and ethnicity: A psychocultural study.* Los Angeles: University of Southern California Press.

Moody, R. A. (1988). *The light beyond.* New York, Doubleday Dell Publishing Group: Inc.

Peck, M. S. (1990). *The road less traveled.* New York: Simon and Schuster.

Peck, M. S. (1993). *Further along the road less traveled.* New York: Simon and Schuster.

Rodabough, T. (1985). Near-death experiences: An examination of the supporting data and alternative explanations. *Death-studies, 9*, 95-113.

Lecture 3: Children and Death

I. Children's understanding of death.

How children view death depends on both age and experience.

A. Age differences.
   1. Age 3. Three-year-olds view death as reversible, unlikely, easily escapable, and not personally relevant.
   2. Age 5. By the time they are 5 years old, children see death as imposing conditions of immobility and separation, but still reversible.
      a. Adults may encourage these notions of death, particularly the idea of reversibility (e.g., they promise to replace a dead pet or they describe a dead grandparent as "sleeping" or "on a long trip").
      b. Such descriptions are consistent with a child's understanding but are unlikely to advance it.
   3. Age 6. By the time they are 6 years old, children understand that death is irreversible and universal. Their interest in death increases, and their anxiety regarding it may also increase.
B. Experience. Children's understanding of death depends on personal experience at least as much as age. Terminally ill children are likely to have a "precocious" understanding of death.

II. Death in children's literature

Depictions of death differ in various kinds of children's literature.

A. Many classic fairy tales mirror preschoolers' conceptions of death.
B. Recently, more children's books convey death-related themes. Such books may help children to deal with deaths in the family, death of friends, etc.
   1. These books present death (e.g., of pets and elderly relatives) as natural.
   2. They may be useful for discussing grief, the idea of immortality as a legacy of fond memories, and perhaps the aging process.

III. Death education

Some death education exists at the secondary and college level.

A. High schools. Death education is not widely available but is usually well received when it is offered.
B. Colleges. Death education is more common at the college level, and it is

usually extremely popular.

References for Lecture 3

Clark, L. R. (1993). Joshua knew. *Journal of the American medical association*, 270(24), 2902.

Cole, D. (1994). When a child dies. *Parents*, 69(3), 144-148.

Glazer, H. & Landreth, G. (1993). When a child is dying. *Education digest*, 59(1), 64-67.

Grollman, E. A. (1994). Straight talk about death for teenagers: How to cope with losing someone you love. *English journal*, 83(2), 80-81.

Kane, B. (1975). Children's concepts of death. (Doctoral dissertation, University of Cincinnati, 1975.) *Dissertation abstracts international*, 36, 2-A.

Krugman, R., Bays, J. A., Chadwick, D., and Kanda, M. (1993). Investigation and review of unexpected infant and child deaths. *Pediatrics*, 92(5), 734-735.

Matko, M. (1993). Do angels cry? *Journal of the American medical association*, 270(5), 548.

TOPIC FOR DEBATE

Should Euthanasia be Legalized?

Background

With advancing medical technology, it is now possible to prolong the lives of many seriously ill patients almost indefinitely. Even when no cognitive awareness or neurological functioning can be detected, physiological functioning can be maintained. Some people feel that if they were in such a situation, they would not want to be kept alive through such "heroic" measures. To them, euthanasia is a far more humane response than treatment in certain situations.

Euthanasia, commonly known as <u>mercy killing,</u> can take one of two general forms. In passive euthanasia, a patient dies as a result of a decision not to take further action or not to use a particular treatment that would prolong his or her life. Active euthanasia involves performing some deliberate action for the purpose of ending a patient's life: for example, administering a lethal dose of a drug. A growing number of physicians acknowledge that they have practiced euthanasia, and many support the use of living wills.

Euthanasia is at present illegal in the United States, and many people feel that it contradicts our cultural system of morality. They argue that human life is sacred and must be preserved at all costs. It is understandable that a person who is seriously ill may feel depressed and believe that life is no longer worth living; if the patient's judgment is being affected by medication, he or she might be even more likely to express a wish to die. However, opponents of euthanasia maintain that medical advances always hold the possibility of new, effective treatments, and that patients' depression or drug-clouded judgment should not provide a basis for denying them that possibility.

Opponents of euthanasia also point out that legalization raises troublesome possibilities. If a patient is comatose, or is too young to make a responsible decision about treatment, then the decision for or against euthanasia would be made by relatives or physicians. The potential for abuse of the patient's fundamental rights in such situations is obvious and frightening.

However, strong arguments in favor of legalizing euthanasia can also be offered. One might argue that a seriously ill person is the only proper judge of the value of his or her own life. If a patient believes that life is not worth living, relatives and medical professionals should be bound to respect and respond to that sentiment. The quality of life and the appropriate time and manner of death are intensely personal matters, and each individual should have the right to make decisions about them.

Proponents of euthanasia also point out that medical practices designed to prolong life may rob a patient of dignity and may impose intense and prolonged grief on the patient's family. More practically, long-term life support can impose immense financial burdens on patients and their families. For these reasons, many people believe that it is immoral to impose medical treatment or maintain life against the wishes of a patient and his or her family.

Debate plan

Using this background, and information from additional sources (selected references appear below), student panels should debate the following positions:

<u>Position A</u>. Euthanasia should be legalized and recognized as a humane approach to

terminal illnesses and in certain other situations.

Position B. Euthanasia should remain illegal.

References for the debate

Anonymous (1994). Netherlands passes liberal euthanasia law. *Christian century,* *111*(6), 194.

Capron, A. M. (1993). For them rather than by them. *Hastings center report,* 23(6), 30-31.

Dworkin, R. (1993). Letting go: death, dying, and the law. *American health,* *12*(6), 83.

Ferrer, I. (1994). Holland's right to die. *World press review,* *41*(3), 23.

Hutchison, F. (1993). Life and death issues: life on the line: ethics, ending patients' lives, and allocating vital resources by John F. Kilner. *Christian century,* *110*(16), 525.

Post, S. G.. (1993). How shall the aged die? Ethics on call (Nancy Dubler); Euthanasia is not the answer (David Cundiff); A good death (T. P. Hill and D. Shirley; Hospice care (B. Hagship, Jr. and J. Leon). in *Gerontologist,* *33*(3), 427-429.

Rong, R. (1993). Euthanasia in the 1990s: dying a "good" death. *Current (GCDC),* 354, 27-33.

Veatch, R. M. (1993). From forgoing life support to aid-in-dying. *Hastings center report,* *23*(6), 7-8.

TOPICS FOR DISCUSSION

Topic 1: Aspects of Death

1. Ask students to summarize the three aspects of death defined in the text (page 589). Ask them to give examples of situations in which only one of these aspects was present.

2. Ask students which of the three aspects of death is likely to be most personally relevant to a medical professional working with a terminally ill patient; to the patient; and to the relatives of the patient. Ask them to explain each selection.

Topic 2: Age Differences in Attitudes toward Death

1. Ask students to summarize the text material on children's awareness of death (pages 589-590). Ask them how children's misconceptions regarding death (e.g., the idea that it is reversible) can be both beneficial and harmful. On that basis, ask students to judge the appropriateness of death education for children.

2. Ask students to describe ways in which attitudes toward death reflect cognitive and personality development during adolescence, young and middle adulthood, and old age (pages 590-592).

Topic 3: Stages of Dying

1. Ask students to summarize Kübler-Ross's model of stages of emotional reactions to dying, and ways in which the model has been criticized (page 593).

2. Ask students to suggest ways in which familiarity with Kübler-Ross's stages of reaction to death could be helpful to professionals who work with seriously ill patients. Ask them to suggest how her model might interfere with professionals' care of these patients.

Topic 4: Grief

1. Ask students to distinguish among bereavement, mourning, and grief (pages 593-594) and to give examples of different situations illustrating these terms.

2. Have students suggest steps society can take to promote resolution of grief after a loss (e.g., educators could discuss death openly with students rather than treating it as a taboo topic).

Topic 5: Suicide

1. Ask students to summarize the information in the text regarding suicide among different age groups, and gender and racial differences in suicide rates (pages 605-608).

2. Ask students to suggest steps that individuals can take to decrease motivations for suicide among children,

teenagers, and adults of various ages. Ask students to suggest changes in society that could decrease motivations for suicide in each of these age groups (pages 608-610).

PROJECTS AND CLASS EXERCISES

Group Exercise: Life Extension

The group should imagine breakthroughs in medical technology that would make unlimited extension of the human life span possible. In this hypothetical situation, physicians would be able to prevent death for virtually unlimited periods; however, they would have no greater power than they do today to maintain or restore health and vigor. Students should discuss the consequences of this situation, considering how such changes in medical technology would affect the family, the economy, the political system, the environment, social services, and personal satisfaction with life. The group should also identify the most positive effect and the most negative effect of this kind of life extension.

Project 1: Children's Views of Death

Students should review a selection of children's books, children's television programs, and children's movies in which death is addressed in some way. Students should write a paper describing how these sources deal with the topic, and identifying the treatments that seem to be most and least adaptive for youngsters.

Project 2: Kübler-Ross's Work

Students should read one or more of Elisabeth Kübler-Ross's books or articles in which she describes the research that formed the basis for her description of stages of dying. Students should write a paper in which they identify the strongest and weakest methodological aspects of her work. They should also comment on the implications of the methodological weaknesses, and on the importance of her work (despite its methodological shortcomings).

Project 3: Hospice Care

Students should visit a hospice in the community and interview at least one employee or volunteer. Students should write a paper describing the hospice and their own reaction to this approach to caring for patients with terminal illness.

ESSAY QUESTIONS

1. Define biological, psychological, and social death.

Answer guideline. Biological death is the cessation of bodily processes; the specific criteria considered vary from state to state. Psychological death is the feelings people have about their own impending death and the death of those close to them. Social death is funerals, mourning rituals, and legal issues and procedures surrounding death.

2. Describe young children's ideas about death.

Answer guideline. Young children have several misconceptions about death. Until about age 5, 6, or 7, children do not understand that death is irreversible or that it is universal. Also, they do not understand that the dead are nonfunctional (e.g., they may believe that the dead can think or feel.)

3. How is adolescents' cognitive functioning related to their ideas about death?

Answer guideline. Although adolescents usually have an accurate intellectual understanding of death and realize intellectually that they will eventually die, adolescent egocentrism can lead to distorted feelings about death. One aspect of adolescent egocentrism is the "personal fable," adolescents' belief that they are unique, special, and even potentially immortal. Thus, adolescents may believe that they are immune to death, and act accordingly.

4. What changes in awareness of death occur in middle adulthood?

Answer guideline. During middle adulthood, most people realize for the first time (at least, on a "gut level") that they will eventually die. This realization may be prompted by the death of parents and peers, as well as by changes in strength, stamina, and other aspects of physical functioning. The realization is often paired with a changed perspective on time, involving a switch from thinking of life in terms of time since birth to thinking in terms of time left to live. Finally, this realization may be an impetus for making substantial life changes, such as a career change or a change in marriage.

5.   What are the stages of dying, according to Elisabeth Kübler-Ross?

Answer guideline. Elisabeth Kübler-Ross, on the basis of interviews with nearly 500 terminally ill patients, proposed that people approaching death experience five emotional stages. In the first stage, denial, these people refuse to accept the reality of their condition; they may believe, for example, that tissue samples were mixed up in a laboratory. The second stage is anger: the patient may be envious of and hostile toward people who are in good health. In the third stage, bargaining, the patient attempts to strike a deal (with God, fate, or some other potent force) for a finite, temporary prolongation of life; for example, the patient may pray to live until a grandchild is born. Depression is the fourth stage: the patient mourns for the impending loss of all loved ones, interests, and ties to life. The fifth stage is acceptance: patients feel at peace with themselves and their condition.

6.   What is death education?

Answer guideline. Death education refers to programs aimed at helping people of various ages to understand dying and grieving, and to deal with these issues as individuals and as professionals. Goals of any specific death education program depend on the age and needs of the students. Common goals for these programs include helping children develop as few death-related anxieties as possible, helping people prepare for their own and their loved ones' deaths, helping professionals feel comfortable with terminally ill people and provide humane care, and helping people understand and prevent suicide.

7.   Describe hospice care.

Answer guideline. Hospice care is patient- and family-centered care for the terminally ill. The care may be provided in the patient's home, in an institution (a hospital or some other medical facility), or in some combination of these settings. Care is provided by a variety of professionals, including doctors, nurses, social workers, psychologists, and members of the clergy; also, by nonprofessional volunteers. The emphasis is not to cure the patient but to provide the greatest comfort possible to the patient and the patient's family.

8.   Define euthanasia, active euthanasia, and passive euthanasia.

Answer guideline. Euthanasia is commonly known as mercy killing. In active euthanasia, deliberate action is taken in order to shorten a patient's life and thereby minimize the patient's suffering. In passive euthanasia, treatment that could extend the patient's life is withheld.

9.   Discuss reasons why teenagers commit suicide.

Answer guideline. Some teenagers apparently commit suicide in response to the increased stress of contemporary adolescence; others feel lonely and unloved by their friends and even their parents. Some teenagers commit suicide in response to depression or drug abuse, and some are diagnosed as having unstable personalities. Suicidal adolescents are frequently in conflict with their parents, unable to call on them for support when they feel lonely. Many come from dysfunctional families, and many have been abused or neglected.

10.   Define life review.

Answer guideline. A life review is a process of reminiscence which ideally enables a person to identify the significance of his or her life. Through thinking and talking about people, events, and feelings of the past, individuals can attain an enhanced perspective on their lives and may be prompted to complete "unfinished business" (e.g., resolving a quarrel or reestablishing an estranged relationship).

APPENDIX

GENERAL RESOURCES

INTRODUCTION

In this **General Resources** appendix, you will find several practical features:

- A selected bibliography of handbooks and readers.

- Information about selected distributors of audiovisual materials and suggestions for using such materials.

- Suggestions for incorporating guest speakers into your course.

- Suggestions for implementing and evaluating student debates and class discussions.

- Suggestions for getting feedback on your course.

The main purposes of the appendix are to provide references for background reading and to offer possibilities for designing the course, establishing requirements, and developing grading procedures.

SELECTED BACKGROUND READINGS

This section is a selected bibliography of recent, readily available handbooks and readers on teaching and on life-span development. These references should be useful for background reading on topics outside your own area of specialization or as a review within your area. They are not intended to provide in-depth coverage of human development (as would be needed for preparing a scholarly article, for example); however, they should provide more than enough information for answering students' questions on topics outside your own area of expertise.

These references might also provide useful suggestions for students' further reading (although some of them are rather technical), in addition to the readings listed at the end of each chapter of the textbook. Also, a selected list drawn from these references could be provided to students to help them research a topic for a debate, project, or group exercise.

References on Teaching

Benjamin, L. T. & Lowman, K. D. (Eds.) *Activities handbook for the teaching of psychology*. Washington, DC: American Psychological Association.

Fuhrmann, B. S. & Grasha, A. F. (1983). *A practical handbook for college teachers*. Boston, MA: Little, Brown.

Johnson, D. W., et al. (1984). *Circles of learning: Cooperation in the classroom*. Alexandria, VA: Association for Supervision and Curriculum Development.

McKeachie, W. J. (1986). *Teaching tips* (8th ed.). Lexington, MA: Heath.

Notterman, J. M. (1993). *Psychology and education: Parallel and interactive approaches*. New York: Plenum Press.

Postlethwaite, K. (1993). *Differentiated science teaching: Responding to individual differences and to special education needs*. Philadelphia, PA: Open University Press.

Rabinowitz, M. (1993). *Cognitive science foundations of instruction*. Hillsdale, NJ: Lawrence Erlbaum Associates.

Rheingold, H. L. (1994). *The Psychologist's Guide to an Academic Career*. Hyattsville, MD: American Psychological Association, Inc.

Teaching of Psychology. This quarterly journal is published by Division 2 (Teaching of Psychology) of the American Psychological Association. Most issues include course descriptions, articles on teaching, reviews of books and films, and suggestions for class demonstrations. Although the journal is not devoted exclusively to the life-span development course, ideas for such a course appear regularly. For information about subscriptions, contact the American Psychological Association, Inc., 750 First Street, NE, Washington, DC 20002-4242.

General References on Life-Span Development

Baldwin, A. L. (1981). *Theories of child development*. New York: Wiley.

Dacey, J. (1991). *Lifespan development*. Fort Worth, TX: Harcourt, Brace, Jovanovich.

Datan, N., Greene, A. L., & Reese, H. W. (1986). *Life-span developmental psychology: Intergenerational relations*. Hillsdale, NJ: Erlbaum.

Flavell, J. H. (1993). *Cognitive development*. (3rd ed.). Englewood Cliffs, NJ: Prentice-Hall.

Globerson, T. (Ed.) (1989). *Cognitive style and cognitive development*. Tel Aviv Annual Workshop in Human Development, Norwood, NJ: Ablex.

Greenspan, S. I. (Ed.). (1989). *The course of life*. Madision, CT: International Universities Press.

Hauert, C. (Ed.) (1989). *Developmental psychology: Cognitive, perceptuo-motor, and neuropsychological perspectives*. New York, NY: Elsevier Science.

Hurrelmann, K. (1989). *Human development and health*. Berlin, NY: Springer-Verlag.

Levin, I. & Zakay, D. (Eds.) (1989). *Time and human cognition: A life-span perspective*. New York: Elsevier Science.

Mercer. J. (1991). *To everything there is a season: Development in the context of the lifespan*. Lanham, MD: University Press of America.

Pratt, M., Hunsberger, B., & Pancer, S. M. (1993). Thinking about parenting: Reasoning about developmental issues across the life span. *Developmental psychology*, 29: 585-595.

Smuts, A. B. & Hagen, J. W. (1986). History and research in child development. *Monographs of the Society for Research in Child Development*, 50, Nos. 4-5, Serial No. 211.

220

Thomas, R. M. (Ed.) (1990). *The Encyclopedia of human development and education: Theory, research, and studies* (1st ed.). Oxford, England: New York: Pergamon.

Turner, J. (1991). *Lifespan development.* Forth Worth, TX: Harcourt Brace Jovanovich College Publishers.

Valsiner, J. (1989). *Human development and culture: The social nature of personality and its study.* Lexington, MA: Lexington.

Van Hasselt, V.B. & Hersen, M. (Ed.) (1992). *Handbook of social development: A lifespan perspective.* New York: Plenum Press.

References on Prenatal and Infant Development

Bayley, N. (1993). *Manual for the Bayley scales of infant development.* (2d ed.). New York: Psychological Corporation. McGraw-Hill.

Bornstein, M. H. (1992). *Development in infancy: An introduction.* New York: McGraw-Hill.

Brazelton, T. B. (1990). *The earliest relationship: Parents, infants, and the drama of early attachment.* Reading, MA: Addison-Wesley.

Colombo, J. (1993). *Infant cognition: Predicting later intellectual functioning.* Newbury Park, CA: Sage.

Cramer, B. G. (1992). *The importance of being baby.* Reading, MA: Addison-Wesley.

Ever, D. (1992). *Mother-infant bonding: A scientific fiction.* New Haven, CT: Yale University Press.

Fox, N. A., Kimmerly, N. L., & Schafer, W. D. (1991). Attachment to mother/attachment to father: A meta-analysis. *Child development, 62*: 210-215.

Harris, J. R. (1992). *Infant & child: Development from birth through middle childhood.* Englewood Cliffs, NJ: Prentice-Hall.

Kline, J. (1989). *Conception to birth: Epidemiology of prenatal development.* New York: Oxford University Press.

Lamb, M. E. & Campos, J. J. (1987). *Development in infancy: An introduction* (2d ed.). New York: Random House.

Morrison, G. S. (1990). *The world of child development: Conception to adolescence.* Albany, NY: Delmar Publishers.

Nilsson, L. (1982/1966). *A child is born.* New York: Delacorte/Seymour Lawrence.

Osofsky, J. J. (1987). *Handbook of infant development* (2d ed.). New York: Wiley.

Rutkowska, J. C. (1993). *The computational infant: Looking for developmental cognitive science.* New York: Harvester Wheatsheaf.

References on Development in Childhood and Adolescence

Anderman, E. M. & Maehr, M. L. (Summer 1994). Motivation and schooling in the middle grades. *Review of educational research, 64*(2): 287-300.

Aseltine, R. H. (1993). Mental health and social adaptation following the transition from high school. Special Issue: Late adolescence and the transition to adulthood. *Journal of research on adolescence, 3*(3): 247-270.

Atwater, E. (1988). *Adolescence.* Englewood Cliffs, NJ: Prentice-Hall.

Benasich, A., Curtiss, S., & Tallal, P. (1993). Language, learning, and behavioral disturbances in childhood: A longitudinal perspective. *Journal of the American academy of child and adolescent psychiatry, 32*: 585-594.

Biller, H. B. (1993). *Fathers and families: Paternal factors in child development.* Westport, CT: Auburn House.

Burnand, G. (1993). *Human development: Childhood, adolescence, and personality in terms of a unifying theoretical system.* High Wycombe: Leadership.

Eagle, C. J. & Schwartz, L. (1994). *Psychological portraits of adolescents: An integrated developmental approach to psychological test data.* New York: Lexington Books.

Elder, G. H., Modell, J., & Parke, R. D. (1993). *Children in time and place: Developmental and historical insights.* New York: Cambridge University Press.

Elkind, D. & Flavell, J. H. (1969). *Studies in cognitive development: Essays in honor of Jean Piaget.* New York: Oxford University Press.

Flavell, J. H. (1993). *Cognitive development* (3d ed.), Englewood Cliffs, NJ: Prentice-Hall.

Flavell, J. H. (1963). *The developmental psychology of Jean Piaget.* New York: Van Nostrand Reinhold.

Fuligni, A. J. & Eccles, J. S. (1993). Perceived parent-child relationships and early adolescents' orientation toward peers.

Developmental psychology, 29: 622-632.

Ginsburg, H. P. & Opper, S. (1988). *Piaget's theory of intellectual development (3d ed.).* Englewood Cliffs, NJ: Prentice-Hall.

Gruber, H. E. & Veneche, J. J. (1977). *The essential Piaget.* New York: Basic Books.

Hughes, D. & Brand, M. (1993). Myths or truths of adolescence. *Journal of the American academy of child and adolescent psychiatry, 32*: 1077.

Kelly-Byrne, D. (1989). *A child's play life: An ethnographic study.* New York: Teacher's College Press.

Kessler, J. W. (1988). *Psychopathology of childhood* (2d ed.). Englewood Cliffs, NJ: Prentice-Hall.

LeCroy, C. W. (1994). *Handbook of child and adolescent treatment manuals.* New York: Lexington.

Levitt, M. J., Guacci-Franco, N., & Levitt, J. L. (1993). Convoys of social support in childhood and early adolescence: Structure and function. *Developmental psychology, 29*: 811-818.

Meadows, S. (1993). *The child as thinker: The development and acquisition of cognition in childhood.* London; New York: Routledge.

Rice, F. P. (1992). *The adolescent: development, relationships, and culture.* Boston: Allyn and Bacon.

Sroufe, L. A. (1992). *Child development: Its nature and course.* New York: McGraw-Hill.

Sroufe, L. A., Egeland, B., & Kreutzer, T. (1990). The fate of early experience following developmental change: Longitudinal approaches to individual adaptation in childhood. *Child development, 60*: 1363-1373.

References on Adult Development, Aging, and Dying

Binstock, R. H. & Shanas, E. (1990). *Handbook of aging and the social sciences* (3d ed.). New York: Van Nostrand Reinhold.

Birren, J. E. & Schaie, K. W. (1990). *handbook of the psychology of aging* (3d ed.). New York: Van Nostrand Reinhold.

Chrisler, J. C. (1993). Body image issues of older women. Special Issue: Faces of women and aging. *Women & therapy. 14*(1-2): 67-75.

Deeg, D. J. (1991). Experiences from longitudinal studies of aging: An international perspective. *Journal of cross-cultural gerontology, 6*(1): 7-22.

Dubler, N. & Nimmons, D. (1993). How shall the aged die? *Gerontologist, 33*(3): 427-429.

Edwards, A. J. (1992). *Dementia.* New York: Plenum Press.

Finch, C. E. & Schneider, E. L. (1990). *Handbook of the biology of aging* (3d ed.). New York: Van Nostrand Reinhold.

Francis, L. P. (1993). Advance directives for voluntary euthanasia: A volatile combination. *Journal of medicine and philosophy, 18*(3): 297-322.

Gilligan, C. (1982). *In a different voice: Psychological theory and women's development.* Cambridge, MA: Harvard University Press.

Gomez, C. F. (1993). *Regulating death: Criminal justice ethics, 12*(1): 71-77.

Greenberg, V. E. (1994). *Children of a certain age: Adults and their aging parents.* New York: Lexington Books.

Jackson, J. S., Chatters, L. M., & Taylor, R. J. (1993). *Aging in black America.* Newbury Park, CA: Sage.

Lester, D. & Tallmer, M. (1994). *Now I lay me down: Suicide in the elderly.* Philadelphia: Charles Press.

Lock, M. (1993). *Encounters with aging mythologies of menopause in Japan and North America.* Berkeley: University of California Press.

Lucas, E. T. (1991). *Elder abuse and its recognition among health service professionals.* New York: Garland.

McIntosh, W. A. (1993). Life events, social support, and immune response in elderly individuals. *International journal of aging and human development, 37*(1): 23-26.

Neugarten, B. L. (1972). *Middle age and aging: A reader in social psychology.* Chicago, IL: University of Chicago Press.

Parks, R. W., Zec, R. F., & Wilson, R. S. (1993). *Neuropsychology of Alzheimer's disease and other dementias.* New York: Oxford University.

Rose, M. R. (1991). *Evolutionary biology of aging.* New York: Oxford University Press.

Salthouse, T. A. (1991). *Theoretical perspectives on cognitive aging.* Hillsdale, NJ: Erlbaum.

Sand, G. (1993). *Is it hot in here or is it me? A personal look at the facts, fallacie, and feelings of menopause.* New York: HarperCollins.

222

Sargi, B. J. (1992). Grandparenting, life satisfaction, and retirement homes. *Dissertation abstracts international, 53*(6-A): 1804.

Schulz, R. (1993). *Adult development and aging: Myths and emerging realities.* New York: Macmillan; Toronto: Maxwell Macmillan Canada.

Thomas, J. L. (1990). The grandparent role: A double bind. *International journal of aging and human development, 31*3): 169-177.

Urosfsky, M. I. (1993). Letting go: Death, dying, and the law. *American health, 12*(6): 83.

Zwilling, R. & Balduini, C. (Eds.) (1992). *Biology of aging.* Berlin, NY: Springer-Verlag.

AUDIOVISUAL MATERIALS

Selected Distributors

An abbreviation follows each distributor's name; this is the abbreviation that appears in the list of films and videos given for each chapter in this manual. Instructors might contact distributors to request a catalog and information on rates and preview policies. However, beware of relying on catalog descriptions rather than previewing a video or film; catalog descriptions can be inaccurate.

ABC Merchandising (ABC)
American Broadcasting Co. TV
1330 Avenue of the Americas
New York, NY 10019

American Journal of Nursing (AJN)
Educational Services Division
555 West 57th Street
New York, NY 10019

Beacon Films (BCN)
930 Pinter Avenue
Evanston, IL 60202
1 (800) 323-5448

Benchmark Films (BF)
145 Scarborough Road
Briarcliff Manor, NY 10510

**Corporation for Public Broadcasting
The Annenberg/CPB Project (CPB)**
c/o Intellimation
Attn: Psychology Department
P.O. Box 1922
Santa Barbara, CA 93116-1922

Coronet/MTI Film and Video (CORT)
Supplementary Education Group
Simon and Schuster Communications
108 Wilmot Road
Deerfield, IL 60015
1 (800) 323-5343

CRM/McGraw-Hill Films (CRM)
2233 Faraday Avenue
Carlsbad, CA 92008
1 (619) 431-9800

Davidson Films (DAV)
3701 Buchanan Street
San Francisco, CA 94123

Educational Development Center (EDC)
Distribution Center
55 Chapel Street
Newton, MA 02160

**Far West Laboratory for Educational
Research and Development (FWL)**
Hotel Clairmont
41 Tunnel Road
Berkeley, CA 94705

**Films for the Humanities and
Sciences (FFHS)**
PO Box 2053
Princeton, NJ 08543-2053
1 (800) 257-5126
FAX (609) 275-3767

Filmmakers Library, Inc. (FML)
124 East 40th Street, Suite 901
New York, NY 10016

Films, Inc., Public Media Inc. (FI)
5547 Ravenswood Avenue
Chicago, IL 60640
1 (800) 323-4222

Harcourt Brace Jovanovich (HBJ)
7555 Caldwell Avenue
Chicago, IL 60648

Health Sciences Communication Center (HSCC)
Case Western Reserve University
University Circle
Cleveland, OH 44106

Insight Media
121 West 85th Street
New York, NY 10024
1 (212) 721-6316
FAX (212) 799-5309

Milner-Fenwick, Inc. (MF)
2125 Green Spring Drive
Timonium, MD 21093

PBS Video (PBS)
1320 Braddock Place
Alexandria, VA 22314
1 (800) 344-3337

Pennsylvania State University
Psychology Cinema Register (PSU)
AV Services
6 Willard Building
University Park, PA 16802

Perspective Films,
 Education Group (PER)
Simon and Schuster Communications
108 Wilmot Road
Deerfield, IL 60015

Polymorph Films, Inc. (PFV)
118 South Street
Boston, MA 02111

Psychological Films (PSYCHF)
3334 East Coast Highway, Suite 252
Corona Del Mar, CA 92625

Pyramid Film & Video (PF)
2801 Colorado Avenue
Santa Monica, CA 90404
1 (213) 828-7577

Research Press (RP)
Box 31775
Champaign, IL 61821

Simon & Schuster Communications (SSC)
(now PER--see above)

Time-Life Film & Video (TLF)
100 Eisenhower Drive
Paramus, NJ 07652

University of California
Extension Media Ctr. (UCEMC)
2176 Shattuck Avenue
Berkeley, CA 94704
1 (415) 642-0460

University of Minnesota (UFV)
Media Resources
540 Rarig
Minneapolis, MN 55455

Michigan State University (WK)
WKAR-TV
600 Kalamazoo Street
E. Lansing, MI 48824

Yale University Media Design Studio (YU)
305 Crown Street
New Haven, CT 06520

Using Audiovisual Materials

With careful choice and preparation, films and videos can enhance students' interest in and appreciation of the course content. Indiscriminate or unplanned use of these media, however, will have (at best) no impact. Selection of videos and films should be guided by at least two sets of considerations.

Content. Can the topic be addressed more effectively through this video or film than by other means? Is the approach taken in the video or film consistent with your learning objectives? Does the video or film present current information accurately? Is its level of difficulty or abstraction appropriate for your students? Does it complement (rather than reiterate) material presented in the text, in lectures, or in other classroom activities? Are your students "visual" learners?

Cost. Is the film or video worth its cost? Cost should be considered not only in terms of rental or purchase fees but also in terms of class time?

Even well-chosen films and videos require careful preparation. To prepare yourself, *preview* the selection: make notes of points you consider important, and plan a brief introduction. In your introduction, you may want to identify correspondences between the video/film and the textbook, lectures, etc. Identify important points in the video/film. Write important terms or concepts on the board.

224

To prepare your students, introduce the video/film and explain the purpose for which it is being used. In addition to the points outlined above for your introduction, you should include points that the students should look for and explain how their understanding of the content will be evaluated (exam questions, class discussion, etc.). In some cases, you may want to distribute an outline of the material to guide students' note-taking. Remember, however, that taking notes is much easier for a video than for a film, since the room does not have to be darkened for videos.

Guest Speakers

Many instructors find that guest speakers can enrich a course in many ways. Perhaps their most important contribution is giving students concrete examples of how scholarly information about human development can be applied. Occasionally, a guest speaker becomes a valuable contact for students seeking practicum, internship, volunteer, or work experience.

Suggestions for guest speakers are noted in the "Audiovisual Materials" section of each chapter in this manual. Resources for locating guest speakers include local chapters of certain national organizations (e.g., March of Dimes, Urban League, Association of Retarded Citizens, American Cancer Society). The community service or community education offices of local hospitals, state or municipal human services agencies (e.g., Child and Family Services, Office of the Aging, Hospice, and self-help groups like Parents without Partners).

Deriving maximum benefit from guest speakers requires careful preparation. You should contact potential speakers well in advance (preferably before the semester or quarter begins) to schedule a visit and later confirm the appointment with the speaker two to five days beforehand. When you contact a potential speaker, explain the nature of the course and the kind of students who are enrolled in it, the topic or topics you would like the speaker to address, the approximate size of the class, and the length of the class period. When you confirm the appointment, you should also find out about any audiovisual or duplicating needs the speaker may have. Ask if an honorarium is expected.

The class should be prepared to give the speaker an attentive reception, at the very least. During the class period before the speaker's visit, explain the purpose of the presentation and the speaker's background, and ask the class to prepare questions for the speaker. You may or may not want to collect these questions and give them to the speaker; but in any case, it is important that students be prepared to ask questions.

You should also identify aspects of the presentation for which students will be held responsible and explain how their understanding will be evaluated.

DEBATES AND DISCUSSIONS

Debates

Each chapter in this manual includes a topic for debate by the students. A brief background statement is followed by statements of two contrasting viewpoints to be debated and a short list of references. These debates are probably best implemented using two panels of no more than five students each. Each panel should be assigned one of the two viewpoints; the panel members' task is to develop arguments in support of it and to do the library research necessary to document their arguments.

When the debate is presented in class, allow 10 to 15 minutes for the members of each panel to state their arguments; these statements should be followed by a 5-minute rebuttal period for the opposing panel. There should be adequate time remaining for other members of the class to direct questions (or their own rebuttals) to members of either panel.

As a follow-up to the debate, you might require (or offer as an extra-credit option) a short paper explaining which set of arguments the students found most convincing and why.

Class Discussions

Guiding a meaningful class discussion can often be difficult or frustrating. One excellent reference regarding skills in leading discussion is by McKeachie (1986), listed in "References on Teaching," above. His suggestions include effective ways to start a discussion and phrase questions, approaches to dealing with nonparticipants and monopolizers, and ways to identify and overcome barriers to discussion. Perhaps his most important question, though, is simply to be patient: if the questions that you have posed as a starting point are at all challenging, don't forget to give students time to think about them.

One other point to consider is that it is rare for all members of a class to participate verbally in any discussion. Some students are quiet by nature. As frustrating as that may be for the instructor, such students may still be participating in the discussion: eye contact and other nonverbal signals to students who are speaking should be considered forms of participation. Don't be tempted to judge the success or failure of a class discussion by the number of different voices heard or by the number of silences during it.

Remember that, in general, if students are going to want to participate in a discussion, the topic must have some relevance and meaning for them. From a learning perspective, this means that students must be able to see a relationship between the topic to be learned ("new learning") and ideas and concepts about which they already know something ("old learning"). For example, if the discussion is on the merits of Maslow's concept of "self-actualization," the instructor can promote the discussion by starting out with a brief presentation on humanistic psychology and its relationship to the changes going on in Russia--a current topic which should be familiar to most college students.

GETTING FEEDBACK ON THE COURSE

Most departments require instructors to give their students some sort of "consumer satisfaction" questionnaire/evaluation at the end of a semester or quarter. Although these questionnaires can provide useful information, that information is obtained too late to correct any problems that arise during the course. The suggestions in this section are intended as supplements to the end-of-course evaluation.

At the beginning of the course, you may find it useful to get background information about your students. This information might include the student's year in school, major or expected major, reason for enrolling in the course, special learning considerations (e.g., an auditory impairment or a learning disability), and any topics that he or she would like to see addressed in the course. Many undergraduate schools are seeing a large increase in the number of adults returning to college. These adult students are usually highly motivated but may require some developmental services (e.g., reading or writing assistance) from the learning support center at your institution.

At approximately the midpoint of the semester (after at least one examination), an anonymous, open-ended questionnaire can be a valuable way to evaluate the course. You can ask for students' reactions to various aspects of the course, such as the textbook, exams, the *Study Guide* (if your students are using it), opportunities for discussion, lectures, guest speakers, and videos/film/laser discs/software. The objective here is to encourage students to offer suggestions on how the course could be improved and to monitor students' participation in their own learning.

- NOTES -

- NOTES -

- NOTES -

- NOTES -